Law's Politics: The Cyprus Troubles, 1960–1968

Nadia Kornioti

Law's Politics: The Cyprus Troubles, 1960–1968

palgrave
macmillan

Nadia Kornioti
School of Law
University of Central Lancashire - Cyprus (UCLan Cyprus)
Pyla, Larnaca, Cyprus

ISBN 978-3-031-93368-4 ISBN 978-3-031-93369-1 (eBook)
https://doi.org/10.1007/978-3-031-93369-1

This Palgrave Macmillan imprint is published by the registered company Springer Nature Switzerland AG.
The registered company address is: Gewerbestrasse 11, 6330 Cham, Switzerland

To my grandparents,
who lived parallel lives, in opposite worlds,
during a Cold War.

A Note on Names, Language, and Terminology

Talking and writing about the Cyprus Question calls for a number of linguistic and terminological clarifications. The below points serve as guidance for the reader.

Cyprus/ Republic of Cyprus/ Island of Cyprus

According to article 1 of the 1960 Treaty of Establishment, the Republic of Cyprus comprises of 'the Island of Cyprus, together with the islands lying off its coast' except for the two Sovereign British Areas, defined in Annex A of the same Treaty (the Akrotiri and Dhekelia Sovereign Base Areas). The same distinction between 'the Republic of Cyprus' (the RoC/ the Republic) and 'the Island of Cyprus' (the island) has been retained throughout the present book.

Areas Under / Not Under the Control of the Republic

Today, the term refers to the internationally unrecognised 'Turkish Republic of Northern Cyprus' (TRNC) unilaterally declared on 13 November 1983. Under public international law, the northern territory of the Island of Cyprus has been occupied by the Republic of Turkey since 1974. This book deals with the preceding decade. Therefore, 'areas not under the control of the Republic' in this book refers to the Turkish Cypriot-administered enclaves, established after 21 December 1963.

Community/ Greek Cypriot/ Turkish Cypriot

According to article 2 paragraphs (1) and (2) of the Constitution of the RoC, all RoC citizens shall belong to either of two communities of 'Greeks' or 'Turks'. The terms 'Greek Cypriot' and 'Turkish Cypriot' are usually employed to distinguish the Cypriots from the citizens of Greece and Turkey, respectively. For simplicity, the terms 'Greek Cypriot' and 'Turkish Cypriot' are used throughout the book, except for direct quotations. Reference to 'Cypriots' includes members of both communities. The term 'religious groups' is used to distinguish the 'Greek Orthodox' population, from other Christian denominations.

Topographical and Personal Names

Due to displacement and resettlement, many towns and villages in Cyprus are known with various names. Thus, archives are inconsistent in the topographical names utilised. These names have been reproduced directly here without prejudice to RoC legislation forbidding the use and publishing of names other than those officially assigned by its authorities.

The book refers throughout to Turkey, and not Türkiye, in line with all archival material and literature consulted for the present research, with no prejudice to that State's current name.

Greek names have been transliterated into the Latin alphabet. Special characters of the Turkish alphabet have been omitted in the main text but retained in bibliographical information. All names have been adjusted to pronunciation, where necessary.

Languages and Translations

All translations from texts in Greek, French, and German are by the author, unless stated otherwise. Alternative sources in English or Greek have been sought for texts originally in the Turkish language.

Terminology

Many of the terms used in the present book are employed across neighbouring disciplines in law, the social sciences, and the humanities. Where no distinction is explicitly mentioned in the text, it shall be assumed that the term is used in its legal sense.

Citations and Bibliographical Information

At the end of each chapter the reader can find bibliographical information on archival and secondary sources. Since the book is not intended for a legal audience only, the citation of legal sources has been kept to a minimum, and inserted in the main body of the text, where possible, without always aligning with the detailed demands of regular legal practice.

Acknowledgements

The present book is the product of many questions that preoccupied my mind for years. They first appeared during my earliest introduction to public international law as a law student, and then matured during my first experiences as a legal professional, before taking the form of a concrete research project towards the writing of a doctoral thesis. Until then, the thoughts and observations included here were scattered mental notes, gathered over lengthy discussions with family, friends, and colleagues. This book, therefore, is the systematisation of those scattered thoughts, through concrete archival research, enriched with past and current theoretical debates in legal scholarship. As such, I am first and foremost thankful to all those who dedicated their time to share their views, their knowledge, and—some in particular—their own personal and family memories, at a time that I was not yet certain this book would ever be written. These stories have been a valuable source of information and a constant motivation towards the completion of this project.

At UCLan Cyprus, I would like to thank my Director of Studies, Dr Klearchos A. Kyriakides, for the feedback he has offered based on his legal and historical expertise, throughout my doctoral research. His resourcefulness in the middle of the COVID-19 pandemic, when all scheduled travelling for research was indeterminately cancelled, is particularly appreciated. I would also like to thank my second supervisor Dr Ian Turner at UCLan, UK, for all the help in navigating the many administrative and organisational demands a doctoral degree has. Next, I am grateful to my PhD examiners, Prof. William A. Schabas, Dr. Gregoris Ioannou, and

Dr. Demetra Loizou, for engaging with my work, for the constructive discussion and feedback, and for their concrete advice towards improving what would become the first draft of this book. Lastly, I could certainly not leave behind Prof. Stéphanie Laulhé Shaelou, Head of the School of Law at UCLan Cyprus, for supporting me in my academic and professional development during the many years we have now been working together, and the rest of the UCLan Cyprus School of Law team for the various ways they have been part of my journey over the last years.

This book would not have been so rich in information without my valuable participation at the 2019 Global Humanitarianism Research Academy, organised by the Leibniz Institute of European History, the University of Exeter, and the International Committee of the Red Cross. For this incredible opportunity, I am forever grateful to Prof. Stacey Hynd, Prof. Julia Irwin, Prof. Dr. Fabian Klose, Dr. Mark-William Palen, Prof. Dr. Johannes Paulmann, and Prof. Andrew Thompson. I could of course not omit to thank Daniel Palmieri, Fabrizio Bensi, Damian Gonzalez Dominguez and Guy Thomas, for their patient guidance and assistance during the study visit to the ICRC Archives in Geneva.

In the process of completing the book, I am thankful to Isobel Cowper-Coles and the rest of the team at Palgrave Macmillan for their guidance, patience and understanding in extending the deadline for submission over the last few months. In Nicosia, Cyprus, I would like to extent my thanks to the staff at the 'Stelios Ioannou' Learning Resource Centre at the University of Cyprus, for the countless 'good mornings' and 'good nights' we have been sharing over the years, and their immediate help when help was needed. I could hardly find a richer collection of resources and a more comfortable studying environment anywhere else on the island.

Special thanks are due to Dr. Jason Beckett for supervising me as an undergraduate law student at the University of Leicester and for introducing me to critical international legal scholarship all those years ago. A separate set of special thanks are due to Shirin Jetha, who gave me the opportunity to work with her at the Association for Historical Dialogue and Research in Nicosia for a short but brilliant time, and for remaining the supportive friend and mentor she has been ever since. Because of her I had the chance to be part of exciting projects and meet people whose diverse backgrounds, academic research, and life experience have been a constant source of inspiration.

Lastly, I am grateful for the constant support of my close friends and family, who for years have been offering a space where I could share my excitement or surprise for the latest discovery, for listening and asking hard questions, and for sharing their thoughts. Finally, I am forever indebted to my parents, for instilling in me a constant curiosity for what is yet to be learnt, whereas the most special thank you is reserved for my best friend and partner in life for his endless patience, constant encouragement, and his eagerness to see this book published. Both his enthusiasm and his sober realism over the last two years were essential towards its completion.

The responsibility for any mistakes and omissions in the text remains mine.

Nicosia, 31 January 2025 Nadia Kornioti

Competing Interests The author has no competing interests to declare that are relevant to the content of this manuscript.

Contents

1 **The Cypriot Question: A Problem of Many Angles** 1
Legal Theory, History, and Interdisciplinary Research 7
Overcoming Silence and Abstraction 16
Reference List 20

2 **International Law, Empire and Cyprus, 1878–1959** 25
Imperial Humanitarianism and the Civilising Mission 27
Cypriot Society and Politics, 1878–1949 31
War and Peace After the United Nations, 1945–1949 38
Use of Force and the United Nations Collective Security System 39
Regulating Conduct and Allocating Responsibility During Armed Conflict 43
Reconfiguring Civil War as Non-international Armed Conflict 51
The Final Decade of the Crown Colony of Cyprus, 1950–1959 61
Cyprus and the Global Anti-colonial Movement 62
The EOKA Emergency and Early Inter-communal Violence 68
Conclusion 80
Reference List 81

3 **Fragile Independence, 1960–1963** 93
International Law and the Constitution of the Republic of Cyprus 95
The Three Constituent Treaties of the Republic of Cyprus 96
International Humanitarian Law and Human Rights in the Cypriot Legal Order 102

Bi-communal Challenges and the Constitutional Deadlock 109
The Internal Mechanics of the Principle of Bi-communality 111
Early Constitutional Challenges 116
Crime and Provocation Before December 1963 121
Conclusion 125
References 125

4 The Cyprus Troubles, 1963–1964 131
Humanitarianism and Peacekeeping in the Pursuit of Law and Order 132
Bloody Christmas 132
The Arrival of the International Committee of the Red Cross 138
The Establishment of the United Nations Force in Cyprus 143
Conflict Qualification 150
Assessing Intensity: Violence in the First Half of 1964 150
Assessing Organisation: The Establishment of the National Guard 159
The Tylliria Air Raids: The Internationalisation of the Conflict? 163
Legal Questions Deriving from Turkey's 1964 Intervention 170
Constitutional Survival Through Necessity 178
The Judiciary's Position on Internal Violence 180
The 1949 Geneva Conventions During the Ibrahim *Case* 186
The Broader Significance of the Ibrahim Case 188
Conclusion 190
References 192

5 Politics Before Everything, 1965–1968 201
Cypriot Society After 1964 202
The Effective End of Bi-communality 205
The Enclaves and the Turkish Cypriot Community 212
Legal Issues Relevant to Communal Segregation 223
Shifting Diplomatic and Military Balances 230
Diplomacy over Law 231
Military Controversies and Further Interventions 238
The Kophinou Operation 244
New Parameters 248
Conclusion 255
References 255

6 Epilogue 263
References 265

7 Conclusion 267
References 273

Appendix I: Article 3 Common to Geneva Conventions I–IV 1949 275

Appendix II: Security Council Resolution 186 (4 March 1964) 277

Index 279

Abbreviations

CIA	Central Intelligence Agency.
CLR	Cyprus Law Reports.
DoN	Doctrine of Necessity.
ECHR	European Convention on Human Rights.
ECmHR	European Commission of Human Rights.
ECtHR	European Court of Human Rights.
EOKA	National Organisation of Cypriot Fighters (Εθνική Οργάνωση Κυπρίων Αγωνιστών).
GC I	Geneva Convention I for the Amelioration of the Condition of the Wounded and Sick in Armed Forces in the Field 1949.
GC II	Geneva Convention II for the Amelioration of the Condition of the Wounded, Sick and Shipwrecked Members of Armed Forces at Sea 1949.
GC III	Geneva Convention III relative to the Treatment of Prisoners of War 1949.
GC IV	Geneva Convention IV relative to the Protection of Civilian Persons in Time of War 1949.
HORM	Minutes of the House of Representative (Plenary Sessions).
ICJ	International Court of Justice.
ICRC	International Committee of the Red Cross.
ILA	International Law Association.
NATO	North Atlantic Treaty Organisation.
PCTA	Provisional Cyprus Turkish Administration.
PIO	Public Information Office (succeeded by the Press and Information Office / Γραφείο Τύπου και Πληροφοριών).

RoC / the Republic	Republic of Cyprus.
SBA(s)	Sovereign Base Area(s).
ToA	Treaty of Alliance.
ToE	Treaty of Establishment.
ToG	Treaty of Guarantee.
TMT	Turkish Resistance Organisation (Türk Mukavemet Teşkilatı).
TRNC	Turkish Republic of Northern Cyprus.
TWAIL	Third World Approaches to International Law.
UK	United Kingdom of Great Britain and Northern Ireland.
UN	United Nations.
UNA	United Nations Archive.
UNCIVPOL	UN Civilian Police.
UNFICYP	United Nations Force in Cyprus.
UNGA	United Nations General Assembly.
UNSC	United Nations Security Council.
USA	United States of America.
WWI	First World War.
WWII	Second World War.

List of Tables

Table 2.1 Indicators suggesting the levels of 'Organisation' and 'Intensity' in cases of internal armed violence may have reached the threshold of a non-international armed conflict 56
Table 5.1 RoC Population per ethnic group (RoC Census December 1960) 203

CHAPTER 1

The Cyprus Question: A Problem of Many Angles

For decades, the so-called Cyprus Question has been at a standstill. Though many are aware that Cyprus is divided in a 'northern' and a 'southern' part, few are familiar with the background story to this state of affairs. Even fewer with the fact that the issue has been holding a semi-permanent position at the United Nations Security Council's (UNSC) agenda for six full decades. The suppression of some of the darkest periods of Cypriot history in public discourse has had a tremendous impact on Cypriot society. This has not only distorted the historical record, but it has also had a direct political impact, domestically and internationally, through the sustenance of resentment, fear and mistrust between members of each Cypriot community.

There is no simple way to engage with modern Cypriot history without acknowledging the complex matrix of internal and international actors that have vested interests in a pending resolution of the Cyprus Question. British-Cypriot anthropologist Peter Loizos, who spent most of his career at the London School of Economics and one of the most influential academics on the experience of displacement,[1] had used the analogy of a car accident in bad weather to illustrate how the many different variants of the accident may prevent a straightforward recognition of who is to be held accountable for it. Was it the bad weather conditions, a technical failure, or

[1] Loizos, *The Heart Grown Bitter.*

N. Kornioti, *Law's Politics: The Cyprus Troubles, 1960–1968*,
https://doi.org/10.1007/978-3-031-93369-1_1

a malicious, or negligent, or contingently fatal act by each of the drivers involved? Similarly in the Cyprus case, he argued, the different levels of engagement within a complex period of rapid global developments prevent the unambiguous restructuring of the events that took place. Loizos, therefore, systematised the different actors involved in the Cyprus Question as follows:

(a) the mass of 'ordinary' Turkish Cypriots and Greek Cypriots, most of whom lived together with people from the other community, developing social and economic relations despite their 'consciousness of difference', 'antagonism' and 'mistrust';
(b) the formal and informal relations between the political leaders of the two communities;
(c) the foreign policy-makers of the United Kingdom (UK), Greece and Turkey, the Guarantor Powers of Cypriot independence, who would be driven by their own interests; and
(d) the priorities of the UN, NATO, and the Warsaw Pact in the Eastern Mediterranean, in the context of their long-term competition.[2]

Starting from this premise, the present book seeks to enrich the existing literature and the public discourse on inter-communal violence in Cyprus. Unlike most of the literature on the Cyprus Question, which deals with foreign policy and the interests of foreign actors, the book turns the spotlight internally, on inter-communal relations, and the experience of ordinary people.

The entry point towards achieving this, from a primarily legal perspective, is common article 3 of the 1949 Geneva Conventions I-IV Relating to the Protection of Victims of Armed Conflicts.[3] The first and only public international law provision dealing with 'armed conflict not of an international character' until 1977, when Additional Protocol II to the 1949 Geneva Conventions Relating to the Protection of Victims of Non-International Armed Conflicts was adopted. The focus on a single international legal provision is of significance considering the chronological focus on the book, from the establishment of the Republic of Cyprus (RoC) in 1960 to 1968. The 1960s constitute a very particular period in the development of international law in the shadow of the Second World War

[2] Loizos, *Unofficial Views*, 77–79.

[3] For the full text of common article 3 see Annex I.

(WWII), the period of decolonisation, the Cold War, and the rise of the Civil Rights movement. Thus, the book serves as an opportunity to situate the events in Cyprus within a broader framework, showing how the most complex aspects of the Cyprus Question are a product of a particular time, impacted directly by global political and legal developments of the 1960s, but also earlier.

Through common article 3, the direct question raised in the book is whether armed violence between the Greek Cypriot and the Turkish Cypriot communities did in fact reach the level of non-international armed conflict, as defined legally, starting from the first major wave of violence between the two communities in December 1963. The book then concludes in March 1968 when measures were adopted by the first President of the Republic towards the restoration of order, ahead of the first formal cycle of inter-communal negotiations in search of a settlement. Thus, the book addresses the most definitive years of the rising tension in inter-communal relations on the island, constituting the prologue to the coup d'état and the Turkish invasion of summer 1974, which led to the division of the island as it currently stands. Kypros Chrysostomides, former Minister of Foreign Affairs of the RoC and an international lawyer, had admitted that inter-communal violence after the establishment of the RoC could generally be described as a 'civil conflict' or 'even "civil war"'[4] without engaging in a complete legal analysis, but other sources have left the topic majorly unaddressed. In the literature, the period from 1963 onwards is referred to in various ways, such as 'the uneasy years', 'civil strife', 'internal conflict' and 'internal crisis', among others, whereas references to a 'civil war' are extremely rare. The same applies to international studies on armed conflict with reference to Cyprus, but retain the same ambiguity on the pre-1974 period.

To the readers unfamiliar with the Cyprus Question, the main premise upon which this book is based may come across as curiously simplistic. Surely, an event as severe as a civil war could not go unnoticed in global affairs or historiography. As already mentioned, however, common article 3 serves only as the legal mechanism through which the book seeks to address the broader interplay between law and politics, and the consequences this has had for Cyprus, the region and international law itself, in terms of public discourse and the predominant historical record. The book follows years-long observations on how along with the fragmented

[4] Chrysostomides, *The Republic of Cyprus*, 93.

historical record that has survived in the public discourse over the decades, there is a parallel fragmentation of the legal questions that dominate local politics. The fragmented historical narrative stems from decades-long physical division of the Turkish Cypriot and Greek Cypriot communities, which started in the late 1950s, was reinforced as of the last days of 1963, and was solidified in the summer of 1974, leading to two separate historical narratives by each community. According to anthropologist Rebecca Bryant, this is also the result of a 'tacit complicity' on behalf of academia, not only in Cyprus but also in conflict situations in general, as there are often topics that scholars simply 'do not dare to touch'.[5] In that regard, whereas the book would be of interest to those who seek to obtain a deeper understanding of inter-communal relations and violence in Cyprus, the case of Cyprus itself is one of the many, yet lesser-known, case studies stemming from the period of decolonisation, addressing issues of broader theoretical concern at the crossroads of law, politics, history, and historiography.

The starting point for the inquiry that has led to this book lies with the dominant Greek Cypriot narrative's reference to the events of the 1960s as 'the troubles' *(οι φασαρίες)*, or the 'Turkish insurrection' *(τουρκική ανταρσία, τουρκοανταρσία)*. The term 'Troubles', which has been employed most notably with reference to the events in Northern Ireland from the 1960s to 1998, carries no legal connotations. Sociologists, however, distinguish between 'troubles'—personal problems or matters that have to do with one's self—from 'issues', whose use extends to problems 'beyond the individual and local environment', such as 'crises' in an institutional context.[6] This sociological differentiation is arguably applicable here in an international context, if one looks at the 'international community' of states as 'a society', where every state is a separate 'individual'. Then, 'troubles' could suggest that an ongoing problem falls within the internal (private) affairs of the State, meriting no involvement from outside actors, while an 'issue' would call for the raise of concern and involvement from other actors external to the State, meaning the international community. In either case, the impact of the decades-long reference to 'troubles' on Greek Cypriot public consciousness is obvious, especially in light of the better-known, more dramatic, and more impactful Turkish invasion of 1974.

In English, the Greek word *ανταρσία (an-dar-see-ah)* has multiple overlapping meanings in its plain and ordinary meaning, including 'uprising',

[5] Bryant, "State of Cypriot Silences"

[6] Alexander and others, C*ontemporary introduction to Sociology* 13.

'sedition', 'mutiny', 'insurgency', insurrection', 'rebellion' and 'revolt'.[7] Thus, the term *Τουρκοανταρσία*, carries more direct political connotations, since it implies that the events in question were nothing more than a 'Turkish insurrection'.[8] The adjective 'Turkish' already disclosing 'who started it', and subsequently, who carries bigger responsibility for what followed. Legal literature, on the other hand, refers to *ανταρσία* as 'insurgency', which is a legally charged term, even though its colloquial use in Greek downplays the seriousness of the events, from which no exact legal meaning can be deduced. As perceived in the mainstream Greek Cypriot narrative, *ανταρσία* suggests a spontaneous 'taking of arms' against the government, but which was not severe enough to suggest this was a 'civil war', or an 'internal armed conflict'. To an external observer this careful engagement and scrutiny of specific terminology may seem superfluous. In the Cypriot context, however, the choice of specific terms over others plays a paramount role in every aspect of all discussions concerning the Cyprus Question. To a certain extent this carefully curated vocabulary has helped build a series of uncritically accepted facts that form the basis for the mainstream narrative of each community for decades.[9]

On the other end of the argument made in this book is the history of international law itself, as a discipline. As recognised by Anghie, the histories of international law express also the history of broader ideas.[10] Thus, given law's alleged ability to impact the conduct of various actors and hold them accountable, a study of the history of public international law also addresses questions pertaining to the way a particular history is written. Thus, one's understanding of the events that unfolded in Cyprus in the 1960s shifts once clarified that until the mid-twentieth century each of the terms 'rebellion' and 'insurgency' had a very specific meaning under international humanitarian law, as the milder phases of what is usually understood by 'civil war'.[11] Considering, therefore, the legal weight carried by some of the various terms *ανταρσία* can be translated into, and the calls for a deeper engagement with the 'Cypriot civil war',[12] the book problematizes the use of the law during this period, through a little-known case

[7] *Modern Greek-English Dictionary Vol. I* (Aristide D. Caratzas 2005)

[8] PIO, *Problem in Perspective*, 7

[9] Ioannou, *Normalisation of Cyprus' Partition*, 49–53, 123–142; Kızılyürek, *Resentment*, 499; Panayiotou, "Hegemony, Permissible Public Discourse" 71

[10] Anghie, "Basic principles of international law" 48.

[11] Orford, "Civil Wars".

[12] Varnava, "Renembering the Cypriot Civil War".

study. Namely, the experience of inter-communal armed violence in the RoC, during the 1960s.

I would hereby like to raise four points of clarification, to better illustrate the argument made in this book. Firstly, when looking at inter-communal violence in Cyprus, the book is in agreement with other commentators who have stated that one cannot comprehend fully the issues that led to extensive inter-communal violence within three years from the establishment of the RoC, unless the broader historical context, and in particular the pre-independence decades of Cypriot history, are also taken into account.[13] For this reason, the book starts with a scene-setting chapter on the relevance of nineteenth-century imperialism, colonialism and the global movement for decolonisation to Cyprus.

Secondly, the book rejects the dominant view that post-independence armed violence arose in 1963–1964, and then again in 1974. While this is not wrong in terms of the *intensity* of violence witnessed, the book looks at violence and its consequences holistically, over a rather extended and coherent timeline, introducing earlier signs and manifestations of tension before the establishment of the RoC. A similar view has been expressed by Gregoris Ioannou, according to whom inter-communal violence 'climaxed' in 1964, but the violent environment was 'maintained' until 1967.[14] Even then, one cannot tell with certainty whether the relative lack of inter-communal violence from 1968 to 1974 was a time of inter-communal 'peace', and not the first stage of a 'frozen' deadlock, considering that the internal and international mechanisms employed to deal with the exceptional circumstances on the island from December 1963 onwards remained in place then, and some of them are still in place today.

Thirdly, aligned with those views that call for more research on Cypriot history from a serious, systematic, critical and reflective perspective, the present research adopts a critical international legal position, according to which the primary concern is not whether one has behaved lawfully or unlawfully, but whether certain behaviour is or not *legally justifiable*.[15] Hence, the aim of the book is not to 'adjudicate' the violence that took place in Cyprus and allocate responsibility for the atrocities committed. Instead, considering the global historical background, the aim is to problematise how the local and the international legal culture, along with

[13] Hatzivassiliou, *The Cyprus Question*, 72.

[14] Ioannou, *The Normalisation of Cyprus' Partition*, 20–21.

[15] Klabbers, *International Law*, 22.

the surrounding political and diplomatic discourse, have contributed to the maintenance of a 'state of Cypriot silences'.[16]

Lastly, due to language constraints, the present book has relied more heavily on materials in Greek, English, and French and occasionally German, even though views and experiences recorded in the Turkish language would have undoubtedly enriched it. An anthropological perspective is once again instructive here, since as demonstrated by social anthropologist Olga Demetriou, in research cross-fertilising 'politics' and 'science', the 'threshold of objectivity', is often a 'conscious negotiation' between one's understanding of 'their subjective positioning and that of the objective analysis they are expected to present'.[17] Thus, given my own positionality, the book may at certain points inevitably engage with, assess, and analyse the events presented from a Greek Cypriot perspective, despite the fact that every effort has been made to present an as broad range of views and contextual information as possible.

Legal Theory, History, and Interdisciplinary Research

Internal armed violence or conflict is a notoriously complicated topic to study from an international law perspective, primarily due to the overarching role of the principle of sovereignty, which in its classical sense precludes external actors from engaging with the internal politics of a sovereign State. Moreover, as elaborated in detail in the following chapter, there was an 'interlude' regarding common article 3 from 1949 to 1968,[18] during which colonial powers and new States were reluctant to accept the application of international humanitarian law, the sub-area of international law dealing with conduct during armed conflict, in internal conflicts. The plethora of internal conflicts during that period however, most recognisable among them the Vietnam War, led to renewed efforts to strengthen the protection of non-combatants in non-international armed conflicts, and the adoption of the additional provisions regulating internal armed conflict under Additional Protocol II to the 1949 Geneva Conventions. Since then, there have been multiple studies on the phenomenon from various disciplinary perspectives.

[16] Bryant, "Cypriot Silences," 113.

[17] Demetriou, "Paratexts of the Cyprus Conflict," 95.

[18] Mantilla, "Origins and Evolution," 49.

With some notable exceptions, interest in the topic in international law resurged primarily in the 1990s, in the context of the armed conflicts in former Yugoslavia and Rwanda, during what has been called the 'great renaissance'[19] of international criminal law, the area of international law that deals with the criminal responsibility of individuals accused of misconduct during atrocities, and the renewed debates over the establishment of a permanent International Criminal Court. The topic obtained such significance that in 1999 the American Journal of International Law (AJIL) organised a symposium on 'Method in International Law', on 'individual accountability for violations of human dignity committed in internal conflict, with respect to both the substantive law and the mechanisms for accountability'.[20]

Traditionally legal scholarship does not engage with 'methodology' in the same way the Social Sciences do. As a matter of fact, the boundaries between legal philosophy, theory, and method are rather obscure. Legal positivism, the dominant theoretical paradigm since the nineteenth century, has detached legal analysis from engaging with 'extra-judicial considerations', such as economic, social, moral, and political factors. Instead, what is called a 'doctrinal' or 'black letter' approach is preferred,[21] which seeks to apply a set of facts to a relevant set of laws, without a critical engagement with other factors. Albeit 'modern positivism' is less 'extreme' in its detachment from extra-judicial factors and recognises that the law is not independent from context in a given situation, lawyers remain generally confined to 'clarify[ing] the legal side of things', and not to facilitate a decision-maker's 'dilemma' between law, politics, and morals.[22] Hence, the lawyer is either called to take the lead in a formal judicial or quasi-judicial setting, for example a tribunal or a fact-finding commission, or they take the backstage and let the final decision (and the assumption of responsibility) to an appointed or elected decision-maker.

In the Cypriot context, the persistence of an extremely politicised and volatile environment left virtually no room for a constructive and reflective engagement with deeper questions of legal theory and practice, turning the Cyprus Question in a considerably under-theorised and rather marginalised case study internationally. Claire Palley's observation that 'a Greek Cypriot

[19] Schabas and Bernaz, "Introduction," 1.

[20] Slaughter and Ratner, "Appraising the Methods of International Law," 295.

[21] Bianchi, *International Law Theories*, 21.

[22] Simma and Paulus, "The Responsibility of Individuals," 306–307.

writer, who presents facts and general community views on their significance, risks being accused of bias, with any strong opinions being singled out as evidencing prejudice',[23] is especially true for those academically inclined Cypriot lawyers of the older generations, who may have had an interest to examine the facts at face value, and not in pursuit of one-sided legal arguments. Not to mention early precedents of persecution and impunity before and after the establishment of the Republic, for those who deviated from the dominant policy line of their respective community, at a time when the domestic criminal justice system proved repeatedly ineffective in bringing alleged perpetrators to justice.

Moreover, contrary to today, up until the 1990s, there were no international tribunals that could have complemented the jurisdiction of domestic Cypriot courts in the pursuit of accountability. Despite various calls for the introduction of State-led transitional justice mechanisms, like 'fact-finding' or 'truth' commissions, such initiatives were never properly introduced. Thus, with the exception of the well-known and rather influential case law of the European Court of Human Rights (ECtHR), which addresses only some aspects of the Cyprus Question, the formalist framework within which lawyers can traditionally offer their input beyond the politically charged environment of the Executive and the Legislature, never materialised.[24] Though Transitional Justice initiatives elsewhere have not always been convincing in reconciling the opposing parties to a conflict, their informative potential is undeniable,[25] and the complete lack of any such mechanisms in Cyprus, has led to a significant gap in the preservation of a common Cypriot historical memory. This explains why this book requires an interdisciplinary analysis, taking with equal seriousness the extensive examination of historical facts on the one side, and a legal and legal-historical analysis on the other. Nevertheless, even though the binary division between *questions of fact* and *questions of law* are present in any legal proceeding, the intertwining of past facts (the realm of history) and law, is not always straight forward in the relative abstractness of *academic* legal writing.

Lastly, even though the present book is telling 'a story', it cannot claim to be saying 'the whole story'. The events that follow the chronology of the book post-1968, are equally important in order to obtain a comprehensive

[23] Foreword by Claire Palley in Soulioti, *Fettered Independence: Narrative*, xvi.
[24] Hadjigeorgiou, "A one-sided coin".
[25] Teitel, *Transitional Justice*, 69–117.

understanding of the full spectrum of legal and socio-political elements entangled in the Cyprus Question. Here, the priority has been to enrich the abundant literature on the Cyprus Question with overlooked legal observations, with the objective to draw attention to the domestic, inter-communal aspects of the Republic's early history, moving away from the predominantly international relations-dominated literature of the last decades. It is within this context that the need for interdisciplinarity emerged, as a means to integrate the input from different relevant disciplines within a history-oriented legal research project. In the words of political geographer Richard Patrick, author of the first and potentially most complete account of the events discussed here to date, had stated that 'we all accept that conflict and peace research, by its very nature, is an inter-disciplinary hybrid'.[26]

While legal philosophy had already started questioning legal formalism in the nineteenth century, stronger deviation from the positivist approach in international law occurred in the 1940s in law schools in the United States of America (USA), following international law's failure to prevent the atrocities of WWII. The same trend, however, was not immediately observed across the Atlantic. A phenomenon that further reduced the intellectual space that would have potentially allowed for a non-positivist theoretical engagement with international law (and law in general) in Cyprus, where leading Greek and Turkish legal academics joined forces with Cypriot lawyers in all efforts to overcome the legal complexities associated with the Cyprus Question. This was despite the fact that a considerable number of prominent Cypriot lawyers in the period surrounding Cypriot independence were educated and qualified as Barristers in England and, as seen further, were not oblivious to the colonial prejudices of their discipline.

It must be further clarified that until recently there was no Cyprus-based Law School that would be able to engage with the matter on a more academic base. The very first university on the territory controlled by the RoC post-1974, the University of Cyprus, was established in 1989, admitting its first students in 1992, whereas the first Law Department was established at the same institution in 2006.[27] The above comes in striking antithesis to the rich contribution of international lawyers from other former colonies, many of whom from the 1960s onwards revolutionised international legal

[26] Patrick, *Political Geography and the Cyprus Conflict*, 400.

[27] Ioannou and Sonan, *Inter-Communal Contact*.

thought, through the so-called Third World Approaches to International Law (TWAIL) movement,[28] by identifying and contextualising the recurring colonial biases of public international law, maintained in the new post-colonial States.[29]

From a legal theoretical perspective, the Cyprus Question is an obvious 'hard case'. A case in which the result cannot be 'clearly dictated by statute or precedent'[30] or, in international law terms, by treaty or customary law. According to Finnish Professor of International Law and former diplomat Martti Koskenniemi, in such cases a decision can be reached either through broad outlines of justification which accept that sometimes there are gaps in the law, a 'weak justification', or through a 'strong justification' rooted in the ability of legal principles to be used in a way which would eventually determine and justify a final outcome. These two contradictory approaches result in 'any international dispute becom[ing] a hard case by the simple fact that disputing States are *always* able to make a *prima facie* justification of their action by referring to their sovereign liberty'.[31]

On this basis, the international legal argument is characterised by a dualism that makes international law both inherently indeterminate and political.[32] One of the examples Koskenniemi offers lies at the epicentre of many international disputes, including the Cyprus Question. This is no other than the tension between the opposing principles of 'self-determination' and 'territorial integrity', which are 'ultimately the same', since 'When a group of people call for territorial integrity, they call for respect for their identity as a self-determining entity and *vice-versa*'.[33] In this way, since the 1990s, Koskenniemi's work has offered new impetus and an innovative framework for international legal reach, through which one can examine how the two Cypriot communities eventually 'neutralised' each other,[34] through their diametrically opposed aspirations for the governance of Cyprus, based on contradictory claims of territorial integrity and self-determination.

[28] Gathii, "TWAIL: A Brief History of Its Origins," 26.

[29] Abi-Saab, "The Newly Independent States"; Anand, "Role of the '"New" Asian-African Countries".

[30] Dworkin, "Hard Cases".

[31] Koskenniemi, *From Apology to Utopia,* 41–47.

[32] Koskenniemi, *From Apology to Utopia,* 590–591.

[33] Koskenniemi, *From Apology to Utopia,* 510.

[34] Kızılyürek, *Resentment,* 580.

With a distance of more than half a century from the events addressed here, the book inevitably also raises the question of *why* the substantially relevant area of international humanitarian law has been absent from the general discussion on the Cyprus Question, despite the fact that the use of armed violence during the most tense days of inter-communal 'strife' is undisputed. It is in order to shed light on this question that the present research turns to both the work of the Critical Legal Studies (CLS) and TWAIL movements, given the impact the two have had on the 'historical turn' in international law over the last two decades. From that perspective, one can look at Cyprus as a case study illustrating over an extended period of time how when international law's *'tekhne'*, its skill, fails to give an answer to a 'hard case', legal formalism's inability or reluctance to integrate a broader, extra-legal perspective into the debate leads to 'silence'.[35] A 'silence' which derives from the marginalisation of a seemingly irrelevant international legal practice.

Admittedly, assuming a critical approach in a research project focusing on international humanitarian law may come across as a paradox. Critical legal scholarship has often employed a cynical stand vis-à-vis the employment of a 'humanitarian language', which is used by military, political, and humanitarian professionals alike, despite the contradicting priorities these professional groups have.[36] It is here conceded that problems with humanitarianism are many and, as seen in the next chapter, some of them can be traced to the very foundations of the idea of 'humanitarianism'. It has been observed, however, that in situations of use of force (and by extension in international humanitarian law too) 'it tends to be non-lawyers rather than lawyers whose expectations are unreasonably elevated and who attack international law as having no significant role when there is anything less than perfect compliance'.[37] Hence, unless the lawyers take it on themselves to insist participating in the discussion and keep the legal debates alive and present in the public discourse, those who international humanitarian law claims to protect are usually kept in the dark about law's challenges and shortcomings, oftentimes misled by absolute claims to 'truth' and promises of exaggerated notions of an unattainable ideal of 'justice'.

Another tension between this research and the above theoretical approach is that scholars usually associated with the CLS movement reject

[35] Korhonen, "New International Law," 12–18.

[36] Kennedy, *Dark Side of Virtue.*

[37] Gray, *Use of Force*, 25.

the idea of interdisciplinarity, and yet the book has already admitted to an interdisciplinary approach. Such criticisms have been expressed for instance against early efforts in the 1990s to develop a 'dual agenda' that would bring together public international law and international relations research under a single methodology.[38] This was a warning against developing increasingly complicated technical vocabularies,[39] leading to 'overblown expectations'.[40] This is not the kind of interdisciplinarity the present thesis promotes. The purpose of interdisciplinarity here is rather to illustrate how other disciplines have found it easier to engage with some of the most controversial aspects of Cyprus' history, and use public international law and legal history as a means to address persisting arguments with legal contributions.

The debates between the realist and the critical approaches, are pertinent to the events discussed in the book, since a considerable number of US-based legal commentators who had written about the Cyprus Question in the 1960s and the 1970s, were linked to the policy-oriented 'New Haven' or 'International Legal Process' schools of thought in public international law.[41] Apart from the early TWAILers mentioned above, these were the only other group of scholars who systematically engaged with the problematic non-application of the limited (but formally enforceable) common article 3 in the 1960s, and the problems this led to in instances of internal violence. A subtle reminder, perhaps, of the fact that the CLS movement itself, like the 'New Haven' and the 'International Legal Process' movements, derived from pre-WWII American Legal Realism.

Among the various theoretical streams and schools of thought developed in international legal scholarship, TWAIL is described as a 'distinctive way of thinking about international law'.[42] Even though the term was coined in 1997, the origins of this way of thinking lie in the work of the first generation of post-colonial international lawyers, who wanted to show how international law 'legitimiz[ed] the subjugation and oppression of Third World peoples'.[43] Its scope of interest has expanded since then, but at its core the approach retains a distinctive historical re-examination of

[38] Dunnoff and Pollack, "International Law and International Relations," 3.

[39] Koskenniemi, "Miserable Comforters"; Klabbers, "The Bridge Crack'd".

[40] Klabbers, 'Whatever Happened to Gramsci?," 478.

[41] Miller, *Cyprus: Law and Politics*; Ehrlich, *Cyprus 1958–1967*; Falk, *International Law of Civil War*.

[42] Gathii, "TWAIL: A Brief History of Its Origins."

[43] Anghie and Chimni, "Individual Responsibility in Internal Conflict," 186–187.

international law, including a critique of nation-State formation processes in the Third World and the resulting resort to violence in many cases. Even before the RoC joined the European Union (EU) in 2004, its perception as a post-colonial State was interrupted by its proximity to Europe. However, Cypriot history shares many of the colonial and post-colonial tensions experienced in many Afro-Asian States, along with Malta and Ireland; the other two cases of post-colonial 'peripheral' Europe.[44] This is a validation of the ascertainment that 'history matters' and 'the South moves';[45] meaning the constant change of our perception of the world under generic geographical or other terms, like current references to a 'Global South' and a 'Global North', or alternative references to 'developed' and 'developing' States, or a 'First World' and a 'Third World'.

The theoretical frameworks and schools of thought that have been guiding international legal scholarship for the most part of the second half of the twentieth century are illustrative of how international legal theoretical frameworks have been feeding into debates concerning the relevance of legal thought to practical issues. There are also, however, recognised 'law and …' approaches, which relate more directly to social scientific notions of methodology, including 'law and history',[46] among various alternatives, such as 'law and economics' or 'law and anthropology'. These approaches to law are interdisciplinary by default and require engagement with both law and the other discipline on an equal basis.[47] Thus, the 'law and history' approach, is separate from the field of legal history, where the latter constructs a linear study of the development of a specific law or field of law.[48]

The present book draws from both legal history and the 'law and history' approach. This is achieved through a more descriptive engagement with international law's history, but also by employing history-related methodologies, through an extensive assessment of archival materials. The book follows in the footsteps of other legal historians like Brian Simpson, who is not only one of the leading legal historians of the development of the common law, but also wrote a detailed account on the history of the European Convention on Human Rights (ECHR) in the 1950s, based on the Cypriot experience with human rights advocacy during the anti-colonial

[44] Reynolds, "Peripheral Parallels?," 247.
[45] Eslava, Luis, "TWAIL Coordinates."
[46] Cammiss and Watkins, "Legal research in the humanities".
[47] Hervey et al., *Research Methodologies,* 76–77.
[48] Handler, "Legal History".

EOKA emergency of 1955–1959.[49] To complete the puzzle, despite the many debates on law, history, and their politics in international law,[50] international lawyers are yet to come to overriding conclusions on an exact methodology that shall be applied in research at the intersection of law and history.[51] Hence, history's relationship with international law is currently in flux, and debates among international lawyers, but also between international lawyers and historians, are still ongoing.[52]

Lastly, the increasing comfort of international lawyers to expand their disciplinary horizons has led to another parallel development, which is no other than the increased blending of international legal analysis with internal law, as a means to situate international law's abstractions in the 'empirical world of ordinary life', in order to improve international law and its institutions.[53] This is particularly true in a study on 'internal' violence, such as the present, where internal developments play an equally important, if not more determinate, role than the various international actors with an interest in the conflict. Thus, apart from extensive references to public international law, the book also contains extensive information on how inter-communal violence affected the socio-legal landscape in Cyprus, including *intra-disciplinary* references to the Republic's domestic constitutional and criminal legal frameworks.

Speaking of history and time merits also a note on geography and space. Despite the numerous linkages one can establish between Cyprus and other regions of the world due to similar experience, one must not overlook that Cyprus as an island experiences an 'apparent paradox, between isolation and linkage',[54] with historians observing that insularity constitutes island-territories as:

> a bridge or a stepping stone; a frontier outpost or an imperial backwater province; a realm marked by parochialism or a meeting point of civilizations; a place of exile or a laboratory.[55]

[49] Simpson, *Human Rights and the End of Empire*.
[50] Orford, *International Law and the Politics of History*.
[51] Vadi, "International Law and its Histories"; de la Rasilla, *International Law and History*.
[52] Orford, "On International Legal Method"; Benton, "Beyond Anachronism".
[53] Chimni, "The Past, Present and Future".
[54] Nicolini and Perrin, "Geographical Connections," 8.
[55] Hadjikyriacou, "Insularity in the Ottoman World," viii-ix.

Island studies have also recognised island-territories as ideal 'laboratories' for the sociogeographical study of communal social relations, given their tendency to develop unique features; a follow through to nineteenth-century recognition of islands as excellent laboratories for evolutionary research in the natural sciences.[56] Hence, with Cyprus being the third largest island in the Mediterranean Sea, located at the Mediterranean basin's north-eastern corner at the 'crossroads of three continents' (Europe, Africa and Asia), the island's geographical location allows for an empirical 'micro-history'[57] of the phenomenon of protracted, complex conflicts.[58] The lack of continental borders, which often serve as continuous points of tension between the opposing parties in an armed conflict, and more importantly without a serious violent incident having taken place since the late 1990s, there is a maintenance of 'laboratory conditions', which is rarely available in situations where upheavals are common.

Overcoming Silence and Abstraction

The plethora of question marks that still exist in the general understanding of 'what exactly happened' in Cyprus in the 1960s, contrasts sharply with the vast amount of general literature, concerning the island's history in the second half of the twentieth century. Overall, existing literature varies in terms of the origin of the authors, the language, the scope, focus, and disciplinary angles chosen. Hence, given the gaps in the historical narratives regarding the period examined in the present thesis, the consultation of archival material was of paramount importance in order to connect the dots between those incidents broadly discussed in the literature, and those issues that have not attracted the same level of attention.

For decades research conducted on Cyprus had relied heavily on materials stored at The National Archives in Kew, London, due to an overall lack of culture, on behalf of the Cypriot State, to meticulously preserve and make publicly available archival information. During the period under consideration here, the situation was described by former RoC Minister of Justice, Stella Soulioti, as follows:

[56] Pungetti, "Islands, culture, landscape," 53.
[57] Vadi, "International Law and its Histories," 330–331.
[58] Policinski and Kuzmanovic, "Editorial."

> There was [in the 1960s] no Public Record Office and no official historian. As a member of the first Council of Ministers, I therefore felt a compulsion to collect, copy and classify all documents and to record all meetings, conversations and events which I thought were significant. [...] On the other side of the scales, however, was the President of the Republic, Archbishop Makarios, who could not bear to keep a document. Anything other than a strictly official document of state he consigned to the fire. He was particularly ruthless with his own manuscripts. [...] It was not until 1964 that Archbishop Makarios realised the value of archives. [...] Even after I stopped being a Minister in 1970, he would give me copies of documents and relate to me conversations and events which he thought should be [on] record.[59]

Hence, significant amount of historical memory has been preserved and published by private individuals, including former State officials like Soulioti. Moreover, from 1960 to 1974 there was no centralised, high-level, government-led international policy in the Republic, given the volatile and peculiar circumstances on the island.[60] This has been an additional hurdle towards the evaluation of decisions taken by State-actors during the same period.

The RoC Constitution does enclose a Right to Petition under article 29, which enables individuals or groups to address requests or complaints to any public authority, including the legislature, the judiciary, local authorities, and semi-governmental organisations, which need to be replied to within 30 days. However, the application of this provision has been problematic for decades, and the legal framework on accessing public information was only strengthened much later. First in 1991 with the Law on the Establishment of a State Archive (Law 208/1991), and more recently, through the Law on the Right of Access to Public Sector Information 2017 (Law 184(I)/2017), which has been enforceable since 22 December 2020, and reflects the provisions of the UK equivalent Freedom of Information Act 2000.

As a result of such recent developments, it was not clear at the beginning of the present research, in January 2018, what information would be readily available. For this reason, at the planning stages of the research, this project too relied heavily on the possibility to consult The National Archives. In that regard, a short introductory study visit to London took place in June 2018, and in July 2019, I had the privilege to be selected for

[59] Soulioti, *Fettered Independence: Narrative*, xix.
[60] Kouskouvelis, "Small state strategy".

participation at the *Global Humanitarianism Research Academy 2019*, organised by the Leibniz Institute of European History, in Mainz, Germany, the University of Exeter, UK, and the International Committee of the Red Cross (ICRC), in Geneva, Switzerland, through which I had the opportunity to obtain full access and study the ICRC archive on the ICRC's mission to Cyprus from January 1964 to December 1965. Material from the ICRC has not been previously published, and the information contained therein has been a valuable contribution to the book and a unique source on concrete developments on the field.

The detailed information available in the ICRC archive was further enhanced once combined with a thorough study of the archival material readily available online from the United Nations (UN). Such information includes documents from the UN online documentation database, which contains formal correspondence submitted to UN organs, General Assembly and Security Council verbatim records, and the periodical reports of the UN Secretary-General on the activities of the United Nations Force in Cyprus (UNFICYP), from 1964 to 1968. Among these, the UN Secretary-General reports on peace operations have been recognised as 'critical contributions'[61] to the work of the UNSC, and despite being descriptive and diplomatic in nature, they have been instrumental in rebuilding a coherent timeline of events. Though the Secretary-General reports have been relied on by other researchers, they had rarely been used for the extraction of information on Cypriot society at the time, or for the purpose of collecting data of legal significance. Reference must be made also to the limited use of the UN Online Archive, originally stored in New York, which according to the information available on the website contains an astonishing amount of 765 boxes on UNFICYP alone up to 1974. Yet, the vast majority of them are still classified as 'Strictly Confidential'. A testimony to the lack of a political settlement and the ongoing relevance of this historical period to developments today.

The findings in the above archives have been further complemented by additional archival material available online. Namely, selected declassified reports from the USA Central Intelligence Agency (CIA), as well as the USA State Department's Office of the Historian. In Cyprus, the online Press Releases' Archive of the RoC Press and Information Office (PIO) containing information from 1962 onwards, as well as the complete Official Record of the Plenary Sessions' Minutes of the House of Representatives

[61] Johnstone, "Role of the UN Secretary-General," 447.

(HORM) since the establishment of the RoC, served as valuable digitally accessible Cyprus-based sources. One should not omit to also mention online access to the minutes, the Hansard, of the Westminster Parliament in London. There is, of course, a plethora of archives that have not been studied yet, including the Turkish Cypriot public archive located in Kyrenia, of which I have been informed informally by UNFICYP officers and Turkish Cypriot researchers.

To the archival material mentioned above, one needs to add the vast number of books, journal articles, policy reports, and personal accounts on the Cyprus Question, illustrating even more starkly the disbalance in the comparatively limited amount of materials produced in (international) law, as opposed to the plethora of materials of other genres and disciplines. Contrary to the plethora of materials engaging with the international elements of the Cyprus Question published for decades, such as the 'Cyprus triangle' of Greek, Turkish, and British relations, most of the internal aspects, including the inter-communal armed violence in the decade preceding 1974, have been overlooked. Extensive cross-reference to the materials available from the ICRC and the UN in this book, make the two international organisations—along with the 'ordinary people of Cyprus', in the wording of Peter Loizos—the book's core protagonists.

Law is a discursive discipline and a powerful political tool. For decades the mainstream political and historical narratives developed in the Greek Cypriot and the Turkish Cypriot community supressed the violence perpetrated by each group, emphasising instead primarily the political and diplomatic aspects of the conflict, leading to an overall silence or a very abstract understanding of this period. Thus, the ambition of this book, and the research that preceded it, has not been to draw final conclusions on issues of legal violations and accountability, but rather to offer a legal interpretation of this controversial period in Cypriot history, to help overcome both the silence and the dominating abstraction. In doing so, the book also reflects critically on the history of international law itself. In the broader scope of things, the book envisages to contribute in both legal and historical debates on issues of war, peace, and ethnic disputes, that have their root in the post-colonial period and the Cold War, while setting the Cyprus Question on a broader global map of historical developments.

The book is organised in four substantive chapters which follow a chronological order, an epilogue, and a conclusion. Chapter 2 is a scene-setting chapter, introducing a brief history of international law and the establishment of both the ICRC and the UN, along with a summary of the colonial history of Cyprus. Chapter 3 introduces the constitutional arrangement which founded the RoC and the internal political turmoil of the first three years of the Republic's existence, while Chaps. 4 and 5 deal with the core years of inter-communal violence, from 1963 to 1968. The historical narrative is intertwined with reflections on the development of international law across this period.

Reference List

Books

Alexander, Jeffrey, Jeffrey C. Alexander, Kenneth Thompson, Laura Desfor Edles and Moshoula Capous-Desyllas. *A contemporary introduction to Sociology: Culture and Society in Transition.* 3rd ed., Routledge, 2018.

Bianchi, Andrea. *International Law Theories: An inquiry into different ways of thinking.* Oxford University Press, OUP 2016.

Chrysostomides, Kypros. *The Republic of Cyprus: A study in International Law.* Martinus Nijhoff, 2000.

de la Rasilla, Ignacio. *International Law and History: Modern Interfaces.* Cambridge University Press, 2021.

Drohan, Brian. *Brutality in an Age of Human Rights: Activism and Counterinsurgency at the End of the British Empire.* Cornell University Press, 2018.

Ehrlich, Thomas. *Cyprus 1958–1967.* Oxford University Press, 1974.

Gray, Christine. *International Law and the Use of Force.* 3rd edn, Oxford University Press, 2008.

Hatzivassiliou, Evanthis. *The Cyprus Question, 1878–1960: The Constitutional Aspect.* University of Minnesota, 2002.

Hervey, Tamara, Robert Cryer, Bal Sokhi-Bullley and Ali Bohm. *Research Methodologies in EU and International Law.* Hart, 2011.

Ioannou, Gregoris. *The Normalisation of Cyprus' Partition Among Greek Cypriots: Political Economy and Political Culture in a Divided Society.* Palgrave, 2020.

Kennedy, David. *The Dark Side of Virtue: Reassessing international humanitarianism.* Princeton University Press, 2005.

Niyazi Kizilyurek. *Μια ιστορία βίας και μνησικακίας: Η γένεση και η εξέλιξη της εθνοτικής διένεξης στην Κύπρο Vol 2* (A story of violence and resentment: The genesis and evolution of the ethnic conflict in Cyprus) (Heterotopia 2019) (in Greek)

Klabbers, Jan. *International Law.* 2nd edn, Cambridge University Press, 2017.

Koskenniemi, Martti. *From Apology to Utopia: The Structure of International Legal Argument.* Reissue with New Epilogue, Cambridge University Press, 2005.

Loizos, Peter. *The Heart Grown Bitter: A Chronicle of Cypriot War Refugees.* Cambridge University Press, 1981.
Loizos, Peter. *Unofficial Views: Cyprus: Society and Politics.* Intercollege Press, 2001.
Miller, Linda. *Cyprus: The Law and Politics of Civil* Strife. Center for International Affairs, Harvard University, 1968.
Orford, Anne. *International Law and the Politics of History.* Cambridge University Press, Cambridge University Press 2021a.
Patrick, Richard. *Political Geography and the Cyprus Conflict, 1963*–1971. University of Waterloo, 1989.
PIO, *The Problem in Perspective.* PIO, 1968.
Simpson, A W Brian. *Human Rights and the End of Empire: Britain and the Genesis of the European Convention.* Oxford University Press, 2004.
Soulioti, Stella. *Fettered Independence: Cyprus, 1878–1964 Vol 1 - The Narrative.* University of Minnesota Press, 2006.
Teitel, Ruti G. *Transitional Justice.* Oxford University Press, 2000.

Chapters in Edited Volumes

Anghie, Antony. "Basic principles of international law: A historical perspective." In *International Law for International Relations,* edited by Başak Çalı. OUP, 2010.
Cammiss, Steven and Dawn Watkins. "Legal research in the humanities." In *Research Methods in Law* edited by Dawn Watkins and Mandy Burton. 2nd edn, Routledge, 2018.
Dunnoff, Jeffrey and Mark Pollack. "International Law and International Relations: Introducing an Interdisciplinary Dialogue" *Interdisciplinary Perspectives on International Law and International Relations: The State of the Art*, edited by in Jeffrey Dunnoff and Mark Pollack. Cambridge University Press, 2013.
Hadjikyriacou, Antonis. "Envisioning Insularity in the Ottoman World" In *Islands of the Ottoman Empire*, edited by Antonis Hadjikyriacou. Markus Wiener, 2018.
Hadjigeorgiou, Nasia. "A one-sided coin: A critical analysis of the legal accounts of the Cypriot conflicts." In *The Palgrave Handbook of State-Sponsored History After 1945*, edited by Berber Bevernage and Nico Wouters. Palgrave, 2018.
Handler, Philip. "Legal History." In *Research Methods in Law* edited by Dawn Watkins and Mandy Burton. 2nd edn, Routledge, 2018.
Kouskouvelis, Elias I. Στρατηγική μικρών κρατών στο διεθνές σύστημα: η περίπτωση της Κύπρου' (Small state strategy in the international order: The Case of Cyprus). In *Το Κυπριακό και το Διεθνές Σύστημα, 1945–1974: Αναζητώντας θέση στον κόσμο* (The Cyprus Problem and the International System, 1945–1974: In search of a position in the world), edited by Petros Papapolyviou, Aggelos Syrigos and Evanthis Hatzivassiliou. Patakis, 2013.

Mantilla, Giovanni. "The Origins and Evolution of the 1949 Geneva Conventions and the 1977 Additional Protocols." In *Do the Geneva Conventions Matter?*, edited by Matthew Evangelista and Nina Tannenwald. Oxford University Press, 2017.

Panayiotou, Andreas. "Hegemony, Permissible Public Discourse and Lower Class Political Culture." In *Cyprus and the Politics of Memory*, edited by Rebecca Bryant and Yiannis Papadakis. Tauris I.B, 2012.

Reynolds, John. "Peripheral Parallels? Europe's Edges and the World of Bandung" In *Bandung, Global History and International Law: Critical Pasts and Pending Future*, edited by Louis Eslava, Michael Fakhri and Vasuki Nesiah. Cambridge University Press, 2017.

Schabas, William A. and Nadia Bernaz. "Introduction." In *Routledge Handbook of International Criminal Law*, edited by William A. Schabas and Nadia Bernaz. Routledge, 2013.

Journal Articles

Abi-Saab, Georges. "The Newly Independent States and the Rules of International Law: An Outline." *Howard Law Journal* 8 No. 2 (1962): 95–121.

Anand, Ram Prakash "Role of the 'New' Asian-African Countries in the Present International Legal Order" *American Journal of International Law* 56 No. 2 (1962): 383–406.

Anghie, Antony and BS Chimni, "Third World Approaches to International Law and Individual Responsibility in Internal Conflict" *Studies in Transnational Legal Policy* 36 (2004) 185–210.

Benton, Lauren, "Beyond Anachronism: Histories of International Law and Global Legal Politics" *Journal of the History of International Law* 21 (2019) 7–40.

Bryant, Rebecca, "The State of Cypriot Silences." *The Cyprus Review* 22, No. 2 (2010): 113–22.

Chimni, B.S, "The Past, Present and Future of International Law: A Critical Third World Approach" *Melbourne Journal of International Law* 8 No. 2 (2007): 499.

Demetriou, Olga, "Reading the paratexts of the Cyprus Conflict: Policy, Science, and the Pursuit of 'Objectivity." *The Cyprus Review* 20 (2008): 93–113.

Dworkin, Ronald, "Hard Cases." *Harvard Law Review* 88 No. 6 (1975): 1057–1109.

Falk, Richard A., ed. *The International Law of Civil War.* John Hopkins Press, 1971.

Gathii, James Thuo, "TWAIL: A Brief History of Its Origins, Its Decentralized Network, and a Tentative Bibliography." *Trade Law and Development* 3 (2011): 26–48.

Johnstone, Ian "The Role of the UN Secretary-General: The Power of Persuasion Based on Law" *Global Governance* 9 No. 4 (2003): 441–458.
Klabbers, Jan "The Bridge Crack'd: A Critical Look at Interdisciplinary Relations" *International Relations* 23 (2009): 119–125.
Klabbers, Jan "Whatever Happened to Gramsci? Some Reflections on New Legal Realism" *Leiden Journal of International Law* 28 No. 3 (2015): 469–478.
Koskenniemi, Martti "Miserable Comforters: International Relations as New Natural Law" *European Journal of International Relations* 15 No. 3 (2009): 395–422.
Korhonen, Outi, "New International Law: Silence, Defence or Deliverance?," *European Journal of International Law* 7 (1996): 1–28.
Nicolini, Matteo and Thomas Perrin, "Geographical Connections: Law, Islands, and Remoteness" *Liverpool Law Review* 42 (2021) 1–14.
Orford, Anne, "On International Legal Method" *London Review of International Law* 1 (2013): 166–197.
Policinski, Ellen and Jovana Kuzmanovic, "Editorial – Protracted Conflicts: The Enduring Legacy of Endless War" *International Review of the Red Cross* 101 (912) (2019): 965–976.
Pungetti, Gloria, "Islands, culture, landscape and seascape" *Journal of Marine and Island Cultures* 1 (2013): 51–54.
Slaughter, A-M and Steven Ratner, "Appraising the Methods of International Law: A Prospectus for Readers," *American Journal of International Law* 93 (1999) 291–302.
Simma, Bruno and Andreas Paulus, "The Responsibility of Individuals for Human Rights abuses in Internal Conflicts: A positivist view," *American Journal of International Law* 93 (1999) 302–316.
Vadi, Valentina, "International Law and its Histories: Methodological Risks and Opportunities" *Harvard International Law Journal* 58 No. 2 (2017): 311–352.
Varnava, Andrekos, "Remembering the Cypriot Civil War 50 Years On" *The Cyprus Review* 25 No. 2 (2013) 113–116.

Other

Ioannou, Gregoris and Sertac Sonan. *Inter-Communal Contact and Exchange in Cyprus' Higher Education Institutions: Their Potential to Build Trust and Cooperation – Report 8/2019.* PRIO Cyprus, 2019.
Orford, Anne. "Civil Wars: A History in Ideas." Review of *Civil Wars: A History in* Ideas, by David Armitage, *American Journal of International Law*, 2021b, https://doi.org/10.1017/ajil.2021.37
Eslava, Luis "TWAIL Coordinates" (*Critical Legal Thinking*, 2 April 2019) https://criticallegalthinking.com/2019/04/02/twail-coordinates/

CHAPTER 2

International Law, Empire and Cyprus, 1878–1959

Cypriot history is a centuries-long study of imperialism and colonialism in light of the conflicts for domination across the eastern Mediterranean region. Themes that have been increasingly drawing the interest of international legal scholarship in the last few decades. From the Greek expansion across the Mediterranean and the Black Sea in antiquity, to the establishment of Greek and Phoenician city-states on the island, followed by the Roman and Byzantine Empires, only to be succeeded by the Knights Templar, the Frankish Lusignan Dynasty, and then the Venetians in the Middle Ages, it is understood why in the first half of the twentieth-century historians looked at Cyprus as the 'land where races have always met, yet rarely mingled'.[1] The multitude of occasionally competing cultures that make up the social fabric of the island to this day has been evident at all turns of social, public, economic, and institutional life in Cyprus for centuries.

At the time when the Venetian Republic competed over control in the Mediterranean with the Ottoman Empire, Cyprus came under the rule of the Serenissima for 82 years, before entering a new three-century-long phase as an Ottoman province in 1571. The conquest of Cyprus was a primary goal of Sultan Selim II, who had expressed an interest in conquering the island even before acceding to the throne following the

[1] Luke, *A Portrait*, 17.

N. Kornioti, *Law's Politics: The Cyprus Troubles, 1960–1968*,
https://doi.org/10.1007/978-3-031-93369-1_2

death of Sultan Suleiman the Magnificent in 1566.[2] Thus, by early 1570 the Ottomans had initiated a series of diplomatic negotiations with Venice explicitly requesting ownership over the island. When their demands were not met, the first Ottoman forces disembarked on Cyprus on 3 July 1570, leading to a year-long war between existing and aspiring rulers. Despite the violent transit from Venetian to Ottoman rule, the Ottomans were not completely unwelcome by the predominantly Christian Greek-Orthodox local population, since the arrival of the Ottomans would entail the restoration of the primacy of the Autocephalous Greek-Orthodox Church of Cyprus, which had been abolished by Papal Bull in 1260,[3] and would abolish feudal serfdom, which had constituted the basis of socio-economic organisation since Byzantine times.[4]

One cannot discuss the events upon which this book focuses without an introduction to the history of the island and how historical events formed the ethnic and ideological identities of the Greek and Turkish communities, as well as the nationalist political priorities they pursued in the decades before and after the establishment of the RoC. This being a law-oriented study, however, requires also an introduction to the conceptual framework within which this book has been written, touching upon the history of international law itself, the history of humanitarianism as an idea, and brief account of the evolution of the two in the aftermath of the WWII.

Whereas the establishment of the UN is seen as a threshold moment in the development of international law, this view is today challenged by both historians and international lawyers.[5] In recent years, attention has turned, instead, to the 'imperial humanitarianism' enclosed in the colonial 'civilising mission' of the European Powers of the nineteenth century.[6] Within that context, the establishment of the UN is seen as a transition from the League of Nations, the organisation founded at the end of the First World War (WWI) which collapsed in the eve of WWII,[7] with the UN inheriting elements of that failed firtst initiative. As stated by others, 'over-emphasizing the rupture' between the pre- and post-WWII international

[2] Soucek, "Naval Aspects".
[3] Hill, *History of Cyprus Vol.3*, 1059–1104.
[4] Sakellaropoulos, *Cypriot Social Formation*, 42–43, 54–56.
[5] Rodogno, "European Legal Doctrines"; Tzouvala "These Ancient Arenas".
[6] Barnett, *Empire of Humanity* 9; Green, "Humanitarianism in the nineteenth-century".
[7] Khan, "Drafting History" 21.

legal order, fails to consider continuities that persisted, in particular with regard to statehood, minority protection, and ethnic nationalism.[8] For the Cyprus Question, which relates to events and political choices relevant to the dissolution of the Ottoman Empire in the late nineteenth century and the fall of colonialism following WWII, such debates are particularly enlightening and provide an enriched contextual scope of analysis.

Imperial Humanitarianism and the Civilising Mission

Though a body of law regulating inter-State relations, known as *jus gentium*, had been in existence since antiquity, and a 'Law of Nations' had preoccupied a number of thinkers since the Middle Ages,[9] it was only in the nineteenth century that international law started to obtain the form of a professionalised 'amateur science'.[10] This coincided with two interlinked phenomena which dominated the international agenda in the second half of that century. The European Powers' expanding 'civilising mission' in the territories they colonised, and secondly, the rise of humanitarianism.

The 'civilising mission', which served as the justification for colonisation, claimed to foster progress for the whole of humanity. It was based on a 'standard of civilisation' categorising peoples into 'civilised', 'barbarian' and 'savage', wherein the 'civilised Europeans' based their perceived 'superiority' on a combination of the classical Greek and Roman civilisations, with the ideals of the Enlightenment. This bias was then internalised by international law, influencing the discipline's development thereafter. Recent studies on the history of international law see the development of classical international law as an intellectual project of liberal and cosmopolitan jurists of nineteenth-century Germany, France, Britain, Belgium, and Switzerland, who envisaged a 'European international law', that would 'articulate' and 'represent', the 'legal conscience of the civilized world'.[11]

At the same time, even though the 1648 Treaty of Westphalia, the founding document of the principle of sovereignty, included rules on the peaceful settlement of disputes,[12] in the nineteenth century war was still an

[8] Tzouvala "These Ancient Arenas," 1170.
[9] Koskenniemi, *Uttermost Parts of the Earth*.
[10] Koskenniemi, *Gentle Civilizer*, 28.
[11] Koskenniemi, *The Gentle Civilizer* 47.
[12] Gross, "Westphalia," 25.

acceptable means for dispute settlement, despite the fact that its *raison d'être* directly contradicted humanitarianism's liberal aspirations.[13] As a result, in the late nineteenth century, the laws of armed conflict evolved into two separate sets of rules: the rules on the conduct of war, known as the *jus in bello*, and the rules dictating when use of force was permissible, the *jus ad bellum*.[14] This distinction had already existed for centuries,[15] but obtained reinforced clarity from the late nineteenth century onwards through the development of new legal instruments.

It was against this background that the year 1863 saw the codification of some basic norms to govern the conduct of military forces during warfare. In February 1863, a five-member Committee of the Geneva Public Welfare Society met for the first time, upon the initiative of local businessman Henry Dunant, with the aim to make suggestions for an international treaty which would oblige States to take care of wounded soldiers on the battlefield.[16] In April, amidst the American Civil War, German-American jurist Francis Lieber published the 'Lieber Code', which is considered the first codification on the rules of warfare in modern times. It took only a year for the Geneva-based Committee, the future ICRC, to convince a handful of governments to support the scheme, and adopt the first Geneva Convention on the Amelioration of the Condition of the Wounded in Armies in the Field.[17] In the same spirit, a few years later the St. Petersburg Declaration of 1868 became the first legal document prohibiting the use of specific weapons, followed by the first and second Hague Conferences of 1899 and 1907, which led to the Hague Conventions and Hague Regulations, regulating the conduct of hostilities on land, at sea and in the air. As a result, *jus in bello*, the rules of conduct during war, was subdivided into two additional directions. The 'Hague rules' focusing on the methods of active warfare, and the 'Geneva rules' on the protection of those not participating in the fighting, those *hors de combat*.

Recent research has been cautious not to give extensive credit to the humanitarian sensitivities of nineteenth-century European Powers. As af Jochnick and Normand have argued, despite their humanitarian rhetoric, all these new international legal rules achieved was the legitimation and

[13] Koskenniemi, *Gentle Civilizer*, 83–88.

[14] Bugnion, "*Jus ad bellum*," 171.

[15] Grotius, *The Rights of War and Peace*.

[16] Barnett, *Empire of Humanity*, 76–80.

[17] ICRC, 'The ICRC and the Geneva Convention (1863–1864)' (*ICRC*, 29 December 2004).

ultimately, the promotion of use of force. For instance, during the American Civil War it was the Lieber Code that justified the starvation and the bombardment of civilians under the justification of military necessity, while the explosive bullets prohibited under the St. Petersburg Declaration were already an obsolete weapon by that time.[18] Moreover, as Daniel Palmieri, the ICRC's in-house historian par excellence, observed, in the late nineteenth century States were reluctant to use new technologies of warfare, not due to humanity or a willingness to legally constrain the military methods available to them, but driven by a reluctance to appear 'uncivilised' among their counterparts. He admits that even the ICRC might have been 'carried away by the pacifist message' out of ambition rather than conviction, since for years the organisation addressed humanitarian matters only from a theoretical perspective, as opposed to engaging in direct action.[19]

In the meantime, the Empires east of Europe had already been struggling for decades to become equal members of the 'international club' of the West. [20] Hence, when in 1865 the Ottoman Sultan informed the ICRC that his Empire was ready to accede to the 1864 Geneva Convention, but it would replace the emblem of the Red Cross against a white background with that of a Red Crescent, the ICRC responded with disbelief, unconvinced that a a predominantly Muslim State would abide to the 'uniquely Christian values' of the organisation. Similar concerns arose also when Japan expressed an interest to join.[21] While the 'barbarian' 'Orientals' had obviously developed social structures and cultures of their own, surely they could not be quite as 'civilised'. Along these lines, the majority Christian population of the eastern European territories of the Ottoman Empire, were a challenge for the rulers of Europe, since they were positioned at an intermediate zone, between 'civilisation' and 'barbarity', at the crossroads of Europe and Asia.[22]

WWI was the first major test for the newly-codified humanitarian principles. That was when the ICRC had to initiate field operations for the first time, putting into practice the humanitarian values the organisation had been promoting for half a century since its establishment.[23] At the same

[18] af Jochnick and Normand, "The Legitimation of Violence" 56–66.

[19] Palmieri, "How warfare has evolved," 986–997.

[20] Koskenniemi, *Gentle Civilizer*, 132–136.

[21] Barnett, *Empire of Humanity*, 81–82.

[22] Tzouvala, "These Ancient Arenas," 1149; Mazower, *Balkans*, 9.

[23] Palmieri, "Standing the test of time?," 1273.

time, the whole decade from the Balkan Wars (1912–1913) up to the signing of the Peace Treaty of Lausanne (1923), was definitive for Greco-Turkish relations and the competing nationalisms in the broader region. Though the violent events of this decade had no direct impact on daily life on Cyprus, Cypriot volunteers of both Greek and Turkish ethnicity did travel to the continent to join the armed forces of their respective 'motherlands'.[24] At the same time, the violent persecution of the Armenian and Greek populations led many survivors to seek protection on British-ruled Cyprus, and the memory of those events became part of the collective consciousness of a significant proportion of the Cypriot population. As such, the events on the Balkans contributed to the formation of the socio-political balances which dominated in the first half of the twentieth century,[25] already leading to sporadic incidents of violence between the two dominant ethno-religious groups of Cyprus.

On 12 March 1964, the ICRC delegate in Cyprus wrote to the organisation's *Conseil de Presidence* in Geneva:

> Remember, first of all, that the Turkish invasion, in 1571, is still present in the memory of this unfortunate island, as well as the remembrance of the severe Ottoman occupation.[26]

There is no way of finding out to what extent the Cypriots during this time appreciated the difficulty they posed to 'white gentlemen', who did not wish to shake hands with the 'betwixt'—not quite white, not quite black—native gentlemen of the island.[27] Orientalist accounts from western travellers and historians visiting or living on the island in the first half of the twentieth century often contradicted the wondrous period of the Franks and the non-barbarity of the Greek language, to how the island 's[u]nk into a long sleep' with the arrival of the Ottomans.[28] Whatever benefits there may had been during the island's transition from Venetian to Ottoman rule, by the mid-twentieth century these were long-forgotten. Between the competitive nationalisms of their two 'motherlands', further inflamed by a civilisational bias that cut right across the island's diverse

[24] Papapolyviou, *Cyprus and the Balkan Wars.*

[25] Kornioti, "The Island of Cyprus."

[26] ICRC, B AG251 049-004, Summary of Report Presented by Mr. A. De Cocatrix, Head of the ICRC delegation in Cyprus, to the Council of the Presidency, 12 March 1964.

[27] Heacock, "The Framing of Empire."

[28] Luke, *A Portrait*, 8, 73.

culture, religions, languages and ethnic identities, there was limited chance for the local population not to be embroiled in the competition.

Cypriot Society and Politics, 1878–1949

Cyprus' transit from Ottoman to British rule relates directly to a definitive moment for the Balkan region. The 1878 Congress of Berlin, where Europe's imperial powers gathered to decide how to curve Russian influence in South-East Europe and ultimately determine the future of its peoples.[29] In secret and in parallel to the formal proceedings, Britain and the Ottoman Empire negotiated and signed the Cyprus Convention of Defensive Alliance between Great Britain and the Ottoman Empire of the 4th of July 1878. A secret treaty of alliance, which aimed securing British support for the Ottomans at the Congress and protection from Russia's expansionist policies in the Black Sea and the Caucasus, in exchange for British administration of Cyprus.[30] Thus, whereas the Porte retained its sovereignty over the island, the British occupied and administered it in exchange of an annual 'Tribute', which served as compensation for the Ottoman Empire's lost tax revenue, collected from the local population.[31] This peculiar arrangement remained in place until November 1914, when Turkey entered WWI on the side of the Central powers, and the UK annexed the island on 5 November 1914 (Cyprus (Annexation) Order in Council, 5 November 1914). A move facilitated by its ongoing military presence on it. This annexation was recognised by Turkey in articles 20 and 21 of the 1923 Peace Treaty of Lausanne, and it was only then that it became possible to formally give Cyprus the status of a Crown colony on 10 March 1925 (Letters Patent,10 March 1925, No 1691 *The Cyprus Gazette*).

The Ottoman period undoubtedly had a major impact on the socio-economic landscape of the island. The 'luckless peasantry' of Cyprus (Christian and Muslim),[32] who on a number of occasions had revolted against exploitation in the hands of corrupted Ottoman officials and the elite Greek-speaking leadership, including the powerful Autocephalous

[29] Van den Bogaert, "Berlin Congress (1878)."
[30] Hill, *History of Cyprus Vol 4,* 285.
[31] Markides, *The Cyprus Tribute*, 25–51.
[32] Luke, *A Portrait*, 78.

Church of Cyprus, remained greatly impoverished and highly illiterate.[33] Yet, until 1914, the British being aware of the Sultan's continuing sovereignty, refrained from undertaking any major reforms. Such reforms were only initiated after 1925,[34] when the British adjusted the existing administrative structures, albeit retaining elements of the Ottoman socio-cultural *millet* system in public institutions. Examples include the retention of separate educational systems for each religious group, and the establishment of separate community councils in mixed villages, headed by separate *mukhtars* (local community leaders). The judicial system initially retained the jurisdiction of Sharia and Ecclesiastical courts for family law matters,[35] while Ottoman law continued to apply in most property-related disputes. Such elements survived the harmonisation of the Cypriot legal order with the English Common Law in 1935, and were eventually inherited by the RoC.[36]

Following the signing of the Lausanne Treaty in 1923, foreign commentators soon recognised that the protection of minorities on Cyprus remained an outstanding issue.[37] Greek Cypriot hopes for union with Greece—*enosis*—had already surfaced during the Greek War of Independence (1821–1830) and were reiterated immediately upon the arrival of the first British High Commissioner in 1878. This raised obvious concerns among the Turkish Cypriot population, as well as the other smaller Christian denominations, notably the Armenian and the Latin Roman Catholics, who not only opposed *enosis*, but also opposed the autonomy of the island fearing oppression of their respective identities.[38] Ever since, the issue of *enosis* lies at the core of any discussion over the 'Cyprus Question', along with the diametrically opposing objective of partition—*taksim*—that came to dominate Turkish Cypriot politics in the following decades.

The Legislative Council established in the first years of Britain's administration of Cyprus became a forum for early political rivalries, but also collaboration on a few occasions, between the two main religious communities of the island. According to the internal Cyprus Constitution of

[33] Hill, *History of Cyprus Vol 4*, 263.
[34] Georghallides, *1931 crisis*, 5, 14–28.
[35] Serghides, 43–53; Demetriadou, "Legal Discourse and Social History."
[36] Pikis, *An analysis of the English Common Law*.
[37] Toynbee, "The East after Lausanne."
[38] Georghallides, *1931 crisis*, 87–88.

1882, the Legislative Council consisted of 12 elected members (9 Christian/ 3 Muslim) and 6 officially appointed British officials (Order in Council, 30 November 1882).[39] Thus, the majorities within it were thin, with the British *ex officio* members compensating for the numerical difference between Greek Cypriot and Turkish Cypriot members. Eventually, therefore, the declaration of Cyprus as a Crown colony brought limited amendments to the governing structure, with no substantial social impact.

Despite early competition among the Greek Cypriot and the Turkish Cypriot elites regarding the governance of the island, the additional financial burden from the contributions to the 'Tribute' combined with the global economic depression of the late 1920s, led Christian Orthodox and Muslim leaders for a brief moment in time to set aside their conflicting aspirations and focus on the fiscal burdens of the island.[40] Even though the Tribute was eventually abolished on 1 January 1928, the lack of any improvement in the financial state of the colony reinforced the pursuit of national aspirations,[41] which reached peak tension in the last quarter of 1931.

In the afternoon of 21 October 1931 an initial gathering of 300 individuals turned into a mass of 3,000 Greek Cypriot demonstrators marching to the Governor's House in demand for *enosis*. The crowd clashed with the Police and military reinforcements arrived to Nicosia the next day. By then, anti-Government protests had broken out in all major towns, and the riots could only be suppressed three days later, when on 24 October ten Greek Cypriot leaders, believed to have incited the violence, were arrested and eventually expelled from Cyprus.[42] Among them were four pro-unionist politicians, two members of the Communist Party of Cyprus (*Κομμουνιστικό Κόμμα Κύπρου*—KKK), established in 1926, and two Christian Orthodox Bishops. The message that similar conduct would not be tolerated had to be clear across the political spectrum. These 'October Riots', the *Oktovriana*, were later recorded as the 'only situation in the history of British Cyprus at all comparable with the era of terrorism that began in the spring of 1955'.[43]

[39] Zannetos, *History of the Island of Cyprus*, 329–345.

[40] Kyriakides, *The Cypriot Legislative Council*.

[41] Markides, *The Cyprus Tribute*, 125–137.

[42] Cyprus Government, *Ταραχαί εν Κύπρω*.

[43] Luke, *A Portrait*, 175.

Casualties included six killed and 30 wounded among the protesters, as well as 39 injured police officers, while the Governor's House was completely burnt down. The biggest price paid by the British, however, was the damage to their image as a colonial power. The Cypriots on the other hand, were subjected to punitive measures, including a fine of 34,315 GBP imposed only on the Greek-Orthodox population, and the criminal conviction of 2,606 individuals.[44] A series of measures which impacted the political rights and civil liberties of the whole population were also put in place, including the abolition of the Legislative Council and the suspension of the internal Constitution of the colony. Amendments to the Criminal Code and the laws on local administration abolished the election of local authorities, and a strict curfew was put in place. These aimed directly at preventing pro-nationalist propaganda, including through the educational system, the prohibition of the tolling of church bells and the flying of national Greek and Turkish flags, as well as a strict censorship of press, telegrams, correspondence, and cinema.[45]

The Turkish Cypriots were not exempted from any of the measures apart from the fine, despite the fact that they neither participated in the *Oktovriana*, nor assumed an official position. Their community was facing a dilemma, since they were also unhappy with many aspects of British policy in Cyprus, yet they were aware that the British prevented the domination of the majority Greek-speaking population. This coincided with a general rise of Turkish nationalism, and the adoption of a series of Kemalist reforms which aimed at severing the Turkish Cypriots' ties with the Ottoman past.[46] Such reforms included the establishment of a number of Turkish Cypriot institutions, like the 'Cyprus Turkish National Council', in May 1931.[47] According to Turkish Cypriot economist Ozay Mehmet, the emotional, identity-related, development of nationalism among the Turkish Cypriots was only one aspect of a broader picture, which entailed the rational, economic anxieties of a numerically smaller community.[48]

Some commentators view the *Oktovriana* as the starting point for the island's twentieth century violent history, inter- and intra-communally. Though this view has often been expressed in public, there is no

[44] Georghallides, *1931 crisis*, 702–708.
[45] Pastella, "Criminal Checks."
[46] Hatzivassiliou, *The Cyprus Question*, 17.
[47] Sakellaropoulos, *Cypriot Social Formation*, 176.
[48] Mehmet, *Sustainability of Microstates*, 22–23.

comprehensive research drawing direct linkages between these and later events. Nevertheless, there is limited doubt that the *Oktovriana* riots solidified the nationalist movements which dominated Cypriot politics in the following decades. Indeed, the socio-political correlations are many, seen in conjunction with the intensified anti-colonial sentiment which was reinforced from this moment onwards and over the following oppressive decade; a period known as 'Palmerocracy' *(Παλμεροκρατία)*, from the Governorship of Sir Richmond Palmer (1933–1938), even though in practice, Palmer had merely implemented the policies imposed by his predecessor, Governor Stubbs.[49]

Whereas violence during the EOKA struggle and the inter-communal violence of 1958 are directly relevant to the violence from 1963 onwards, the same cannot be said for the *Oktovriana*. In 1931, contrary to the planned and strategic action of the military and paramilitary groups involved in later events, the *Oktovriana* were spontaneous riots, repressed by the British authorities within days, and legally dealt with through the ordinary criminal justice system of the colony.

One exceptional incident, that draws analogies and potentially set a precedent for impunity and silence in later instances of politically motivated violence was the assassination of politician Antonios Triantafyllides in January 1934. Triantafyllides was a high-profile qualified Advocate, former member of the Legislative Council, and a supporter of co-operation with the British authorities as a means towards pursuing the interests of the local people, until a political solution was found. Following his assassination, suspicions that this was a politically motivated killing rose when his father-in-law claimed that Triantafyllides received threats against his life, asking him to stop serving on the Advisory Council. A governing body established in November 1933, whose members were directly appointed by the colonial Government, and whose four Greek Cypriot members were under attack for cooperating with the colonial authorities. One suspect was prosecuted for the crime and eventually acquitted.[50]

During WWII, the colonial government took measures for the safety and welfare of the local population in anticipation of potential attacks, given the island's proximity to the Middle East. The territory of Cyprus was once again not directly affected by the hostilities. By mid-October 1940, the first group of Cypriot volunteers to the Royal Army Service

[49] Markides, *The Cyprus Tribute*, 174–175.
[50] Varnava, *Assassination in Colonial Cyprus*.

departed to join British forces in Egypt, and by early 1941 a total of 6,000 men, comprising of Cypriots from various religious groups, had volunteered.[51] At the end of WWII, the position of the British vis-à-vis their Cyprus policy was difficult. *Enosis* was ruled out by the Colonial Office, thus, attention turned towards the establishment of a new internal constitution, despite the fact that the British were highly disappointed with the Legislative Councils from 1878 to 1931.

Among the Greek Cypriots and the Greeks, public expectations for *enosis* were high considering that Greece and the UK had fought WWII on the same side, and many colonies and mandates were moving towards independence. This was not an absurd aspiration, considering that Britain had offered Cyprus to Greece in the early stages of WWI to ensure the latter's support. That offer was at the time rejected by the Greeks, and all diplomatic efforts towards unification thereafter failed.[52] To make matters more complicated, in 1947, Italy ceded to Greece the Dodecanese Islands in the Aegean Sea. Most prominent among them was the island of Rhodes, which shared more than few cultural and historical elements with Cyprus, including the fact that Rhodes was capital of the *villaet* (Ottoman territorial department) to which Cyprus had belonged to in 1878.[53] Archival evidence suggests that in 1947 thoughts about *enosis* were entertained by officials in the British Foreign Office, but these contravened the priorities set by the Colonial Office.[54]

To fully comprehend the weight of some of the events mentioned in the next chapters, a brief commentary is needed on the political polarisation in both communities along the right-left political spectrum during the 1940s. An exercise which is usually considered irrelevant to legal research. For both communities, the period after WWII sees the gradual entry into the scene of some of the protagonists that would dominate Cypriot politics until the early twenty-first century, and the development of political intra-communal divisions which are yet to eclipse. Whereas historically these intra-communal divisions are of particular significance against the background of the Cold War, it is important for the reader to have in mind that these political divisions have been a constant factor in local public life since.

[51] Yiangou, "British Diplomacy and the Cyprus Issue," 26.

[52] Loizou and Loizides, 7–10.

[53] Zannetos, *History of the Island of Cyprus*, 52.

[54] Yiangou, "British Diplomacy and the Cyprus Issue," 27.

During the late 1930s, there were efforts towards the establishment of political unions and increased syndicalisation involving both Greek and Turkish Cypriots.[55] Within this context, the Progressive Party of the Working People (*Ανορθωτικό Κόμμα Εργαζόμενου Λαού*—AKEL) was established in April 1941 and by 1944 merged with KKK.[56] Even though AKEL was supported by many Turkish Cypriots, the party's ambiguous position regarding *enosis* caused uneasiness and alienated many of them, who soon thereafter faced persecution from within their own community, due to their political allegiance with the left. Across the political spectrum, the Cypriot National Party (*Κυπριακό Εθνικό Κόμμα*—CNP) was established in 1943, as an answer to the growing influence of AKEL, as evident in the strong support the latter received with the restoration of municipal elections in the same year, for the first time since the *Oktovriana*.[57]

In the same year, the first large Turkish Cypriot party was established, under the name Turkish Minority Association of the Island of Cyprus (*Kıbrıs Adası Türk Azınlığı Kurumu*—KATAK), a founding member of which was the first and only RoC Vice-President, Dr Fazil Kutchuk. This opened the way for leadership struggles involving a number of leading figures, with different visions on economic and social development. Among them, was also Dr Ihsan Ali, who following the events of 1963 maintained a constant opposition to the separatist tendencies of his community's leadership.[58] These divisions would lead to the split of KATAK as early as 1944, giving rise to the Turkish Cypriot National Popular Party (*Kıbrıs Millî Türk Halk Partisi*-KMTHP). By then, the riots of 1931 had led the British to shift their earlier pro-Christian orientation, and show more interest towards the concerns of the Turkish Cypriots, resulting in the establishment of the Commission on Turkish Cypriot Affairs, in 1948. This was headed by future President of the RoC Supreme Court Mehmet Zekia, and supported by the young, at the time, long-term Turkish Cypriot leader Rauf Denktash (1975–2005).

With the departure of Palmer in 1938, and his replacement with the more liberal William Battershill, expectations for constitutional reform were renewed. A petition expressing trust in the new Governor was handed

[55] Hatzivassiliou, *The Cyprus Question*, 41.

[56] Ioannou and Sonan, "Trade unions."

[57] Kalantzopoulos, "Cyprus in the 1940s"; Yiangou, *Cyprus in World War II*.

[58] PIO, 'Dr. Ihsan Ali Protests to General Thimayya Against the ill-treatment of moderate Turks' (PIO, 4 August 1964).

to him in London, before Battershill's departure to Cyprus. Among the members of the delegation was Glafkos Clerides, first Chair of the RoC House of Representatives and future President of the Republic (1993–2003). Rauf Deknтash and Glafkos Clerides would become the main protagonists of the negotiations towards a solution to the Cyprus Question, until the early 2000s.

The socio-political developments during the 82 years of British rule set the stage for the events which occurred in the aftermath of Cypriot independence. As accurately described by Peter Loizos, the Cyprus Question is in fact 'several problems, differently defined by different persons'.[59] In parallel to the events discussed above, global and international legal developments also took place. International law has its own separate history that interacts, is impacted by and contributes to the way events unfold. Thus, leaving aside developments in Cyprus, we shall now turn to the ways WWII impacted the development of those branches of public international law which are most relevant to questions of war and peace.

War and Peace After the United Nations, 1945–1949

Despite the minimum codification of the 'laws of war' briefly presented above, the extent of the atrocities of WWII was unparalleled, and in between the end of WWII in Europe and the deployment of the atomic bombs in Japan, on 26 June 1945 the UN Charter was signed in San Francisco, with a renewed rhetoric for global peace and prosperity. Articles 1 and 2 of the UN Charter, set the purposes and the principles of the UN. Even though their drafting history suggests that they were meant to be legally binding, this is contradicted by the highly political language of the text.[60] Rarely, however, in a political context, the one raising the argument is ready to accept what international lawyers have known all along: that these are provisions whose capacity to resolve conflicts among States as standalone legal rules of public international law is extremely limited. Their primary objective, therefore, is no other than to guide the conduct of the UN organs when deliberating solutions for problems of international concern, and subsequently, whenever a legal argument is

[59] Loizos, *Unofficial Views*, 77.
[60] Wolfrum, "Article 1," 107.

based on the purposes and the principles of the UN Charter, controversy arises.

As a British colony, Cyprus initially joined the UN infrastructure as a non-self-governing territory under article 73(e) of the UN Charter, which gave minimum supervisory powers to the UN to collect technical and statistical information on economic, social, and educational issues.[61] In terms of law, the domestic law of the colonies was understood as 'peripheral' to the domestic law of the colonising State, in this case the UK. Hence, the exact relationship between a colony and the UK for the purposes of international law was a matter of domestic law, where all colonial territories were constituent of the commonwealth network, which took the form of a single 'unitary State' held together by the Crown on the international arena.[62]

Use of Force and the United Nations Collective Security System

The maintenance of 'international peace and security' is considered the primary purpose of the UN, and can be pursued through various policies and measures, primary among them being the implementation of collective security measures, and the 'adjustment or settlement' of international disputes, under article 1(1) of the Charter.[63] The distinction between 'adjustment' and 'settlement' appears not to have attracted particular attention in the Cypriot context, yet it is significant, considering that the UNSC has been 'adjusting' the ongoing dispute in relation to the island since 1964, whereas responsibility for the actual 'settlement' remains with the parties to the conflict. Thus, clarifying the exact role of the UNSC under the UN framework of collective security, and distinguish this from the pool of other branches of public international law relevant to 'war and peace', is of particular use here.

When the first codified modern laws regulating warfare were introduced in the late nineteenth century, whether or not a State would resort to force remained a sovereign prerogative, despite efforts to make war 'more humane'. War was only formally 'outlawed' with the 1928 General Treaty for the Renunciation of War, broadly known as the Kellogg-Briand Pact, but as the Pact proved unsuccessful at the start of WWII a second

[61] Fastenrath, "Chapter XI," 1829.
[62] Fawcett, "Treaty Relations," 89–91.
[63] Hyde, "Peaceful Adjustment of Disputes".

attempt was introduced through the UN Charter, and in particular article 2(4), which prohibits the 'threat or use of force against the territorial integrity or political independence of any State'. This provision is broader in scope than the 1928 Kellogg-Briand Pact which only outlawed 'war', but not the occasional 'use of force' against another State.[64]

The exact interpretation of article 2(4) of the UN Charter has been long-debated, and its application in practice has been problematic, despite the fact that it is a recognised rule of customary international law; i.e. its enforcement is not dependent on a State having signed and ratified an international treaty. The provision is also a peremptory norm of international law (*jus cogens*), which means that it represents a principle so fundamental that does not allow States to derogate from it under any circumstances. In the case of article 2(4) the UN Charter allows for one clear exception. The exercise of the right to self-defence under article 51 of the Charter. Problems with this provision's interpretation have been clearly illustrated in the literature, including a suggestion that article 2(4) can be seen as enclosing (or justifying) two separate and opposing 'codes' of action. The first, the 'institutional code', applied by formal international bodies and organisations aiming to completely restrict the unilateral recourse to force, and the second, the 'State code', which describes how States in some cases may tolerate unilateral uses of force by other States.[65] Nuances like these are often observed, acknowledged and discussed among lawyers, but they are rarely the subject of debates beyond legal academia.

The prohibition of the use of force under article 2(4), is closely related to the customary principle of non-intervention in the internal affairs of the State. Some have equated the provision under article 2(7) as representative of the principle of non-intervention, but that particular provision only restraints *the UN as an organisation* from intervening in issues within the domestic jurisdiction of any State.[66] Hence, article 2(7) is most clearly understood to apply in terms of the actions of the organs of the UN, including peacekeeping operations, such as the UNFICYP. As far as *inter-state relations* are concerned, the non-intervention principle is not mentioned in the UN Charter,[67] but it derives directly from interpretations of

[64] Randelzhofer and Dörr, "Article 2(4)," 200, 206–207.
[65] Hakimi and Katz Cogan, "The Two Codes".
[66] Nolte, "Article 2(7)," 284.
[67] Kunig, "Intervention, Prohibition of."

the classical principle of State sovereignty,[68] which prevents one State from intervening in the internal affairs of another.

Non-surprisingly, the principle of non-intervention is not an absolute one. In the context of the UN, as the primary international organisation concerned with the maintenance of international peace and security, the UNSC has been given powers to exercise collective action either through the pacific settlement of disputes, like negotiation, mediation and good offices (article 33 UN Charter), or through collective action aiming to prevent 'threats to the peace', 'breaches of the peace' or 'acts of aggression', under Chapter VII of the Charter (articles 31–43 UN Charter). Such action *may* entail the collective use of force authorised and coordinated by the UNSC, if other measures like economic sanctions, or the severance of diplomatic relations prove ineffective.

Misgivings about the UN collective security system under Chapter VII had been expressed from the beginning. As the Cold War intensified, the UNSC tended to respond to civil conflicts based on political ideology and superpower motives, as opposed to abiding to a specific policy or legal norms.[69] This of course is in line with the fact that both the UNSC, and the United Nations General Assembly (UNGA) are political organs, whereas the sole judicial, and therefore, exclusively law-oriented organ of the UN is the International Court of Justice (ICJ). Thus, the tension between law and politics is inherent to the available UN mechanisms aiming to maintain international peace and security. For decades international adjudication was not considered a suitable forum for the resolution of issues involving questions of war and peace, until the late 1980s, when and the ICJ delivered its landmark judgment in the case of *Military and Paramilitary Activities in and against Nicaragua*,[70] in which the Court found the USA in breach of its international law obligations for its involvement in paramilitary activities in Nicaragua. Hence, international tribunals and international cases addressing issues relevant to armed conflict are a relatively recent phenomenon in the development of international law. Thus, recourse to an international tribunal during the period discussed here was virtually unavailable.

[68] Besson, "Sovereignty."

[69] Samuels, *Political Violence*, 2.

[70] *Military and Paramilitary Activities in and against Nicaragua* (*Nicaragua* v *United States of America*), Judgement [1986] ICJ Rep 14.

Peacekeeping, another major key term in the Cyprus context, has not been introduced in international affairs through the UN Charter. Peacekeeping forces are a tool developed by the UN to enable limited collective action by the organisation itself in light of the political difficulties that existed during the Cold War to launch collective action in the way envisaged in Chapter VII. Following an experimental approach for most of the 1950s, it was the establishment of the UN Emergency Force (UNEF) during the 1956 Suez Crisis that led Dag Hammarskjöld, UN Secretary-General at the time, to draft a document which enclosed 'certain basic principles and rules which would provide an adaptable framework for later operations'.[71] The very first principle sharply distinguished peacekeeping from action under Chapter VII, and explicitly required the consent of the host State for the deployment of peacekeeping forces on its territory, in line with the principle of State sovereignty. To date, there is no exact legal definition for 'peacekeeping', yet it is known that form and structure have changed over the decades with forces after 1990, becoming highly 'multidimensional' and 'complex'.[72]

When UNFICYP was established by virtue of UNSC Resolution 186 in March 1964, in a statement which played down the limited but fundamental role military components play in peacekeeping, U Thant, UN Secretary-General from 1961 to 1971, had explicitly mentioned that the establishment of UNFICYP did not constitute collective action against aggression under Chapter VII, but it was:

> an attempt on the international level to prepare the ground for the permanent, freely agreed solution of a desperate and dangerous situation by restoring peace and normality. The nature of this operation is far nearer to a preventive and protective police action; it is not repressive military action.[73]

UNFICYP is, therefore, a subsidiary organ of the UN,[74] and a 'first generation' peacekeeping force, reflecting other simple peacekeeping forces introduced during the Cold War, primarily tasked with observing developments and maintaining ceasefire lines.[75] At the time of its establishment, UNFICYP was only the eighth such force, and today it is the third longest

[71] A/3943, paras 54–193.

[72] Bothe, "Peacekeeping," 1171.

[73] Miller, *Cyprus: Law and Politics*, 34 citing UN Press Release SG/SM/76, 26 May 1964.

[74] UNA, S-0869-0001-07-00001, 25 April 1964 (Released 6 June 2006).

[75] Wilde, "Taxonomies."

in service in the world. Hence, many of the limitations it faced in the 1960s, and many of those it potentially still faces today, need to be assessed in the context of broader problems the UN faced with this highly experimental mechanism at the time.[76]

More details on UNFICYP's establishment and action are examined in following chapters. However, it is worth noting that following the adverse experience in Vietnam and the Biafra Civil War in Nigeria, by the end of the 1960s the situation in Cyprus had been generally assessed as a fairly successful case of UN intervention in confining violence.[77] The confining of violence, however, is not to be interpreted as successfully resolving the dispute. The problem with many of the internal conflicts that were ongoing in the mid-twentieth century, among which commentators also included Cyprus, was the limited ability international law had to drive 'effective legal regulation'. States, it has been argued, used international law as a means to establish a 'verbal position in relation to critics', as opposed to a tool in the forming of policies.[78] Though this observation still holds true today, this practice was particularly prevalent during the decolonisation period.

Regulating Conduct and Allocating Responsibility During Armed Conflict

The Interwar period and the immediate aftermath of WWII saw rapid developments in three distinct but interlinked areas of public international law, which relate to but constitute separate legal regimes from the rules on the use of force. Due to their subject matter these areas of international law are sometimes indistinguishable in non-legal discourse, despite the fact that each has separate objectives, targets different individuals or groups of people, and may vary regarding enforcement and accountability measures. In the chronological order of development after WWII, these are the fields of (i) international criminal law, (ii) international human rights law, and (iii) international humanitarian law; the latter also referred to as *jus in bello*. In view of the analysis that follows in the book, it is important to hereby distinguish and clarify the differences among the

[76] Tudor, *Blue Helmets Bureaucrats*.
[77] Falk "Introduction," 8.
[78] Falk "Introduction," 4–6.

three. Before doing so, however, it is important to make three clarifications at the outset.

Firstly, up to 1945 individuals were *not* considered subjects of public international law, and therefore, individuals had no obligations and held no rights under international law. This has been long-recognised also by Cypriot commentators,[79] and lies in direct contrast to the way humanitarian and human rights issues are addressed nowadays, with an emphasis on a rhetoric of individual rights and liberties. In that regard, the 1960s are a peculiar period in the development of public international law, with a persisting lack of clarity on many aspects in the application of the three legal regimes mentioned above.

Secondly, the development of international criminal law, international human rights law and international humanitarian law, does not absolve States, the primary subjects of public international law, from potential legal responsibility. A State can be held liable under the doctrine of State responsibility, and if an international crime is committed by 'an agent of a State', meaning a high-ranking official of that State, then the unlawful act can be attributable to the whole State, as well. However, since a State's responsibility under international law depends on its obligations under conventional and customary non-written rules in each particular case, there is no 'uniform code [...] reflecting the obligations of all States'.[80]

Lastly, when dealing with legal matters within a historical context, one needs to be constantly aware of the complex relationship law has with time, both philosophically and practically. For whereas history is comfortable with looking to the past, the law is primarily expected to pre-empt the 'myriad cases that are always still to come'.[81] This is evident by the general principle of legality which forbids the retroactive application of the law, and the criminal legal principle *nullum crimen sine lege*; or no crime without law. Temporality always plays a central role in legal cases of historical relevance, such as issues pertaining to past atrocities,[82] or post-colonial questions on sovereignty.[83] Though a relatively simple concept, rules on temporality are subject to technical complexity in their practical application, which requires careful consideration of various details attaching to

[79] Tornaritis, *Individual as Subject*, 16–18.

[80] Crawford, "State Responsibility," para 2.

[81] Douzinas, "Theses on Law, History and Time."

[82] Schabas, "Retroactive Application"; von Arnauld, "How to Illegalize Past Injustice."

[83] Wheatley, "Revisiting the Doctrine of Intertemporal Law."

the facts of a case. Hence, even though issues of retroactivity have been considered in the analysis undertaken in the present book, where relevant, the level of detailed examination that would be necessary if the questions arising here were before a tribunal or another judicial or quasi-judicial body has not necessarily been undertaken.

Returning to the three interrelated branches of public international law, international criminal law is often described as an 'amalgam' of the principles of international and (domestic) criminal law, aiming to allocate direct criminal responsibility to *individuals* for massviolence.[84] Early efforts to try individuals for criminal acts relevant to war took place with regard to German Kaiser Wilhelm II, at the 1919 Paris Peace Conference. In terms of Greco-Turkish relations, it is worth mentioning that the 1920 Treaty of Sèvres, which never came into force, also envisaged the prosecution of 'persons accused of having committed acts in violation of the laws and customs of war' in Turkey during WWI. A fact that could have had considerable impact on later developments in Cyprus as well as the broader region. As these post-WWI efforts never took shape in practice, the next opportunity to implement individual prosecution for war atrocities arose with the end of WWII and the International Military Tribunals (IMTs) in Nuremberg and Tokyo in 1946. After the completion of the works of the two tribunals, however, international criminal law was once again marginalised until the 1990s and the conflicts in former Yugoslavia and Rwanda.

International criminal law is directly linked to international humanitarian law since under the 1949 Geneva Conventions I–IV, specific acts constituting 'grave breaches' in the wording of the Conventions, were codified as 'war crimes' under article 8 of the Rome Statute, the treaty that established a permanent International Criminal Court based in The Hague, in 1998. Other international crimes under the same instrument include 'Genocide', which is also criminalised under the separate Genocide Convention of 1948, 'Crimes against humanity', an additional Convention for which is still being negotiated at the time of writing, and the crime of 'Aggression', which was first defined by the UNGA in 1974, and then in the Rome Statute as recently as 2010.

Considering the non-retroactive application of the law, none of the provisions of the Rome Statute were of course applicable to atrocities that took place in the 1960s. The 1949 Conventions provide that the burden remained with each 'High Contracting Party' to 'enact any legislation

[84] Cryer, "International Criminal Law."

necessary to provide effective penal sanctions for persons committing, or order others to commit, any grave breaches under the 1949 Geneva Conventions I–IV (arts 49/50/129/146). The scope of these provisions, however, is further narrowed by the fact that they are only applicable under an *international armed conflict* between two or more States.

It is exactly at this point where the distinction between a non-international armed conflict and an international armed conflict is of high importance, since under the 1949 Geneva Conventions, no international crimes were recognised under an internal armed conflict.[85] The sole relevant international law provision on such conflicts until 1977, was common article 3, which only provides a guarantee under the criminal justice system of the State on whose territory the non-international armed conflict takes place. Therefore, in terms of prosecutions for crimes committed in Cyprus during the period addressed in this book, jurisdiction remained at all times with the RoC criminal justice system.

For historical clarity, it is worth mentioning that arguably there is only a single exception to the above through the 1948 Genocide Convention, which made genocide an international crime punishable during peacetime and international armed conflicts (article I), and provided that suspects could be tried 'by a competent tribunal of the State in the territory of which the act was committed, or by such international penal tribunal as may have jurisdiction' (article IV). The reference to 'peacetime' in this instance is understood to include situations of internal armed conflicts in the absence of an intra-State conflict,[86] yet the threshold for satisfying the criteria for Genocide has been set so high by international tribunals that it is extremely difficult to have a finding of Genocide in cases of internal violence. Though allegations of 'genocide' appear sporadically in the historical record regarding the events examined in this book,[87] it must be mentioned that the RoC only acceded to the Convention on 29 March 1982, and according to the UN database has not yet ratified it. Therefore, the Genocide Convention was not applicable on the territory of the RoC in the 1960s.

Regarding international human rights law, historians have traced its development to the League of Nations' failure to protect minorities in

[85] Schabas, "Non-State Actors" 474–475.

[86] Schabas, "Non-State Actors" 477.

[87] E.g. Necatigil, *The Cyprus Question*, 44.

Europe in the years leading up to WWII,[88] which is indicative of a continuity in the humanitarian trends of the late nineteenth century. After WWII, on 10 December 1948, the UNGA adopted Resolution 270(III), better known as the 1948 Universal Declaration of Human Rights. A comprehensive 'International Bill of Human Rights', as stated in the document's full title, which UN member States at the time did not wish to be legally binding.[89] To this day its status as a binding legal instrument of customary international law remains debatable.[90] Two years later, a regional legal instrument, the ECHR was passed, and soon thereafter obtained particular significance for Cyprus' anti-colonial struggle, whereas a decade later was embedded in the Constitution of the RoC.

International human rights instruments do not in principle contain provisions on individual criminal responsibility, but it is possible to hold a State accountable for failures to protect human rights.[91] There are, however, some limited exceptions to the lack of individual responsibility, in the Genocide Convention of 1948 mentioned above, as well as the 1966 Convention on the Elimination of All Forms of Racial Discrimination, the 1973 Apartheid Convention, and the 1984 Convention Against Torture, most of which were adopted after the chronology examined here.

Contrary to the present popularity of human rights as legal principles, in fact international human rights law is a latecomer in the development of international law. The literature recognises three distinct but cumulative, phases of human-rights-related activity at the UN. The 'setting-standard' period from 1947 to 1954, the human rights 'promotion' period from 1955 to 1966, and the 'protection' period from 1967 onwards.[92] Like other areas of public international law, during the Cold War international human rights law was 'paralysed', especially in the UNSC, with the exception of a few twentieth-century mass violations of law in the context of the apartheid regime in South Africa, and the occupation of Palestine.[93] The chronology of the present book, therefore, falls primarily within the period of the promotion of human rights, and as seen in the following chapters, the fact that human rights at the time were not afforded the same level of

[88] Mazower, "The strange triumph."
[89] Alston and Mégret, "Introduction," 8.
[90] Schabas, *Customary International Law*, 15–18.
[91] Schabas, "Non-State Actors," 466–467.
[92] Alston and Mégret, "Introduction," 8.
[93] Alston and Mégret, "Introduction," 8.

protection one would expect today, was definitive in how the legal-historical narrative in Cyprus developed in later decades.

International humanitarian law, to which we turn last, is in fact the oldest regime in contemporary public international law. With the adoption of two earlier Geneva Conventions in 1929, one on the Amelioration of the Condition of the Wounded and Sick in Armies in the Field and another on the treatment of prisoners of war, WWII interrupted the process of codifying additional laws on the conduct of hostilities and the protection of those *hors de combat*. Work on the matter resumed in July 1946, but it took three years of negotiations before the four 1949 Geneva Conventions relating to the Protection of Victims of Armed Conflict (Geneva Conventions I–IV) were formally adopted. In the meantime, WWII had brought the ICRC at the brink of bankruptcy, while new conflicts, such as the Greek Civil War (1946–1949) and the Korean War (1950–1953), further drained the organisation's limited resources.[94] For most of the 1950s and the 1960s, while the organisation never ceased its field operations, the ICRC was nearly bankrupt, under-stuffed, and demoralised. It is under these circumstances that ICRC one-man delegations were present in Cyprus from January 1964 to December 1965. Things for the ICRC only started improving during the 1967 Six-Day Arab-Israeli War and the Nigerian (Biafra) Civil War, at a point when a general shift on humanitarian matters started being observed in public international law.[95]

This change was initiated with the UN International Conference on Human Rights in Tehran, in 1968,[96] which culminated with the adoption of UNGA Resolution (XXIII) on the 'Respect for human rights in armed conflicts', directly linking international human rights law to the Geneva and Hague rules of international humanitarian law.[97] The relationship between the two legal regimes, however, was anything but clear. In an article published on the occasion of the twentieth anniversary from the signing of the 1949 Geneva Conventions, Jean Pictet, one of the main drafters of the Conventions, held the view that international humanitarian law 'describe[d] the large body of public international law derived from humanitarian sentiments and centred upon the protection of the individual', whereas 'human rights' was a separate branch of humanitarian law,

[94] Palmieri, "Standing the test of time?," 1286–1290.
[95] Nolte, "Different Functions."
[96] A/CONF.32/41 (Teheran, 22 April to 13 May 1968).
[97] UNGA, Res 2444(XXIII) (19 December 1968) para 5.

additional to the 'law of war'.[98] Historians and international lawyers today agree that in the first half of the twentieth century, what we refer to today as international human rights law and international humanitarian law were far more closely integrated, than what more recent practical application suggests.[99] It was the proliferation of regional instruments on human rights such as the ECHR, and the establishment of a parallel international human rights law regime through the adoption of the 1966 Covenants on Civil and Political Rights, and on Economic, Social and Cultural Rights (both in force since 1976), that enhanced the drifting apart between the two.

The separate development of these two areas of law, has led to long-term theoretical debates on which takes precedence if both humanitarian and human rights law are applicable. The most popular position is that international humanitarian law is a specialised area of law (*lex specialis*), which in times of armed conflict assumes precedence over the generally applicable principles of human rights law (*lex generalis*). This discussion, though of direct and paramount significance in the context of the unresolved Cyprus conflict has not taken place in Cyprus, where international human rights law—through the ECHR—has been the preferred course of legal action. It is estimated here that this comes as a result of various factors, notwithstanding a piecemeal approach to public international law, but also the limited options for recourse to other judicial bodies with jurisdiction over the violent events which unfolded in Cyprus up to 1974. This in turn has been further enabled through the historical lack of clarity in the period in question, the fragmentation of public international law in multiple highly specialised areas of law, and the long-term approach of the ECtHR to refrain from engaging with facts concerning active hostilities and issues of international humanitarian law.[100] Incidentally, the latter point is linked to the first inter-state case under the ECHR, *Greece v UK* (1958) which also happens to concern Cyprus and the EOKA emergency, discussed in detail in the following pages.

Lastly, in terms of politics, international humanitarian law is unpopular due to its equal applicability to all parties to an armed conflict. Dealing

[98] Pictet, "The need to restore the laws."

[99] Fortin, "Complementarity between the ICRC and the United Nations"; Alexander, "A Short History"; Van Dijk, "Human rights in war."

[100] Bowring, "Fragmentation."

specifically with the conduct of hostilities, international humanitarian law is not concerned with the *jus ad bellum* and therefore, with the question who carries the legal (and moral) responsibility for initiating an armed conflict. An issue which is at the epicentre of any debate on who is the prime perpetrator of human suffering in any armed conflict. Consequently, humanitarian law applies to all parties involved in an armed conflict, regardless of whether the use of force as such can be legally justified, or not.[101] Therefore, a government cannot seriously invoke the violation of humanitarian law by the opponent State or armed group, without anticipating from their opponent to turn a mirror back on them. As a result, humanitarian law does not always play out well in terms of politics, for who would admit openly they are victims of an armed attack *and* the perpetrator of horrendous war crimes or other international crimes, before an international or a domestic audience. It is here that the individual criminal responsibility under international criminal law acknowledges that whereas a State's or an armed group's conduct may be justifiable under international law, criminal misconduct can still be attributed to specific individuals, even if their uniform suggests they belong to the morally less culpable party to the conflict.

The lack for clarity in the relationship between international humanitarian, criminal and human rights law regimes has had a direct impact on the Cypriot historical narrative, including in the present chronology. The present book concludes at March 1968, just a month before the Tehran Conference took place. Later quests for justice in the Cyprus context included scuttered elements of all three of the above interrelated branches of public international law, without any known efforts to systematise the various legal arguments in public discourse. There are dangers in a narrative that 'mixes everything' and blurs the line separating 'ordinary' human rights violations and violations that threat or breach international peace and security.[102] This approach allows for 'dubious interventionist agendas', makes legal rules virtually inoperative and blurs the separate responsibilities that arise. It is this 'blurring' that this book attempts to detangle, starting from the less-known and less-discussed aspects of the Cyprus Question.

[101] Schabas, "Belt and suspenders?".

[102] Mégret, "The Security Council," 97–98.

Reconfiguring Civil War as Non-international Armed Conflict

Historically, sovereign rulers had developed a common code of customary rules regulating conduct during hostilities among themselves. Yet the courtesy of a minimum protection was not afforded to their own subjects, in case the latter rebelled against the sovereign's authority. In an analogous manner, nowadays States are reluctant to accept that the threshold of a civil war has been reached, in the belief that this would legitimise the standing and the actions of the non-State rebelling group. This trend has been a constant obstacle in the effective implementation of international humanitarian law during non-international armed conflicts, like in the case of the Northern Ireland 'troubles', where the UK government continuously denied that a non-international armed conflict was taking place there.[103] We have previously examined the breadth of legal norms and doctrines that are relevant to armed conflict, international or internal. However, the history of the normative framework regulating 'civil war' or 'internal' or 'non-international' armed conflict has its own insights to provide.

In classical international law the laws and customs of war recognised three distinct categories of civil war. In order of intensity, starting from the least tense situation, the first is the state of 'rebellion', which involved violence of limited duration and could be easily suppressed by a State's law enforcement agencies without the involvement of the military. A rebellion would turn into an 'insurgency', if violence expanded in terms of duration, geographical scope, and numbers, and the government became increasingly unable to control it. Thus, whereas the actions of the 'rebels' would have been subjected to ordinary criminal law, an insurgency was a more 'fluid' state of affairs between the insurgents and the State. There are no objective criteria to definine a situation as an insurgency. However, whereas during a rebellion other States were prohibited from assisting the rebels, as that would amount to interfering in the domestic affairs of the State in a state of rebellion, during an insurgency, insurgents could form 'a factual relation' with outside States, 'for reasons of convenience, of humanity, or of economic interest'.[104]

The third and last stage of intensity would be that of a 'belligerency', where violence would reach such levels of intensity that the relationship

[103] Milanovic, "Transnational and Mixed Conflicts," 48.

[104] Sivakumaran, *Law of Non-International Armed Conflict*, 10.

between the government and the belligerent party would be regulated by the laws of war; i.e. inter-state armed conflict. This is the same doctrine that applied to 'revolutions'.[105] Belligerency was subject to recognition of the situation as such based on four criteria: (i) an ongoing civil war, accompanied by general hostilities, (ii) occupation and 'orderly administration of a substantial part of national territory' by the insurgents, (iii) observance of the rules of warfare on the part of the insurgents, and (iv) the need for third States to expressly take a position vis-à-vis the civil war. This was necessary to ensure protection from abuse of 'a gratuitous manifestation of sympathy with the cause of the insurgents'.[106] Moreover, this served as a means to enable third States to protect their own interests if they were affected by the ongoing civil war, either in terms of their rights as neighbouring States, or when maritime relations were involved, since the recognition of belligerency would give neutral States protection from potential harm during commercial activities at sea.[107] By the early 1970s, however, these criteria were considered 'misleading' by some, since there were no procedures for third-party actors to estimate the situation and governments would define their relationship with insurgent factions depending on 'political preferences' as opposed to any other set of criteria.[108]

The above formula was applied during the nineteenth century, and yet, there are few recognised instances of belligerency, except for the Greek War of Independence (1821–1830) and various other conflicts in Latin America during the same period. Formal recognitions of insurgency and belligerency have not been recorded in the early twentieth century. Examples include the Spanish Civil War (1936–1939), but also the Nigerian (Biafra) Civil War in 1967. Both of these conflicts played a significant part in the development of international humanitarian law and the legal framework governing non-international armed conflicts, in particular. The ICRC's experience in Spain, reinforced the organisation's determination to ensure the protection of civilians in internal conflicts, but these were interrupted during WWII.[109] The Nigerian Civil War, on the

[105] Greenman, "Common Article 3 at 70."

[106] Oppenheim, *International Law*, 249–250.

[107] Greenman, "Common Article 3 at 70."

[108] Falk "Introduction," 12.

[109] Draft International Convention on the Condition and Protection of Civilians of Enemy Nationality Who are on Territory Belonging to or Occupied by the Belligerent (Tokyo Draft) 1934; Draft Convention for the Protection of Civilian Populations against new Engines of War (Amsterdam Draft) 1938.

other hand, was a definitive moment that led to innovation in ICRC practices and the broader humanitarian sector.[110] The Nigerian conflict was a catalyst for the reform of international humanitarian law in the 1970s, which led to the adoption of supplementary Additional Protocols I and II to the 1949 Geneva Conventions in 1977. These two supplementary legal instruments complete the 'Geneva rules' of international humanitarian law, but they are not addressed in detail here since they are not applicable to the 1960s chronology of the book.

The ICRC first attempted to draw attention to the humanitarian needs arising during a civil war as early as the 1912 International Red Cross Conference. However, the delegates refused to give the matter any consideration.[111] It would take almost four more decades until this objective was achieved through common article 3 to the 1949 Geneva Conventions; the 'Convention in miniature'.[112] To some common article 3 was 'revolutionary', and to others a 'legal heresy'.[113] To ICRC's Jean Pictet it was an 'almost unhoped for extension' to common article 2,[114] which provides that the 1949 Geneva Conventions 'shall apply to all cases of declared war or of any other armed conflict which may arise between two or more of the High Contracting Parties'. Like common article 2, common article 3 is identical in all four 1949 Conventions, safe for the addition of the word 'shipwrecked' in 1949 Geneva Convention II for the Amelioration of the Condition of the Wounded, Sick and Shipwrecked Members of Armed Forces at Sea. Despite efforts during the drafting process to set specific criteria for what would constitute a non-international armed conflict, the text contains little information on the substance on what a non-international armed conflict is, other than being an 'armed conflict not of an international character'.

In Pictet's 1952 Commentary some indicative legally non-binding criteria were given to help assess whether the 'threshold' for a non-international armed conflict was crossed by the level of violence observed. The first criterion required the existence of an armed group revolting against the de jure government. Such a group should possess an organised military force, act under specific authority and within a determinate

[110] Marie-Luce Desgrandchamps, "Organising the unpredictable".
[111] Elder, "The Historical Background of Common Article 3".
[112] Pictet, *Commentary GCI 1952*, 48.
[113] Greenman, "Common Article 3 at 70."
[114] Pictet, *Commentary GCI 1952*, 38.

territory, with 'the means of respecting and ensuring respect for the Convention'. A second criterion addressed the government, stating that given the level of violence the government would be 'obliged' to have recourse to the 'regular military forces'. Other indicators for an ongoing non-international armed conflict would be the recognition of the revolting group as belligerents, the fact that the dispute appeared on the agenda of the UNSC or the UNGA as a 'threat to international peace, a breach of peace or an act of aggression', or that the insurgents had obtained the characteristics of a State, such as the exercise of '*de facto* authority over persons within a determinate territory'.

The obligation not to act in a way that is prohibited under common article 3 is absolute and the insertion of a reciprocity clause was omitted on purpose. However, whereas the legal government of a State-party to the Conventions was obviously obliged to comply with common article 3, justifying the obligation of an insurgent party to do so was less straight forward, due to their lack of a formal status under international law, since insurgent forces are non-State entities. Thus, already at the Diplomatic Conference negotiating the Conventions, many participating States doubted that the Conventions could bind insurgent groups. In the commentary, Pictet agreed that binding a non-State actor through a Convention would have been unthinkable in earlier times, but shall the insurgents exercise 'effective sovereignty' over a territory, then their claim to represent the State, or part of the State in question would suffice to bind them under common article 3. In practice, if the insurgents did apply common article 3 it would benefit the civilians and those *hors de combat*, and if not, then that would be used against them, as it would have an obvious impact on the image of the insurgent party. If they were not serious about their international obligations, then they would fail to convince other actors, like UNSC members for instance, of being in control of the situation.

By the early 1960s, following some failed attempts to apply common article 3, concerns over its inadequacy increased given the brevity of the provision and the fact that in internal conflict the opposing forces usually refuse to recognise each other's official status.[115] This is also reflected in the text of the four available commentaries, one per each 1949 Geneva Convention published from 1952 to 1960, which are almost identical in terms of common article 3. The one on Geneva Convention III, on the

[115] Jakovljević and Patrnogic, "Urgent need," 256.

protection of prisoners of war, for instance, stated in 1960 in more certain terms that 'Applications by [...] the [ICRC] for permission to engage in relief work have more than once been treated as unfriendly attempts to interfere in the domestic affairs of the country concerned'.[116] Thus, by the 1960s there was an abundance of lack of clarity not only on how the 1949 Conventions would be applied in practice, but also on what the role of the ICRC was.

In early recognition of the problems posed by the ambiguity of common article 3, the ICRC convened three Expert Commissions to give opinions on specific questions relevant to common article 3, in 1953, 1955 and 1962, which dealt with (i) political detainees, (ii) the application of humanitarian principles in 'internal disturbances', and (iii) the availability of aid to victims of said disturbances, respectively.[117] Hence, when the third Expert Commission was asked 'In which cases is article 3 legally applicable?', the 1962 Commission, offered some additional clarity, reiterating the importance of setting certain, yet still rather ambiguous, criteria for the determination of the existence of an internal armed conflict:

> a minimum amount of organisation, [...] the length of the conflict, the number and framework of the rebel groups, their installation or action on a part of the territory, the degree of insecurity, the existence of victims, the methods employed by the legal government to re-establish order, etc.[118]

Among the members of all three Expert Commissions was Professor Nihat Erim,[119] future Prime Minister of Turkey in the early 1970s, who in 1959 was member of the Turkish/ Turkish Cypriot drafting team for the RoC Constitution. In fact, Erim presided over the ICRC's 1962 Expert Commission, where he was joined by Greek Law Professor George Tenekides, who also had a long-term involvement in the Cyprus Question.[120] This is proof that both Cypriot communities had direct access to in-depth international humanitarian law expertise during the period of the 'Cyprus troubles'.

[116] Pictet, *Commentary GCIII 1960,* 29.

[117] ICRC, "Commission aux détenus politiques"; ICRC, "Commission de l'application des principes humanitaires"; ICRC, "Victims of Internal Conflicts."

[118] ICRC, "Victims of Internal Conflicts," 82–83.

[119] Erim, *Cypriot Dimensions.*

[120] Tenekides, *Cyprus: Recent Histories.*

Pictet's criteria never crystallised into customary international law, and when the ICRC reissued the commentary on Geneva Convention I in 2016, it developed a more extensive list of criteria based on Pictet's commentary, the report of the 1962 Expert Commission, and the additional experience gathered over more than 60 years. These criteria were then grouped under two overarching criteria of *'organisation'* and *'intensity'* (Table 2.1). The criteria are meant to be considered cumulatively, suggesting that the more of these indicators are present in a violent context, the higher the possibility of establishing that a non-international armed conflict is taking place.[121] These criteria have been chosen and presented in a manner that protects a State's sovereign interests.

Notably there are no criteria qualifying an 'international armed conflict', since the purpose of the term in the Geneva Conventions was simply to replace the concept of inter-state 'war', as understood historically.[122]

Table 2.1 Indicators suggesting the levels of 'Organisation' and 'Intensity' in cases of internal armed violence may have reached the threshold of a non-international armed conflict

Level of Organisation of armed forces/ groups	*Level of Intensity of violence*
i. Command structure and capacity to sustain military operations	i. Seriousness of attacks
ii. Disciplinary rules/mechanisms	ii. Increase in armed clashes
iii. Headquarters	iii. Spread over territory, over a given period of time (duration)
iv. Control over certain territory	iv. Distribution of weapons among both parties
v. Access to weapons/ equipment	v. Attention and resolutions from the UNSC
vi. Recruits and military training	vi. Number of civilians forced to flee
vii. Planning, coordination and carrying out of operations	vii. Type of weapons and equipment (e.g. tanks)
viii. Use of military tactics	viii. Blocking, besieging, and shelling of towns
ix. Negotiation and conclusion of agreements (e.g. ceasefire)	ix. Number of casualties
	x. Quantification of troops/units deployed
	xi. Deployment of government forces
	xii. Ceasefire orders and agreements
	xiii. Attempts of representatives from international organisations to broker and enforce ceasefire agreements

[121] ICRC, *Commentary GCI 2016*, paras 434–435.
[122] Milanovic, "Transnational and Mixed Conflicts," 29.

The above criteria have also guided the present research. It must be clarified, however, that they are used as factual indicators aiming to restore an, as accurate as possible, illustration of the narrative of violence in Cyprus up to 1968, for the purposes of academic research. Only formal bodies vested with the power to make legally binding decisions can take authoritative decisions on the matter. Moreover, a formal judicial or quasi-judicial procedure that would aim at allocating legal responsibility for the events that took place would depend on the arguments raised, which could relate to all or any combination of the relevant areas of law described above, depending on the forum and the purpose of the formal procedure. Such a formal procedure would also require an authoritative determination on issues of time in view of the exact applicable law.

The Cypriot case is not alone in its ambiguous disposition or outward disregard of international humanitarian law in the 1960s. One of the most significant obstacles to the application of common article 3 in the two decades after 1949 came from the colonial powers, which already during the drafting process had reservations over new international legal rules which would allow foreign intervention at times of increasing violence in the colonies. As already mentioned, even though colonial territories did not enjoy equal status to the metropolis of the colonial ruler for the purposes of international law, the colonial power along with its colonial territories were seen as a single unitary state. Positions on common article 3, however, varied. Whereas France had a dubious approach and eventually accepted a compromise affected by the experience of its own resistance fighters during the German occupation of France in WWII,[123] the UK, Belgium, the Netherlands and Portugal resisted the proposal throughout. The UK and Portugal were the last from the group to ratify and make the 1949 Conventions enforceable in their domestic legal order in 1957 and 1961, respectively.[124]

Major 'testing grounds' for the ICRC and common article 3 proved the Mau Mau insurgency in Kenya (1952–1960) and the Algerian War of Independence (1954–1962), when the UK and France consistently refused to apply international humanitarian law in the anti-colonial context. Instead, they resorted to a rhetoric of 'fight against terrorism', 'emergency', 'civil disturbance', *'actions de maintien de l'ordre'*, and *'entreprises*

[123] Klose, "The Colonial Testing Ground," 109.

[124] Thompson, "Humanitarian Principles to the Test."

de pacification'.[125] An approach which was also evident a few years later, in the context of the EOKA struggle in Cyprus. The Mau Mau insurgents, on the other hand, showed a willingness to make use of humanitarian legal principles, when in January 1954 they adopted rules of conduct, which prohibited acts like the killing of children, the raping of women, and the attacking of hospitals or schools.[126] A few years later, Algerian international lawyer and diplomat Mohammed Bedjaoui, wrote his famous book on colonialism and self-determination, advocating for the applicability of international humanitarian law in the Algerian war.[127] These developments were not unknown or indifferent to the Cypriots, with both Greek Cypriot and Turkish Cypriot MPs expressing their solidarity with Algeria at the House of Representatives in 1961.[128]

Of relevance is also the fact that during the 1950s the British used to refer to the military actions in the colonies as 'counterinsurgencies' without acknowledging the existence of 'civil war' or 'non-international armed conflict'. This was in spite of the obvious connection between the non-legal term 'counterinsurgency', understood as the 'broad set of strategies and practices intended to halt insurgency', and insurgency, which included acts like guerrilla warfare, terrorism, and non-violent resistance, with the intention to 'destroy or replace the existing structure of authority'.[129] Here, the tension between 'insurgency' in the legal sense, as the second stage of intensity in a civil war, and a broader colloquial meaning is once again evident, leading Brian Drohan, a historian with a military background, who has undertaken extensive research on the Cyprus 'counterinsurgency' of 1955–1959, among others, to observe that only recently the 'myth of British counterinsurgency' is being increasingly disputed.[130]

This predisposition of the colonial powers was not unique to international humanitarian law. As human rights and international criminal law expert William Schabas has indicated, in preparation of the Nuremberg Charter the British and American negotiators showed an uneasiness with the potential precedent the Nuremberg trial could lead to, had the Nazi officials been prosecuted in regard to the persecution of minority groups on German territory, since that would constitute interference with German

[125] Klose, "The Colonial Testing Ground," 107–117.
[126] Drohan, *Brutality in an Age of Human Rights*, 12.
[127] Bedjaoui, *Law and the Algerian Revolution*.
[128] Chamatsou, "Reflections."
[129] *Arreguín-Toft, "Counterinsurgency"*.
[130] Drohan, *Brutality in an Age of Human Rights*, 6–9.

sovereignty.[131] Antony Anghie and B.S. Chimni, two of the most prominent international legal scholars in (post-)colonial international law, concur with Schabas that the distinction between atrocities committed in international and internal conflicts, derived from concerns over the Allies' treatment of minorities within their own territory, or atrocities in the colonies.[132] In the same regard, the UN did not interfere on issues concerning non-self-governing territories until 1961, following the adoption of the 'Declaration on the Granting of Independence to Colonial Countries and Peoples'.[133]

It was not until 1977 and the adoption of Additional Protocol I to the 1949 Geneva Conventions that, under article 1(4), international law defined and regulated anti-colonial conflicts as 'wars of national liberation'. Meaning international armed conflicts 'in which peoples are fighting against colonial domination and alien occupation and against racist regimes in the exercise of their right of self-determination'. This provision essentially recognised non-self-governing territories as separate entities with international standing.[134] At the same time, Additional Protocol II 1977, gave more elaborate and detailed rules on the conduct of non-international armed conflicts that 'take place in the territory of a High Contracting Party between its armed forces and dissident armed forces or other organized armed groups' (article 1(1)). This is a narrower scope of applicability than common article 3, since it explicitly states that for Additional Protocol II to apply one side to the non-international armed conflict has to be the government armed forces of a High Contracting Party, whereas common article 3 can apply also in conflicts between non-State armed groups. Additional Protocol II today 'supplements' common article 3, which is still valid law but no longer the sole provision regulating conduct during a non-international armed conflict. Nevertheless, common article 3 is the only provision that was in force during the timeframe of the present book.

The long-term involvement of Turkey, Greece, and the UK in Cyprus, as Guarantors of Cypriot independence since 1960, makes the task of qualifying the violence in Cyprus since 1963 even more challenging. This

[131] Schabas, *Unimaginable Atrocities,* 50.

[132] Anghie and Chimni, "Individual Responsibility in Internal Conflict," 195–196.

[133] Declaration on the Granting of Independence to Colonial Countries and Peoples, UNGA Res 1514(XV) (14 December 1960).

[134] Rosas, 'Wars of National Liberation"; Cassese, *Self-Determination of Peoples,* 393.

difficulty is rooted in the 'binary' categorisation of armed conflict as international or non-international. The very term 'armed conflict' is not a 'generic term', from which the qualification into international or non-international derives. Used on its own, the term is a shorthand for the one type of conflict *or* the other, which may be especially convenient in cases where 'one wants to ***avoid*** qualifying the conflict' because that would be 'politically or legally difficult' (emphasis in the original).[135] The issue of external intervention cannot be avoided in the Cypriot context, and subsequently, the exercise of conflict qualification is a highly complex legal and political matter with potential impact on every State involved.

Despite the recognised customary status of the 1949 Geneva Conventions today, which means that the Conventions bind all States regardless of whether they have signed them or not, and the recognition by the ICJ that common article 3 is reflective of 'elementary considerations of humanity' in 1986,[136] for the purposes of this book common article 3 is employed as a conventional (i.e. treaty-based) rule of public international law, since it was only in the 1990s and through a series of international cases that the status of the law was further clarified. Those developments, however, fall beyond the scope of the events studied here.[137]

The above analysis shows the multiple levels of complexity in determining whether a certain level of internal violence reaches the threshold of civil war or non-international armed conflict from the first place, and how this has been made even more challenging through a politicised (non-) application of the law in the 1960s. According to the literature, in 1949 the intention was for common article 3 to cover situations traditionally termed 'civil war'. Gradually, however, common article 3 acquired a lower threshold of application than initially anticipated.[138] This could explain why the Cypriot *historical* narrative from 1963 onwards developed in terms of 'rebellion' and 'insurgency', foregoing the term 'civil war'. Cases of persisting doubt on whether common article 3 was applicable or not were envisioned even in 1962, when the ICRC Expert Commission stated that in such situations the ICRC retained a right of initiative to deal with humanitarian matters, regardless of the legal status of ongoing violence.

[135] Milanovic, "Transnational and Mixed Conflicts," 28–31.

[136] *Nicaragua v United States of America, 1986*, para 218.

[137] Greenwood, "International Humanitarian Law"; Cassese, "The *Nicaragua* and *Tadić* Tests".

[138] Moir, "Concept of Non-International Armed Conflict," 409.

For this reason, the presence of the ICRC in itself, like in the case of the Cyprus mission of 1964–1965, does not automatically suggest that the threshold of a non-international armed conflict had been crossed.

Furthermore, the above analysis has shown the extent at which anti-colonial struggles and colonial policy impacted the applicability of international law in the mid-twentieth century. The Greek Cypriot anti-colonial movement played a significant role by setting several precedents, both domestically and internationally. It is therefore addressed here in some detail, in order to bridge and offer clarifications in the gaps between the legal and the historical records.

The Final Decade of the Crown Colony of Cyprus, 1950–1959

At the end of WWII, the colonial Empires trembled, while the Cold War gained force. Indeed, in the period after WWII, all actors in international affairs had to adapt to the process of decolonisation. A process which impacted, and impacts to this day, millions around the globe, unexpectedly established a plethora of new States, and altered significantly the institutional and normative framework of public international law. All this, in a relatively short period of time, during which Cyprus obtained renewed geopolitical significance in the Eastern Mediterranean region, as captured accurately in a quote by a Sunday Times commentator, in December 1947. He was writing on the impact of the anticipated evacuation of British troops from Palestine, and the quote is reproduced by Hill at the very last lines of his four volumes on the History of Cyprus, published in 1952:

> It is, I think, a good guess that, when the evacuation starts, not all of our troops will be brought home from Palestine. Of India, Egypt and Cyprus only Cyprus is left, and common sense indicates that it will become a Middle East base.

Indeed, at that point in time, the British were determined to not lose control over Cyprus in light of regional developments in the Middle East and the gradual dismantling of the British Empire. Of course, other colonial powers faced or would soon be facing analogous challenges, as seen by the Angolan (1961–1991) and Mozambican (1962–1992) wars of independence against Portugal, and the war of Algerian Independence

(1954–1962) against France. At the same time, the Cold War gave rise to multiple civil wars elsewhere, such as the Greek Civil War (1946–1949), the Korean War (1950–1953), and the war in Vietnam (1957–1975).

These armed conflicts, international or internal, carry their individual socio-political complexities and continue to impact daily life in those countries today, like in the case of Cyprus. In this context, literature from the TWAIL movement has been instrumental in contextualising global developments during the peak of decolonisation, from 1955 to 1965, reviving and reassessing overlooked aspects from that time. TWAIL insights have also proven enriching in contextualising the events which unfolded in Cyprus in the 1950s and the 1960s. We shall, therefore, turn to a brief examination of the role the global decolonisation movement played for and in Cyprus.

Cyprus and the Global Anti-colonial Movement

The 1950s were off to an eventful start in the Crown colony of Cyprus. In January 1950 the Greek-Orthodox Church of Cyprus organised a plebiscite for the Greek Cypriots on the question of whether *enosis* (union with Greece) was desirable. An overwhelming 95.7% of the Greek-Orthodox Cypriots voted in favour, in what was seen as an undisputed exercise of their right to self-determination; an event that can still lead to political tension.[139] In September 1950, the young Bishop Makarios of Kition was elected Archbishop Makarios III of Cyprus, assuming the roles of Head of the Church of Cyprus and—as per Ottoman custom—de facto political leader of the Orthodox-Greek Cypriots. He would soon become the most widely recognised political figure of the island, and eventually the first elected President of the RoC. Roles he kept for almost three decades, until his death in 1977.

It is within this atmosphere that after consistent efforts the Greek Cypriots convinced the Greek government to raise the issue of Cyprus on their behalf, before the UNGA for the very first time in August 1954 (A/2703). An initiative which gave Greece the opportunity to come out of the marginalisation it had been experiencing internationally, ever since its own civil war in the late 1940s. The Greek motion drew directly from the UN Charter, and the UN purpose of developing 'friendly relations

[139] Suksi, "The referendum as an instrument" 97.

among nations based on respect for the principle of equal rights and self-determination of peoples' (article 1(2) UN Charter).

The British were anxious to prevent a successful outcome for Greece and the Greek Cypriots, as the topic was of existential significance for the British Empire and its role in the region. They were also reluctant to address the issue of self-determination *per se*, knowing that the majority of the island's inhabitants were not supportive of British rule.[140] This led them to bring to the table, for the first time in an international forum, Turkey's interests in Cyprus. Until then Turkey had taken no position on the matter, after recognising the British annexation of Cyprus in 1923 through the Treaty of Lausanne. The emphasis on applying the principle of self-determination regarding Cyprus was reiterated in the draft resolution submitted by Greece (A/2881). However, any opportunity to discuss the topic at the General Assembly was lost when New Zealand introduced, on behalf of the UK, a second draft resolution, before the General Assembly's First Committee on Disarmament and International Security, which took precedence and determined that the time was not yet appropriate for the General Assembly to be seized on the matter (UNGA A/RES/814(IX) 17 December 1954).

In parallel to the above developments, when one by one the former colonies of Africa and Asia started gaining independence, a general concern rose among them that they had been 'left out' of the 1945 San Francisco Conference establishing the UN, and therefore, excluded from the development of a new global order.[141] In San Francisco, only 12 out of 50 delegations came from these two regions. In an attempt to make up for the omission, the first ever Afro-Asian inter-state Conference was organised in Bandung, Indonesia, from 18–24 April 1955. The initiative was led by Sir John Kotelawala, Prime Minister of Ceylon (today, Sri Lanka), President Sukarno of Indonesia, and Indian Prime Minister Jawaharlal Nehru.

Though majorly marginalised in mainstream European historiography of the twentieth century, the conference—which gathered, among others, 29 newly independent Asian and African States—is considered by many the foundational moment of 'the Third World as a political entity'.[142] The Conference produced a 'Final Communiqué' which set down common

[140] Faustmann, "The Internationalization of the Cyprus Conflict," 13–15.

[141] Anghie, "The Origins of Third World Sovereignty."

[142] Burke, "The Compelling Dialogue of Freedom."

standards among the signatory States, on issues of economic and cultural co-operation, human rights and self-determination, the 'problems of dependent peoples', meaning those who still lived under colonial rule, and the promotion of world peace and co-operation.[143] It also set in motion the process towards the foundation of the Non-Aligned Movement, which in 1961 the RoC joined as a founding member, and from which it withdrew upon joining the European Union in 2004.

Among the participating States and signatories of the Communiqué was Turkey. Among the delegates, representing the Greek-Orthodox population of the Crown colony of Cyprus, was Archbishop Makarios III. Even though EOKA had just started its armed action against the British on 1 April 1955 Makarios was not precluded from attending, irritating contemporary commentators:

> ...Orthodox [Christians] make a great deal of Holy Week, but in 1955 that fact did not deter Makarios from abandoning his ecclesiastical responsibilities and from flying on Good Friday of all days to Bandoeng, where his presence had no raison d'être.[144]

Makarios' objectives at the conference were to gain support for EOKA, to demonstrate solidarity with the Afro-Asian States, and enhance all efforts to internationalise the Cyprus Question.[145] He was eventually disappointed, since the Final Communiqué made no explicit reference to the British colonies, even though it explicitly referred to the right of self-determination of the peoples of French-administered Algeria, Morocco, and Tunisia. Despite the fact that the conference in Bandung failed to lead to formal and immediate developments, its symbolism across the post-colonial world was immediately recognised.[146] Issues of sovereignty and non-intervention, as well as colonialism and self-determination (including the self-determination of minority groups) were of particular importance to the future of Cyprus, as well.

In the mid-twentieth century, the principle of sovereignty lay at the epicentre of the decolonisation process, and although the States in Bandung upheld the western model of nation-state sovereignty, their

[143] Final Communiqué of the Asian-African Conference of Bandung (Indonesia, 24 April 1955).

[144] Luke, *A Portrait*, 177.

[145] Reynolds, "Peripheral Parallels?," 252.

[146] Eslava, Fakhri and Nesiah, "The Spirit of Bandung," 7.

sovereignty was guided by *Panchsheel*, the 'Five Principles of Peaceful Coexistence', proclaimed by Nehru in 1954.[147] The *Panchsheel*, which were foundational for the Non-Aligned Movement too, contained the principles of mutual respect for sovereignty and territorial integrity, non-aggression, noninterference in internal affairs of other States, equality and mutual benefit, and peaceful coexistence. The principles relate to some of the most fundamental doctrines of classical international law, reflected also in articles 1, 2(1), 2(4), and 2(7) of the UN Charter.

Retaining the western 'nation-state' conceptualisation of sovereignty, however, implied that the new States were relatively homogenous, in spite of the fact that the alleged homogeneity of European States was itself the result of violent revolutions, oppression and the subject matter of numerous international judicial procedures in the early twentieth century. Moreover, despite the well-established obligation to protect minority groups within one's sovereign territory by the 1950s, this was not addressed in the Five Principles. The threat and fear of minorities developing their own nationalist aspirations through claims to self-determination was present back then, and still exists in many instances today. In paraphrasing Anghie, the precolonial past endured, ancient battles were revived and replaced by new political entities,[148] not unlike in South-East Europe, including Cyprus, where Byzantine, Ottoman and other rivalries have been revived on the Balkan peninsula across the twentieth century and sometimes still persist, though in Cyprus one cannot disregard the distinctive colonial 'twist'.

Thus, among the conflicting legacies of Bandung were a series of unresolved tensions that many post-colonial States inherited, including issues concerning the presence of various minority groups in virtually all States with a colonial past. 'Minorities' in this context do not refer merely to 'numerically smaller demographic or communal entities', but rather 'signify the domestic presence of ethnic and religious communities *seen as having non-local origins*' (emphasis in original).[149] In Burma (Myanmar) and Malaya (Malaysia) for instance, the combined number of residents of Indian and Chinese origin, amounted for as much as 50% and 60% of the

[147] Kim, Fidler and Ganguli, "Eastphalia rising?"

[148] Anghie, "The Origins of Third World Sovereignty," 543–551.

[149] Abraham, "Bandung and State Formation," 48.

total population, respectively,[150] leading to an 'understanding [of] the "minority" as an ethnic phenomenon' in international law.[151]

Like in Asia, the establishment of the Turkish Cypriot community was to a significant extent the result of migrations within broader imperial borders, centuries earlier. Thus, non-suprisingly the above examples resonate with occasional, now less met, arguments dismissing the Turkish Cypriot community as non-local to a 'Greek Cyprus'. The same hostility, however, is not observed vis-à-vis other religious groups in Cyprus, such as the Armenian Cypriots and the Maronite Cypriots, whose settlement on the island from the fifth and seventh centuries respectively, does not generally cast them 'non-local'. And these are not all the minority groups that have existed historically. Being an island located at a historical hotspot of imperial conflicts and conquests, it is not surprising that the literature identifies a minimum of 20 small religious, ethnic, or geographical groups, that permanently or temporarily found refuge on the island, during the British colonial rule alone, from 1878 to 1960.[152]

Under public international law, minorities (ethnic, religious or both) are intrinsically linked to the right of self-determination; 'the right of peoples under colonial, foreign, or alien domination to self-government, whether through formation of a new State, association in a federal State, or autonomy or assimilation in a unitary (non-federal) State'.[153] In its political sense, self-determination is broader, putting an emphasis on criteria such as common history, race, ethnicity, and language, often associated with 'nation' and subsequently, nationalism. As a result, the majority of cases raising claims of self-determination are not necessarily recognised as such under public international law.[154]

The principle of self-determination has a long history, which can be traced back to at least the seventeenth century. After it resumed prominence in the early twentieth century, through Lenin's claim to 'national self-determination' during the Bolshevik revolution and through US President Woodrow Wilson's famous 1918 'Fourteen Points' speech before Congress, self-determination found its way into the Peace Treaties of WWI, which included complex schemes of minority protection within

[150] Abraham, "Bandung and State Formation," 54–58.

[151] Shahabuddin, *Ethnicity and International Law*.

[152] Hadjilyras, *The Religious Groups*, 30–32.

[153] Crawford, *Brownlie's Principles*, 621.

[154] Quane, "The Evolving Right to Self-Determination," 538.

the new borders drawn on the European continent. With minorities engaging in a 'tripartite interaction' with their 'host-state' and their 'kin-state',[155] self-determination started transforming from a 'revolutionary concept' into a principle of 'international diplomacy and international legal discourse'.[156]

This process of legalisation was completed with the explicit inclusion of self-determination in the UN Charter (article 1(2)). In 1945, however, self-determination was not synonymous to independence as it is often assumed today. When the UN was established, no rights were recognised for those in the colonial territories other than the limited duties towards them under the UN Charter, which at no point imposed a duty to grant them independence.[157] Even so, following WWII it was the decolonisation process that turned self-determination into a '*cri de guerre* [a war cry] of third world nations' in the following decades,[158] and decolonisation's moral and legal force.[159] Adding to complexity, in 1954, Josef Kunz interpreted the rise of human rights as a substitute to self-determination in cases where the application of the self-determination principle was impossible or undesirable.[160] Twelve years later, this was taken a step further when in 1966 self-determination was codified as a human right in the International Covenants on Human Rights.

Although today self-determination is a recognised peremptory norm of public international law, its exact content and application is less than clear. Legal literature recognises that self-determination has multiple components. These include an 'external' and an 'internal' dimension, the first as applied to the colonies, and the latter as applicable to 'racial groups denied equal access to government' within a single State.[161] Depending on the context, self-determination does hold the potential of unification with a third State and a right to secession from an existing State, but the law fails to offer further guidance on the matter.[162]

Like sovereignty, self-determination shifts constantly between its legal and its political conceptions. Legally as a 'right', and politically as a

[155] Shahabuddin, *Ethnicity and International Law*, 98–135.
[156] Koskenniemi, "National Self-Determination Today," 255–256.
[157] Higgins, *Problems and Process*, 111–114.
[158] Tomuschat, "Self-determination," 1.
[159] Shahabuddin, *Ethnicity and International Law*, 136.
[160] Kunz, "The Present Status of of Minorities," 282.
[161] Cassese, *Self-Determination of Peoples*.
[162] Stefan Oeter, "Self-determination," 329.

'principle', each time qualified based on the contextual environment of the claim raised.[163] Hence, self-determination has developed a plurality of concrete meanings, ranging from 'external' to 'internal', 'democratic', 'national', 'socialist', and 'colonial'.[164] As a human right self-determination is illustrative of the complexities of the legal process, and is also known for generating high levels of tension within societies, often 'used by rulers to rule the minds of the ruled'.[165] Thus, when questions on self-determination reach a level where political leaders 'throw [their] peoples against each other', a formal legal setting like a trial, is unlikely to lead to closure, because self-determination has already constructed a particular framework, which supports people's own interpretation of what self-determination means.[166] As the following pages show, self-determination's multiple dimensions stand at the exact intersection of the law with the politics and history of Cyprus, across the diametrically antithetical objectives of *enosis* and *taksim*.

Makarios's presence at Bandung repositions Cypriot politicians within the global framework of this period. According to some, the British saw in Makarios a supporter of Arab nationalism. However, his approach went beyond mere sympathy or solidarity with Cyprus' Mediterranean neighbours. Instead, Makarios participation in Bandung is a sign of strong awareness among Cypriot politicians of the island's peculiar position at the intersection of the European, Asian and African peripheries, and how each connection, if properly exploited, could bring the Greek Cypriots a step closer to the dominant political objective of *enosis*.

The EOKA Emergency and Early Inter-communal Violence

Historically, the Greek Cypriot movement for *enosis* can be separated into two periods, which followed separate patterns of actions. The first one, called by Hatzivassiliou the 'Ionian model', was non-violent, more institutional and lasted until 1931, whereas after WWII, the 'Cretan model' put an emphasis on a violent claim for liberation akin to the model followed in the long Cretan violence towards the unification of the island of Crete

[163] Knop, *Diversity and self*-determination, 29–49.
[164] Hilpold, *Autonomy and self-determination*, 7.
[165] Allott, "Absolute right or social poetry?," 209.
[166] Koskenniemi, "Impunity and Show Trials," 1.

with Greece in 1913.[167] This shift was driven to some extent by the futility of all diplomatic efforts to promote the Cyprus Question as an international issue of self-determination, eventually leading to the launch of an offensive against the British administration of the island on 1 April 1955. With the objective being *enosis*, as opposed to independence, the Greek Cypriot anti-colonial struggle is an 'anomaly in the colonial empire' distinguishing the case of Cyprus from other anti-colonial movements.[168]

At the epicentre of the uprising lay the National Organisation of Cypriot Fighters (*Εθνική Οργάνωση Κυπρίων Αγωνιστών*—EOKA). A guerrilla armed group, consisting of Greek Christian Orthodox Cypriots, led and organised underground by Georgios Grivas, who a decade later would become Commander of the RoC armed forces. He was a Cyprus-born officer of the Greek Army, who had received formal military training in Greece. He was pro-*enosis* throughout his life and, though not formally a politician, his views and actions impacted Cypriot politics until his death in January 1974. In preparation, Grivas had drawn a 'Preliminary General Plan of Insurrectionary Action', which contained tactics like sabotage, surprise attacks and popular passive resistance, a plan of action in anticipation of counter-attacks 'by the Turks', and instructions on the manufacturing of explosive devices.[169] The strategic objective was not total defeat, but a 'moral victory through a process of attrition, by harassing, confusing and finally exasperating the enemy forces'.[170] An approach which Grivas would later follow on at least some occasions in his role as National Guard Commander.

Even though preparations had been underway since 1953,[171] and the British authorities had caught a small fishing boat smuggling arms to Cyprus as early as January 1955, the bombings across the island on 1 April did catch them off guard.[172] While a spontaneous uprising like the one in 1931 was anticipated, 'cool, premeditated, terrorism', was not.[173] The complexity of the overall situation in spring 1955 is evident in the first long debate on the subject, held in the House of Commons in London, which touched upon all aspects of the problems that existed. The long-

[167] Hatzivassiliou, *The Cyprus Question*, 13–15.
[168] Simpson, *Human Rights and the End of Empire*, 893.
[169] Grivas, *Guerrilla Warfare*, 91–106.
[170] Grivas, *Guerrilla Warfare*, 5.
[171] Varnava, *The History of EOKA*, 31–34.
[172] Crawshaw, *The Cyprus* Revolt, 114–115.
[173] Holland, *Britain and the Revolt*, 55.

term restrictions on daily life since 1931, issues on identity and self-determination, and the potential effect of these events on British interests in NATO, Malta, Palestine, and Egypt, in light of a earlier plan, which eventually never materialised, to move Britain's Middle East headquarters from Suez to Cyprus.[174]

EOKA operated under a centralised chain of command that led directly to its leader. Members were divided in autonomous regional cells, each comprising of 'sabotage', 'execution', 'ambush', and 'anti-Turkish' sub-groups, as well as a Youth and a Political division. Non-armed mass mobilisation was an important aspect of the organisation's action, often recruiting school children to spread leaflets and organise riots in urban areas. Evangelos Averoff, the Greek Foreign Minister at the time, wrote in his memoir that it was all coordinated by Grivas himself, and gives detailed information on how he himself was involved in the smuggling of arms from Greece.[175]

Initially the violence involved only the bombing of public buildings and installations, but by August 1955 violence increased in intensity with several assassinations of Police officers, and attacks directed at civilians who EOKA believed had collaborated in some way with the authorities. By the end of the emergency, the fight was fought at four levels: 'the British', 'the traitors', 'the Communists', and 'the Turks'.[176] Yet, comparatively speaking, some Cypriot commentators have estimated that EOKA was less violent than the Mau Mau insurrection, and the Algerian National Liberation Front.[177] Grivas himself expressed the view that those who had collaborated with the authorities were Communists, whom EOKA could not 'allow' to exploit the circumstances for the promotion of Soviet-backed communism, as the case was in China, North Vietnam, Kenya and Latin America, among others.[178] Thus, two and a half decades since the *Oktovriana* riots of 1931, in the late 1950s society was as divided as ever, and the legacy of these ideological divisions would continue impacting Cypriot politics for decades to come. An analogous division was brewing simultaneously within the Turkish Cypriot community.

[174] HC Deb 05 May 1955 vol 540 cols 1910–97.

[175] Averoff-Tossizza, *Lost Opportunities,* 149–163.

[176] Averoff-Tossizza, *Lost Opportunities,* 163.

[177] Karyos, "The influence of international actors in the strategic options," 105.

[178] Grivas, *Guerrilla Warfare,* 1–3.

Early efforts to deal with security matters turned towards the strengthening of the Police Force, despite earlier experience in Kenya and Malaya suggesting that local civilian authorities would most likely prove ineffective. In that regard, an auxiliary Special Police Unit was introduced, consisting primarily of Turkish Cypriot officers. A temporary Detention of Persons Law was passed on 16 July 1955, under which individuals could be detained without a public hearing, a right to counsel or a right to examine witnesses, and without a duty on the authorities to disclose the evidence upon which the detention order was made. Governor Robert Armitage however, proved unable to respond effectively to the situation, and for this reason, on 3 October 1955 he was replaced by a career military man, Field-Marshal Sir John Harding.

Harding increased efforts to strengthen the police, but also asked London for military reinforcements, which brought the total number of troops stationed on the island to over 12,000.[179] More importantly from a legal perspective, within a week from Harding's arrival, on 7 October 1955, the UK communicated a *Note Verbale* to the Council of Europe (CoE) Secretary-General, stating that:

> A public emergency within the meaning of Article 15(1) of the [ECHR] exists in the following territory for whose international relations Her Majesty's Government in the United Kingdom are responsible.
>
> Cyprus – Certain emergency powers were brought into operation in the Colony of Cyprus on the 16th July 1955, owing to the commission of acts of violence including murder and sabotage and in order to prevent attempts at the supervision of the lawfully constituted Government.[180]

Article 15(1) ECHR allows for derogations from certain human rights and freedoms protected under the Convention, in 'time of war or other public emergency threatening the life of the nation [...] to the extent strictly required by the exigencies of the situation, provided that such measures are not inconsistent with its other obligations under international law'. This meant that the UK, the nation threatened under the circumstances, could reduce the standard of protection regarding certain rights. The British willingness to notify the Secretariat of its derogations led to certain awkwardness in Strasbourg, the city hosting the Council of

[179] Holland, *Britain and the Revolt*, 100.

[180] As reproduced in: *Greece v UK* (Application No 176/56) Report by the European Commission of Human Rights, 26 September 1958, para 102.

Europe and the ECtHR, since neither the Convention provided instructions as to what needed to be done in such cases, nor any other such notice had ever been made before. To add to complexity, the situation in Cyprus was of direct concern to two more State parties to the Convention; Greece and Turkey.

A Declaration of Emergency under *domestic* colonial law was made by Harding on 26 November 1955, when he enacted the Emergency Powers (Public Safety and Order) Regulations (No. 731), and the Emergency Powers (Collective Punishment) Regulations (No. 732). He was acting under emergency powers conferred to him by a 1952 Emergency Powers (Amendment) Order in Council. Regulation No. 732 contained a total of 76 clauses referring, among others, to arrest without warrant, stop and search powers, and restrictions on movement. These were expanded in 1956 to prevent dissent, enhance the protection of interrogators and intelligence officers, and induce the provision of information from prisoners. In the same year, the death penalty was extended to offences beyond treason and murder, for acts like the discharging of an arm at a person, or the deposition of bombs with the intention to cause death, injury, or damage to property.[181]

Different 'emergency modalities'[182] or regimes were used throughout decolonisation, for colonial authorities to reconcile earlier forms of 'martial law' with concerns on the maintainance of the rule of law.[183] Considering the peculiar, from today's point of view, position of colonial laws in the 'periphery of [British] municipal law',[184] the emergency regulations were a direct product of that colonial legal order. The UK was aware that such measures contravened common article 3, given the fact that the frequent employment of 'collective punishment' by the colonial authorities had already posed particular difficulties for the British during the drafting of the 1949 Geneva Conventions s almost a decade earlier.[185] Therefore, the issuing of a notification under the ECHR and a declaration of emergency, constitute another practical example of how common article 3 and international humanitarian law were disregarded by colonial administrators who favoured a human-rights-oriented counterinsurgency

[181] Simpson, *Human Rights and the End of Empire*, 874–923.
[182] Reynolds. *Empire*, Emergency, 20.
[183] Reynolds. *Empire*, Emergency, 71–93.
[184] Fawcett, "Treaty Relations," 89.
[185] Simpson, *Human Rights and the End of Empire*, 955.

approach, the overriding objective most likely being to shield themselves from international scrutiny.

Similarly, Drohan's comparative historical research on 'human rights activism' in different British counterinsurgency campaigns, speaks of 'cooperative manipulation' on behalf of the authorities, in an effort to shield the practices employed from public view. During this time, the concerted efforts of the Cyprus Bar Association to defend EOKA fighters in the domestic Courts have been of paramount significance, and even triggered the efforts towards the establishment of Amnesty International in 1961.[186] Among those involved were future core protagonists of Cypriot history, like Glafcos Clerides on the defence side, and Rauf Denktash as prosecutor.[187] However, local judicial remedies proved insufficient. Following the detention and exile of Makarios to the Seychelles on 9 March 1956 as well as the first executions of EOKA fighters Michael Karaolis and Andreas Demetriou, Greece lodged an application against the UK to the European Commission of Human Rights (ECmHR) on account of the Greek Cypriots,[188] after renewed failed attempts to bring up the matter before the UN.[189]

The case of *Greece* v *UK* is of historical significance for various reasons also beyond the Cypriot context. Not only it is the first ever inter-State case under the ECHR to be lodged in Strasbourg, but it serves as a preview to many challenges which arose under the Convention at a later stage. Mainly, regarding the deference and prioritisation of State sovereignty and national security interests over individual rights, during derogations under article 15 ECHR.[190] This is is the case that led the way towards the establishment of the legal doctrine of the 'margin of appreciation'.[191] This is a doctrine which has been developed extensively by the case law of the ECtHR over the decades, through which the Strasbourg Court has been allowing State parties to the Convention to exercise a certain level of discretion on policy matters relating to human rights. Whereas the Convention itself does not refer to such a doctrine, the literature identifies the origin of the doctrine in the case discussed here,

[186] Drohan, *Brutality in an Age of Human Rights*, 25–34, 101.

[187] Crawshaw, *The Cyprus* Revolt, 141.

[188] Madsen, "Protracted Institutionalization of the Strasbourg Court," 43.

[189] Simpson, *Human Rights and the End of Empire*, 929.

[190] Reynolds. *Empire, Emergency,* 171–184.

[191] *Greece* v *UK 1958*, para 136; Simpson, *Human Rights and the End of Empire*, 1000; Reynolds. *Empire, Emergency,* 175.

and the case of *Lawless* v *Ireland*,[192] which concerned the claims to human rights violations during the Irish Troubles.[193]

The Cypriot case before the ECmHR addressed practices like whipping, collective punishment, illegal arrest, detention, deportations, the violation of privacy, and the freedoms of expression and assembly. It is worth noting that a small delegation of ICRC representatives also visited Cyprus at the time, to investigate methods of detention and punishment. In their submissions to the ECmHR the Greek government argued, among other things, that since article 15 ECHR allowed for derogations from the Convention only where the measures employed were not inconsistent with other obligations under international law, then the derogations announced by the UK were in breach of the Convention since they contradicted other international law treaties. Specifically, the Greek government drew attention to international humanitarian law, and more concretely article 50 of the 1907 Hague Convention, which refers to general penalties 'inflicted upon the population on account of the acts of individuals', article 87 of 1949 Geneva Convention III on the protection of prisoners of war, similarly prohibiting collective punishment for individual acts, and articles 2, 32 and 33 of Geneva Convention IV 1949 on the protection of civilians, where articles 32 and 33 concern the prohibition of measures involving corporate and collective punishment, respectively. In addition to the above provisions, the Greek government also invoked the argument that the measures were not in line with the UK's obligation under common article 3, under Geneva Conventions III and Geneva Conventions IV, essentially arguing that the ongoing armed violence in Cyprus did constitute a non-international armed conflict within the international boundaries of the British Empire.[194] The focus on Geneva Conventions III and IV result from the particular concern on the treatment of prisoners of war and the civilian population.

The UK counter-argued that 'obligations under international law' in article 15(1) ECHR referred to the scope of a State's right to derogate under international law, and not to public international law rules, in general.[195] A position that was rejected by the Commission.[196] Regarding

[192] *Lawless* v *Ireland* (Application No 332/1957) Report of the European Commission of Human Rights,19 December 1959.

[193] Hutchinson, "The Margin of Appreciation."

[194] *Greece* v *UK 1958*, paras 147–221.

[195] *Greece* v *UK 1958*, para 148.

[196] *Greece* v *UK 1958*, para 149.

common article 3, the UK stated that the provision was not applicable in the case of Cyprus, since the article was intended for conflicts like the one 'experienced in Spain', where a party to the conflict was also a High Contracting Party 'with a capital "P"' (i.e. a State) and was not applicable to 'individual acts of violence or to the activities of [a] terrorist organisation'.[197] The argument links directly to the colonial policy of not recognising the application of common article 3 in the colonies.

Full examination of the arguments on each side is beyond the subject matter of the present book. It needs to be noted though, that the ECmHR eventually decided by majority vote not to give conclusions on the compatibility of the measures that potentially violated international humanitarian law with the ECHR.[198] It, therefore, avoided engaging in depth with the question of the overlapping principles between international humanitarian law and international human rights law. As already discussed above, this overlap has today been addressed in the context of a *lex specialis / lex generalis* relationship between the two areas of law, but the problem persists. Recent case law of the ECtHR caused controversy due to the Court's obvious reluctance to engage with human rights violations during active armed violence.[199] As a non-judicial body, the ECmHR used to give opinions instead of legally binding judgments. Its approach does raise the question, however, to what extent this early precedent contributed to the future institutional approach followed by the ECtHR.

Despite the fact that the use of torture and other brutal acts by the British security forces during decolonisation is well-known and well-documented today, torture allegations were not mentioned in the first application to the ECmHR. However, constant allegations for the use of torture during interrogation quickly drew additional attention and a second application to the ECmHR was lodged on 17 July 1957, concerning 49 individual cases of ill-treatment. These proceedings were terminated on 12 May 1959, upon the mutual agreement of Greece and the UK, after a settlement on the future of Cyprus had been achieved through the London-Zurich Agreements in February 1959.[200] The application had led, however, to increased concerns among the British authorities, who

[197] *Greece* v *UK 1958*, para 184.

[198] *Greece* v *UK 1958*, paras 235–236.

[199] *Georgia* v *Russia (II)* 2021; Dzehtsiarou, '*Georgia* v *Russia* (II).

[200] *Greece v UK (Application 299/57)* Report of the European Commission of Human Rights, 8 July 1959, 18–20.

considered the withdrawal of all colonial jurisdictions from the protections under the ECHR, to prevent applications from other countries on behalf of the colonies.

The violence between EOKA and the British constitutes only one part, the better-known part, of armed violence during the period 1955–1959. However, as seen above, a reaction of some kind by the Turkish Cypriots was already anticipated during the preparatory stage of EOKA and the organisation had warned the Turkish Cypriots not to become involved. Soon after violence erupted however, the internal affairs of the island, which were never fully 'internal', had a spill-over effect over politics in Greece and Turkey, and the relations between the two. A process of 'diffusion',[201] that persists at various levels of intensity to this day. Among the events that took place beyond Cyprus during this period stand out the September Riots in Istanbul and Izmir on 6 and 7 September 1955, when the Turkish State Radio announced a bomb attack at the birth house of Kemal Ataturk in Thessaloniki, Greece, leading to riots and extended destruction of property of non-Muslims in both cities.[202] Since then, Turkish and Greek researchers have presented evidence suggesting that the riots were planned by the Turkish State with the contribution of the British government, linking the event to the developments in Cyprus.[203]

Within a year from the start of EOKA's campaign, the chasm between the two communities grew further. Already by May 1956, the New York Times reported on battles between Greek Cypriots and Turkish Cypriots,[204] whereas another article from the same source describes the separation of the Greek and Turkish quarters of Nicosia with barbed wire to end riots between members from each group.[205] The second half of 1957, saw the establishment of the paramilitary 'Turkish Resistance Organisation' (*Türk Mukavemet Teşkilatı*—TMT). Its objectives were to defend the security of life and property of the Turkish Cypriots, to deter attacks targeting Turkish Cypriots, to confront EOKA and stop the spreading of communism, while strengthening the bond between the Turkish Cypriots and Turkey. TMT was divided in six regional sectors, each commanded by an officer of the

[201] Gurr, *Minorities at risk,* 133.

[202] Güven, "Riots against the Non-Muslims of Turkey," 3–4.

[203] Hatzivassiliou, "The Riots in Turkey"; Soulioti, *Fettered Independence: Documents,* 31–83.

[204] Anon, "2 Cypriotes die in village fights."

[205] Haff, "Barrier to Divide Cyprus' Capital."

Turkish Army, responsible for the smuggling of arms and the training of TMT members.[206]

Diplomatic negotiations ran in parallel to the spreading of armed violence on the island, and while they initially addressed only Greece and Turkey, Governor Harding initiated a dialogue also with Archbishop Makarios, as soon as he arrived in Cyprus in October 1955, without success.[207] Thus, the British turned their efforts towards achieving an international agreement involving the two 'motherlands', leading to the Radcliffe Proposal in 1956, and the Macmillan Plan of 1958. Upon presenting the Radcliffe Proposal to the House of Commons, which envisaged a form of self-government for the island, Secretary of State for the Colonies Lennox-Boyd informed the House that should self-government work satisfactorily, then the UK was ready to reconsider self-determination, favouring partition as an option.[208] The Macmillan proposal on the other hand, retained the element of self-governanment of the Radcliffe proposal in terms of internal affairs, according to which each community would have autonomy on communal affairs through two separate Houses of Representatives,[209] yet issues of external policy, defence and internal security would be reserved for the Governor, who would act in consultation with the governments of Greece and Turkey.[210] The whole scheme would be tested for an interim period of seven years.

Both plans were eventually rejected and according to Kizilyurek, the fact that the British government withdrew its promise for separate self-determination, led to a first climax in inter-communal violence in 1958. Initially, from 26 to 28 January 1958, Turkish Cypriot rioters clashed with the police, leading to the death of seven members of their community.[211] Following this event, Turkish Cypriot nationalism too started to openly turn against the British, leading Harding's successor and last Cyprus Governor, Sir Hugh Foot, to be on guard for threats coming from each ethno-religious community, separately but simultaneously.

Inter-communal violence in 1958 had direct impact on the institutional structure of local authorities. A contested issue which became a source of constant tension in the first three years of the RoC and the following

[206] Chrysostomou, *Establishment of the National Guard*, 218–219.
[207] Novo, "Harding-Makarios Negotiations."
[208] HC Deb 19 December 1956 vol 562 col 1267; Hakki, *A Documentary History*, 28–29.
[209] HC Deb 19 June 1958 vol 589 cols 1316–17.
[210] HC Deb 19 June 1958 vol 589 col 1317.
[211] Kızılyürek, *The Dark 1958*, 14–23, 34.

decade. Already in the early 1940s, the Turkish Cypriots were dissatisfied with the fact that the existing legislation on local authorities prevented them from holding any positions as mayors or deputy mayors and in light of the quest for *enosis* of many Greek Cypriot mayors, the issue was a source of additional friction.

The initiation of a campaign for *taksim* by the Turkish Cypriot leadership in May 1957, led within a year to a Turkish Cypriot demand for separate municipalities. The ongoing EOKA and TMT violence, combined with political intra-communal tension was a particularly difficult situation for the British government, who were reluctant to confront the Turkish Cypriots with violence, especially in light of Turkish Cypriot threats to withdraw from the security forces. As a result, on 3 July 1958 Governor Foot reported that 'unofficial pilot corporations' were set up in all main towns of the island, initiating a process of unofficial geographical division in all main urban centres.[212] During the same period, the Turkish Cypriot leadership initiated a campaign for economic 'self-resilience' and modernisation, with the slogan 'From Turk to Turk', which constituted the starting point for future socio-economic detachment and isolation between the two communities.[213] A sample of what was to follow to a larger scale some five years later.

With armed violence on the rise within each and between the two groups, June 1958 was the most violent month during this period. On 7 June 1958, a bombing attack on the Turkish Information Office triggered renewed violence across the island, leading to damage against private property, a series of murders, and the first major wave of displacement. Among the casualties during this period alone, according to British archival information cited by Kizilyurek, there were 13 to 15 Greek Cypriots and 2 Turkish Cypriots, while some 600 to 700 families had to leave their homes, including Armenian Cypriot families residing in the Turkish quarter of Nicosia.[214]

One of the most violent incidents throughout the 1950s occurred in the same month, when on 12 June 1958 eight Greek Cypriots from the village of Kondemenos died and five others were severely wounded, following an ambush by a group of 50 to 100 Turkish Cypriot men from the nearby Turkish Cypriot village of Gyoneli; a few miles north-west of

[212] Markides, *The Municipal* Issue, 13–25.
[213] Mehmet, *Sustainability of Microstates*, 33–35.
[214] Kızılyürek, *The Dark 1958*, 78–83.

Nicosia. The victims were part of a 35-strong group of Greek Cypriots, among them also minors, who earlier that day had set off to the mixed village of Skylloura to attack its Turkish Cypriots residents. Upon being arrested by the British security forces, the group of 35 were left a few miles away from their village to return there on foot; a regular practice of the British military known as 'bussing'.

The fact that these men were left unarmed and unescorted to walk through the fields in such proximity to a Turkish Cypriot village was a major miscalculation. A formal inquiry investigating whether the British security forces had intentionally left the group of the detainees there, found that the British military had acted with 'utmost good faith', and that the actions of the Turkish Cypriots were intentional.[215] Despite the fact that arrests were made, no known trials have been reported. It appears, however, that the Gyoneli incident set a precedent for future inquiries that took place in the early years of the Republic, where inquiries served as a substitute for a judicial process, contributing to the poor judicial record observed regarding the most horrendous crimes in the following 15 years.

The short period from 1955 to 1959 set the foundation for many of the institutional challenges and the violence inherited by the RoC. If we follow suggestions in the literature that in 1949 common article 3 was intended to cover situations traditionally termed as 'civil war',[216] and that violence between EOKA and the British forces was in fact an insurgency which was not addressed as such due to colonial policy, one is left wondering whether the violence between EOKA and TMT could also be analysed in light of common article 3. Considering that common article 3 can be applicable in situations between two non-State armed groups, then there is no reason to reject that assumption, subject to further analysis. The State here would of course be the UK, as opposed to later violence on the territory of the RoC. Hence, despite the continuity in the causal chain of events that took place from 1958 to 1963, it must be emphasised that the violence of 1958 and the wave of violence from 1963 onwards constitute two separate legal cases, with separate legal entities involved.

[215] HC Deb 10 December 1958 vol 597 col 345; Soulioti, *Fettered Independence: Documents,* 183.

[216] Moir, "Concept of Non-International Armed Conflict."

Conclusion

The nineteenth-century history of public international law, inseparable from the 'civilising mission' and 'imperial humanitarianism', has given us new perspectives on the history of Cyprus. Located at the intersection of the Middle East and Europe, developments in Cyprus have been impacted by a diversity of factors, which are not always obvious at a first glance. As a former Ottoman province, at the turn of the twentieth century the island's population was directly affected by developments on the Balkans, and in particular the harrowing Greco-Turkish conflicts before and after WWI. However, once Cyprus became a British colony in 1925 developments within the British Empire and the broader colonial world started having a more direct effect, especially in the aftermath of WWII and the establishment of the UN. Cyprus' relation to the post-colonial world reached a peak moment with Makarios' participation at the Bandung Conference. The sources consulted have shown a strong awareness among the Cypriot leadership of the tensions caused because of the Cold War, which by the 1950s had already led to intra-communal hostility across different political groups, whereas the rise of anti-colonial sentiment in the 1950s can be directly linked to the various anti-colonial struggles around the world, such as in Algeria, Kenya, and Ireland.

Like elsewhere, also in Cyprus the British refrained from applying international humanitarian law in the context of the EOKA emergency, yet we have seen how Greek Cypriot lawyers and Greece turned to human rights as an alternative legal framework. In his memoirs, UK Prime Minister Macmillan admitted that the EOKA emergency 'was, in effect, a military campaign'.[217] Even though the UK signed the Geneva Conventions as early as 1949, it only deposited an instrument of ratification on 23 September 1957. Thus, the 1949 Geneva Conventions were not applicable in Cyprus at the start of the EOKA emergency, and as seen through the UK counter-arguments before the ECmHR, neither the pre-1949 provisions of international humanitarian law successfully drew any attention to the strong military element of the emergency. As a result, the only way to challenge the emergency regulations introduced under 'peripheral' domestic British law, was through the ECHR by virtue of article 63 (today article 56), the 'colonial clause', which extended the application of the ECHR to all colonial territories.

[217] Macmillan, *Riding the Storm,* 684.

The 1949 Geneva Conventions were only incorporated into British domestic law on 31 July 1957, yet it took two more years to pass an Order in Council (SI 1959/1301) under the Geneva Conventions Act which expressly extended the applicability of the Conventions to most colonies, including Cyprus. By then, Cyprus was already governed by a transitional government which was negotiating the Constitution of the RoC to be. This is an additional rather technical detail that would lead to an examination of armed violence during the EOKA period, which differs from the assessment of the armed violence of the 1960s.

During this period the two main Cypriot ethno-religious groups imitated the long history of 'banditry, politics, and paramilitarism' of their respective 'motherlands'.[218] Violence was justified under a 'folk-legal doctrine', which by its very nature marginalises legal formality, is hostile to individual responsibility and contextual specificity, and in its simplest form is expressed through the idea that 'Some of them have harmed some of us, so some of us may take vengeance on any of them'.[219] In his anthropological analysis, Peter Loizos did not omit to mention that in fact most modern European nation-states had been born in violence, hinting that neither 'barbarity', nor 'savagery' are historically exclusive to the 'non-European', however one chooses to define 'non-European' racially, culturally, or geographically.

Reference List

Books

Averoff-Tossizza, Evangelos. *Lost Opportunities: The Cyprus Question, 1950–1963.* Translated by Timothy Cullen, Susan Kyriakidis. Aristide Caratzas, 1986.

Barnett, Michael. *Empire of Humanity: A history of humanitarianism.* Cornell University Press, 2011.

Bedjaoui, Mohammed. *Law and the Algerian Revolution.* International Association of Democratic Lawyers. 1961.

Cassese, Antonio. *Self-Determination of Peoples: A Legal Reappraisal.* Cambridge University Press, 1995.

Crawford, James. *Brownlie's Principles of International* Law. 9th edn, Oxford University Press, 2019.

[218] Üngör, *Paramilitarism*, 26–29.

[219] Loizos, *Unofficial Views*, 163.

Crawshaw, Nancy. *The Cyprus Revolt: An account of the struggle for union with Greece*. George Allen & Unwin, 1978.

Chrysostomou, Aggelos. *Από τον Κυπριακό Στρατό μέχρι και τη δημιουργία της Εθνικής Φρουράς* (1959–1964) (From the Cyprus Army until the establishment of the National Guard (1959–1964). 2015.

Cyprus Government. *Κυβέρνηση Κύπρου, Ταραχαί εν Κύπρω κατ' Οκτώβριον, 1931- Λευκή Βίβλος κατατεθείσα υπό του επί των Αποικιών Υπουργού εις το Κοινοβούλιον κατά Διαταγήν της Αυτού Μεγαλειότητος κατά Μάρτιον 1932* (Disturbances in Cyprus in October, 1931 - White Book submitted to the Secretary of the Colonies before the Parliament, upon an Order by His Majesty in March 1932). Government Press, 1932.

Drohan, Brian. *Brutality in an Age of Human Rights: Activism and Counterinsurgency at the End of the British Empire*. Cornell University Press, 2018.

Erim, Nihat. *Bildiğim ve gördüğüm ölçüler içinde Kıbrıs* (Cypriot dimensions that I know and see). Ajans-Turk Press, 1975.

Georghallides, Georgios S. *Cyprus and the Governorship of Sir Ronald Storrs: The causes of the 1931 crisis*. The Cyprus Research Centre, 1985.

Grivas, Georgios, *General Grivas on Guerrilla Warfare*, Translated by Alexandros A Pallis. Frederick A. Praeger, 1965.

Grotius, Hugo. *The Rights of War and Peace* (De Jure Belli ac Pacis) Books II and III. First published in 1625, Richard Tuck ed., Liberty Fund, 2005.

Gurr, Ted R., *Minorities at risk: A Global View of Ethnopolitical Conflicts*. United States Institute of Peace Press, 1993.

Hadjilyras, Alexander-Michael. *Η Κυπριακή Δημοκρατία και οι Θρησκευτικές Ομάδες* (The Republic of Cyprus and the Religious Groups). 2012.

Hakki, Murat Metin. *The Cyprus Issue: A Documentary History, 1878–2007*. I.B. Tauris, 2007.

Hatzivassiliou, Evanthis. *The Cyprus Question, 1878–1960: The Constitutional Aspect*. University of Minnesota, 2002.

Higgins, Rosalyn. *Problems and Process: International Law and How We Use It*. Oxford University Press, 1994.

Hill, George F. *A. History of Cyprus Vol 3: The Frankish Period 1432–1571*. First published 1948, Cambridge University Press, 2010a.

Hill, George F. *A. History of Cyprus Vol 4: The Ottoman Province. The British Colony, 1571–1948*. First Published 1952 and edited by Harry Luke, Cambridge University Press, 2010b.

Holland, Robert. *Britain and the Revolt in Cyprus 1954–1959*. Clarendon Press, 1998.

ICRC. *Commentary on the First Geneva Convention for the Amelioration of the Condition of the Wounded and Sick in Armed Forces in the Field*. Cambridge University Press, 2016.

Kızılyürek, Niyazi. *Μια εποχή της βίας: Το σκοτεινό 1958* (An Age of Violence: The Dark 1958). Translated by Michalis Theodorou. 2nd edn, Heterotopia, 2016.

Knop, Karen. *Diversity and self-determination in international law.* Cambridge University Press, 2002.

Koskenniemi, Martti. *The Gentle Civilizer of Nations: The Rise and Fall of International Law 1870–1960.* Cambridge University Press 2001.

Koskenniemi, Martti. *To the Uttermost Parts of the Earth: Legal Imagination and International Power 1300–1870.* Cambridge University Press, 2021.

Kyriakides, Christos K. *Το κυπριακό Νομοθετικό Συμβούλιο (1878–1931)-Ίδρυση, Λειτουργία και Κοινοβουλευτικές Ελευθερίες υπό περιορισμός και αμφισβήτηση* (The Cypriot Legislative Council (1878–1931) - Establishment, Function and Parliamentary Rivalries: Constitutional Freedoms under constraint and doubt). Republic of Cyprus House of Representatives, 2016.

Loizos, Peter. *Unofficial Views: Cyprus: Society and Politics.* Intercollege Press, 2001.

Luke, Harry CJ. *Cyprus: A Portrait and an Appreciation.* George G Harrap, 1957.

Macmillan, Harold. *Riding the Storm 1956–1959.* Macmillan, 1971.

Markides, Diana. *Cyprus 1957–1963: From Colonial Conflict to Constitutional Crisis – The key role of the Municipal Issue.* University of Minnesota, 2001.

Markides, Diana. *The Cyprus Tribute and Geopolitics in the Levant, 1875–1960.* Palgrave, 2019.

Mehmet, Ozay. *Sustainability of Microstates: The Case of North Cyprus.* University of Utah Press, 2010.

Miller, Linda. *Cyprus: The Law and Politics of Civil Strife.* Center for International Affairs, Harvard University, 1968.

Mazower, Mark. *The Balkans.* Phoenix Press, 2001.

Necatigil, Zaim M. *The Cyprus Question and the Turkish position in International Law.* 2nd edn, Oxford University Press, 1993.

Oppenheim, Lassa. *International Law: A Treatise Vol II: Disputes, War and Neutrality.* Edited by Hersch Lauterpacht, 7th edn, Longmans, 1952.

Papapolyviou, Petros. *Η Κύπρος και οι Βαλκανικοί Πόλεμοι: Συμβολή στην ιστορία του κυπριακού εθελοντισμού* (Cyprus and the Balkan Wars. Contribution to the History of Cypriot Volunteers). Center of Scientific Research Sources and Studies of Cypriot History XXVI, 1997.

Pictet, Jean. *Commentary on the First Geneva Convention for the Amelioration of the Condition of the Wounded and Sick in Armed Forces in the Field.* ICRC, 1952.

Pictet, Jean. *Commentary on the Third Geneva Convention relative to the Treatment of Prisoners of War.* ICRC, 1960.

Pikis, George M. *An analysis of the English Common Law, Principles of Equity and their application in a former British Colony, Cyprus.* Brill Nijhoff, 2017.

John Reynolds. *Empire, Emergency and International Law.* Cambridge University Press, 2017.

Kirsti Samuels. *Political Violence and the International Community: Developments in International Law and Policy.* Martinus Nijhoff, 2007.

Sakellaropoulos, Spyros. *Ο Κυπριακός Κοινωνικός Σχηματισμός (1191–2004) Από τη συγκρότηση στη διχοτόμηση* (The Cypriot Social Formation (1191–2004): From the Establishment to the Partition), Topos, 2017.

Serghides, George A. *Internal and External Conflict of Laws in Regard to Family Relations in Cyprus.* 1988.

Schabas, William A. *Unimaginable Atrocities: Justice, Politics, and Rights at the War Crimes Tribunals.* Oxford University Press, 2012.

Schabas, William A. *The Customary International Law of Human Rights.* Oxford University Press, 2021.

Shahabuddin, Mohammad, *Ethnicity and International Law: Histories, Politics and Practices.* Cambridge University Press, 2016.

Simpson, A W Brian. *Human Rights and the End of Empire: Britain and the Genesis of the European Convention.* Oxford University Press, 2004.

Sivakumaran, Sandesh. *The Law of Non-International Armed Conflict. Oxford University Press,* 2012.

Soulioti, Stella. *Fettered Independence: Cyprus, 1878–1964 Vol 1 - The Documents.* University of Minnesota Press, 2006.

Tenekides, Georges. *Chypre: histoire récente et perspectives d'avenir* (Cyprus: Recent history and future perspectives). Nagel, 1964.

Tornaritis, Criton G. *The Individual as a Subject in International Law.* Press and Information Office, 1972.

Tudor, Margot. *Blue Helmets Bureaucrats: United Nations Peacekeeping and the Reinvention of Colonialism, 1945–1971.* Cambridge University Press, 2023.

Üngör, Uğur Ümit *Paramilitarism: Mass Violence in the Shadow of the State.* Oxford University Press, 2020.

Varnava, Andreas *Ιστορία του Απελευθερωτικού Αγώνα της ΕΟΚΑ (1955–1959)* (The History of the EOKA Liberation Struggle (1955–1959). Foundation of the EOKA Liberation Struggle, 2002.

Varnava, Andrekos. *Assassination in Colonial Cyprus in 1934 and the Origins of EOKA: Reading the Archives against the Grain.* Anthem Press, 2021.

Yiangou, Anastasia. *Cyprus in World War II: Politics and Conflict in the Eastern Mediterranean.* I.B Tauris, 2010.

Zannetos, Filios. *Ιστορία της νήσου Κύπρου: Από της αγγλικής κατοχής μέχρι το 1911 Vol 2* (History of the Island of Cyprus: From the British Occupation to the Present Vol 2). 2nd reprinted ed., Epiphaniou, 1997. (Original Filokalias, 1911)

Chapters in Edited Volumes

Itty Abraham. "Bandung and State Formation in Post-colonial Asia." In *Bandung Revisited: The Legacy of the 1955 Asian-African Conference for International*

Order, edited by Seng Tan and Amitav Achary. National University of Singapore Press, 2008.

Allott, Phillip. "Self-Determination – Absolute right or social poetry?." In *Modern Law of Self-Determination*, edited by Christian Tomuschat. Martinus Nijhoff 1993.

Alston, Philip and Frédéric Mégret, "Introduction: Appraising the United Nations Human Rights Regime." In *The United Nations and Human Rights: A Critical Appraisal*, edited by Frédéric Mégret and Philip Alston. 2nd edn, Oxford University Press, 2020.

Anghie, Antony. "Bandung and the Origins of Third World Sovereignty." In *Bandung, Global History, and International Law*, edited by Luis Eslava, Michael Fakhri, Vasuki Nesiah. Cambridge University Press, 2017.

Bothe, Michael. "Peacekeeping." In *The Oxford Commentary on the Charter of the United Nations Vol 1,* edited by Bruno Simma, Daniel-Erasmus Khan, Georg Nolte and Andreas Paulus. 3rd edn, Oxford University Press, 2012.

Chamatsou, Anastasia. "Αντικατοπρισμοί: Η πρόσληψη και η αντιμετώπιση του Αλγερινού από τη νεοσύστατη Κυπριακή Δημοκρατία" (Reflections: Perceptions and Reactions to the Algerian [Problem] from the newly-established Republic of Cyprus). In *Το Κυπριακό και το Διεθνές Σύστημα, 1945–1974: Αναζητώντας θέση στον κόσμο* (The Cyprus Problem and the International System, 1945–1974: In search of a position in the world), edited by Petros Papapolyviou, Aggelos Syrigos and Evanthis Hatzivassiliou. Patakis, 2013.

Cryer, Robert. "International Criminal Law." In *International Law*, edited by Malcolm D Evans. 3rd edn, Oxford University Press, 2010.

Peter Hilpold. "Introduction." In *Autonomy and self-determination: Between Legal Assertions and Utopian Aspirations*, edited by Peter Hilpold. Edward Elgar, 2018.

Eslava, Luis, Michael Fakhri and Vasuki Nesiah. "The Spirit of Bandung." In *Bandung, Global History and International Law: Critical Pasts and Pending Future*, edited by Louis Eslava, Michael Fakhri and Vasuki Nesiah. Cambridge University Press, 2017.

Falk, Richard A. "Introduction." In *The International Law of Civil War,* edited by Richard A. Falk. John Hopkins Press, 1971.

Fastenrath, Ulrich. "Chapter XI Declaration Regarding Non-self-governing Territories." In *The Oxford Commentary on the Charter of the United Nations Vol 2* edited by Bruno Simma, Daniel-Erasmus Khan, Georg Nolte and Andreas Paulus. 3rd edn, Oxford University Press, 2012.

Faustmann, Hubert, "The UN and the Internationalization of the Cyprus Conflict, 1949–1958." In *The Work of the UN in Cyprus: Promoting Peace and Development*, edited by Oliver P Richmond and James Ker-Lindsay. Palgrave, 2001.

Kalantzopoulos, Dimitris. "Cyprus in the 1940s: The Nationalization of Greek Cypriot Politics." In *Cypriot Nationalisms in Context: History, Identity and Politics*, edited Thekla Kyritsi and Nikos Christofis. Palgrave, 2018.

Karyos, Andreas, "Η επίδραση του διεθνούς παράγοντα στις στρατηγικές επιλογές του ένοπλου ενωτικού κινήματος (ΕΟΚΑ), 1955–1959" (The influence of international actors in the strategic options of the armed unitary movement (EOKA), 1955–1959). In *Το Κυπριακό και το Διεθνές Σύστημα, 1945–1974: Αναζητώντας θέση στον κόσμο* (The Cyprus Problem and the International System, 1945–1974: In search of a position in the world), edited by Petros Papapolyviou, Aggelos Syrigos and Evanthis Hatzivassiliou. Patakis, 2013.

Khan, Daniel-Erasmus. "Drafting History" In *The Oxford Commentary on the Charter of the United Nations Vol 1*, edited by Bruno Simma, Daniel-Erasmus Khan, Georg Nolte and Andreas Paulus. 3rd edn, Oxford University Press, 2012.

Madsen, Mikael Rask. "The Protracted Institutionalization of the Strasbourg Court: From Legal Diplomacy to Integrationist Jurisprudence." In *The European Court of Human Rights between Law and Politics*, edited by Jonas Christoffersen and Mikael Rask Madsen. Oxford University Press, 2011.

Mégret, Frédéric. "The Security Council." In *The United Nations and Human Rights: A Critical Appraisal*, edited by Frédéric Mégret and Philip Alston. 2nd edn, Oxford University Press, 2020.

Milanovic, Marko. "The Applicability of the Conventions to 'Transnational' and 'Mixed Conflicts'." In *The 1949 Geneva Conventions: A Commentary*, edited by Andrew Clapham, Paola Gaeta, and Marco Sassòli. Oxford University Press, 2015.

Moir, Lindsay. "The Concept of Non-International Armed Conflict." In *The 1949 Geneva Conventions: A Commentary*, edited by Andrew Clapham, Paola Gaeta, and Marco Sassòli. Oxford University Press, 2015.

Nolte, Georg. "Article 2(7)." In *The Oxford Commentary on the Charter of the United Nations Vol 1*, edited by Bruno Simma, Daniel-Erasmus Khan, Georg Nolte and Andreas Paulus. 3rd edn, Oxford University Press, 2012.

Nolte, Georg. "The Different Functions of the Security Council with Respect to Humanitarian Law." In *The United Nations Security Council and War: The evolution of thought and practice since 1945*, edited by Vaughan Lowe, Adam Roberts, Jennifer Welsh, and Dominik Zaum. Oxford University Press, 2010.

Oeter, Stefan. "Self-determination." In *The Oxford Commentary on the Charter of the United Nations Vol 1*, edited by Bruno Simma, Daniel-Erasmus Khan, Georg Nolte and Andreas Paulus. 3rd edn, Oxford University Press, 2012.

Randelzhofer, Albrecht and Oliver Dörr. "Article 2(4)." In *The Oxford Commentary on the Charter of the United Nations Vol 1*, edited by Bruno Simma, Daniel-Erasmus Khan, Georg Nolte and Andreas Paulus. 3rd edn, Oxford University Press, 2012.

Reynolds, John. "Peripheral Parallels? Europe's Edges and the World of Bandung" In *Bandung, Global History and International Law: Critical Pasts and Pending Future*, edited by Louis Eslava, Michael Fakhri and Vasuki Nesiah. Cambridge University Press, 2017b.

Schabas, William A. "Non-State Actors and International Law." In *Non-State Actors and International Law*, edited by Andrea Bianchi. Ashgate, 2009.

Suksi, Markku. "The referendum as an instrument for decision-making in autonomy-related situations." In *Autonomy and self-determination: Between Legal Assertions and Utopian Aspirations*, edited by Peter Hilpold. Edward Elgar, 2018.

Tomuchat, Christian. "Self-determination in a post-colonial world." In *Modern Law of Self-Determination*, edited by Christian Tomuschat. Martinus Nijhoff 1993.

Wolfrum, Rüdiger. "Article 1." In *The Oxford Commentary on the Charter of the United Nations Vol 1*, edited by Bruno Simma, Daniel-Erasmus Khan, Georg Nolte and Andreas Paulus. 3rd edn, Oxford University Press, 2012.

Yiangou, Anastasia. "Βρετανική Διπλωματία και Κυπριακό Ζήτημα, 1945–1950" (British Diplomacy and the Cyprus Issue). In *Το Κυπριακό και το Διεθνές Σύστημα, 1945–1974: Αναζητώντας θέση στον κόσμο* (The Cyprus Problem and the International System, 1945–1974: In search of a position in the world), edited by Petros Papapolyviou, Aggelos Syrigos and Evanthis Hatzivassiliou. Patakis, 2013.

Journal Articles

af Jochnick, Chris and Roger Normand, "The Legitimation of Violence: A critical history of the Laws of War", *Harvard International Law Journal* 35 (1994): 49–95

Alexander, Amanda, "A Short History of International Humanitarian Law", *European Journal of International Law* 26 (2015): 109–138.

Anghie, Antony and BS Chimni, "Third World Approaches to International Law and Individual Responsibility in Internal Conflict" *Studies in Transnational Legal Policy* 36 (2004): 185–210.

Bowring, Bill, "Fragmentation, '*Lex Specialis*'' and the Tensions in the Jurisprudence of the European Court of Human Rights," *Journal of Conflict and Security Law* 14, No. 3 (2009): 485–489.

Bugnion, François, "*Jus ad bellum, jus in bello* and non-international armed conflicts" *Yearbook of International Humanitarian Law* 6 (2003): 167–198

Burke, Roland, "'The Compelling Dialogue of Freedom': Human Rights at the Bandung Conference," *Human Rights Quarterly* 28 No.4 (2006): 947–965.

Cassese, Antonio, "The *Nicaragua* and *Tadić* Tests Revisited in Light of the ICJ Judgment on Genocide in Bosnia" *European Journal of International Law* 18 No. 4 (2007): 649–668.

Chimni, BS, "The International Court and the maintenance of Peace and Security: The Nicaragua decision and the United States response" *International and Comparative Law Quarterly* 35, No. 4 (1986): 960–970.

Demetriadou, Ersi, "Legal Discourse and Social History in Cyprus: An Inductive Inguiry [sic] 1878–1982" *Cyprus Law Tribune* (1989): 127.

Desgrandchamps, Marie-Luce, "'Organising the unpredictable': the Nigeria-Biafra War and its Impact on the ICRC" *International Review of the Red Cross* 94 (2012): 1409–1432.

Douzinas, Costas, "Theses on Law, History and Time" *Melbourne Journal of International Law* 7 (2006): 13–27.

Dzehtsiarou, Kanstantsin "*Georgia* v *Russia (II)* (App No 38263/08) European Court of Human Rights (Grand Chamber) (Judgement, Merits, 21 January 2021) (note)" *American Journal of International Law* 115 No. 2 (2021) 288–294.

Elder, David A, "The Historical Background of Common Article 3 of the Geneva Convention of 1949," *Case Western Reserve Journal of International Law* 11 (1979) 37–69.

Fawcett, James E S, "Treaty Relations of British Overseas Territories" *British Yearbook of International Law* 26 (1949): 86–107.

Fortin, Katharine, "Complementarity between the ICRC and the United Nations and International Humanitarian Law and International Human Rights Law, 1948–1968" *International Review of the Red Cross* 94 No. 888 (2012): 1433–1454.

Green, Abigail "Humanitarianism in the nineteenth-century context: religious, gendered, national" *The Historical Journal* 57 No. 4 (2014): 1157–1175

Greenman, Kathryn, "Common Article 3 at 70: Reappraising Revolution and Civil War in International Law," *Melbourne Journal of International Law* 21 (2020): 88–114.

Greenwood, Christopher, "International Humanitarian Law and the *Tadic* Case" *European Journal of International Law* 7 (1996): 265–283.

ICRC, "Commission d'Experts chargée d'examiner la question de l'assistance aux détenus politiques" *International Review of the Red Cross* 414 (1953): 440

ICRC, "Commission d'Experts chargée d'examiner la question de l'application des principes humanitaires en cas de troubles intérieurs" *International Review of the Red Cross* 443 (1955): 722.

ICRC, "Humanitarian Aid to the Victims of Internal Conflicts: Meeting of a Commission of Experts in Geneva" *International Review of the Red Cross* 3, No. 23 (1963): 79–91.

Gross, Leo, "The Peace of Westphalia, 1648–1948" *American Journal of International Law* 42 (1948): 20–41.

Güven, Dilek, "Riots against the Non-Muslims of Turkey: 6/7 September 1955 in the context of demographic engineering" *European Journal of Turkish Studies* 12 (2011) 1–18.

Hakimi, Monica and Jacob Katz Cogan, "The Two Codes on the Use of Force" *European Journal of International Law* 27 No. 2 (2016): 257–291.

Hatzivassiliou, Evanthis "The Riots in Turkey, in September 1955: A British Document" *Balkan Studies* 31 (1990): 165–76.

Heacock, Roger, "The Framing of Empire: Cyprus and Cypriots through British Eyes, 1878–1960." *The Cyprus Review* 23 No. 2 (2011): 21–37

Hutchinson, Michael R., "The Margin of Appreciation Doctrine in the European Court of Human Rights," *International and Comparative Law Quarterly* 48, No. 3 (1999): 638–50.

Hyde, James N, "The United Nations and the Peaceful Adjustment of Disputes" *Proceedings of the Academy of Political Science* 25 No. 2 (1953): 80–89.

Ioannou, Gregoris and Sertac Sonan, "Trade unions and politics in Cyprus: a historical comparative analysis across the dividing line" *Mediterranean Politics* 22 No. 4 (2017): 484–503.

Jakovljević, Boško and Jovića Patrnogic, "The urgent need to apply the rules of humanitarian law to so-called internal armed conflicts" *International Review of the Red Cross* 5 (1961) 250–57.

Kim, Sung Won, David P. Fidler and Sumit Ganguli, "Eastphalia rising? Asian influence and the Fate of Human Security" *World Policy Journal* 26, No. 2 (2009): 53–64.

Klose, Fabian, "The Colonial Testing Ground: The International Committee of the Red Cross and the Violent End of Empire," *Humanity* 2 (2011): 107–126.

Kornioti, Nadia, "The Island of Cyprus, Sovereignty and International Law in the Early Decades of British Rule." *The Cyprus Review* 32 No. 2 (2020): 105–128.

Koskenniemi, Martti, "National Self-Determination Today: Problems of Legal Theory and Practice" *International and Comparative Law Quarterly* 43, No. 2 (1994) 241–269.

Koskenniemi, Martti, "Between Impunity and Show Trials" *Max Planck Yearbook for United Nations Law* 6 (2002): 1–35.

Kunz, Josep J., "The Present Status of the International Law for the Protection of Minorities," *American Journal of International Law* 48, No. 2 (1954): 282–287.

Mazower, Mark, "The strange triumph of human rights, 1933–1950," *The Historical Journal* 47, No. 2 (2004): 379–398.

Novo, Andrew R., "An insoluble problem: The Harding-Makarios Negotiations, Turkey, and the Cause of Cypriot *Enosis*" *Journal of Mediterranean Studies* 24 (2015): 89–105.

Palmieri, Daniel "An institution standing the test of time? A review of 150 years of the history of the International Committee of the Red Cross" *International Review of the Red Cross* 94 (888) (2012): 1273–1298.

Palmieri, Daniel "How warfare has evolved – a humanitarian organization's perception: The case of the ICRC, 1863–1960" *International Review of the Red Cross* 97 (2015): 985–998.

Pictet, Jean, "The need to restore the laws and customs relating to armed conflicts," *International Review of the Red Cross* 102 (1969): 459–483.

Quane, Helen, "The United Nations and the Evolving Right to Self-Determination" *International and Comparative Law Quarterly* 47, No. 3 (1998) 537–572.

Rodogno, Davide, "European Legal Doctrines on Intervention and the Status of the Ottoman Empire within the 'Family of Nations' throughout the Nineteenth Century," *Journal of the History of International Law* 18 (2016) 5–41

Rosas, Allan, "Wars of National Liberation – International or Non-International Armed Conflicts?" *Instant Research on Peace and Violence* 4 (1974) 31–37

Schabas, William A, "*Lex Specialis*? Belt and suspenders? The parallel operation of human rights law and the law of armed conflict, and the conundrum of *jus ad bellum*" *Israeli Law Review* 40, No. 2 (2007): 592–613.

Schabas, William A, "Retroactive Application of the Genocide Convention," *University of St. Thomas Journal of Law and Public Policy* 4, No. 2 (2010): 36–59.

Soucek, Svatopluk, "Naval Aspects of the Ottoman Conquests of Rhodes, Cyprus and Crete," *Studia Islamica* 98/99 (2004): 219–261.

Thompson, Andrew, "Humanitarian Principles put to the Test: Challenges to Humanitarian Action during Decolonization," *International Review of the Red Cross* 97 (2016): 45–76.

Toynbee, Arnold, "The East after Lausanne" *Foreign Affairs* 2 (1923): 84–98.

Tzouvala, Ntina, "'These Ancient Arenas of Racial Struggles': International Law and the Balkans, 1878–1949," 29 No. 4 *European Journal of International Law* (2019): 1149–1171.

Van Dijk, Boyd, "Human rights in war: On the entangled foundations of the 1949 Geneva Conventions" *American Journal of International Law* 112 No. 4 (2018): 553–582.

von Arnauld, Andreas, "How to Illegalize Past Injustice: Reinterpreting the Rules of Intertemporality," *European Journal of International Law* 32, No. 2 (2021): 401–432.

Wilde, Ralph, "Taxonomies of International Peacekeeping: An Alternative Narrative" *ILSA Journal of International and Comparative Law* 9 (2003): 391.

Wheatley, Steven, "Revisiting the Doctrine of Intertemporal Law," *Oxford Journal of Legal Studies* 41, No. 2 (2021): 484–509.

Other

Arreguín-Toft, Ivan *'Counterinsurgency' (Oxford Bibliographies*, 28 September 2020) <www.oxfordbibliographies.com/view/document/obo-9780199743292/obo-9780199743292-0064.xml> accessed 20 December 2021

Besson, Samantha 'Sovereignty' in *MPEPIL* (December 2009) https://opil.ouplaw.com/view/10.1093/law:epil/9780199231690/law-9780199231690-e1472, accessed 28 March 2021.

Crawford, James 'State Responsibility' *MPEPIL* (September 2006) https://opil.ouplaw.com/view/10.1093/law:epil/9780199231690/law-9780199231690-e1093?prd=OPIL, accessed 22 August 2021

Philip Kunig, 'Intervention, Prohibition of' in *MPEPIL* (April 2008) https://opil.ouplaw.com/view/10.1093/law:epil/9780199231690/law-9780199231690-e1434?rskey=QpSev6&result=2&prd=OPIL, accessed 28 March 2021

Loizou, Constantinos and Antonios Loizides, "O Ελευθέριος Βενιζέλος και το Κυπριακό Πρόβλημα" (Eleftherios Venizelos and the Cyprus Problem) 69 *Χρονικό*, 23 June 2019

Pastella, Ioanna G "Ποινικός έλεγχος και θεσμικές παρεμβάσεις στην πολιτική ζωή και την ελευθερία έκφρασης στην αποικιακή Κύπρο, 1931-1939" (Criminal checks and institutional interventions in the political life and the freedom of expression in colonial Cyprus, 1931–1939). PhD Thesis, University of Cyprus, 2016.

Van den Bogaert, Sina, "Berlin Congress (1878)" *MPEPIL* (2011). https://opil.ouplaw.com/view/10.1093/law:epil/9780199231690/law-9780199231690-e687 accessed 24 August 2020.

ICRC, 'The ICRC and the Geneva Convention (1863–1864)' (*ICRC*, 29 December 2004) https://www.icrc.org/en/doc/resources/documents/misc/57jnvt.htm accessed 8 November 2021.

Archival Materials

Anon, '2 Cypriotes die in village fights; Greek and Turkish Factions Each Lose a Man Slain Before British Arrive' (*The New York Times*, 27 May 1956).

Haff, J O 'Barrier to Divide Cyprus' Capital; Barbed Wire Will Separate Greek and Turkish Areas of Nicosia to End Riots' (*The New York Times*, 29 May 1956)

Hansard, HC Deb 05 May 1955 vol 540 cols 1910–97.

Hansard, HC Deb 19 December 1956 vol 562 col 1267.

Hansard, HC Deb 19 June 1958 vol 589 cols 1316–1317.

Hansard, HC Deb 10 December 1958 vol 597 col 345.

ICRC, B AG 251 049-004, Mission d'une délégation du CICR à Chypre, du 31 décembre 1963b au 27 novembre 1965, activités diverses de la délégation en faveur des victimes des troubles entre chypriotes grecs et chypriotes turcs, première partie (16/01/1964-02/12/1965)

UN Documents

UNGA A/2703 Application Under the Auspices of the United Nations, of the Principle of Equal Rights and Self-Determination of Peoples in the Case of the Population of the Island of Cyprus (16 August 1954a)

UNGA A/2733 Adoption of the Agenda of the Ninth Regular Session and Allocation of Items to Committees, and Organization of the Session (23 September 1954b)

UNGA A/2881 Report of the First Committee (16 December 1954c)

Court Cases

Military and Paramilitary Activities in and against Nicaragua (*Nicaragua* v *United States of America*), Judgement [1986] ICJ Rep 14

Greece v UK (Application No 176/56) Report by the European Commission of Human Rights, 26 September 1958

Greece v UK (Application 299/57) Report of the European Commission of Human Rights, 8 July 1959

Lawless v *Ireland* (Application No 332/1957) Report of the European Commission of Human Rights, 19 December 1959

CHAPTER 3

Fragile Independence, 1960–1963

The series of dead-end negotiations between Greece, Turkey and Britain in the period 1955 to 1959 took an unexpected turn in the last month of 1958, when the foreign ministers of Greece and Turkey held a brief two-day meeting in Paris, on 16–18 December, to discuss their respective views on Cyprus. This was followed by another meeting between Greek and Turkish representatives in Zurich, from 5 to 11 February 1959, where Greece and Turkey agreed, in the absence of Cypriot and British representatives, the 'Basic Structure' of what would become the Constitution of the RoC. The agreement was so unexpected, that Prime Minister Macmillan would later write that the days that followed were 'like a film than real life'.[1]

Following the Zurich meeting it became clear that Cyprus would become an independent Republic, governed through a rigid collaboration between the island's 'Greeks' and 'Turks'. In addition to the Zurich Agreement, Prime Ministers Karamanlis of Greece, and Menderes of Turkey signed a non-binding 'Gentlemen's Agreement', according to which they would support Cyprus' entry to NATO, to which both States already belonged. This was followed by a conference in London, organised by the UK who still held sovereign power over Cyprus. The event, which took place from 17 to 19 February 1959, attended delegations of all parties involved, with Archbishop Makarios III representing the Greek

[1] Macmillan, *Riding the Storm*, 693.

N. Kornioti, *Law's Politics: The Cyprus Troubles, 1960–1968*,
https://doi.org/10.1007/978-3-031-93369-1_3

Cypriots, and Dr Fazil Kutchuk representing the Turkish Cypriots.[2] The resulting London Agreement, added additional points to the issues agreed upon in Zurich, of which the most significant was the retention of limited territory by the UK in the form of two military Sovereign Base Areas (SBAs).

Shortly thereafter, a transitional government was set up, and three committees took over the preparations for the establishment of the new Republic. The London Joint Committee was tasked with drafting the three constituent international treaties of the RoC and to decide over the delimitation of the UK's SBAs. A Transitional Committee was based in Cyprus and assumed the role of a quasi-government for the duration of the transitional period. Lastly, the Constitutional Committee was in charge of drafting the final text of the Constitution.[3] The calm however, was only superficial, and as early as 18 October 1959 a British naval patrol found ammunition on a Turkish vessel heading to Cyprus. By February 1960, US officials estimated that there was 'at least a possibility that the settlement might collapse'.[4]

On 29 July 1960, the House of Commons of the Westminster Parliament adopted the Cyprus Act, through which the UK handed over its sovereignty over the territory of the island to the future Republic, with the exclusion of the territory of the two SBAs. The Republic was finally established 18 months after the singing of the London-Zurich Agreements, at midnight on the evening of 15 to 16 August 1960. The three international treaties which set the international framework for the establishment of the RoC and the new Constitution were solemnly signed in Nicosia by the last Governor of the Crown Colony of Cyprus Sir Hugh Foot, the first President of the Republic Archbishop Makarios III, the first (and only holder of the seat) Vice-President Dr Fazil Kutchuk, and the General Consuls of Greece and Turkey.

On the same day President Makarios sent a telegram to the UN Headquarters in New York, requesting from UN Secretary-General Dag Hammarskjöld to communicate to the UNSC the Republic's application for admission to the organisation.[5] A draft resolution, co-sponsored by the UK and Ceylon, recommending the Republic's admission for membership to the UNGA was approved unanimously by the UNSC, and the process was completed with the approval of the UNGA on 20 September 1960.

[2] Foreign and Commonwealth Office, *Conference on Cyprus:* (Cmnd 679, 1959).

[3] Faustmann, 'Independence Postponed."; Emilianides, *The secret negotiations.*

[4] US State Department, *Foreign Relations Vol X*, 347.

[5] S/4435.

On that day the RoC joined the UN along with 13 other newly-proclaimed African States, among them Cameroon, Congo (Leopoldville), Congo (Brazzaville), the Central African Republic, and Somalia, taking a seat in the Asia-Pacific regional group. Within a year from joining the UN the Republic also joined the Commonwealth, the Council of Europe, and the Non-Aligned Movement. From an international perspective the future could not have been evaluated as more promising, as the case was for all other former colonies.

The transitional period from February 1959 to August 1960, as well as the first three years within the establishment of the Republic, has only recently attracted the interest of researchers. These years however, are crucial in order to connect the dots between the early inter-communal violence of 1958 to the inter-communal violence which broke out in December 1963. From a legal perspective, the first three years of the Republic are equally important for being the only time when the constitutional order existed and functioned in its originally envisaged form.

International Law and the Constitution of the Republic of Cyprus

The violence of the preceding years combined with the decades-long competition between the two main ethno-religious groups of the island left the local population and the respective leadership in a state of mistrust, still eager to pursue their separate agendas of *enosis* and *taksim*. Like elsewhere in the colonial world, the RoC too was the result of 'scattered proposals aimed at avoiding the logic of national self-determination and popular sovereignty',[6] raising from the very beginning serious doubts over the compatibility of the Republic's constitutional order with the principle of sovereignty.[7]

The exact meaning of the term 'sovereignty' is rather elusive, with 'internal sovereignty' linked to 'self-determination', and 'external sovereignty' relating to a State's 'independence'.[8] State sovereignty often lies at the core of most international disputes and the Cyprus Question is no different. Already in the 1960s, it was extensively argued that the detailed regulation through the Republic's constitutive treaties restricted and

[6] Chatterjee, "The Legacy of Bandung," 670–671.
[7] Constantinou, "Cypriot In-dependence."
[8] Besson, "Sovereignty," paras 69–73.

subjected the exercise of State power, domestically (internally) and internationally (externally), directly to the will of Greece, Turkey and the UK, who assumed the position of Guarantor Powers. In that regard, Cyprus was not unique. Limitations and disadvantages were commonly attached to 'Third World sovereignty' in the post-colonial context, weakening severely the sovereign power allocated to the new post-colonial States, when compared to western conceptions of sovereignty.[9]

The Three Constituent Treaties of the Republic of Cyprus

Before the establishment of the UN, treaties of guarantee aiming towards the maintenance of a specific 'state of affairs' were not uncommon.[10] Indeed, the use of nineteenth-century colonial practices in the management of twentieth-century conflicts had not been adequately recognised in the literature until recently,[11] and the Cypriot Treaty of Guarantee (ToG) is one good example of such practice.

The ToG was signed by the RoC on the one side, and by all three Guarantor Powers, Greece, Turkey and the UK on the other, with each party carrying the obligation to ensure the maintenance of the Republic's 'independence, territorial integrity and security' (articles I and II). The Treaty imposed a separate obligation on the RoC, Greece and Turkey to 'respect the integrity' of the SBAs (article III). The principle of 'territorial integrity' and the notion of 'security' are integrally related to 'independence' and 'sovereignty', and mentioned in article 2 of the UN Charter which contains the guiding principles of the organisation. Territorial integrity is understood as the inviolability of the territory of a State,[12] whereas the exact meaning of 'Security' depends on the context within which 'security' is referred to, and therefore, lacks a legal definition.[13] All of the above are of direct relevance to issues associated with the use of force, and the accompanying principle of non-intervention under public international law.[14]

Article IV ToG, potentially the most controversial article to date, states that:

[9] Anghie, *Making of International Law*, 2.

[10] Wippman, "Pro-democratic intervention," 809.

[11] Shahabuddin, *Ethnicity and International Law*, 4; Zotiades, *Intervention by treaty right*, 21–24; Rodogno, "European Legal Doctrines."

[12] Blay, "Territorial Integrity and Political Independence."

[13] McDonald and Brollowski, "Security."

[14] Philip Kunig, "Intervention, Prohibition of."

> In the event of a breach of the provision of the present Treaty, Greece, Turkey and the United Kingdom undertake to consult together with respect to the representations or measures necessary to ensure observance of those provisions.
>
> In so far as common or concerted action may not prove possible, each of the three guaranteeing Powers reserves the right to take action with the sole aim of re-stablishing the state of affairs created by the present Treaty.

This article has been the subject of great controversy due to Turkey's interpretation of the article, according to which the provision gives unilateral rights for intervention, including a right to military intervention, if there is no consensus between the three Guarantors. There were three legal opinions issued on the ToG between 1959 and 1964, each by a well-known lawyer. The famous Austrian-American legal theorist Hans Kelsen,[15] British barrister and politician Frank Soskice[16] and Elihu Lauterpacht, the international law practitioner and scholar, son of Hersch Lauterpacht, the lawyer behind the conceptualisation of the international crime of crimes against humanity.[17] For the purposes of this research, the original texts of the opinions could not be located, and according to one author the full text of Kelsen's opinion is unavailable.[18] Therefore, the present research depends on the text reproduced in the book of Stella Soulioti, the first and only woman, an Advocate by occupation, sitting on the Republic's first cabinet of ministers. Though each opinion assumed a different approach and focused on different legal questions arising within the Cypriot context, they did share some common points.

Starting from article 103 UN Charter, on the prevalence of Charter provisions over other conflicting obligations of UN member States under other international agreements, all three opinions recognised that the ToG was likely to give rise to conflicting interpretations, in regard to articles 2(4), 52 and 53 of the Charter. Article 2(4) is the general prohibition on the use of force, discussed in the previous Chapter, adopted after WWII. Thus, *a priori* an interpretation of article IV which would allow the use of force by any of the contracting parties to the treaty, could not be sustained.[19] The latter two articles provide that States may undertake

[15] Soulioti, *Fettered Independence: Documents,* 253.

[16] Soulioti, *Fettered Independence: Documents,* 261.

[17] Soulioti, *Fettered Independence: Documents,* 267.

[18] Constantinides, "Hans Kelsen's Opinion," 169.

[19] Soulioti, *Fettered Independence: Documents,* 256–257, 269–270.

'regional arrangements' for the 'pacific settlement of local disputes' without referring them to the UNSC (article 52), but under such regional agreements States are explicitly precluded from using force without the authorisation of the UNSC (article 53). Therefore, even if the ToG was understood to constitute a 'regional agreement' for the purposes of the UN Charter, a unilateral right to use force could not have been exercised without the consent of the UNSC.

Writing in 1963 and 1964, Soskice and Elihu Lauterpacht appeared more certain than Kelsen that ToG, arguably along with the accompanying Treaties of Establishment and Alliance, could constitute a 'regional settlement'. They did, however, had the benefit of writing their legal opinions a few years after the agreements were implemented in practice. Kelsen, on the other hand, had no facts against which to base his arguments. Already a renowned legal theorist by that time, he remarkably worked his way through a number of hypotheses instead, estimating the parties' legal obligations in 'a situation which might arise if the constitution of Cyprus were overthrown by internal revolution aimed at either limiting minority rights or union with another State, or partition'.[20] Under this scenario, he argued, an armed attack against any guarantor troops could potentially justify the use of force by that Guarantor in self-defence. However, if the (hypothetical) disturbances did *not* lead to an armed attack against the Guarantors, then the legal situation would be more complex, giving rise to an examination under articles 41 (UNSC measures not involving the use of force), 53 (UNSC enforcement actions under regional arrangements), 2(3) (on the peaceful settlement of disputes) and 2(4) (prohibition of the use of force) of the UN Charter.

Following onto the second treaty, the Treaty of Establishment (ToE) was signed by all three Guarantors on the one side, and the RoC on the other, containing six lengthy annexes, and supplemented by 14 additional exchanges of notes between the UK and the RoC only. Overall, this Treaty can be seen as the act constituting the RoC's succession over the Crown colony of Cyprus and the latter's sovereignty over most of the territory of the Island of Cyprus.[21] Article 1 of the ToE defines the exact territory of the RoC, as 'the Island of Cyprus, together with the islands laying off its coast with the exception of the two areas defined in Annex A',

[20] Soulioti, *Fettered Independence: Documents*, 256.
[21] Chrysostomides, *The Republic of Cyprus*, 62–64.

meaning the 'Akrotiri' and the 'Dhekelia' SBAs.[22] Article 2 binds the RoC to accord to the UK various rights including complete control within the SBAs, on issues relevant to their guarding, defending and policing, the movement of aircraft, vessels and vehicles, the erection and construction of installations, and the use of roads, and article 3 imposes a duty among all four parties to 'consult and cooperate in the common defence of Cyprus'. Importantly, this treaty, contrary to the other two, has no constitutional force under RoC domestic law.

Even though it may come across as the least controversial of the three, the ToE and the existence of the two SBAs have diachronically maintained immense significance for British defence and foreign policy.[23] In the 1960s their importance was accentuated in the context of the Cold War and the Bagdad Pact (CENTO), signed among the UK, Turkey, Pakistan, Iraq and Iran,[24] whereas to this day the SBAs remain entangled in pursuit of dubious and often-criticised military and other objectives of the UK and its allies across the Middle East.[25]

Moreover, the Treaty relates to normative questions of global importance deriving from the process of decolonisation, such as the ones that arose in the ICJ Advisory Opinion on the *Legal Consequences of the Separation of the Chagos Archipelago from Mauritius in 1965*.[26] The Advisory Opinion had already been preceded by the case of *Bashir and others*[27] before the UK Supreme Court, where the Court stated that the 1960 Cyprus Act had not changed the colonial status of the territory of the SBAs, but simply excluded them 'from the transfer of territory to the new Republic of Cyprus', implying that legally today the SBAs are a continuation of the former Crown colony of Cyprus.[28] On a relevant note, the factual overview provided by the ICJ in its *Chagos* Advisory Opinion is indicative of the 'independence—territorial integrity—self-determination—defence' nexus that is also characteristic of the Cyprus case. At the same time, it illustrates how the historical legacy and practical

[22] Hadjigeorgiou, "Sovereign Base Areas (SBA)."

[23] Kyriakides, "The Sovereign Base Areas."

[24] Chourchoulis, "Western strategy, British bases." Dimitrakis, "The Value of CENTO."

[25] Serveta, "Cyprus in the eye of the storm."

[26] *Legal Consequences of the Separation of the Chagos Archipelago from Mauritius in 1965*, Advisory Opinion [2019] ICJ Rep 95; Hadjigeorgiou, "Decolonizing Cyprus."

[27] *R (on the application of Tag Eldin Ramadan Bashir and others)* v *Secretary of State for Home Department* [2018] UKSC 45.

[28] *Bashir and Others*, paras 69–70.

effect of politico-legal decisions and agreements made in the 1960s is only just now starting to be investigated academically and institutionally. These developments have no direct relevance to the events studied here, but they certainly strengthen the argument in favour of a historico-legal analysis with regard to outstanding, post-colonial, geopolitical, and accompanying legal issues across the globe.

The last constitutive treaty of the RoC, the Treaty of Alliance (ToA), is in line with the assessment of Emer de Vattel, the eighteenth-century Prussian philosopher and jurist, that alliances among smaller States may be formed with the objective to prevent one State from dominating and subjugating the other parties of the alliance. Indeed, this appears to have been the rationale behind the signing of the ToA between Greece and Turkey on the one side, and the RoC on the other.[29] In its Preamble the ToA claims to be an expression of the signatories' 'common desire to uphold peace and to preserve the security of each of them', binding each other under article II to 'resist any attack or aggression, direct or indirect, directed against the independence or the territorial integrity' of the Republic. The ToA and its two Additional Protocols, all of which enjoy constitutional force under article 181 of the Constitution, were supplemented by a separate Agreement for the Application of the Treaty of Alliance (the 'Agreement'), setting the complete legal framework of Greek, Turkish, and Cypriot military presence and collaboration on the island.

According to article 129(1) of the Constitution, the Republic would have its own Army, with a force of 2,000 men, on a ratio of 60:40 allocation of positions between the Greek Cypriot and Turkish Cypriot troops, respectively. Paragraph 2 of article 129 provides that there would be no compulsory conscription, unless otherwise agreed in common by the President and Vice-President of the Republic. In addition to the Cyprus Army, the Treaty provided for the presence of a Greek and a Turkish contingent, numbering 950 and 650 'non-commissioned officers and men', respectively. These were tasked explicitly with the provision of training to the Cyprus Army. The alliance was structured around the establishment of a Tripartite Headquarters on the territory of the RoC, the Command of which was to rotate on an annual basis among a Greek, Turkish and Cypriot General Officer appointed by each corresponding government, whereas the 'supreme political body' of the alliance would be a committee consisting of the Ministers of Foreign Affairs of the three signatories, each

[29] Tornaritis, *The Treaty of Alliance.*

of whom would preside over it, once again based on an annual rotation. Ordinary sessions would be held once a year, with the possibility of convening emergency sessions, if needed.

Contrary to the ToA and its Additional Protocols, the supplementary Agreement is a significantly longer document, providing detailed practical and logistical information, including the measures that should have been taken in preparedness for an attack against the RoC, and the structure, tasks and responsibilities of the Tripartite Headquarters and its Commander. It provided further for the organisation, the equipment, the rotation, and the chain of command of the Greek and the Turkish contingents, as well as the procedure to be followed in case each of the two States was requested *jointly* by the Republic's President and Vice-President to make available troops in addition to the numbers prescribed in the Treaty.

Compared to the many controversial and contested points raised by the ToE and the ToG, the highly technical provisions of the ToA appear clear and straightforward. However, different aspects of the ToA and the subsequent lawful presence of foreign troops in Cyprus during the 1960s is directly relevant to legal questions and factual points examined in depth in the next two chapters. By virtue of all three treaties which constituted, guaranteed and protected the newly established Republic, it is inevitable that more than one army were eligible to be stationed on the territory of the island, and the territory of the Republic more concretely.

The position on the unfairness and the alleged illegality of the three multilateral treaties, became a core position within the Greek Cypriot community, and by extension of the RoC. The argument is a fundamental element of the common narrative on the establishment of the Cypriot constitutional order since. Combined with criticisms on the rigidity of the Constitution, since many substantial parts cannot be amended under article 182 of the Constitution, according to then Attorney-General Criton Tornaritis, 'impaired and almost destroyed' the independence of the Republic. He argued that the Constitution deprived the RoC of 'one of the prerequisite qualities of a State as an international person',[30] stretching the argument further by writing that a State that did not yet exist could not possibly join treaties.[31]

[30] Tornaritis, *Constitutional and* Legal, 12–13.
[31] Tornaritis, *The Treaty of Alliance*, 4–5.

This position was rejected, rightly so, by Chrysostomides who argued that the existence of the ToG and ToA set no restriction on the sovereignty of the RoC, since the treaty itself recognised the 'independence and territorial integrity' of the Republic. Moreover, empirically, had there been any doubts or objections to the sovereignty of the RoC, these would have certainly been raised in the debates concerning the admission of the Republic to the UN.[32] Prominent international legal scholar and practitioner James Crawford acknowledged the particular nature of Cypriot sovereignty, classifying the island's case as an example of a post-1945 territorial internationalisation. 'Internationalized territories', he explained, are special cases in the application of the classical criteria for statehood; defined territory, permanent population, effective government and capacity to enter into relations with other States. He defined 'internationalized territories' as a 'form of organization of territories disputed between States on strategic, ethnic or other grounds' through the 'establishment of autonomous entities under a form of international protection, supervision or guarantee'. Examples are numerous, deriving primarily from the nineteenth and the first half of the twentieth centuries, with the most recent example being the case of the administration of Kosovo from 1999 onwards. Importantly, Crawford did not deny the political nature of this type of entities. On the contrary, he stated specifically that there appears to be no legal, as distinct to political, concept of 'internationalized territory', adding further that 'Politically none of [the] earlier experiments in internationalization were very successful'.[33]

International Humanitarian Law and Human Rights in the Cypriot Legal Order

In contrast to the strong English common law influence in the Republic's legal system as a whole, the Republic obtained a rigidly written Constitution, which prioritised the maintenance of a thin socio-political balance. This resulted in a mixed legal system sharing the characteristics of both the common law and the continental civil legal tradition.[34] According to Malcolm Shaw however, written constitutions in common law jurisdictions, other examples including the Indian and the Irish Constitutions,

[32] Chrysostomides, *The Republic of Cyprus*, 72–74.
[33] Crawford, *The Creation of States*, 233–244.
[34] Symeonides, "Mixed Legal System."

lead to serious questions of Constitutional Law in terms of the relationship between the domestic and the international legal orders. To offer clarification on such questions, engagement with the relevant political context is inevitable.[35]

The provision relevant to the incorporation of conventional public international law in the domestic legal order of the RoC is article 169 of the Constitution. The article distinguishes between two types of international agreements. First, those concerning commercial matters, economic co-operation and temporary agreements (*modus vivendi*) which fall exclusively under the responsibility of the Council of Ministers, and require no further action by any organ of the State. Second, international agreements of any other nature which are to be domestically enforceable only after they are 'approved by a law made by the House of Representatives', following negotiations and a decision to sign by the Council of Ministers. With limited scope for oversight by the Legislature, even in the latter case the primary power and responsibility remains with the Council of Ministers. In order to complete the process, regardless of the nature of a treaty, article 169(3) requires the publication of the international agreement in the official Gazette of the Republic, at which point the international agreement becomes hierarchically superior to any ordinary law adopted by Parliament. International agreements, however, by no means obtain force superior to the Constitution itself, which is the 'supreme law' of the Republic by virtue of article 179 of the Constitution.

Article 169 imposes the additional requirement that any other party to an international agreement joined by the RoC needs to apply reciprocally all terms of the agreement. However, in 1987 the RoC Supreme Court held that the reciprocity principle applied primarily to bilateral conventions, and recognised that some treaties exclude the condition of reciprocity.[36] Treaties of humanitarian nature, like the 1949 Geneva Conventions, often forgo the application of the principle of reciprocity, binding each party separately, regardless of the acts of their counterpart.[37] This indicates that no State can claim that they have not abided to a humanitarian provision on the basis that another State has failed to do so. At least on paper, this practice seems to endorse an accentuated significance for humanitarian treaties within the international legal order.

[35] Shaw, *International* Law, 130.
[36] *Malachtou v Armefti and another* (1987) 1 CLR 207, para 4.
[37] Simma, "Reciprocity."

In terms of customary (non-written) international law, the RoC Constitution is silent.[38] The general position under common law is that customary law is already 'incorporated' in the domestic legal system.[39] Along this line, Tornaritis supported that customary international law had always been part of the common law of England, and thus, was inherited by the RoC Constitution by virtue of article 188(1), which provides that all laws which were in force on the date of the establishment of the Republic, would continue to be in force until amended or abolished.

The question of the incorporation of international law in the Cypriot legal order is directly relevant to the question of whether the 1949 Geneva Conventions were enforceable in the domestic legal order of the Republic after independence. In the 1960s the 1949 Geneva Conventions were yet to crystallise into customary international law, and the fact that they were not formally ratified by the House of Representatives until 1966 (Law 40/1966), blurs their exact status under Cypriot law until then.

Despite the fact that the UK's 1957 Geneva Conventions Act, which applied to the Crown colony of Cyprus as of 1959 and should continue to apply to the Republic, by virtue of article 188 of the Constitution as mentioned above, the RoC signed and acceded to the Geneva Conventions on 23 May 1962.[40] The Ministry of Foreign Affairs communicated an 'Instrument of Accession' to the Swiss Federal Council, the depository of the 1949 Geneva Conventions, on 3 May 1962, and this was then forwarded to the ICRC Headquarters on 15 November 1962. This sufficed for the ICRC to 'give immediate effect' to the notified accession, when in late December 1963 it made an offer of service to the RoC, without reference to a concrete legal basis.[41]

As clarified by McNair, there is no legal duty on a State to ratify a Convention domestically. However, McNair also noted that 'It is not the practice of an enlightened Government to sign a treaty unless, subject to new circumstances intervening, it means to ratify it in due course'.[42] The events of 1963–1964 could justify a delay in ratification, but the fact that

[38] Constantinides "International Law in the Cypriot Legal Order," 236.

[39] Crawford, *Brownlie's Principles*, 63–64.

[40] ICRC Archive, B AG 041-088, Letter from the Swiss Political Federal Department to the ICRC concerning the participation of Ireland, Cyprus, Malaysia and Mauritania to the 1949 Conventions (15 November 1962); ICRC, *IHL Databases*, "Cyprus".

[41] ICRC Archive, B AG 251 049-009, Telegram to RoC MFA, Offer of Service (27 December 1963).

[42] McNair, *The Law of Treaties*, 135.

the Republic had already acceded to the Conventions in 1962 sufficed to bind it at the international level in good faith. In line with the wording of articles 61/60/140/15 of Geneva Conventions I-IV, even without formal ratification the Republic became bound by the provisions of the treaties six months following accession. This six month period was completed on the 3rd of November 1962.

As seen in the previous chapter, in the 1960s humanitarian language had not yet clearly separated between international human rights law and international humanitarian law, and given the relevance of human rights matters in situation of 'internal disturbances' or non-international armed conflicts, a brief reference to the human rights framework applicable in the RoC is inevitable. Firstly, for reasons of clarity and secondly, due to the type of alleged and evident violations that took place during the period under investigation. Moreover, Cypriot lawyers were already very familiar with human rights provisions, due to their engagement in human rights litigation during the EOKA emergency. A fact that suggests a central law for human rights in the Cypriot legal culture at the time.

The Zurich Agreement between Greece and Turkey, did not provide for human rights protections. It was, however, a prerequisite of the London Agreement and article 5 ToE, that the RoC secured the protection of human rights and fundamental freedoms to everyone within its jurisdiction in a manner comparable to the standards set by the ECHR. Similar to the case of the 1949 Geneva Conventions, the ECHR had entered the colonial legal order of Cyprus ahead of independence, albeit some years earlier, in 1953. Nonetheless, like with the Geneva Conventions, the Republic signed the ECHR and Protocol I of the Convention on 16 December 1961, within six months of becoming the 16th member state of the Council of Europe, on 24 May 1961. According to the Council of Europe database, both instruments were ratified and entered into force on 6 October 1962 without any reservations, albeit the ratification law had already been published in the Official Gazette of the Republic five months earlier (Law 39/1962; Official Gazette no. 157 (24 May 1962)).

The ECHR is not the sole legal instrument on human rights applicable to Cyprus at the time, however. Part II of the Constitution, entitled 'Fundamental Rights and Freedoms', lists the fundamental rights protected directly under the Constitution, considered by some commentators as one of the greatest achievements of the Constitutional

Committee.[43] More than half of the 30 articles constituting Part II of the Constitution correspond in full or in part to the text and the protections enshrined in the ECHR and its Protocol I. Some articles however, have been drafted in a way that would better reflect the Cypriot realities. Examples include article 22 on the Right to Marry, which contains additional provisions on marriage between persons of different religious backgrounds, and article 23 on the Right to Property, which makes special reference to the property rights of religious authorities. Moreover, drawing inspiration from the Constitutions of Italy Japan, Ireland, and the Federal German *Grundgesetz*,[44] according to Tornaritis, the Cyprus Constitution is further enriched with a number of socio-economic rights, to better align with the requirements of a modern society.[45]

In correspondence with the Cypriot political context, article 6 of the Constitution prohibits discrimination against 'any of the two Communities or any person as a person or by virtue of being a member of a Community', by any State organ or authority. In addition, article 34 sets an internal guarantee, analogous to that in the three multilateral treaties of Establishment, Guarantee and Alliance, which prohibited the interpretation of Part II of the Constitution in a way which would imply 'for any Community, group or person' a right to engage with activities that aim at undermining or destructing the 'constitutional order established by this Constitution'. A separate overarching protection from discrimination on the grounds of 'community, race, colour, religion, language, sex, political or other convictions, national or social descent, birth, wealth, social class or other', is also enclosed in article 28, according to which everyone is to enjoy equal protection and treatment before 'the law, administration and justice', unless otherwise provided for elsewhere within the Constitution.

The previous chapter examined, in the context of EOKA, how the ECHR allowed for derogations from human rights protections during an emergency. A similar provision was adopted under article 183 of the Constitution, which empowers the Council of Ministers to declare an emergency in case of war or other public danger threatening the Republic or any section of its territory. Any declaration of emergency has to refer specifically to the articles of the Constitution being suspended, and the Council of Ministers is not free to choose the articles to be suspended.

[43] Emilianides, *The secret negotiations*, 256.

[44] Tornaritis, *Human Rights*, 55.

[45] Emilianides, *Constitutional Law in Cyprus*, 169.

Instead, the Constitution provides clearly that derogable rights include: article 7 (Right to Life, only as far as it concerns death caused by a permissible act of war), article 10 paragraphs (2) and (3) (Protection from Forced Compulsory Labour), articles 11 (Right to liberty and security of person), 13 (Right to free movement), 16 (Inviolability of dwelling house), 17 (Secrecy of correspondence), 19 (Freedom of Speech), 21 (Freedom of Assembly), article 23(8)(d) (Requisition of property on payment of prompt compensation in cash) and articles 25 (Right to carry on business) and 27 (Right to Strike).

The President and the Vice-President of the Republic retained the right to veto such a declaration, jointly or separately, within 48 hours from communicating the declaration to their respective Offices. The proclamation of emergency should then be promulgated by publishing it in the Official Gazette, before forwarding the said proclamation to the House of Representatives. Upon publication of the approval of the House of Representatives in the Gazette, the Proclamation of Emergency would be valid for a two-month period, with possibility of extension by the House of Representatives, upon the request of the Council of Ministers. In case the House of Representatives rejected an emergency declaration, then the declaration would have no legal force.

To date there is no recorded incident of this procedure to have ever been put in practice, despite the fact that all States ought to declare a 'state of war'—a subcategory of a state of emergency—in the context of internal disturbances and cases of inter-state armed conflict.[46] In 1964, as seen in more detail in the next chapter, the (reformed) Supreme Court of the Republic was called to answer whether there was a state of emergency in Cyprus following the violence which erupted in December 1963. Given the limited derogations allowed under the Constitution, the Court remarked that whereas there was no emergency according to the Constitution, it would be unreasonable to declare that a state of emergency did not exist altogether.[47] Besides, military threats and a state of war constitute the 'core' of the very concept of a state of emergency.[48]

The resistance of the RoC authorities towards accepting that an emergency existed after 1963 was not without criticisms. In one relevant example, Professor Buergenthal, a holocaust survivor, human rights expert, and a Judge of the ICJ from 2000 to 2010, had written in 1966:

[46] Milanov, "State of War", para 11.

[47] *Mustafa Ibrahim and others* (1964).

[48] Greene, *Permanent States of Emergency* 22.

> In view of the existing civil war in Cyprus and the *de facto* suspension of its Constitution it is unfortunately abundantly clear that in that country the [ECHR] has so far remained a document devoid of any legal significance.[49]

These allegations, which are directly relevant to the subject matter of the next two chapters, were dismissed by Attorney-General Tornaritis, who held the view that not only the Courts continued to grant effective remedies in violation of human rights, but also that the constitutional protection of human rights had proven 'extremely satisfactory'.[50]

The status of *de facto* emergencies was recognised two decades later by the International Committee on the Enforcement of Human Rights of the International Law Association (ILA), at the 1988 ILA Conference in Warsaw. The situation in Cyprus post-1974, was one of the cases studied by the Committee. In its Interim Report, the Committee defined a '*de facto* emergency' as one 'when conditions are grave enough to justify the imposition of emergency measures but, for whatever reason, the government has declined or failed to invoke emergency powers'. It further acknowledged, using Cyprus and Iraq as likely cases, that governments often claim to maintain the ordinary legal regime formally and in practice. As a result, such situations are neither classified as states of emergency, nor trigger any extraordinary international scrutiny of human rights conditions, constituting the task of determining whether such governmental claims are 'truly credible' especially difficult.[51]

This proves that declarations of emergency are essentially a political matter which the law only comes to regulate, when and if desirable by the government concerned. Secondly, it shows how the general confusion, lack of clarity and lack of implementation observed with international humanitarian law during the 1960s was also characteristic to international human rights law, at a time when individuals played extremely limited role as subjects of public international law. As shown in the next two chapters, this was part of a broader culture, with direct impact on everyday life in violent societies. The events studied in this book are a case in point on the observations made by the Committee twenty years after the completion of the present book's chronological scope.

[49] Tornaritis, *Human Rights*, 70 citing Thomas Buergenthal, 'The Domestic Status of the European Convention on Human Rights: A second look' (1966) 2(1) *Journal of the International Commission of Jurists* 55, 66.

[50] Tornaritis, *Human Rights*, 70–73.

[51] ILA, "Second Interim Report (1988),", 148–149.

The extensive 'Charter of Fundamental Rights'[52] integrated in the RoC Constitution, with the enhanced protection from discrimination at individual and collective levels as well as the reinforced protection of socio-economic rights, set the legal conditions for a potentially prosperous and progressive Republic. However, the ineffectiveness of formal rules aiming to establish democratic institutions in 'new democracies' has been commonly observed, either as a result of a weak civil society, a lack of a democratic culture, or a lack of diverse political parties, among others.[53] As seen below, in Cyprus too the formal law 'in the books' did not lead to the envisaged results, since the material conditions, including the necessary political will, did not exist.

There is limited doubt that the peculiar sovereignty of the RoC has contributed to the violence and, more importantly, to the broader political environment which still precludes the resolution of the ever more complex Cyprus Question. Every Constitution has a moment of establishment, and that moment is rarely questioned, critiqued, and challenged, as it is strongly connected to a State's sense of identity.[54] In Cyprus, the narrative of the establishment of the RoC offered an arena for political scapegoating across all political actors involved, allowing for the development of sub-narratives neatly aligning with the political interests, priorities, and objectives of each community domestically, and each Guarantor Power internationally.

Bi-communal Challenges and the Constitutional Deadlock

The complex internal and external power-dynamics which were at play in the decade preceding the independence of Cyprus, eventually led to the establishment of a Republic with a unique constitutional structure of complex, detailed and rigid check and balances.[55] In the earliest period of its application the arrangement had been a potential template for other cases, such as the protection of the French minority in Algeria.[56] Political science

[52] Emilianides, *Constitutional Law in Cyprus*, 59.

[53] Siems, *Comparative Law*, 315.

[54] Frankenberg, *Comparative Legal Studies.*

[55] Emilianides, *Beyond*, 35 citing Stanley A de Smith, *The New Commonwealth and its Constitutions* (Stevens & Sons, 1964) 282.

[56] Papastamkou, "A prototype for the Algerian Issue," 151.

has developed various theories to attempt overcoming the tensions in pluralistic societies. Among them is the theory of 'consociationalism', which refers to democracies where the principle of majority rule does not apply and State mechanisms are designed in a way which complements the interests of the groups involved.[57] In the case of Cyprus, a primary example of a consociational democracy, the principle of majority rule was replaced by the so-called principle of bi-communality, which enshrines the idea that the governance of the State was divided between two equal but distinct communities.

Sociologists have also been following up on parallel inquiries, examining how group dynamics may lead to tensions, which once they increase in severity may lead to outright violence, and eventually in some cases, grave crimes and atrocities of the most deplorable character.[58] State-centric public international law, on the other hand, still struggles with the position of individuals within the international system. Whereas international legal scholarship has recognised a dichotomy between the principle of sovereignty and community-based goals,[59] the international legal system is yet to resolve this tension in a satisfactory manner. Therefore, international law is at a disadvantage vis-à-vis constitutional law in terms of the analytical and practical tools that could be employed in situations of conflicting community objectives.

This problem is of particular significance to non-international armed conflicts, due to the limited relevance of the laws of armed conflict to internal legal and political developments, other than the conduct of hostilities. Notably, the very terminology employed by international and constitutional lawyers often tends to differ at times of war. Constitutionalists, for instance, have not replaced the term 'war' with the term 'international armed conflict' employed by international lawyers.[60] This is telling of the extent at which law's distinction between international and domestic areas of law leads to separate areas of analysis and separate narratives with limited overlaps between the two. It is this normative distinction that allowed the complete marginalisation of international law in the mainstream understanding of the events of the 1960s in Cyprus. The present book

[57] Lijphart, "Consociational Democracy," 214; Loizides, "Lijphart and Consociationalism in Cyprus."

[58] Mann, *Dark Side of Democracy*, 13.

[59] Korhonen, "New International Law," 3.

[60] Milanov, 'State of War' *MPECCoL* (June 2023), para 11.

envisages to bridge the gap, also advocating for a common analytical approach encompassing both international and constitutional developments in cases of internal violence.

The Internal Mechanics of the Principle of Bi-communality

The Constitution of the RoC is often described as one of the longest constitutional texts in the world, encompassing 199 Articles and three additional Annexes. According to Article 1:

> The State of Cyprus is an independent and sovereign Republic with a presidential regime, the President being Greek and the Vice-President being Turk elected by the Greek and the Turkish Communities of Cyprus respectively as hereinafter in this Constitution provided.[61]

Hence, from the very first Article, the Constitution makes clear that the RoC is 'independent and sovereign', ruled by a presidential regime with significant executive power vested in the two highest officials of the State, the President and the Vice-President, each of whom had to belong to a specific community.

At no point within the Constitution there is a reference to 'Greek Cypriots' and 'Turkish Cypriots, or to a 'Cypriot people'. Instead, Article 2(1) of the Constitution defines the 'Greek Community' and Article 2(2) the 'Turkish Community', on the basis of the identical criteria of mother tongue, cultural traditions, and religion. Criteria closely aligned to the criteria of 'race, religion, language and traditions', identified by the Permanent Court of International Justice in 1930, when it was called to define what 'community' meant in the context of transfer of populations across the Greco-Bulgarian borders.[62] The same article provided for a procedure that would allow smaller religious communities to choose to which constitutionally defined community they would belong. Namely, this procedure concerned the Maronite, Armenian, and Latin religious groups, who through voting in intra-group referenda on 13 November 1960, opted for membership to the Greek Cypriot Community.[63] Naturalised

[61] For an almost complete official English text of the Constitution, translated from Greek and Turkish see: Foreign Office, Colonial Office and Ministry of Defence, *Cyprus* (Cmnd 1093, 1960).

[62] *Greco-Bulgarian 'Communities'*, Advisory Opinion [1930] PCIJ Series B, No 17, 4.

[63] Hadjilyras, *The Religious Groups,* 87.

citizens of the Republic were also given three months from the date they became Cypriot citizens, to choose one of two communities. In short, no Cypriot citizen could avoid being identified as either 'Greek' or 'Turk'. A distinction which today is retained for Turkish Cypriots, but appears to have fallen in disuse for naturalised citizens. Further in Part I of the Constitution, article 3 sets Greek and Turkish as the only official languages of the RoC, excluding English to the surprise of many. Article 4 regulates the use of the Cypriot and the respective Greek and Turkish national flags, and article 5 provides for the right of each community to celebrate the national holidays of each 'motherland', respectively.

Considering the long history of enmity between Greece and Turkey, at least from the early nineteenth century onwards, there is no logic explanation for these provisions other than the fact that the people of the Republic that was established on 16 August 1960 had a closer allegiance to two other States, rather than their own. The absence of a consciousness of a common Cypriot identity is evident, and the strict division of the island's population in 'Greeks' and 'Turks' has since dominated all aspects of the original constitutional architecture of the Republic as well as inter-communal relations to this day. Communal distinctions drew largely from the Ottoman *millet* social system, which had also been retained by the British. However, Cyprus is not unique. The separation of different groups along 'racial' lines was common and had been normalised in the process of State-formation in the colonial context, to the extent they were eventually often formalised into dominant political institutions and practices.[64]

The principle of bi-communality infiltrated the structure of all State organs, services, and official offices of the Republic. With one exception, all services had a quota of 70:30 ratio of allocation of positions between the two communities, whereas in the case of individual official positions, the Head and Deputy Head could not come from the same community. This, however, did not apply for the position of the Head of State. Even though, Head and Deputy Head of the Republic were the Greek Cypriot President and the Turkish Cypriot Vice-President, in case of absence of the President, his position was to be taken over by the Greek Cypriot President of the House of Representatives, and not by the Deputy Head of the State, whose position in case of absence would be taken by the Turkish Cypriot Vice-President of the House of Representatives.

[64] Abraham, "Bandung and State Formation," 64.

The offices of the President and Vice-President of the Republic carried separate privileges and identical immunities. Elections for each would take place on the same day, through separate electoral rolls, every five years. In terms of the exercise of power, the Constitution allocated joint and separate responsibilities. A point of contention was the veto power they held, jointly or separately, in part or in whole, regarding any law or other decision taken by the House of Representatives or the Council of Ministers, based on an exhaustive list of situations relevant to 'foreign affairs', 'defence' and 'security', including the recognition of States, the import of war materials and explosives of all kinds, and the declaration of emergency measures and martial law, among others (article 50, RoC Constitution). All issues that could potentially be subjected to a veto related to the multilateral treaties of Establishment, Guarantee and Alliance, indicating the treaties' direct relevance to the internal affairs of the State, as well as the length at which the constitutional framework aimed at ensuring that the established status quo would not be disturbed. On the other hand, considering the contrasting long-term political objectives of each community, the veto powers were also a recipe for disaster, if used in bad faith.

The two leading officials of the State were jointly tasked with safeguarding the Executive power, by jointly appointing the Council of Ministers, the main executive organ of the Republic.[65] In a clear reflection of the bi-communality principle, in its original form the Constitution provides under article 46 for seven Greek Cypriot and three Turkish Cypriot ministers, among whom at least one of the 'core ministries' (Foreign Affairs, Defence, and Finance) was to be allocated to a Turkish Cypriot minister. Apart from these three ministries the Constitution is silent on the thematic portfolios of the other Ministers. Analogous bi-communal balances as in the Executive had to be maintained also in the Legislature, where a mono-cameral House of Representatives of 50 Members of Parliament (MPs) would share its power between 35 Greek Cypriot and 15 Turkish MPs.

In terms of the Judiciary, detailed provisions were made for the representation of each community on the bench across the court hierarchy. The Supreme Constitutional Court, which had extensive jurisdiction over Constitutional matters and administrative recourses, was presided by a neutral non-Cypriot judge, sitting with two Cypriot judges; one from each community. The High Court, which would act as the Supreme Council of

[65] Tornaritis, *Constitutional and Legal*, 45.

Judicature for matters not under the exclusive responsibility of the Supreme Constitutional Court, principal Appeal Court and a first instance court in some cases, followed in hierarchy and was composed of a non-Cypriot neutral President and three Cypriot judges; two Greek Cypriots, one Turkish Cypriot. The composition of the bench in all subordinate civil and criminal District Courts was determined by the community of the parties to the case or the accused. Where the parties belonged to both communities, a decision on the composition would be taken by the High Court. Even during a coroner's inquest, the procedure had to be conducted by a Coroner belonging to the same community as the deceased. According to Polyviou, this was contrary to any 'considerations of utility', since traditionally in Cyprus the legal profession enjoyed a 'cohesion', which protected the administration of justice from 'the influence of communal factors'.[66] Indeed, as seen in the following chapters, despite the difficulties and the reforms undertaken, the judiciary was the last branch of power that gave in to the growing political and military pressure.

The Constitution also introduced two Communal Chambers, whose members were elected separately by each community. The basis for the Chambers' formation lay in the Macmillan Plan of 1958, in pursuit of 'communal autonomy'.[67] One cannot but notice once again the modernised resemblance with the Ottoman *millet* system, under which personal law matters, for instance family and inheritance, fell within the jurisdiction of each religious group separately;[68] leading to the application of a distinct legal framework for Greek-Orthodox, Muslim, Maronite, Armenian, and Latin citizens.

The competences of the Communal Chambers consisted of a combination of Executive and Legislative powers, on issues closely aligned to one's 'personal status', in terms of religion, education, and social affairs. They could go as far as developing policy and imposing community-specific taxes, and exercise control over producers' and consumers' cooperatives, among others. Thus, the principle of bi-communality was not only rigid in theory, but also required a skilful practical implementation in the daily works of the Republic, if one were to follow closely the letter of the Constitution. The autonomous function of the Communal Chambers was instrumental in facilitating the segregation between the Greek and the

[66] Polyviou, *Cyprus on the edge*, 33.
[67] HC Deb 26 June 1958 vol 590 col 616.
[68] Demetriadou, "Legal Discourse and Social History," 128.

Turkish Cypriots, since they handled a broad range of policy areas relevant to everyday life. Especially in the case of the Turkish Cypriots, as we will see further below, the significance of the Turkish Communal Chamber became starker after 1963.

Last but not least, the rigidness and the continuous check and balances required by the Constitution are also reflected in the provisions concerning the Constitution's amendment under article 182. In its first paragraph article 182 sets an absolute prohibition in amending 'by way of variation, addition, or repeal' any of the 'basic Articles' of the Constitution. These were the articles incorporated into the text of the Constitution from the Zurich Agreement of 11th of February 1959, and came to be known as its 'Basic Structure'. For maximum clarity, these provisions—many of which are as concrete as specific paragraphs within a single article—are explicitly listed in Annex III of the Constitution, which contains a total of 48 out of 199 articles. All remaining provisions could be amended or removed completely from the Constitution, provided that this was approved by an overall majority and separate two-thirds majorities by each community's MPs. The articles under the 'Basic Structure' of the Constitution proved to be the most challenging to implement.

As observed by Emilianides, paradoxically article 179 on the supremacy of the Constitution was not listed as a basic article, despite the fact that it was 'by its nature the most fundamental article of the Cypriot Constitution'.[69] This could have been justified, he argues, on the basis that the provision in question was not included in the London-Zurich Agreements, but the omission (on purpose or otherwise) remains puzzling, since less important articles were included in Annex III. One example given by Emilianides is article 173 on the prerequisite for the establishment of separate municipalities. which was one of the core issues that led to the Constitutional deadlock of 1963. Indeed, even though in practice the existence or not of separate municipalities would have been of limited importance, their establishment was of utter significance for the Turkish Cypriot community, indicating that, like most of the Constitution, Annex III was non-surprisingly drafted on the basis of political and not practical criteria.

[69] Emilianides, *Beyond*, 53.

Early Constitutional Challenges

In addition to the contrasting political objectives of each community, in practical terms the Constitutional deadlock of November 1963 was the result of four basic challenges in the application of the Constitution. These related to difficulties in achieving a 70:30 proportional representation within the Public Service, disagreements over the structure of the Cypriot Army, as well as problems pertaining to tax collection, and the establishment of separate municipalities in the five main urban centres of the island. Without expanding in detail into all four issues here, each of them contributed towards an environment that eventually led to the disintegration of the original constitutional structure once armed violence erupted in December 1963.

The issue of the establishment of the Cyprus Army had already caused some commotion before the Republic was established, given its centrality to the ToA. The Constitution provided for a 2,000-men force, representing both communities at a 60:40 ratio. An additional number of 2,000 men would be employed in the Security Forces of the Republic, the Police, and the Gendarmerie, each of which would have a composition based on the usual 70:30 ratio. Nonetheless, in the earliest period of its application, article 130(2) of the Constitution explicitly allowed for a Greek/Turkish representation of 60:40 in the Security Forces, as a means to absorb more than half of the Turkish Cypriot men released from the Police Force and the Auxiliary Police established during the EOKA emergency, also as a broader policy aiming towards reducing unemployment among men.[70] Depending on the community the Heads of the army, police, and gendarmerie belonged to, their Deputies had to belong to the other community. As such, the first Commander of the Cyprus Army was a Greek Cypriot and his Deputy was a Turkish Cypriot. Both of them were retired officers who had served for years in the Greek and Turkish armies, respectively.

A Law on the Army of the Republic (Constitution and Enlistment) was passed in January 1961 (Law 8/1961), but the army's internal structure remained a pending issue. The Commander favoured a mixed composition across ranks and units, and the Deputy Commander supported the establishment of ethnically homogenous units.[71] The issue was to be resolved by the Council of Ministers. There, the Turkish Cypriot Minister

[70] Chrysostomou, *Establishment of the National Guard*, 55–56.
[71] Chrysostomou, *Establishment of the National Guard*, 128–130.

of Defence, Osman Orek, argued that a mixed composition would lead to practical problems, given a number of issues, such as differences in language. The Greek Cypriot Minister of Foreign Affairs, Spyros Kyprianou, insisted that article XVI(8) of the supplementary agreement to the ToA, implied a mixed composition, providing that 'the principle of mixed organizational structure' should be 'adhered to also in training'. Despite the lack of consensus, it was decided by vote on 10 August 1961, with the seven Greek Cypriot ministers outnumbering the three Turkish Cypriots, that the army would have a mixed composition at all levels.

Upon notification of the above decision, the Vice-President invited the Council to reconsider the matter, by the power given to him under article 58 of the Constitution. Kutchuk argued against the mixed structure of the army on the basis of a number of logistical issues, citing differences in language, religion, and consequent differences in eating habits and traditions, potential disciplinary problems, as well as the subsequent increase in costs this arrangement would inevitably lead to. In addition, he argued that a mixed structure would be contrary to article 132 of the Constitution, according to which in areas where residents belonged almost 100% to one of two communities, the forces stationed in the vicinity should belong to that community.[72]

The competing arguments by Kyprianou and Kutchuk could potentially have been resolved, had the question been referred jointly by the President and the Vice-President to the Supreme Constitutional Court of the Republic. Following the logic of the hierarchy of norms in the Cypriot legal order, since under article 179 the Constitution is the supreme law of the Republic, there is high likelihood that the constitutional provision under article 132 would prevail over the international agreement of the RoC with Greece and Turkey, had the Court agreed with Kutchuk's interpetation of article 132. From the summary of the minutes of the meeting offered by Chrysostomou, however, it appears that the legal counter-argument raised by Kutchuk did not draw enough attention. Instead, the debate focused on the logistical issues mentioned, leading to a political choice and avoiding a judicial procedure, which would not have satisfied both positions anyway. By October 1961 the issue of the composition of the Cyprus Army remained unresolved, despite counter-proposals by the Vice-President and the Minister of Defence to abstain from a mixed composition at least at the lowest ranks, given the higher numbers of

[72] Chrysostomou, *Establishment of the National Guard*, 130.

Turkish-speaking soldiers at that level. A similar suggestion was also made by the Greek Cypriot Commander. In a new vote on 13 October 1961, the Greek Cypriot Ministers insisted on their earliest position of a mixed composition across all ranks. This led the Vice-President exercised his right to raise a veto on 20 October 1961.

While the above debate took place, enlistment to the Cyprus Army had already started as of 3 March 1961, followed by the commencement of training by Greek and Turkish officers, on 11 September 1961. The implementation plan envisaged that the army would have been fully functional within 23.5 months. The veto by the Vice-President, however, stopped all further planning and by 14 November 1963, the Cyprus Army's 381 recruits corresponded to only one fifth of those provided for in the Constitution. The events of 21 December 1963 led to its de facto dissolution. Had the issue of the structure of the army been submitted to the Supreme Constitutional Court for interpretation, experience suggests that it may still not have been resolved.

The Supreme Constitutional Court was instead called upon to interpret article 173 of the Constitution, on the establishment of separate municipalities. Not unlike other regions formerly under Ottoman rule, all mixed residential areas of the island, urban or rural, were separated into different quarters along religious grounds.[73] This concerned Cyprus' five out of six main towns, and 120 out of 619 villages, according to UN Records.[74] Diana Markides, who has written the most authoritative historical account on the matter, locates the origin of the problem of separate municipalities to the early 1940s. At the time, in the absence of an elected legislature during the period of 'Palmerocracy', local authorities obtained extraordinary political significance for Cypriot society. However, by the 1950s, the issue became closely associated to the increasing demands for separate self-determination by the Turkish Cypriot community. The issue was a major point in the negotiations leading up to the establishment of the Republic, and eventually article 173 of the Constitution provided for the establishment of five separate municipalities in Nicosia, Paphos, Limassol, Larnaca, and Famagusta, where each community would elect a separate municipal council. The Greek Cypriots were not in favour, despite the fact that this was the only bi-communal arrangement for which the Constitution

[73] Calame and Charlesworth, *Divided Cities*.

[74] S/6253 (Galo Plaza Report), para 18.

allowed reconsideration within four years from the Constitution's entry into force.

A separate but equally controversial issue related to taxation. As already mentioned, article 188(1) of the Constitution provides that all colonial laws which were in force upon the establishment of the Republic would continue to be valid until repealed or amended. Laws concerning taxation, duties, and the municipalities, however, were exempted from this provision. Instead, municipal laws would expire six months after independence, whereas tax laws would expire on the last day of 1960, to allow the House of Representatives to enact new legislation. However, the Constitution demanded as new municipal and tax laws were approved by separate majorities by each community's MPs. This allowed each community to take advantage of the uncertainty caused as a means to exercise pressure onto the other.

The situation intensified rapidly from various angles. For example, the Turkish Cypriots took the position that they were discriminated against by the Greek Cypriots, by deliberately failing to achieve the 70:30 ratio in the Public Service. Conversely, the Greek Cypriots accused the Turkish Cypriots that they took decisions that undermined the proper constitutional functioning of the Republic. Within this environment, the issue of the municipalities and taxation remained a central point of contestation, affecting all levels of government and involving the Guarantor Powers. The Council of Ministers and each of the Communal Chambers tried to overcome the gaps caused through the lack of taxation and municipal laws, by passing community-specific taxation laws and attempting the introduction of interim measures based on former colonial legislation.[75] Such measures, however, were eventually challenged before the Supreme Constitutional Court, which declared them unconstitutional.

The judgements on all cases concerning the issue of the separate municipalities were delivered on 25 April 1963. These were the last judgments delivered by the Supreme Constitutional Court of the RoC. Soon thereafter, the political pressure was such that the Court's neutral President, well-known German Constitutional jurist Professor Ernst Forsthoff, who had also participated in the drafting of the RoC Constitution, resigned on 21 May 1963.[76] According to the letter he submitted to President Makarios, the reason for his resignation was the mistreatment of his assistant, who

[75] Soulioti, *Fettered Independence: Narrative,* 153–156, 181–184

[76] Hadjihambis, *Supreme Court and its* Judges, 113.

alleged general obstacles in the conduct of his work, including being shadowed by detectives and being accused of bribery.[77] Eventually, a new Constitutional Court President was found, a common-law-trained judge from a Commonwealth country, who was to be appointed in January 1964. This appointment, however, never took placed. Instead, Forsthoff's duties were performed by Judge John Wilson, the Canadian President of the High Court,[78] until he also left the island in May 1964.

Amidst the growing political and public tension aggravated by the local media and sporadic criminal provocations briefly considered below, on 29 November 1963 Makarios sent to Vice-President Kutchuk, and the three Guarantor Powers letters containing the Greek Cypriots' 13 proposed constitutional amendments, prepared by a committee set up by Makarios.[79] It was during this time that Glafcos Clerides, in his capacity as President of the House of Representatives, requested the legal opinion of Sir Frank Soskice on the interpretation of the treaties establishing the RoC.

The 13 points interfered with some of the most challenging aspects of the Constitution, as evidenced by the documentation reproduced by Soulioti.[80] They proposed, among others, the abolition of the President's and the Vice-President's right of veto, the abolition of the need for separate majorities on some issues in the House of Representatives, and foregoing the provision of separate municipalities. The 13 points also included the abolition of the requirement for communal representation within the justice system, the adjustment of the 70:30 ratio to better reflect the actual 80:20 proportion of each community within the general population, and the abolition of the Greek Communal Chamber. All points contravened the principle of bi-communality, restoring in anything but name the numerical advantage of the Greek Cypriots over the smaller community. Many of these points were later implemented, either through amended legislation justified on the basis of the Doctrine of Necessity (DoN), as discussed in the following chapters, or through historical contingency, like in the case of separate municipalities.

Makarios' '13 Points' remain to this day the topic of legal and political analysis and great speculation, but what is of significance here is the fact that they further aggravated a highly tense political environment. About

[77] Soulioti, *Fettered Independence: Narrative*, 215–216.

[78] Hadjihambis, *Supreme Court and its* Judges, 121.

[79] Clerides, *Deposition Vol. 1*,175–193.

[80] Soulioti, *Fettered Independence: Documents*, 647–668.

two weeks later, on 16–18 December 1963 Cyprus, Greece, and Turkey held in Paris the annual meeting of Ministers of Foreign Affairs as required by the ToA. The talks ended a day earlier instead, among rumours of increased military mobilisation within both communities. The police and the gendarmerie had their leave cancelled, Greek Cypriot police officers started searches on all Turkish Cypriots going in and out of the Turkish quarter of Nicosia, and the British forces in the SBAs were also alerted.[81] At this stage, any further escalation could potentially be avoided, albeit with great difficulty.

Crime and Provocation Before December 1963

As already explained, public international law has a rather simple classification of armed violence: (i) criminal activity, including acts of terrorism, (ii) non-international armed conflicts (previously, civil wars) and (iii) international armed conflicts (i.e inter-sate wars). Sociological research, however, has given a nuanced illustration of violence among ethnic groups, showing how violence can escalate from the level of non-criminal acts of discrimination up to the level of genocide, if the appropriate socio-political conditions for the incubation of ever more grave acts of violence exist.[82] This escalation of violence had also manifested in Cyprus, as the legacies of the political tension and hostility of the past decades and of the inter-communal violence of 1958 were inherited by the Republic. In that regard, Cypriot society was subjected to multiple shocks following a series of criminal provocations from 1960 to 1963, which served as the culmination of the unfavourable political environment discussed above.

The criminal justice system is integral to the application of the international rules on armed conflict. Common article 3 of the 1949 Geneva Conventions, more specifically, prohibits 'the passing of sentences and the carrying out of executions' without a judicial procedure abiding to all appropriate 'judicial guarantees', at times of internal armed conflict. Nonetheless, the 1955 ICRC Expert Commission on common article 3 expressed the view that for the ICRC to retain its neutrality, its delegates should not become involved in either the political or the judicial domain of a State experiencing internal violence.[83] As a result, information on such

[81] Markides, *The Municipal* Issue,147–153.
[82] Mann, *Dark Side of Democracy*, 12–17.
[83] ICRC, "Commission de l'application des principes humanitaires"

matters in the ICRC archives is extremely limited. Moreover, in the 1960s there was no permanent judicial international criminal institution analogous to the International Criminal Court, which was established as recently as 1998. Even today the International Criminal Court's jurisdiction is only complementary to the domestic criminal justice system. Hence, in times of armed violence or conflict, it is the domestic courts that have the primary responsibility to hold perpetrators accountable.

A survey of the reported criminal appeal cases over the period 1960–1968 shows that only some types of criminal cases relevant to the events in the present book reached the courts. Most of them included prosecutions dealing with the illegal possession of arms under the Firearms Law (Capital 57) and the Explosive Substances Law (Capital 54), some even before December 1963. One of the earliest authoritative cases, that of *Stelios Michael Simadhiakos*, is characteristic of the overall situation on the island during this period. Decided on appeal, the appellant police officer was accused of inciting a soldier to 'steal arms for business',[84] with Judge Vassiliades referring also to the unreported case of one *Salih Djemali*[85] in which the appellant, a mason, was sentenced to one year imprisonment for attempting to import pistol ammunition in the heels of his shoes.

Later cases in the 1960s concerned offences under the Military Criminal Code (Law 40/1964), such as the pretending of incapacity, insulting a superior, or desertion. The reports of these cases are telling of the alarming situation on the island, like in the case of *Ahmed Osman*,[86] where the Court underlined the gravity of possessing explosive substances given the ongoing situation, derogating from the rather neutral language observed a few years earlier. Nonetheless, these judgments—as reported—hardly addressed the most vital aspects of the increasing violence or prevented its exacerbation.

In the Cypriot legal system, the role of Prosecution is held by the Law Office of the Republic, headed by the RoC Attorney-General and their Deputy, per article 113 of the Constitution. Unlike England and Wales, both officers are independent non-political, officials of the State, who in the original form of the Constitution had to be appointed jointly by the President and the Vice-President, and to belong to different

[84] *Stelios Michael Simadhiakos* v *The Police* (1961) CLR 64, 89.
[85] *Salih Djemali* v *The Republic* (Cr. Appeal 2305) (1961, unreported).
[86] *Ahmed Osman* v *The Police* (1967) 2 CLR 10.

communities.[87] Common law principles prevail in the criminal justice system and many of the core legislative instruments originate in colonial legislation, including the Criminal Code (Capital 154), the Criminal Procedure Law (Capital 155) and the Law of Evidence (Capital 9).

A series of provocative criminal attacks took place within the same week already in March and April 1962, some 18 months from the establishment of the RoC. The Bayraktar and Omeriye Mosques were bombed on 25 March 1962, Independence Day of Greece, and the Ayios Kassianos School was set on fire on 29 March 1962; a date falling in between Greek Independence Day and the annual EOKA anniversary of 1 April. All three buildings are located within a range of no more than a kilometre on the south-eastern side of the walled mediaeval town of Nicosia. There were no casualties, yet considering the strong political undertones of the crimes in question a Commission of Inquiry was established under the colonial Commission of Inquiry Law (Capital 44).

The Commission acted on instruction by the Council of Ministers, which as the principal Executive organ of the Republic had taken many of the responsibilities previously held by the Governor. It was chaired by judge Wilson, President of the High Court, whereas judges Zekia, member of the High Court, and Triantafillides, of the Supreme Constitutional Court, were appointed Commissioners. The Commission of Inquiry was tasked with making a 'full investigation into the circumstances' of the events in question, 'including all facts connected' with them.[88] Capital 44 set no limitations to the type of inquiry such Commissions undertook. However, it was upon the discretion of the Attorney-General whether to proceed with a prosecution or not, without interference by another person or authority. Such fact-finding inquiries were distinguished in character and procedure from any criminal investigation. The public was kept informed through public sessions and newspaper announcements, which invited them to share relevant information with the Registrars of the High Court and the Supreme Constitutional Court. The Commission visited all three sites, and the inquiry lasted from 3 to 25 May 1962. A total of 54 witnesses gave testimony before the Commission and a report was submitted to the Council of Ministers in October 1962.[89]

[87] Kyprianou, *Attorney General's Office in Prosecutions*, 64; At the time of writing a legal reform is underway, concerning the separation of the advisory and the prosecutorial responsibilities of the the Attorney General and their Deputy.

[88] Soulioti, *Fettered Independence: Documents,* 571.

[89] Soulioti, *Fettered Independence: Documents,* 571.

Just before the Commission of Inquiry initiated its work, two Turkish Cypriot lawyers and newspaper editors, Muzaffer Gurkan and Ayhan Hikmet, were assassinated on 23–24 April 1962.[90] The assassinations were condemned by Makarios,[91] but even though evidence implicating high-ranking politicians, including the Greek Cypriot Minister of Interior, was presented to the Commission of Inquiry in the following month, the process led to no definitive clarifications.[92]

Despite the detailed description of the damages and the methods employed in investigating each of the bombings and the arson, the inquiry failed to give a definitive answer to the most pressing question. Namely, who the suspected perpetrators were. Commissioners Zekia and Triantafyllides delivered separate comments. The former explained how the evidence suggested that the crimes could be perpetrated by members from either community, and suggested the establishment of a 'top-level committee' to periodically find solutions to problems of inter-communal relations. The latter elaborated on the findings of the expert evidence provided by an SBA officer who offered his services upon the request of the Republic.

As expected, the inquiry led to renewed tensions among the public, and not proceeding with prosecutions could be interpreted as an effort to prevent the further stirring of public sentiment. The assassinations of Gurkan and Hikmet were part of a long series of known political assassinations in the following decades, which remain under-investigated and under-researched to this day. They either have been forgotten or have almost assumed the status of urban myths since the perpetrators were never identified and captured, and no trials or public official inquiries ever took place. Such politically motivated crimes, relevant to inter- and intra-communal violence took place within both communities and extend beyond the chronological scope of the present book, yet they are telling of the weakness or the reluctance of the criminal justice system to investigate them.

[90] PIO Press Release, Διπλούς Φόνος εν Λευκωσία (Double murder in Nicosia) (24 April 1962).

[91] PIO Press Release, Statement by the President of the Republic (24 April 1962).

[92] Soulioti, *Fettered Independence: Narrative*, 223; Kızılyürek, *Resentment*, 654–666.

Conclusion

The bi-communal structure of the RoC was implemented for slightly more than three years in total, not without the constant disagreements among the leaders of both communities. Trust was already scarce. However, as Crawford noted, whether another formal arrangement could have been implemented with more success is doubtful. This is especially true considering that the leadership of each community had prepared plans that foresaw the use of violence in order to achieve *taksim* and *enosis* respectively, as a way out of their reluctant partnership.

Beyond Cyprus, the Cuban Missile Crisis in October 1962, the armed violence in the Congo, which would later have an impact on UN peace-keeping efforts in Cyprus, the assassination of John F. Kennedy in November 1963, and the first elections held in Kenya in December 1963, had driven global attention away from the rivalries on Cyprus.[93] Those present in Cyprus, though, seemed to make accurate estimations of the overall situation and tried to raise the alarm. Sir Arthur Clark, British High Commissioner in Cyprus at the time, had written to Duncan Sandys, Secretary of State for Commonwealth Relations, on 6 December 1963:

> Politically the republic cannot go on as it is rent by constant tensions and crises [...] increasingly separatist. That way lies disaster because some stupid move by one side or the other could with these emotional people spark off riot and commotion if not civil war.[94]

The 'move' occurred only 15 days later, triggering a series of recurring violent cycles. Whether these constituted a 'riot', 'commotion' or 'civil war' is examined in the following pages.

References

Books

Anghie, Antony. *Imperialism, Sovereignty and the Making of International Law*. Cambridge University Press, 2005.
Calame, Jon and Esther Charlesworth, *Divided Cities: Belfast, Beirut, Jerusalem, Mostar, and Nicosia*. University of Pennsylvania Press, 2009.

[93] Mark Markides, *The Municipal Issue*, 144.
[94] FO 371/168975 C1015/238, Sir Arthur Clark (HC) to Duncan Sandys, 6 December 1963 as reproduced in Madden, *The End of* Empire, 480.

Chrysostomides, Kypros. *The Republic of Cyprus: A study in International Law.* Martinus Nijhoff 2000.

Chrysostomou, Aggelos. *Από τον Κυπριακό Στρατό μέχρι και τη δημιουργία της Εθνικής Φρουράς* (1959–1964) (From the Cyprus Army until the establishment of the National Guard (1959–1964). 2015.

Clerides, Glafcos, *Cyprus: My Deposition Vol 1.* Alithia Publishing, 1989.

Crawford, James, *The Creation of States in International Law.* 2nd edn, Oxford University Press, 2007.

Crawford, James. *Brownlie's Principles of International* Law. 9th edn, Oxford University Press, 2019.

Emilianides, Achilles C. *Η υπέρβαση του Κυπριακού Συντάγματος* (Beyond the Cyprus Constitution). Sakkoulas 2006.

Emilianides, Achilles C. *Constitutional Law in Cyprus.* Wolters Kluwer, 2019.

Emilianides, Achilles C. Οι μυστικές διαπραγματεύσεις: Η γένεση της Κυπριακής Δημοκρατίας (1959–1960) (The Secret Negotiations: The Birth of the Cyprus Republic 1959–1960). Papazisis, 2022.

Frankenberg, Günter. *Comparative Constitutional Studies: Between Magic and Deceit.* Edward Elgar, 2019.

Greene, Alan, *Permanent States of Emergency and the Rule of Law: Constitutions in an Age of Crisis.* Hart, 2018.

Hadjihambis, Demetrios H, *The Supreme Court of Cyprus and its Judges.* Supreme Court of Cyprus, 2010.

Hadjilyras, Alexander-Michael. *Η Κυπριακή Δημοκρατία και οι Θρησκευτικές Ομάδες* (The Republic of Cyprus and the Religious Groups). 2012.

Kızılyürek, Niyazi *Μια ιστορία βίας και μνησικακίας: Η γένεση και η εξέλιξη της εθνοτικής διένεξης στην Κύπρο Vol 2* (A story of violence and resentment: The genesis and evolution of the ethnic conflict in Cyprus), Translated by Michalis Theodorou. Heterotopia, 2019.

Kyprianou, Despina. *The role of the Cyprus Attorney General's Office in Prosecutions: Rhetoric, Ideology and Practice.* Springer, 2010.

Macmillan, Harold. *Riding the Storm 1956–1959.* Macmillan, 1971.

Madden, Frederick *The end of Empire: Dependencies Since 1948 – Part I: the West Indies, British Honduras, Hong Kong, Fiji, Cyprus, Gibraltar and the Falklands.* Greenwood Press, 2000.

McNair, Arnold D. *The Law of Treaties.* Reprinted 2003, Oxford University Press, 1961.

Mann, Michael. *The Dark Side of Democracy.* Cambridge University Press, 2005.

Markides, Diana. *Cyprus 1957–1963: From Colonial Conflict to Constitutional Crisis – The key role of the Municipal Issue.* University of Minnesota, 2001.

Polyviou, Polyvios G. *Cyprus on the edge: A study in constitutional survival.* 2013.

Shahabuddin, Mohammad, *Ethnicity and International Law: Histories, Politics and Practices.* Cambridge University Press, 2016.

Shaw, Malcolm N. *International Law*. 8th edn, Cambridge University Press, 2017.
Siems, Mathias. *Comparative Law*. 3rd edn, Cambridge University Press, 2022.
Soulioti, Stella. *Fettered Independence: Cyprus, 1878–1964 Vol 1 - The Narrative*. University of Minnesota Press, 2006.
Soulioti, Stella. *Fettered Independence: Cyprus, 1878–1964 Vol 2 - The Documents*. University of Minnesota Press, 2006.
Tornaritis, Criton G. *The Treaty of Alliance: An analysis of the treaty and the reasons that led to its termination in the light of International Law*. Publisher/ Year Unknown.
Tornaritis, Criton G. *The Human Rights as Recognized and Protected by Law with Special Reference to the Law of Cyprus*. 1966.
Tornaritis, Criton G. *Constitutional and Legal Problems in the Republic of Cyprus, Press and Information Office*. 1972.
Zotiades, George B. *Intervention by treaty right: Its legality in present day international law*. Jus Gentium Series of Publications on International Law, 1965.

Chapters and Edited Volumes

Itty Abraham. "Bandung and State Formation in Post-colonial Asia." In *Bandung Revisited: The Legacy of the 1955 Asian-African Conference for International Order*, edited by Seng Tan and Amitav Achary. National University of Singapore Press, 2008.
Chatterjee, Partha. "The Legacy of Bandung". In *Bandung, Global History, and International Law*, edited by Luis Eslava, Michael Fakhri, Vasuki Nesiah. Cambridge University Press, 2017.
Chourchoulis, Dionysis. "Δυτική στρατηγική, βρετανικές βάσεις και Κύπρος, 1960–69" (Western strategy, British bases and Cyprus, 1960–69). In *Το Κυπριακό και το Διεθνές Σύστημα, 1945–1974: Αναζητώντας θέση στον κόσμο* (The Cyprus Problem and the International System, 1945–1974: In search of a position in the world), edited by Petros Papapolyviou, Aggelos Syrigos and Evanthis Hatzivassiliou. Patakis, 2013.
Constantinides, Aristoteles. "Hans Kelsen's Opinion on the Eligibility of the future Republic of Cyprus as a Member of the United Nations." In *Das internationale Wirken Hans Kelsens*, edited by Clemens Jabloner, Thomas Olechowki, and Klaus Zeleny. MANZ, 2016.
Constantinides, Aristoteles. 'Η Θέση του Διεθνούς Δικαίου στην Κυπριακή Έννομη Τάξη' (The Position of International Law in the Cypriot Legal Order). In *Essays of Law and International Relations in Memory of Professor Elias Krispis*, edited by Foundation for International Legal Studies of Professor Elias Krispis and Dr. Anastasia Samara-Krispi. Sakkoulas, 2015.
Kyriakides, Klearchos A. "The Sovereign Base Areas and British Defence Policy since 1960." In *Britain in Cyprus: Colonialism and Post-Colonialism 1878–2006*, edited by Hubert Faustmann and Nicos Peristianis. Bibliopolis, 2006.

Loizides, Neophytos. "Arend Lijphart and Consociationalism in Cyprus." In *Consociationalism and Power-Sharing in Europe: Arend Lijphart's Theory of Political Accommodation*, edited by Michaelina Jakala, Durukan Kuzu, and Matt Qvortrup. Palgrave 2018.

Sophia Papastamkou, 'Παράδειγμα προς μίμηση ή προς αποφυγή; Η πολιτειακή οργάνωση της Κυπριακής Δημοκρατίας ως πρότυπο για την επίλυση του Αλγερινού, 1960–62' (An example to be followed or avoided? The State structure of the Republic of Cyprus as a prototype for the resolution of the Algerian Issue, 1960–62). In *Το Κυπριακό και το Διεθνές Σύστημα, 1945–1974: Αναζητώντας θέση στον κόσμο* (The Cyprus Problem and the International System, 1945–1974: In search of a position in the world), edited by Petros Papapolyviou, Aggelos Syrigos and Evanthis Hatzivassiliou. Patakis, 2013.

Wippman, David. "Pro-democratic intervention" In *The Oxford Handbook of the Use of Force in International Law*, edited by Marc Weller. Oxford University Press, 2015.

Journal Articles

Constantinou, Costas M, "Cypriot In-dependence and the Problem of Sovereignty" *The Cyprus Review* 22, No. 2 (2010) 17–33.

Demetriadou, Ersi, "Legal Discourse and Social History in Cyprus: An Inductive Inguiry [sic] 1878–1982" *Cyprus Law Tribune* (1989): 127.

Dimitrakis, Panagiotis, "The Value of CENTO of UK Bases on Cyprus" *Middle Eastern Studies* 45 No. 4 (2009) 611–624.

Faustmann, Hubert, "Independence Postponed: Cyprus 1959–1960" *The Cyprus Review* 2 (2002): 99–119.

Hadjigeorgiou, Nasia, "Decolonizing Cyprus 60 Years after Independence: An assessment of the legality of the Sovereign Base Areas" *European Journal of International Law* 33, No. 4 (2022): 1125–52.

ICRC, "Commission d'Experts chargée d'examiner la question de l'application des principes humanitaires en cas de troubles intérieurs" *International Review of the Red Cross* 443 (1955): 722.

Korhonen, Outi, "New International Law: Silence, Defence or Deliverance?," *European Journal of International Law* 7 (1996): 1–28.

Lijphart, Arend, "Consociational Democracy" *World Politics* 21, No. 2 (1969) 207–225.

Rodogno, Davide, "European Legal Doctrines on Intervention and the Status of the Ottoman Empire within the 'Family of Nations' throughout the Nineteenth Century," *Journal of the History of International Law* 18 (2016) 5–41.

Symeonides, Symeon C, "The Mixed Legal System of the Republic of Cyprus" *Tulane Law Review* 78 (2003) 441

Other

Besson, Samantha, "Sovereignty" in *MPEPIL* (April 2011) https://opil.ouplaw.com/view/10.1093/law:epil/9780199231690/law-9780199231690-e1472 accessed 28 March 2021

Blay, Samuel K N, "Territorial Integrity and Political Independence" *MPEPIL* (March 2010) https://opil.ouplaw.com/view/10.1093/law:epil/9780199231690/law-9780199231690-e1116?prd=OPIL accessed 28 March 2021

Hadjigeorgiou, Nasia, "Sovereign Base Areas (SBA)" *MPEPIL* (June 2021) <https://opil.ouplaw.com/view/10.1093/law-epil/9780199231690/law-9780199231690-e2261> accessed 30 November 2021.

ILA, Committee on the Enforcement of Human Rights Law, 'Second Interim Report of the Committee' (1988) 63 *International Law Association Conference Report* 129.

Kunig, Philip "Intervention, Prohibition of" in *MPEPIL* (April 2008) https://opil.ouplaw.com/view/10.1093/law:epil/9780199231690/law-9780199231690-e1434?rskey=QpSev6&result=2&prd=OPIL accessed 28 March 2021.

McDonald, Avril and Hanna Brollowski, "Security" in *MPEPIL* (May 2011) https://opil.ouplaw.com/view/10.1093/law:epil/9780199231690/law-9780199231690-e399 accessed 28 March 2021

Momchil Milanov, 'State of War' *MPECCoL* (June 2023) https://oxcon.ouplaw.com/display/10.1093/law-mpeccol/law-mpeccol-e504?rskey=3L1O2s&result=2&prd=OXCON accessed 10 January 2025

Simma, Bruno "Reciprocity" *MPEPIL* (April 2008) https://opil.ouplaw.com/view/10.1093/law:epil/9780199231690/law-9780199231690-e1461> accessed 3 December 2021 accessed 30 November 2021.

ICRC, *IHL Databases*, "Cyprus" https://ihl-databases.icrc.org/applic/ihl/ihl.nsf/vwTreatiesByCountrySelected.xsp?xp_countrySelected=CY, accessed 20 August 2019.

Serveta, Marianna, "Cyprus in the eye of the storm – Militarised geopolitics in the Eastern Mediterranean" (*Swedish Defence Research Agency*, 10 May 2023) https://www.foi.se/rapportsammanfattning?reportNo=FOI%20Memo%208176> accessed 10 January 2025.

Archival Materials

Foreign and Commonwealth Office, Conference on Cyprus: Documents singed and initialled at Lancaster House on 19 February 1959 (Cmnd 679, 1959)

Foreign Office, Colonial Office and Ministry of Defence, *Cyprus* (Cmnd 1093, 1960)

Hansard, HC Deb 26 June 1958 vol 590 col 616.
ICRC, B AG 041-088, Adhésion aux Conventions de Genève de 1949 de la République *de Chypre* (15/11/1962-15/11/1966).
ICRC, B AG 251 049-009, Mission d'une délégation du CICR à Chypre, du 31 décembre 1963 au 27 novembre 1965, activités diverses de la délégation en faveur des victimes des troubles entre chypriotes grecs et chypriotes turcs, sixième partie (13/01/1963-29/11/1965).
PIO Press Release, Διπλούς Φόνος εν Λευκωσία (Double murder in Nicosia) (24 April 1962).
PIO Press Release, Statement by the President of the Republic (24 April 1962).
US State Department, *Foreign Relations of the United States, Vol X, Part 1, Eastern Europe Region; Soviet Union; Cyprus (1958–1960).* National Security Report, Statement of US Policy Toward Cyprus, 9 February 1960 https://history.state.gov/historicaldocuments/frus1958-60v10p1/d347 accessed 23 September 2021.

Court Cases

Greco-Bulgarian 'Communities', Advisory Opinion [1930] PCIJ Series B, No 17.
Salih Djemali v The Republic (Cr. Appeal 2305) (1961, unreported).
Stelios Michael Simadhiakos v The Police (1961) CLR 64.
Ahmed Osman v The Police (1967) 2 CLR 10.
Malachtou v Armefti and another (1987) 1 CLR 207
R (on the application of Tag Eldin Ramadan Bashir and others) v Secretary of State for Home Department [2018] UKSC 45.
Legal Consequences of the Separation of the Chagos Archipelago from Mauritius in 1965, Advisory Opinion [2019] ICJ Rep 95.

CHAPTER 4

The Cyprus Troubles, 1963–1964

There is considerable evidence in the literature that upon independence there were key political figures from both communities who saw independence as an intermediary step to their community's respective aspirations for *enosis* and *taksim*. By late 1963 the Cypriots witnessed the mobilisation of a number of paramilitary groups within both communities, with yet another provocation in the form of a bombing attack taking place in Nicosia on 3 December 1963. The target this time was the statue of former EOKA fighter Markos Drakos.

The period from December 1963 to September 1964 is by all accounts the most violent of Cypriot history post-independence, surpassed only by the events of summer 1974. Though a lot has been written on the 'Cyprus troubles', younger generations of Cypriots, Greek Cypriots in particular, are often oblivious to the extent of displacement, the numbers of casualties and missing persons, the increasing criminal and armed violence, as well as the political and legal manoeuvring that took place, which set the infrastructure and formed the realities we experience on a daily basis today. It is during these months that the ICRC and the UN entered the scene with their respective monitoring mission and peacekeeping force. A testament to the humanitarian crisis and the severity of the violence experienced on the island, by a non-negligible part of the population. Using the criteria of 'organisation' and 'intensity' as guidance, the reference to a

N. Kornioti, *Law's Politics: The Cyprus Troubles, 1960–1968*,
https://doi.org/10.1007/978-3-031-93369-1_4

Cypriot 'civil war'—a term occasionally used in UN reports from that time—becomes more realistic, less remote, and less politically charged.

Humanitarianism and Peacekeeping in the Pursuit of Law and Order

The incident that triggered the spread of violence island-wide on 21 December 1963, was an exchange of fire between Turkish Cypriot civilians and Greek Cypriot police officers in Nicosia, at the intersection between the Turkish Cypriot and the Greek Cypriot quarters in Nicosia's walled mediaeval town. According to the formal press release by the Cyprus Police, the incident took place at 2:10 am, when a police patrol stopped a car, whose passengers were a Turkish Cypriot couple. Upon being asked to produce identification documents, the two passengers refused to comply and the tense discussion drew a crowd of Turkish Cypriot residents from the adjacent neighbourhood. Shots were eventually exchanged. The man died on the scene, and the woman once transferred to the Nicosia General Hospital. From there on violence escalated fast.

Bloody Christmas

By sunrise, the police reported two more shooting incidents, at 3:20 a.m. and 5:30 a.m., while at 9:50 a.m. a patrolling police car escorting the Minister of Transport and Works, a Greek Cypriot, was attacked by high school students from the Turkish Lyceum, who threw 'sticks, stones and bottles' in that direction. The police shot towards the students, causing 'light wound[s]' to two of them.[1] There is additional evidence of dispersed shooting incidents on the same day, such as the shooting of three Turkish Cypriot men at 4:45 p.m., passing by the coffee shop in Nicosia's suburb of Mia Milia (Haspolat),[2] as well as attacks against the security forces, when for instance, a gendarmerie vehicle was fired at in the Turkish Cypriot village of Ayios Sozomenos, at 10:25 p.m.[3] Despite a joint appeal by the President and the Vice-President of the Republic urging the members of both communities 'to go peacefully about their normal

[1] PIO, Αστυνομική Ανακοίνωσης (Police Announcement) (21 December 1963).
[2] PIO, Statement by Gendarmerie (21 December 1963).
[3] PIO, Statement by Gendarmerie (22 December 1963).

business',[4] it was soon clear that this was not the intention of many. By the evening of 22 December, violence spread among members of the mixed constitutionally-established Cyprus Army at the force's Tripartite Headquarters.[5]

In the following week, official government announcements consistently referred to provocations by 'Turkish fanatics',[6] with Minister of Interior Polykarpos Yorkadjis commending the police and the gendarmerie for taking control of the situation.[7] According to information cited from the National Archives in London, however, by 23 December the Greek Cypriot Head of Police had informed the British High Commission that the situation was 'out of control'.[8] Indeed, from 23 to 25 December, the situation on the ground deteriorated progressively, with violence spreading across other regions of the island. Most of the fighting took place primarily in Turkish Cypriot quarters around Nicosia. Casualties were estimated at a few hundred from both sides, but with heavier impact on the Turkish Cypriots.[9]

Given the lack of presence by any international organisations on the ground during these early days, sources describing in detail these early clashes have been scarce, and rarely derive from official documentation. One such personal account is the admittedly partial account of journalist Harry Gibbons, Middle East correspondent for the London Daily Express and potential double-agent for Britain and Russia, who happened to be in Cyprus on a break from his coverage of the war in Yemen, on the occasion of Christmas and New Year celebrations. His book on Cyprus, 'The Genocide Files', which is unavailable for purchase and in public libraries on the territory controlled by the RoC today, claimed that the Public Information Office (PIO) was playing down the events, giving wrongful impressions to foreign correspondents on the island.[10] This view is supported in a comprehensive two-page CIA memorandum issued on

[4] PIO, Joint appeal by the President and the Vice-President of the Cypriot People (21 December 1963).

[5] Chrysostomou, *Establishment of the National Guard*, 235.

[6] PIO, Turkish Cypriots continue their unprovoked attacks (24 December 1963).

[7] PIO, Statement by the Minister of Interior Mr. Polykarpos Yorkatzis (27 December 1963).

[8] Chrysostomou, *Establishment of the National Guard*, 236.

[9] CIA, Doc No CIA-RDP79T00429A001400020022-6, Memorandum: Cyprus, 26 December 1963

[10] Gibbons, *Genocide Files*, 13, 38; Gibbons later claimed he was a double-agent for Britain and Russia. Despite its partiality, his account is useful in appreciating the full range of arguments raised at each side, from the more neutral to the most radical.

26 December 1963, which states that in those days the Greek Cypriots had a 'virtual monopoly' on most information leaving Cyprus.[11] The lack of adequate information is also inferred from the ICRC archives, where it was reported that one Red Cross District Nurse from Limassol, a city some 80 Km south of Nicosia, had arrived to the capital on 4 January 1964 'knowing nothing of trouble'.[12] The press releases issued by the PIO, though referring to specific incidents, they maintain a rather descriptive stand, without engaging with the level of animosity described in non-governmental secondary sources and oral testimonies.

The ICRC archives, though without elaborate details on these early violent incidents, clearly describe the immediate aftermath, informing on hostages held by each side, as well as wounded, missing, and displaced persons from both communities.[13] During those days, descriptions of attacks and clashes have emerged from a number of mixed or Turkish Cypriot-dominated neighbourhoods and villages, as well as an attack on the Nicosia General Hospital located in the Greek Cypriot quarter, which resulted in the death of a number of Turkish Cypriot patients. Following the attack, the hospital's Turkish Cypriot medical staff were safely transferred to the Turkish Cypriot quarter of Nicosia upon the initiative of President Makarios, after they voluntarily withdrew from service, according to government sources.[14]

Another major incident is the clashes in the suburb of Omorphita (Kuchuk Kaimakli), located just to the northeast of the mediaeval town of Nicosia. In 1963 Omorphita had about 7000 inhabitants, among them some 5000 Turkish Cypriots who occupied 1000 houses, compared to 400 houses occupied by 2000 Greek Cypriots of various Christian denominations.[15] The fighting that took place there in December 1963 is considered one of the most severe attacks on civilians, with responsibility usually ascribed to a group of irregular fighters led by Nikos Sampson;

[11] CIA, Doc No CIA-RDP79T00429A001400020022-6, Memorandum: Cyprus, 26 December 1963.

[12] ICRC, B AG 200 049-004, Cyprus 11/1/64: Notes on verbal report made by Miss Jean Gilmour MBE on return from 10 days in Cyprus (Formerly confidential report of the British Red Cross).

[13] ICRC, B AG 200 049-005, Press clippings and images collected by the ICRC.

[14] PIO, Ο Αρχιεπίσκοπος συνόδευσε το Τουρκικόν Νοσοκομειακόν Προσωπικόν εις την Βρεττανικήν Αρμοστεία (The Archbishop has escorted the Turkish Hospital Staff to the British High Commission) (26 December 1963).

[15] S/5764, para 94.

well-known former EOKA fighter, at the time an elected MP, and ten years later the unlawfully appointed 'President' of the Republic following the 15 July 1974 coup d'état. A less-known fact is that on 24 and 25 December, a platoon of the Cypriot Army, consisting of 21 Greek Cypriot men, was also active in the area. This was the 'first and last' operation of the Cyprus Army, which was effectively dissolved once its Turkish Cypriot members withdrew in the Turkish quarter of Nicosia and started fighting against government forces.[16] Thus, with the exception of the little activity recorded by the Cyprus Army, fighting in December 1963 was conducted by irregular armed groups from each community.

Criminologist Lambros Kaoullas, using Cyprus as a case study, has developed a theoretical framework of 'chaotic security structures', to describe the 'structural flux' in situations of internal violence or transitions following the end of an armed conflict. This structural fluidity derives from the inability of the State to centrally control its own security forces, leading it to forgo the Weberian 'monopoly of violence' it usually holds, creating a 'security deficit' which includes, among others, the collapse of the justice system.[17] Though the concept of 'chaos' is insightful as indicated by a controversial 2021 judgment of the ECtHR concerning hostilities between Georgia and Russia,[18] Kaoullas' analysis appears to understate the involvement and complicity of high-ranking members of the government in creating and sustaining the chaotic situation observed. As seen further, this is a dominant issue throughout inter-communal violence in Cyprus. Moreover, the reference on more recent case law of the ECtHR, is also useful to show once again the long-term and persisting inability of judicial mechanisms to deal effectively with active hostilities. In early 1964 in Cyprus the 'security structures' were indeed 'chaotic', and unlawful, since it was not until February 1964 that steps were taken by the government towards regaining some control over the paramilitary groups. A process which took months, and arguably was never successfully completed during this period, considering the controversies that arose in the period 1965 to 1967, discussed in the following chapter.

Developments in the last two weeks of 1963 led to immediate reactions by the three Guarantor Powers, which up to that point unanimously urged

[16] Chrysostomou, *Establishment of the National Guard*, 238–241.

[17] Kaoullas, "Security deficit," 34–37.

[18] *Georgia v Russia (II)* (Application No 38263/08) (Grand Chamber) Judgement (Merits), (ECtHR) 21 January 2021; Dzehtsiarou, '*Georgia* v *Russia (II)*'.

the Cypriot politicians on both sides not to resort to violence. This changed on 25 December, Christmas Day, when Turkish airplanes flew over Nicosia, entrenching the ongoing tension on the ground. According to Zaim Necatigil, Turkish Cypriot lawyer, member of the Turkish Cypriot negotiating team since 1975, and former 'Attorney-General' of the 'Turkish Republic of Northern Cyprus', this was a 'warning flight' aiming to deter the continuation of fighting, and a tactical move to allow for the relocation of the Turkish military contingent, from its original barracks in a Greek Cypriot-dominated area and in proximity to the Greek contingent's camp, north of the Turkish quarter of Nicosia, along the road connecting Nicosia with the northernmost town of Kyrenia.[19] The move of the Turkish contingent blocked the road connecting the two towns, and it was not until ten months later that UNFICYP made arrangements for traffic to resume,[20] while the RoC government has not regained control of that area ever since. Another such flight followed on 28 December. Throughout this period, the Greek contingent remained in their barracks following instructions by the Greek government, despite multiple requests towards them, from the Greek Cypriots, to intervene. This call for action was directly rejected by Greece, whose Minister of Foreign Affairs stated that the Cypriots 'shall not engage Greece in war'.[21] As seen below in detail, the involvement of either Greece or Turkey at any stage was likely to politically lead to a regional armed conflict, and legally give rise to liability under the doctrine of State responsibility for actions taken contrary to the principle of non-intervention.

On 26 December 1963, Zenon Rossides, UN Permanent Representative for Cyprus in New York, called for an emergency meeting of the UNSC, bringing a complaint against Turkey 'for the acts of (a) aggression, and (b) intervention in the internal affairs of Cyprus by the threat and use of force against its territorial integrity and political independence'.[22] Through a separate communication, submitted by the UN Permanent Representative for Turkey, the Cypriot Vice-President complained that Mr. Rossides was 'misrepresenting the situation' and that Turkey's action was a 'warranted conciliatory action' aiming 'to save the Turkish community from a most

[19] Necatigil, *The Cyprus Question*, 34.
[20] S/6102, paras 7–21, 148.
[21] Soulioti, *Fettered Independence: Narrative*, 348.
[22] S/5488.

merciless massacre'.[23] From that day on, the Cyprus Question became a permanent feature on the agenda of the UNSC and occasionally of the UNGA.

The first cycle of violence closed on 30 December, when a ceasefire was agreed in Nicosia, and the infamous Cypriot 'Green Line' was drawn crossing through Nicosia's city centre, delimitating the city's historical Greek and Turkish quarters. Barrels, sandbags, and barricades were erected, with RoC police-controlled designated checkpoints, controlling entry and exit from what became the 'Turkish sector' of the city. Today, checkpoints exist along the UN Buffer Zone which is an extension of the 1964 'Green Line' after 1974, expanding from the eastern to the western coast of the island. Crossing was completely forbidden, with a few exceptions, from July 1974 to April 2003, and the crossing regime is today governed by European Union legislation.

The term 'ceasefire' has no official legal definition,[24] but the concept is significant for both the 'Geneva' and the 'Hague' rules of international humanitarian law, as it has a direct impact on the conduct of hostilities and those protected by the 1949 Geneva Conventions. 'Ceasefire' is used today almost interchangeably with other similar terms, such as 'suspension of arms', 'cessation of hostilities', 'truce', and 'armistice. There are, however, minor differences among them. For instance, whereas an armistice is seen as a temporary suspension of military operations, a ceasefire can be used to describe the freezing of military operations to allow for political negotiations to start. Oppenheim's International Law does not refer to 'ceasefires', but the same situation seems to be described under 'suspension of arms'.[25] Importantly, during a ceasefire, an armed conflict has not ended.

Without access to any official documents from 30 December 1963, it is not possible to draw further conclusions. However, it is worth noting that 'special agreements' under common article 3 to the Geneva Conventions today are understood to include ceasefire agreements, which are considered one of the qualifying criteria for non-international armed conflicts under both 'organisation' and 'intensity'.[26] A number of ceasefire

[23] S/5491.

[24] Bell, "Ceasefire," para 1.

[25] Oppenheim, *International Law*, 547–548.

[26] ICRC, *Commentary GCI 2016*, para 850; Moir, "Concept of Non-International Armed Conflict,", 406.

agreements were agreed upon on various occasions in Cyprus during the 1960s, as seen further below.

Among the general public, military and conflict-related vocabulary and practices quickly flooded the communication and the relationship between the two communities, even though the legal implications of the terminology used is usually beyond the point in daily life under such circumstances. In the Turkish Cypriot narrative, the period from 21 December 1963 to the end of that year is known as the 'Bloody Christmas' (*Kanlı Noel/ Ματωμένα Χριστούγεννα*). A term which never became part of the mainstream glossary of the Greek Cypriot narrative.

The Arrival of the International Committee of the Red Cross

Reference to the ICRC mission to Cyprus during this period in the secondary sources is almost non-existent. Even where such reference is made, this is in passing without any details on the organisation's significant role at the time.[27] According to its Statutes, during an armed conflict and other situations of armed violence, the ICRC is a principal coordinating actor. Hence, the presence of an ICRC mission on a specific territory is indicative of the severity of the violence experienced there, *as a matter of fact*. It is not indicative of whether a situation amounts to a non-international or international armed conflict, *as a matter of law*. It is for this reason that the 1962 ICRC Expert Commission referred to a 'right of initiative' of the ICRC,[28] even in cases were the applicability of common article 3 was in doubt. The Commission held the view that it should not proceed with strictly defining the lower level of armed violence, that of 'internal disturbances'.[29] 'Humanitarian assistance', on the other hand, is not a legally defined term, but it is understood as the provision of emergency relief to people affected by natural or man-made disasters, including armed conflict.[30]

The ICRC Archives in Geneva hold detailed information on developments in Cyprus during most of the period examined in this chapter and the next, containing the majority of the reports written by ICRC delegates

[27] eg Varnava, *Cyprus Before 1974*, 109.
[28] Nishat Nishat, "ICRC Right of Initiative".
[29] ICRC, "Victims of Internal Conflicts," 87–88.
[30] Lattanzi, "Humanitarian Assistance," 232.

in Cyprus for the ICRC headquarters in Geneva, from 1 January 1964 to 25 November 1965. According to information held therein, it is understood that some notes to the ICRC headquarters were destroyed instead of being shipped to Geneva upon closing the mission, due to sensitive information they contained.[31] Even so, the archive serves as a valuable primary historical source, giving a clear picture on how violence had affected daily life and the socio-political atmosphere on the island, during this period. It is also the only source that makes comparatively consistent reference to international humanitarian law on various occasions. Still, one could say that it does not live up to initial expectations, bearing witness to the general international legal culture of the 1960s, and the overall marginalisation of international humanitarian law until the late 1960s.

In his well-known study on the missing persons in Cyprus, anthropologist Paul Sant Cassia claimed that it was the British High Commissioner in Nicosia who 'foresaw the need to bring the ICRC', without reference to an official source.[32] Though consultations with the British High Commission are very likely, the first contact with the ICRC according to the Geneva archive was established by Turkish Cypriot associations in London. On 27 December 1963 at 18:15 the ICRC sent a telegram to RoC Foreign Affairs Minister, Spyros Kyprianou, later second President of the RoC following the death of Makarios (1977–1988), informing they had been following developments in Cyprus and had 'learned with satisfaction that Red Cross on Cyprus is assisting [the] victims [of the] troubles'.[33] They subsequently offered the services of the ICRC and the offer was accepted by the Minister the next day.

In this instance the ICRC made no reference to a legal basis for its offer. However, the archive does contain a draft letter of Offering of Service to the RoC on 19 July 1974, very likely misplaced, where the legal basis referred to there is in fact common article 3, raising the question whether the ICRC held the view in 1974, that the imminent use of force in the eve of the Turkish invasion on Cyprus was a continuation of the violence that had been taking place as of 1963.[34]

[31] ICRC, B AG 251049-005.02, 'Note 286 – Liquidation de la délégation' (11 November 1965).

[32] Sant Cassia, *Bodies of Evidence*, 29.

[33] ICRC, B AG 251 049-009, Telegram to Spyros Kyprianou (27 December 1963).

[34] ICRC, B AG 251 049-001, Letter of 19 July 1974 (potentially a draft).

The British Red Cross had already established a Cyprus Branch in 1950, which held the status of a charity under the pre-independence Charities Law (Capital 41). Following independence, the British Red Cross continued being active in Cyprus, both under Capital 41 and the status of an 'authorised service organisation', according to Annex B of the ToE, which also provided for the activity of The Order of the Knights of St. John and the St. Andrew's Ambulance Association, as acknowledged in the ICRC reports. Other humanitarian organisations explicitly mentioned in primary sources include OXFAM, CARE, and USAID.

Communication was quickly established between the Office of International Relations of the British Red Cross in London and the ICRC Secretariat in Geneva. During this period, Sheegla Patterson, British Red Cross Chief Field Officer, was tasked with coordinating the work of the organisation's Cyprus Branch, whereas Jacques Ruff, a Swiss citizen with previous ICRC experience in Palestine, Japan and Laos was appointed first ICRC delegate to Cyprus.[35] He arrived at Nicosia International Airport at 7 a.m. New Year's Day 1964,[36] where he was received by a small delegation of Greek Cypriot officials and humanitarian workers, including Stella Soulioti, Minister of Justice, and simultaneously President of the Cyprus Branch of the British Red Cross, and Sheegla Patterson.

On the day of his arrival, Ruff joined the British forces on an inspection tour, heading a convoy accompanying medical staff towards Omorphita, where intense fighting had occurred in the last days of December. Describing the situation, he referred explicitly to attacks against civilians by Greek Cypriot armed groups and multiple casualties, empty bullet shells, smashed furniture, abandoned houses, blood stains, and abandoned domestic and farm animals, which gave him 'a clear idea of the violence with which these Greeks and these Turks had confronted each other'.[37] In his first report, he further described how Nicosia was divided into three 'sectors'. A Greek and a Turkish one, each 'held respectively under the control of the police and the contingents of the Greek and Turkish armies', and a 'no man's land' (English term in the original French text), most probably referring to the area surrounding the Ledra Palace Hotel, protecting the British contingent. Each sector had a life of its own, and mov-

[35] ICRC, B AG 200 049-004, ICRC Telephone Conversations with British Red Cross (29–31 December 1963).

[36] ICRC, B AG 251 049-009, ICRC Telegram to BRC (31 December 1963).

[37] ICRC, B AG 200 049-004, First Activity Report (7 January 1964).

ing from one sector to another was not permitted, except for ambulances clearly carrying the Red Cross emblem.

During this period, the issues that required the immediate attention of the Red Cross were identified as 'traditional tasks' *(domaine des tâches traditionnelles)*. These included the visiting of prisoners, the release of hostages, the organisation of a Tracing Bureau for Missing Persons, the regrouping of families, and the organisation of relief operations for Turkish Cypriots isolated in enclaves as well as the displaced population overall regardless of community.[38] A more detailed examination of the ICRC's activities in view of the Turkish Cypriot community is undertaken in the next chapter. Here, it must be noted that Greek Cypriot families where the father or another primary caretaker had been killed or went missing were also beneficiaries of humanitarian relief.[39]

In his first report to Geneva, Ruff concluded that the situation had not yet reached the status of a 'civil war', not excluding that possibility if tension increased. This contradicted the opinion of the Turkish Red Crescent, which became involved through efforts to offer humanitarian assistance to the Turkish Cypriot community, including the setting up of a field hospital 'to serve all Cypriots suffering from the calamity of the inter-communal strife without discriminating race, faith or nationality'.[40] A letter by the Turkish Red Crescent was received in Geneva on 6 January 1964 claiming that civilians were deliberately exposed to 'starvation, disease, oppression and atrocities', while 'great difficulties are shown by the local authorities' in permitting the shipment of aid.[41] This is the earliest document that made direct claims based on international legal provisions, invoking the violation of human rights under the UN Universal Declaration of Human Rights, the ECHR, the 1948 Genocide Convention, and common article 3 of the 1949 Geneva Conventions.

These claims were followed by concrete suggestions to ICRC on the appointment of an impartial committee tasked with undertaking a formal inquiry in the investigation of the claims raised. There is no evidence that these suggestions were followed up with, further contributing to the

[38] ICRC, B AG 200 049-004, Second Activity Report (16 January 1964) Annex 10 (6 January 1964).

[39] ICRC, B AG 251 049-005.02, Note 187-Future relief actions (10 February 1965); Note 217 – Distribution of relief to Greek Cypriot families (22 March 1965).

[40] ICRC, B AG 200 049-004, First Activity Report, Annex 6, Visit to the Mobile Hospital set up by the Turkish Red Crescent (3 January 1964).

[41] ICRC, B AG 200 049-004, Letter from TRC (6 January 1964).

ambiguity of said claims. The humanitarian principles of 'neutrality' and 'impartiality' are at the hard of all international and national Red Cross/ Red Crescent organisations, however they have always been subject to extensive debate.[42] Hence, no direct conclusions can be drawn with certainty based on this letter alone, given the fact that on the one side the Turkish Red Crescent was correct to raise any concerns it may have had, but on the other, one cannot overlook the lack of such concerns raised by other actors. Moreover, there is always the possibility that any such legal concerns were overlooked, following broader trends and practices of the 1960s, with the objective to refrain from any actions that would appear to adjudicate the conflicting legal claims of the parties involved.

In a document dated 12 January 1964, it is stated that the RoC government did not recognise the Turkish Red Crescent 'as an official organisation'.[43] A political statement with no legal basis since, recognition or not, the government would not have been precluded from exercising its sovereign right to withhold consent for any activities of the Turkish Red Crescent on its territory. Something which of course would adversely affect the government's international image.

Regardless of this early statement, the government was eventually compelled to recognise the need for humanitarian relief and the condition that all goods would be documented by the Cyprus Branch of the British Red Cross, a method of distribution was eventually agreed upon, on the condition that all goods would be documented by the Cyprus Branch of the British Red Cross. The overall assessment of the ICRC was that:

> … there was so much fear amongst both communities that it was imperative that non-Cypriots took over relief operations. […] [T]he problem of refugees and persons in need was created because they cannot go to work or to their fields, and therefore cannot earn money, and therefore are hungry. The feeling amongst the Turkish community was that they would not be allowed to accept aid from the Government; if they do they will be threatened, and if they do not they will die for lack of aid.[44]

[42] Harroff-Tavel, "Neutrality and Impartiality."

[43] ICRC, B AG 200 049-004, Third Activity Report (13 January 1964), Annex 1 (12 January 1964).

[44] ICRC, B AG 200 049-004, Third Activity Report (13 January 1964), Annex 3 – Informal interview with British Army Officers (13 January 1964).

Turkish Red Crescent shipments of humanitarian assistance continued even after the ICRC mission left the island, and a total of 13 deliveries of food, clothing, medication and other necessities, weighting few tons each, were made from 1964 to 1968.[45] Once UNFICYP was deployed, the peacekeeping force assumed the task of escorting the movement of food, essential merchandise, and individuals, as necessary.

The collection of archival materials from the first days of ICRC presence on Cyprus gives a detailed overview of the infrastructure of the humanitarian relief network which was set up. At any time for the duration of the ICRC mission on Cyprus, there was one ICRC delegate whose work was logistically and administratively supported by the Cyprus Branch of the British Red Cross. Coordination across both communities took place through a Combined Services Committee, whereas a separate Political Liaison Committee held high-level meetings in the presence of Red Cross representatives, the British High Commissioner in Cyprus, the Ambassadors of Greece and Turkey, and representatives of each community.[46] Their task was to guide the Commander of a Joint Truce Force consisting of British forces stationed on Cyprus under the ToE and the Turkish and Greek contingents,[47] which took the role of a temporary 'peacekeeping force', until further arrangements were made.[48]

Importantly, this arrangement did not invoke the ToG in any way,[49] even though its relevance can hardly be denied. Arguably, the very structure of this arrangement is a reflection of James Crawford's description of the RoC as an 'internationalised territory', where the views of all Guarantors had to be taken into account at all times, further blurring the subtle line between the internal and the international affairs.

The Establishment of the United Nations Force in Cyprus

In mid-January 1964, correspondence between the ICRC Cyprus delegation and Geneva gave away an increasing anxiety over diplomatic developments in London. The UK, already burdened with additional military operations in its declining Empire, did not wish to take sole responsibility

[45] S/8446, para 122.
[46] HC Deb 14 January 1964 vol 687 col 35, para 5; S/6102, paras 47-55.
[47] HC Deb 14 January 1964 vol 687 col 35, para 4; S/5508.
[48] Packard, *Getting it Wrong*.
[49] Crawford, *The Creation of States*, 243.

for the maintenance of order on Cyprus. Though the Joint Truce Force 'markedly reduced the fighting in Nicosia', according to US intelligence, irregular forces from both communities saw the relative calm in January 1964 as an opportunity to strengthen their respective positions.[50] Forceful violence resurged in the first half of February across regions, but evidence from secondary sources suggests that the British force did not interfere to prevent fighting or disarm irregular fighters.

While a humanitarian emergency unfolded on Cyprus, representatives of all involved parties gathered in London from 15 January to 15 February 1964. Even though the Conference started as a 'peace-making' effort, the irreconcilable differences between the two communities by the end of January shifted the attention towards 'peacekeeping'.[51] Initially, a NATO peacekeeping force was envisaged, since all three Guarantors were parties to the alliance, despite the risks entailed due to the potential of a full-scale armed conflict between Greece and Turkey. The proposal was eventually rejected by Makarios, who believed that direct involvement by the USA would contradict the Republic's long-term policy of non-alignment.[52] Another option was the establishment of a Commonwealth force which, however, proved unfeasible given developments in South Asia, where 'India and Pakistan [were] busy watching each other' and China, and Malaysia was preoccupied on its frontier with Indonesia.[53]

Under these circumstances, the RoC, by now represented exclusively by the Greek Cypriot leadership, started pursuing with more determination the idea of a UN peacekeeping force. This was more favourably looked upon also by the Soviet Union, who would be enabled to become more involved through its permanent seat on the UNSC.[54] At this point, the Greek Cypriot politicians sought legal advice from prominent international lawyer Elihu Lauterpacht, who on 30 January 1964 submitted his legal opinion on the Treaties of Guarantee and Alliance. One of the concrete concerns raised was the issue of whether the credentials of Zenon Rossides, Permanent Representative of the RoC to the UN in New York, would have been recognised by the members of the UNSC. An indication of the level of tension reached, the awareness of the Greek Cypriot

[50] CIA, Doc No CIA-RDP79T00429A001400020022-6, Memorandum: Cyprus, 26 December 1963.

[51] Clerides, *My Deposition Vol. 1*, 236–330.

[52] James, *Keeping the* peace, 76–83.

[53] Clerides, *My Deposition Vol. 1*, 306–307.

[54] Mirbagheri, *Cyprus and International Peacemaking*, 38.

politicians that the survival of the Republic as an internationally recognised State was anything but guaranteed at this point. Elihu Lauterpacht was of the view that Rossides' credentials could not be 'seriously challenged'.[55] A reflection of the asymmetrical position international law maintains to this day, vis-à-vis the privileged position held by recognised States on the one hand, and the disadvantageous position of non-state actors, groups, and entities, during international disputes.

Throughout this period, UN Secretary-General U Thant, was closely following the developments.[56] After the unsuccessful conclusion of the London Conference, attention shifted promptly to New York. The debates before the UNSC gave everyone involved the opportunity to put their legal, political, and factual arguments on the table. There, any efforts by the representative of Turkey to shed doubt on the international legal status of the RoC were fended off by the Soviet and Greek delegations.[57] Apart from the UK, the USA, and the Soviet Union, all other UNSC members held a rather neutral position, putting more emphasis on the internal situation on the island, contrary to the international dimension of Turkish involvement, a point which served the interests of the Cypriot government much better.

The 28 February 1964 was a definitive moment concerning the position of the Turkish Cypriot community internationally, when Turkey requested, on behalf of the Turkish Cypriots, for Rauf Denktash, at the time President of the Turkish Communal Chamber, to formally present the Turkish Cypriot position before the UNSC.[58] Only the Soviet Union and Czechoslovakia were openly against the request, with other members being generally favourable, albeit not without reservations. Bolivia, for instance, did express the view that they would rather hear Fazil Kutchuk, in his capacity as Vice-President of the RoC.[59] In the end, a compromise was reached after long debate, which allowed Rauf Denktash to speak in his individual capacity as a lay member of the Turkish Cypriot community, as opposed to the formal representative of any entity.[60] The debate was, once again, telling of the privileged position of the Greek Cypriots as representatives of the recognised government, whereas the Turkish Cypriots

[55] Soulioti, *Fettered Independence: Documents*, 805, 807.
[56] S/5514; S/5516.
[57] eg S/PV.1099, paras 5–13.
[58] S/5556.
[59] S/PV.1098, para 10.
[60] S/PV.1098, para 61.

were too optimistic in their hope for more visibility. It was also clearly noted that the Republic was seen as responsible for its failure to take control of the situation internally.

During his transit in Ankara on the way back to Cyprus, Denktash was informed that the Council of Ministers had published a decision that upon his arrival he was to be arrested and tried for 'offences against the State and other crimes'. Acknowledging this was an internal matter of the Republic, U Thant requested from the Cypriot government to reconsider its decision, since it was likely to have adverse international repercussions for Cyprus. The government never withdrew its statement, but agreed with the proposition that Turkey should host Denktash for an indeterminate duration of time.[61]

In conclusion of the UNSC debates on Cyprus in February 1964, a draft resolution, co-sponsored by Bolivia, Brazil, the Ivory Coast, Morocco, and Norway, was presented to the UNSC on 2 March 1964, and adopted unanimously without amendments two days later. This was UNSC Resolution 186 of the 4th of March 1964,[62] which today holds a paramount position in all communication and public statements on the Cyprus Question, since it constitutes the legally binding instrument that 'seals' the recognition of the sovereignty of the RoC internationally. Over the decades, however, the more nuanced positions expressed within the UNSC have gradually been forgotten, and certainly almost completely abandoned in internal political discussions. These neglected points concern the responsibility allocated to the Republic to stop the violence (paragraph 2) and of each community separately to act with 'utmost restrained' (paragraph 3).

The significance of UNSC Resolution 186 also lies in being the foundational document of UNFICYP and the appointment of a mutually appointed mediator. Early commentary on UNSC Resolution 186, observed that the clear separation of responsibilities between the newly established UN force as per paragraphs 4, 5 and 6, and the separate recommendation on the designation of a UN Mediator, suggested that UN participation in Cyprus was not meant to burden the organisation with the resolution of the problem, but that the burden would be on the parties themselves.[63] Further evidence in that regard is the direct allocation of

[61] Clerides, *My Deposition Vol 2*, 200–201.

[62] S/5571; S/PV.1102, para 28.

[63] Miller, *Cyprus: Law and Politics*, 33.

duties to both Cypriot communities by reference to the Mediator, who according to paragraph 7 of the Resolution:

> shall use his best endeavours with the representatives of the communities and also with the aforesaid four Governments, for the purpose of promoting a peaceful solution and an agreed settlement of the problem confronting Cyprus, in accordance with the Charter of the United Nations, having in mind the well-being of the people of Cyprus as a whole and the preservation of international peace and security.

In setting up UNFICYP, the UN were cautious of their earlier experience with ONUC, the United Nations Operation in the Congo (1960–1964), where UN staff had actively interfered with the political situation in the country.[64] In addition, considering the complex and highly politicised nature of the situation in Cyprus, countries became reluctant to contribute to a mission which may not have been successful, and also held the risk of being accused of partiality, like in Congo.[65] The fact that contrary to other peacekeeping forces UNFICYP was financed by voluntary contributions, posed additional difficulties.[66] Hence, despite the urgency, it was only on 27 March 1964 that the first troops started arriving on Cyprus,[67] while the international agreement between the Republic and the UN was ratified by the House of Representatives a few months later, on 15 June 1964. There has been little change to the force's structure since, which comprises of a military component, a Civilian Police (UNCIVPOL) and a Civil Affairs Unit.[68]

Each side had different expectations of UNFICYP. For the Greek Cypriots, UN presence was regarded as a means towards ending the Turkish Cypriot 'rebellion', assisting the government to restore its rule, and defend itself against a potential Turkish invasion. For the Turkish Cypriots UNFICYP had to protect their community from the threat of Greek Cypriot oppression, and assist splitting the island between the two

[64] Tudor, *Blue Helmets Bureaucrats*, 114–161.

[65] Tudor, *Blue Helmets Bureaucrats*, 223; Miller, *Cyprus: Law and Politics*, 35.

[66] Bothe, "Peacekeeping," 1177.

[67] S/5593; S/5593/Add.1; S/5593/Add.2 S/5593/Add.3; S/5634; UNA, S-0869-0003-03-00001, *Items in Peace-keeping Operation – Cyprus*.

[68] Theodorides, "UNFICYP."

communities.[69] Both positions were wrong and exaggerated for internal consumption, since UNFICYP was tasked with nothing more than:

> preserving international peace and security, to use its best efforts to prevent a recurrence of fighting and, as necessary, to contribute to the maintenance and restoration of law and order and a return to normal conditions.[70]

Misconceptions about UNFICYP's role caused distress among the local population, who on some occasions expressed their dissatisfaction against the force through demonstrations.[71] Politically there was no considerable clarity either, as shown through the lengthy plenary debate at the House of Representatives regarding the ratification of the service agreement between the UN and the RoC (Law 29/1964).[72] Like the UN officials, the Greek Cypriot MPs were also concerned with whether UNFICYP would face the same problems as ONUC did, since many found its terms of reference unclear. More concrete concerns were also raised, like in the case of Ezekias Papaioannou, Secretary-General of AKEL, who expressed the view that accepting UNFICYP's 'temporary presence' should not be interpreted as inability by the Republic to deal with the ongoing situation.

Disagreement about the exact meaning of 'return to normal conditions' in the text of Resolution 186 also persisted. UNFICYP carried just enough arms to act in self-defence shall the need to do so arose. This included '(a) the defence of United Nations posts, premises and vehicles under armed attack', and '(b) the support of other personnel of UNFCYP under armed attack'.[73] Even then, any conduct would be constrained by the 'principle of minimum force', and the rules and general principles of public international law. The regulations issued for UNFICYP by the UN Secretary-General also stated that 'The Force shall observe and respect the principles and spirit of the general international Conventions applicable to the conduct of military personnel'.[74] In practice, therefore, at no point

[69] Kyriakides, *Constitutionalism and Crisis.*

[70] UNSC Res 186, para 5; S/5764, para 1.

[71] Tudor, *Blue Helmets Bureaucrats*, 227 citing Anon, 'Turks Mob U.N. Chief on Cyprus: 150 Women Hurl Rocks and Shout "Death to Gyani, Death to Gyani"' (*The Washington Post*, 27 April 1964).

[72] HORM, Session 1963–1964, 15 June 1964.

[73] S/5653, paras 10, 16, 18.

[74] UNA, S-0869-0001-07-00001, *Items-in-Peace-keeping operations – Cyprus*, para 40.

UNFICYP troops were allowed to act in a way that would bring them into direct conflict with either community, unless compelled to do so because the security of the force itself was at stake.

The Commander of the force was directly accountable to the UN Secretary-General, who in turn could issue directions to the UNFICYP Commander. In case any members of the force were suspected of a criminal offence of any kind, the peacekeeper in question would be subjected to the criminal jurisdiction of their own national State, including their national State's military rules and regulations. In principle bound by 'neutrality' and 'impartiality', UNFICYP commanders had the power to engage with local leaders from either community. In traditional peacekeeping forces, this was often reflected in the composition of a peacekeeping force, where UNSC permanent members or other interested parties were excluded from the contribution of troops.[75] Nonetheless, the UK has been a constant contributing State to UNFICYP from the very beginning, despite its permanent seat on the UNSC and its vested interests in the Cyprus Question as a Guarantor Power for Cypriot independence and territorial integrity. There are two ways to potentially explain this exceptional position of the UK. Firstly, that UK troops were already deeply involved in peacekeeping efforts since the very first days of the conflict and therefore, were unique in their capacity to guide ground operations, while secondly, by maintaining the UK's military role outside the SBAs under the umbrella of peacekeeping, helped to promote internationally the view that the situation in Cyprus was a Greco-Turkish affair only.

The problems arising due to the ambiguity of UNFICYP's mandate were exacerbated by the lack of resources and adequate training for its troops, who often had to improvise regarding their humanitarian response on the ground. This blurred the boundaries between the responsibilities of the ICRC and UNFICYP, and both organisations were reluctant to take responsibility for matters they felt fell out of their respective mandates. For the ICRC the situation was 'too political', while for the UN was 'too humanitarian'.[76]

[75] Tsagourias, "Consent, Neutrality/Impartiality," 478–480.

[76] Tudor, *Blue Helmets Bureaucrats*, 229–234.

Conflict Qualification

While diplomatic developments were taking place in London and New York in the first quarter of 1964, violence persisted on Cyprus. As already discussed, the applicability of common article 3 is conditioned upon establishing the existence of a non-international armed conflict. This in turn is subject to satisfying cumulatively the criteria of 'organisation' and 'intensity', through a comprehensive reading of a number of factual indicators (Table 2.1). A detailed legal examination and analysis of the military violence during this period has never taken place, and the indicators clarified by the ICRC can serve as guidance in the process. Thus, we shall now turn to the most violent series of events from January to September 1964, to legally assess whether these events could amount to a non-international armed conflict. Reference to other relevant aspects of international law is made, as necessary.

Assessing Intensity: Violence in the First Half of 1964

Despite the ceasefire agreed upon in Nicosia at the end of 1963, in the first days of January 1964 grievous crimes continued taking place, with animosity further fed by the political tension that existed in anticipation of the London Conference. One such crime was the killing of three monks and a young man at the Galaktotrophousa Monastery between Kornos and Kophinou villages, on New Year's Day 1964. The attack on the monastery was undertaken by four Turkish Cypriots, who wounded several more civilians staying at the monastery overnight. The Abbot went missing.[77] In the following days, in fear of reprisals many Turkish Cypriots in nearby villages moved towards the majority Turkish Cypriot village of Kophinou, which eventually became the Kophinou enclave.

Within the first week of 1964, the ICRC delegate in Cyprus reported in his first report to Geneva that the Turkish Cypriot community had no updates on the 102 Turkish Cypriots inhabitants of Denya village, located approximately 25 km west of Nicosia, and that nine corpses were found in the vicinity of the village of Ayios Vassilios. By 12 January 1964, it was established that these nine corpses were just few out of a total of 21 bodies belonging to Turkish Cypriots found in a mass grave. Some of the bodies had their arms and legs tied, which suggested that the victims were also

[77] PIO, Turks kill Greek monks (1 January 1964).

tortured. Apart from this being an offence under domestic criminal law, the act of torture and killing carries legal implications under common article 3 of the 1949 Geneva Conventions, article 3 of the ECHR, and article 8 of the Cyprus Constitution. Press publications at the time suggested the attack on Ayios Vassilios may had been a reprisal for the killing of Greek Cypriots outside the Turkish Cypriot village of Gyoneli in 1958. In turn, from 12 to 18 January 1964, six Greek Cypriots were abducted in Paphos district, believed to be a reprisal for the killings in Ayios Vassilios.[78] These crimes were a continuing trend from the violence in the last days of December 1963.

Throughout the first half of 1964 the scattered clashes were led by decentralised groups of irregular fighters active on both sides. These non-state formations enjoyed a certain level of autonomy regarding the control they had in different regions. We see the re-emergence of TMT in the Turkish Cypriot community, as well as a new organisation officially called EOK (*Εθνική Οργάνωση Κύπρου/* Cyprus National Organisation), but better known as 'Akritas', in the Greek Cypriot community, established in secret in 1961[79] or 1962,[80] with the aim to achieve union with Greece after independence. Additional scuttered informal groups acted in addition to 'Akritas' and the formal government-controlled security forces of the RoC. Best known among them were the groups led by Nicos Sampson, which was mentioned above in the context of the Omorphita battles in December 1963, and the Vassos Lyssarides groups, which led the operation at St. Hilarion castle in April 1964, discussed below. Chrysostomou identifies six additional such groups, led by Nikiphoros Ioannou, Costas Christodoulides MP, Renos Kyriakides, Andreas Moustakas, Ioannis Kassinis and Photis Papaphotis all of which could be associated to the regional EOKA sectors of the 1955–1959 emergency, bringing the total number of paramilitary formations on the Greek Cypriot side, including 'Akritas', to ten. Discipline was loose, and some later admitted that there were incidents of 'unacceptable behaviour' among their members.[81]

Within the areas that came under the control of Turkish Cypriot fighters, UN reports distinguish between those Turkish Cypriot police, gendarmerie and army officers who on 21 December 1963 came under the

[78] Kızılyürek, *Resentment*, 512.
[79] Chrysostomou, *Establishment of the National Guard*, 225.
[80] Soulioti, *Fettered Independence: Narrative*, 259; Kızılyürek, *Resentment*, 442–453.
[81] Chrysostomou, *Establishment of the National Guard*, 252–255.

exclusive control of the Turkish Cypriot leadership, and the 'extremists' under direct TMT control.[82] Regardless of this distinction, however, under international humanitarian law all Turkish Cypriot fighters were non-state actors, acting against the legal authority of the State.

The violence did not leave unaffected members of the other religious groups, even though their separate experience has been fused in their constitutional Greek Cypriot communal identity.[83] On 4 March 1964, there was an eviction of all Armenians from the Turkish Cypriot quarters, while there have been reports of collusions also between Armenian Cypriots and Christian Orthodox-Greek Cypriot irregulars.[84] In addition, apart from the 'military incidents', violence between civilians also occurred on the basis of personal grievances, leading to theft, intentional provocations, spontaneous conflict and vendettas.[85] This phenomenon is not surprising, since research has established that there is an intrinsic link between 'civil war' and criminal activity.[86]

Following the establishment of UNFICYP, the earliest UN Secretary-General reports to the UNSC described the situation as 'relatively quiet', even though 'grave incidents' were sporadically noted, including clashes at Ktima in the town of Paphos on 7–10 March, and the village of Ghaziveran (Kazivera) on 19 March. In the meantime, a second 'Green Line', one that does not survive to this day, was drawn in Larnaca. Only days after the first UNFICYP troops arrived, the first major clashes were reported in the Tylliria region on the north-west coast of the Island, from 4 to 8 April. There, UNFICYP had to resort to use of force in self-defence following attacks from both communities, eventually putting an end to the violence by taking control over disputed geographical positions.[87] Despite UNFICYP's success in stopping the violence this time, by the middle of summer the region would become the epicentre of clashes, reaching a climax involving the Turkish Air Force in the first week of August.

The vast majority of casualties during this period occurred during an operation at St Hilarion Castle. The castle overlooks the Nicosia-Kyrenia Road from one of the picks of the Pentadaktylos (Beshparmak/Kyrenia)

[82] S/5950, para 23.

[83] PIO, Turks raid Nicosia Armenian Church (29 January 1964); PIO, Maronite Detained by Turkish Terrorists (12 June 1964).

[84] Patrick, *Political Geography and the Cyprus Conflict*, 74.

[85] Patrick, *Political Geography and the Cyprus Conflict*, 120–125.

[86] Kalyvas, "Civil Wars, Organized Crime," 1521–1522.

[87] S/5679, paras 8–10.

mountain range north of Nicosia, which had been inaccessible to Greek Cypriots since Christmas 1963, when the Turkish army contingent moved its troops in the area. The secretly planned operation took place roughly from 23 to 29 April 1964, with some disparity between the dates mentioned across different sources.[88] The secondary accounts of Ierodiakonou, who is a former military officer, Chrysostomou and Kizilyurek[89] contradict the UN Secretary-General's report, according to which the 'outbreak' occurred on 26 April.[90]

Clarity is given by Ierodiakonou, who explained that the operation took place in two phases. The first phase, which started on 23 April 1964, targeted a nearby area, and only on 25 April attention shifted towards the St Hilarion Castle exclusively. Its overall aim was to restore Greek Cypriot control over the main mountain passage on the road connecting the towns of Nicosia and Kyrenia, but this was only 'partially successful'.[91] It is well-known that this operation was executed by the paramilitary group led by Vassos Lyssarides, but according to Ierodiakonou its planning was supported by the officers of a newly established 'voluntary National Guard', indicating a lack of complete separation between the official forces of the Republic and the paramilitary groups, at this time.

The UN evaluated the incident as 'especially serious', since it was a 'planned and organized military effort'.[92] Crucially, UNFICYP was unprepared to intervene militarily, since the government had not shared relevant information in advance. Nonetheless, they did initiate diplomatic talks with each side immediately. The end of the battle at St Hilarion coincided with the completion of the first month of UNFICYP presence on the island. UN Secretary-General Thant was alarmed by the dilemma UNFICYP found themselves in. On the one side, the need to prevent the Cypriots from killing each other and on the other, the need to defend the UN force, as they could not 'stand idly by and see an undeclared war deliberately pursued, or see innocent civilians of all ages ruthlessly struck

[88] Chrysostomou, *Establishment of the National Guard*, 288; Ierodiakonou, *Stone years*, 71–72.

[89] Ierodiakonou, *Stone years*, 71–72; Chrysostomou, *Establishment of the National Guard*, 288–289; Kızılyürek, *Resentment*, 533.

[90] S/5671, para 1.

[91] Chrysostomou, *Establishment of the National Guard*, 289.

[92] S/5671, paras 6, 8 and Annex II 'Statement by Lt. General Gyani, UNFICYP Commander (28 April 1964).

down by snipers' bullets'.[93] He then added, that his commentary was not to be interpreted as an 'assessment of blame', indicating an early detachment from any form of direct formal assessment of the situation. His approach was in line with the interim aims set by UNFICYP, whose core objectives were:

(a) To prevent a recurrence of fighting.
(b) To contribute to the maintenance and restoration of law and order.
(c) To contribute to a return to normal conditions.[94]

In the first month of UNFICYP's debarkation on the island, a total of 163 shooting incidents were registered in 30 days, with 21 killed, 28 wounded, and 36 missing persons from both communities reported.[95] Throughout this period and until November 1967 the case would often be the following:

> neither side was clear about the feelings or intentions of the other. Finally, some dramatic incident which occurred within 'A' would be misinterpreted by community 'B' as an attack. Community 'B' would rush to its own defence but this action would in turn be misinterpreted by community 'A' as an attack. Fighting then began and each side blamed the other for starting it.[96]

One such incident was the exchange of fire on 22 April 1964, when the Greek Cypriots used fire against a Turkish Cypriot enclave after they heard gun shots. UNFICYP intervened establishing that the gun shots were part of Turkish Cypriot Bayram celebrations.[97]

In the last month of the first three-month period of UNFICYP, from 2 May to 8 June 1964, exchanges of fire were a daily phenomenon, including five cases of grenade attacks or shooting directed at UNFICYP. These incidents included an attack by Turkish Cypriot snipers against UNFICYP personnel escorting Greek Cypriot harvesters, as well as Greek Cypriots shooting against UNFICYP members conducting an investigation in the

[93] S/5671, paras 5, 6.
[94] S/5671, Annex I Objectives and interim aims of a comprehensive programme of action for UNFICYP para 1.
[95] S/5679, paras 15–16.
[96] Patrick, Patrick, *Political Geography and the Cyprus Conflict*, 122.
[97] S/5679, para 13.

death of two bodies found in the St. Hilarion area. A more serious incident concerned the killing of two Greek Army officers and a Greek Cypriot police officer, as well as the wounding of a third Greek Army officer on 11 May 1964, when the four of them entered the mediaeval town of Famagusta (the town's Turkish Cypriot quarter) wearing civilian clothes. According to the ICRC, a series of reprisals by Greek Cypriots followed this event. This was confirmed by the UN Secretary-General, according to whom, following the abduction of 32 Turkish Cypriots in Famagusta district after the killing of the military and police officers, no action was known to him regarding the prosecution of any perpetrators.[98]

The explicit reference to 'reprisals' here and throughout the archives is crucial, since reprisals are regulated under international humanitarian law, where they are allowed only under specific conditions and against specific categories of people or objects.[99] Pictet's 1952 Commentary on common article 3 had already pointed out that the taking of hostages was understood to include the act of reprisals, and today this is seen as customary international humanitarian law under ICRC's customary rule 148.[100] Over the years there have been efforts to expand protection from reprisals beyond the limited protection afforded under articles 46/47/13/33 of Geneva Conventions I-IV 1949, especially with regard to civilian populations.[101] Today, the ICRC has expanded Pictet's earlier position, stating that under common article 3 the prohibition of reprisals is inferred through the prohibition of violence to life and person, the taking of hostages, and outrages upon personal dignity, cruel and degrading treatment and torture, and the overarching principle of 'humane treatment',[102] underlining the relevance of all four Geneva Conventions 1949. In a historical context, these later developments in the law help evaluate the significance of these incidents and emphasise strongly the severity of the marginalisation of these forms of violence within the historical narrative.

Even though the first three-month periodic report to the UNSC made no reference to international humanitarian law, the report gives a good overview of the military preparations, the level of military force engaged, and the lack of freedom of movement. It can be inferred from the

[98] S/5764 paras 14–18.

[99] Henckaerts and Doswald-Beck, *Customary Study: Rules*, 513–529.

[100] Pictet, *Commentary GCI 1952*, 54.

[101] E.g. Basic Principles for the protection of civilian populations in armed conflicts UNGA Res 2675 (XXV) 1970 (9 December 1970).

[102] Henckaerts and Doswald-Beck, *Customary Study: Rules*, 306.

language employed that the Secretary-General was guided in his reporting by *jus in bello* (the rules on the conduct of hostilities) and *jus ad bellum* (the rules on the use of force). Examples include the reference to 'Greek Cypriot authorities', but Turkish Cypriot 'fighting elements',[103] with due regard to military developments, including the increased possession of arms and ammunition on each side, as well as the reference to 'reprisals' and the 'siege' of the school in Polis, where Turkish Cypriot civilians remained for safety, even after their freedom of movement had been restored.[104]

Furthermore, the report described in detail the 'Cypriot Armed Forces', sub-divided into the 'Cyprus Regular Police' and the 'National Guard', distinguishing them from the 'Greek Cypriot irregulars', and the Turkish Cypriot 'armed groups'.[105] There was also a comparison between the 'stronghold' enclave of Louroudjina, south of Nicosia, where 4000 Turkish Cypriots had gathered, with a large proportion of armed men under the influence of TMT, and the situation in the small, predominantly Turkish Cypriot non-enclaved villages of Marki and Kochatis, 7 miles (11 km) to the west of Louroudjina, whose inhabitants were not as armed, and therefore, exposed to Greek Cypriot reprisals in case of provocations by the Turkish Cypriot fighters in Louroudjina.[106]

These indirect international humanitarian law-related references explicitly come to the surface in the concluding remarks, where in paragraph 117, reproduced here in full, it is stated that:

> 117. The practice of *abducting people* and *holding them as hostages or killing* them in *retaliation* is most reprehensible. It has been employed by both communities, but, because of the circumstances, to a considerably greater extent by Greek Cypriots. The taking of hostages is *prohibited by international law*, and the *killing of hostages* is a universally recognized *war crime*. Where such killings have occurred, they have to be branded only as cold-blooded *murders*. It is bad enough that such inhumanity can occur in these times; it is far worse that in *no instance has anyone suspected of guilt been found, charged and tried*. President Makarios has condemned these acts and I agree with him that they create throughout the world a bad image of the people and Government of Cyprus, indicating, as they seem to do, an inabil-

[103] S/5764, paras 22–23.
[104] S/5764, paras 35, 40.
[105] S/5764, paras 43–48, 64, 67.
[106] S/5764, paras 38–40.

ity on the part of governmental authority to check and control shocking excesses of this kind. (emphasis added)

UN Secretary-General's Report S/5764 was drafted and disseminated to the UNSC days after conscription for the National Guard was formally launched (Law 20/1964; published on 2 June 1964). Despite the fact that the report recognised the new conscription law as helpful towards the 'definition of status of those bearing arms in Cyprus' and would likely increase control over the 'present irregulars'—another indirect reference to international humanitarian law—the Secretary-General was cautious to question the consistency of this new legislation with UNSC Resolution 186. Apart from the new conscription legislation, he identified two additional inconsistencies with paragraph 1 in particular, according to which all UN Member States had to 'refrain from any action or threat of action likely to worsen the situation in the sovereign Republic of Cyprus'. He asserted in strong language that 'threats on landing in Cyprus by Turkish military forces' were 'certainly not consistent' with this provision, and that without questioning the right of the sovereign government of the RoC to legally import or manufacture arms, arms smuggling by both communities was 'critical', and incompatible, once again, with paragraph 1, UNSC Resolution 186.[107]

The carefully chosen wording of the report maintains consistency between the law, and the necessities of diplomatic etiquette. The activities mentioned throughout this report are relevant to a broad range of legal obligations under both *jus ad bellum* and *jus in bello*. Thus, they can be interpreted as an effort on behalf of the Secretary-General to indirectly remind the parties, the two communities, of their respective international legal obligations. Moreover, the very fact that he took caution in recognising the Republic's sovereign right to import or manufacture arms suggests that even though the UN Secretariat and the UNSC would refrain from directly invoking all relevant legal provisions, there was a strong understanding of the respective rights and obligations at all sides.

In early June 1964, international humanitarian law considerations were also a priority for the ICRC as seen in the written instructions to newly arrived ICRC delegate Pierre Boissier. Boissier was clearly instructed by the ICRC to ensure the liberation of hostages 'in conformity with common article 3 of the four 1949 Geneva Conventions', and remind 'all

[107] S/5764, para 118–120.

interested parties' of the provisions under article 15 Geneva Convention I,[108] according to which the parties to an armed conflict shall take positive action to collect the sick and wounded, protect them 'against pillage and ill-treatment', and allow for their 'removal, exchange, and transport'.

Common article 3 is silent on the temporal scope of the article's applicability. However, the literature recognises that a non-international armed conflict 'usually results from a progressive series of actions that initially do not amount to armed confrontation'.[109] Thus, following a legal assessment of the earliest days of violence described, and considering the sporadic violence ahead of 21 December 1963, it can be deduced ex post facto that many events qualified as 'internal disturbances' short of reaching the threshold of a non-international armed conflict:

> Internal disturbances are marked by serious disruption of domestic order resulting from acts of violence which do not, however, have the characteristics of an armed conflict. They encompass, for example, riots by which individuals or groups of individuals openly express their opposition, their discontent or their demands, or even isolated and sporadic acts of violence. They may take the form of fighting between different factions or against the power in place.[110]

The debate before the UNSC on 26 December, and the negotiation and conclusion of a ceasefire agreement between the two parties on 30 December 1963, arguably indicate a shift towards a non-international armed conflict, without clarification as to *when* the shift was complete.

However, intensity alone does not suffice to establish the qualification of armed violence as a non-international armed conflict, since an assessment under the criterion of organisation is also necessary. Before turning to organisation, it suffices to conclude that considering the information from the UN and ICRC reports analysed above, there is limited doubt that by early summer 1964 all interested parties were familiar with the relevant international legal framework and that intensity was of such nature that it justified the invocation of common article 3. As seen below, this view is reinforced by the nature of military preparations undertaken by the RoC in the first half of 1964.

[108] ICRC, B AG 251 049-004, Instructions to Mr. Pierre Boissier (4 June 1964).
[109] Venturini, "Temporal Scope," 69.
[110] Harroff-Tavel, "Action taken in Internal Violence," 203–204.

Assessing Organisation: The Establishment of the National Guard

Efforts by the RoC to organise the scattered, autonomous, paramilitary formations were initiated as early as January 1964, with the establishment of a General Chief of Staff Bureau, with the assistance of Greek officers who arrived on the island to support the process. A 'Defence Council' was also set up on 4 February 1964, aiming to coordinate relations between Nicosia and Athens, its members including Greek and Greek Cypriot military high-ranking officers, the President of the Republic, the President of the House of Representatives, and the Minister of Interior, among others.[111]

On 25 February 1964, the Defence Council established a 'voluntary National Guard' (Εθνοφρουρά/ *Ethnofrura*) and a Special Police Force Unit. The aim was for the Special Police Force to be a first step towards recruitment to the voluntary National Guard, and absorb members of the paramilitary formations, into this legalised voluntary semi-military formation (Defence Council, Basic Order 1, 1 March 1964).[112] According to the literature, the aim of this centralised military force was to offer adequate training and strengthen discipline, with the introduction of two 'Military Police Courts'. It is worth noting here that no corresponding law has been found on the establishment of such courts, and the law on the Military Penal Code and Procedure was not adopted until a few months later (Law 40/1964; published on 31 July 1964). Nonetheless, on 16 March 1964, four members of the voluntary force were found guilty and removed from their ranks for undertaking an armed robbery against a Turkish Cypriot. On 30 March, three days after UNFICYP had commenced its operation, an order demanding among others, the 'excellent appearance' of its members in terms of 'uniform, discipline etc.' was issued. The voluntary National Guard was formally presented to the public on 1 April, EOKA's 9th anniversary.[113] These developments suggest a gradual alignment of the Republic's forces with the criterion on 'organisation' under common article 3, and in particular, the indicators of the existence of common structure, disciplinary mechanisms, recruitment and military training, planning and coordination of armed forces.

Despite improvements in the organisational structure, concerns persisted on the voluntary force's potential inability to adequately defend the

[111] Chrysostomou, *Establishment of the National Guard*, 256–258.

[112] Chrysostomou, *Establishment of the National Guard*, 263.

[113] Chrysostomou, *Establishment of the National Guard*, 270–272.

island in the case of a Turkish invasion. Therefore, steps to upgrade the operational capacity of the National Guard were taken, which increasingly resembled a proper army, through the adoption of Law 20/1964 (2 June 1964), on the establishment of the conscription-based National Guard (*Εθνική Φρουρά/ Ethniki Frura*). Section 4 of Law 20/1964 provided for the compulsory conscription of all male 'citizens of the Republic', aged 18 to 50 years old, subject to exceptions.

The law did not expressly exclude the Turkish Cypriots from conscription, and it was only upon the issuing of the first Order for Conscripts that 'the Turks' were expressly excluded.[114] According to Hadjilyras, conscription rules did not apply strictly to the members of the smaller religious groups either, and this vague policy was followed until 1980, when it was officially decided that there would be no compulsory conscription for their members.[115] On 4 June, an additional relevant law was published, which merged the Police and the Gendarmerie into a single Police Force (Law 21/1964), according to its Preamble, due to the 'recent events' and in order to improve the forces' efficiency under a unified administration.

Neither law led to substantial debate in the Plenary sessions of the House of Representatives. The importance given to the National Guard bill, however, is evident by the fact that it was discussed jointly for three consecutive days by the Parliamentary Committees on Defence, Finance, and Legal Affairs. A considerable length of time compared to usual practice, as inferred by the publicly available plenary minutes.[116] Moreover, these deliberations were open to all MPs, regardless of whether they were actual members of the three committees discussing the bill. It is important to clarify that the National Guard did not replace the constitutional Cyprus Army. Rather, the National Guard absorbed the formal army, through the secondment of army officers to the National Guard; a process that was only formalised in 1966 through the Army of the Republic (Composition, Enlistment and Discipline) (Amendment) Law of 1966 (Law 77/1966).

Laws 20/1964 and 21/1964 are the first in a series of legislative acts that directly contradicted the black letter of the Constitution, as discussed more extensively in the next chapter. The dissatisfaction of the Turkish Cypriot community was expressed through a letter from Kutchuk to Makarios on 30 May, wherein the former attempted to raise a veto against

[114] Chrysostomou, *Establishment of the National Guard*, 299.
[115] Hadjilyras, *The Religious Groups*, 115.
[116] HORM, Session 1963–1964, 1 June 1964.

the two laws. The letter, according to Chrysostomou, was simply ignored by the Cypriot government.[117]

The legislative amendments concerning the RoC security forces aimed at enabling the implementation of a complete defence plan presented by Georgios Grivas on 3 May 1964, which included the obtaining of additional equipment, and the setting up of training centres and military barracks. Amendments to the Criminal Code which prohibited the publication of information regarding any defence-related preparations were also made (Law 41/1964). Other measures included the passing of a Military Penal Code (Law 40/1964), and a Law on the establishment of a Civil Defence (Law 42/1964; now repealed). All three laws were published in the Official Gazette of the Republic on 31 July 1964, and they indicate directly the intensive preparation for war.

By mid-June 1964, the UN reported that there were 5000 persons employed in the 'Cyprus Regular Police', the merged police and gendarmerie, and 15,000 volunteer national guards, some of whom 'under very uncertain Government control'.[118] In parallel, the Greek government, with the consent of Makarios, organised the sending of an initial number of 2000 additional Greek soldiers, whose number by 14 July 1964 increased to some 5000 individuals. They arrived on the island gradually and in secret, often presenting fake RoC travel documents. The line of command was linked directly to the Ministry of National Defence of the Kingdom of Greece. Something that led to coordination as well as tension between the Greek Army and the Cypriot National Guard.[119] The practical problems were exasperated by Grivas' return to Cyprus on 12 June 1964, for the first time since he departed from Cyrus upon the end of the EOKA emergency, leading to a series of military controversies.

Considering the criterion of 'organisation', it has repeatedly been stated that fighting between irregular armed groups suffices to qualify a violent situation as a non-international armed conflict under the 1949 Geneva Conventions. Nevertheless, amidst the growing intensity, the Greek Cypriot community—as representative of the State's recognised government—started organising its military forces more diligently in February 1964. By April, the St. Hilarion operation proved a prima facie capacity of the irregular, yet government-supported, armed groups to sustain military

[117] Chrysostomou, *Establishment of the National Guard*, 291–293.
[118] S/5764, paras 43, 44.
[119] Chrysostomou, *Establishment of the National Guard*, 293–294.

operations and use military tactics. As the months moved on, further steps were taken to improve the command structure of its forces, to organise their Headquarters, retain control over specific territory, recruit soldiers, and organise military training. The process was concluded with the adoption of the laws merging the Police and the Gendarmerie, and the final act in the establishment of the National Guard, with the adoption of Law 20/1964. As already discussed, the lengthy sessions of the Parliamentary Committees debating Law 20/1964, indicate that international legal considerations had contributed to the whole enterprise.

Even though a distinction between the 'voluntary' and 'conscription-based' National Guard exists for most of the first half of 1964, the difference is of limited practical significance, since what differed was merely the method of recruitment, with the 'voluntary National Guard' being as much under governmental control as the conscription-based National Guard. This is in fact a matter of domestic law, since under international humanitarian law, and more specifically article 3 of the Regulations Respecting the Laws and Customs of War and Land, annexed to the 1907 Hague Convention IV, each State enjoys a level of autonomy in how to best organise the structure of its armed forces.[120] This is supported by the Geneva provision under article 4(A)(2) Geneva Convention III 1949 on the protection of Prisoners of War, which entitles 'militias and members of other volunteer corps' to the same protection under Geneva Convention III, in case they are captured by enemy forces.[121]

On the Turkish Cypriot side, the fact that less information is available makes such detailed assessment significantly more difficult. We know that the Headquarters of the Turkish Cypriot irregular forces were in Nicosia, but it has not been possible to establish the level of efficacy and collaboration between the different units. Neither has there been clear information on planning, the carrying out of operations, and any potential disciplinary rules and mechanisms. What we do know is that by summer 1964 the Turkish Cypriot leadership had control over a considerable proportion of the Turkish Cypriot population within the enclaves, but their level of organisation only improved from 1965 onwards.

It must be noted that regarding the Turkish Cypriot irregular forces, some of the indicators under the 'organisation' criterion were not fulfilled, partly due to the government's tight control over the items entering the

[120] Ipsen, "Combatants and Non-combatants," 96.

[121] Watts, "Who is a Prisoner of War?" 895–896.

enclaves in the form of humanitarian assistance. These included objects that could be used for the sewing of uniforms, such as camouflage netting, khaki cloth, studs for boots, and 'woollen clothing (if capable of military use)', as well as materials that could be used for the improvement of military infrastructure, like ammonium nitrate, fuel in large quantities, radio sets, iron poles and rods, cables and wire, among other items.[122]

In addition to the organisational issues mentioned above, most of the indicators under 'intensity' did apply to the regular and irregular forces on both sides without distinction. These include the increase in armed clashes, the spread of control over territory, the distribution of weapons, attention of and the adoption of resolutions by the UNSC, displacement, the besieging and shelling of towns or areas within them, the number of casualties, ceasefire agreements, and attempts of representatives from international organisations, here UNFICYP and the ICRC, to facilitate the negotiation and enforce ceasefire agreements. Hence, taking all of the above indicators together, it does appear that the ICRC's criteria of 'organisation' and 'intensity' were gradually fulfilled cumulatively in the spring of 1964 and by summer the latest, a non-international armed conflict was underway at full force.

The Tylliria Air Raids: The Internationalisation of the Conflict?

Throughout the first half of 1964 the USA unsuccessfully urged the Turkish Cypriot officials to return to their official governmental posts. At the time, there was amble sympathy for the Turkish Cypriots, but it was estimated that before long UN officials would turn their favour to the recognised government of the Republic. On 27 March 1964, all Turkish Cypriot ministers were replaced with Greek Cypriots, leading the US officials to conclude that the impasse had reached a 'point of no return'.[123]

When tension reached alarming levels in early June 1964, US Secretary of State Dean Rusk informed US President Johnson that Kutchuk intended to declare an independent State on Cyprus and ask Turkey to intervene.[124] In a letter to Turkish Prime Minister Inonu dated 5 June 1964, Johnson expressed the USA's disapproval towards any potential use of force by

[122] S/6102, Appendix to Annex II – List of prohibited materials (7 October 1964).

[123] Nicolet, "Turkish Cypriot Failure in 1964," 64.

[124] LBJ Presidential Library, Telephone conversation between President Johnson and Dean Rusk #3623 (4 June 1964).

Turkey, since the right to take unilateral action, presumably under the ToG, was 'not yet applicable'.[125] The letter did prevent a military intervention successfully, but it was perceived by Turkish officials as a serious interference with Turkey's sovereign rights. Despite American estimations that this was the 'climax of [the] Cyprus crisis',[126] the situation deteriorated further in the following two months, despite ongoing negotiations on a new plan, the 'Acheson Plan', which collapsed in Geneva on 28 August 1964.

The coastal region of 'Tylliria' (Dillirga), is located in Nicosia District along the north-western coast of Cyprus, encompassing a number of villages of originally mixed and mono-communal population. The region includes the Kokkina (Erenkoy) enclave, which today remains inaccessible to RoC authorities, despite the fact that it is detached and only accessible by sea from the rest of the occupied northern part of the island. From 1963 to 1974, this was the only sea-coast 'exclave' the Turkish Cypriot leadership controlled, which given its geographical position served as a 'bridgehead' for the import of arms, supplies and fighters from Turkey. Its important strategic position was further enhanced by its proximity to two 'particularly sensitive areas'; the enclaves of 'Limnitis' (Yeshilirmak) and Lefka (Lefke). Lefka alone had concentrated some 3000 Turkish Cypriots, among whom were 750 to 900 TMT fighters. All three enclaves had a combined total of 1450–1600 fighters.[127]

Sporadic fighting between Turkish Cypriot irregulars and the National Guard had already started in the region on 16 June 1964. UNFICYP negotiated the movement of posts and fortifications between the two sides throughout the month of July, and reported on the building up of arms and equipment on both sides.[128] With tension growing, on 16 July 1964 the ICRC sent a telegram to the RoC Minister of Foreign Affairs, to remind him of the Republic's duty to facilitate the distribution of and free access to humanitarian assistance under the Geneva Conventions and relevant resolutions of the Red Cross international conferences.[129] The telegram displeased the government, since it gave the impression that the

[125] Lindon B Johnson and Ismet Inonu, "Document" (June 1964).

[126] Office of the Historian, *Vol. XVI.* Telegram from the Embassy in Cyprus to the Department of State (6 June 1964).

[127] S/5950, paras 64–87, 96–99.

[128] UNA, S-0869-0003-08-00001, *Items in Peace-keeping operations, Cyprus.*

[129] ICRC, B AG 251 049-006, Telegram from Pierre Boissier in Nicosia to ICRC, Geneva (16 July 1964).

ICRC accused the RoC of ignoring the Conventions. The resulting diplomatic tensions were of such severity that ICRC delegate Pierre Boissier requested from the ICRC Headquarters in Geneva not to give any publicity to said telegram.[130]

On 25 July, Boisser wrote to Geneva that 'conflict [was] always possible', yet there were almost no preparations towards the application of the Geneva Conventions. One example was the lack of dissemination of identity cards to medical personnel, to make them easily identifiable and protected in case of active warfare. He further informed that he disclosed to the 'Greek authorities' the coordinates of the Turkish Red Crescent field hospital in the Turkish Cypriot sector of Nicosia, presumably to ensure its protection from potential attacks by the National Guard and/or the Greek army. In closing, he asked for the shipment of six more copies of the Geneva and Hague Conventions to Cyprus.[131]

By late July, the Turkish Cypriots had control over five villages of Tylliria; Kokkina, Mansoura, Alevga, Selain t' Api (Selladi tou Appi, Selçuklu), and Ayios Theodoros (Nicosia district). They were surrounded by two National Guard companies through posts installed in the nearby villages of Piyenia (Pigenia), Mosphileri, Kato Pyrgos, and Pakhy Ammos (Pachyammos). These were reinforced with additional troops and heavy equipment from 3 to 7 August, leading to a total of 2000 soldiers, compared to 500 Turkish Cypriot fighters within the Kokkina enclave, who were the direct concern of the National Guard. A company of UNFICYP troops was also deployed nearby.[132] Two Greek patrol vessels, 'FAETHON' and 'ARION', had also been present off the coast of Mansoura village since late July.[133]

Following the month-long accumulation of force, the first exchange of fire between the National Guard and Turkish Cypriot fighters occurred on 5 August. During the same days shootings were recorded also in other regions. For instance, in the afternoon of 6 August, 50 soldiers of the Turkish National Contingent entered the walled city of Nicosia, and by the evening UNFICYP recorded the movement of 100 armed National Guardsmen in the same direction.[134]

[130] ICRC, B AG 251 049-005.02, Note 106 – Activités de la délégation (20 July 1964).

[131] ICRC, B AG 251 049-005.02, Note 108 - Activités de la délégation (25 July 1964).

[132] S/5950 paras 65–68.

[133] Savvides, "Chrysouli Military Base."

[134] UNA, S-0869-0003-08-00001, Summary of Military Action in Cyprus, 5–8 August 1964.

Despite immediate requests for a ceasefire by UNFICYP, fighting continued. According to evidence submitted later by Turkey, UNFICYP recorded fire from 'A Greek Cypriot patrol boat' towards Kokkina at 4:50 a.m. on 7 August. In the afternoon of 8 August, Turkish aircraft started attacking RoC positions across Tylliria and at open sea. 'FAETHON' was completely burned down, resulting in the killing of five of its Greek crew members, and the grievous wounding of everyone else. On the Turkish side, an aircraft exploded mid-air, and even though the pilot managed to eject himself from the plane, he was caught by RoC forces. He eventually died in hospital, from where his body was returned to Turkey through UNFICYP's good offices.[135] He is the only known Turkish citizen held by the Republic as a prisoner of war under article 4 of Geneva Convention III on the protection of prisoners of war.[136]

In the meantime, Turkish Cypriot fighters in the nearby villages retreated into Kokkina, and about 200 Turkish Cypriot civilians were evacuated to the nearby Greek Cypriot village of Kato Pyrgos, where a camp for displaced civilians had been hastily set up. The civilians, however, requested to be transported to the Turkish Cypriot town-enclave of Lefka instead. Despite initial agreement by the government to facilitate the move, government assistance was withdrawn after only the first group of 40 individuals made the transfer, on the basis that the Republic could not guarantee the civilians' safety while passing through the Greek Cypriot village of Xeros. A rather unconvincing argument from a legal perspective, since armed forces have a duty to protect civilians during armed conflict, regardless of the side to which they belong. As the remaining displaced civilians continued fearing for their safety in Kato Pyrgos, they were subsequently transported back into the Kokkina enclave, allegedly upon their own request.[137] This seriously jeopardised the application of the principle of distinction between civilians and combatants under one of the earliest and now customary rules of international humanitarian law, according to which combatants are afforded a lower standard of protection and must therefore, be distinguished from civilians at all times.[138] The decision to transfer them back was also contrary to article 8 of Geneva Convention IV

[135] S/5950, para 78.
[136] Watts, "Who is a Prisoner of War?" 889.
[137] S/5950, paras 76–81.
[138] Henckaerts and Doswald-Beck, *Customary Study: Practice*, 3–4.

on the protection of civilians, according to which no civilians can renounce the rights secured for them by the Convention.[139]

The Turkish air raids according to American estimations, engaged about 65 F-100 planes, initially attacking with rockets and machine guns. On the second day, on 9 August, the attacks were disproportionately more severe, with the employment of heavier weaponry, including napalm bombs.[140] On that day, the village-hospital in Pomos that carried the Red Cross emblem, was bombed by the Turkish Air Force, leading to the death of one doctor, four nurses, and six patients.[141] The ICRC did recognise a potential breach of the Geneva Conventions by the Turkish Army, adding that the plane may had been targeting a Greek Cypriot tank positioned against the wall of the hospital. According to the same report, the Greek Cypriot side admitted the position of the tank, but 'in their defence, the Greeks affirmed that the tank was so well-camouflaged that the Turkish aviation could not have noticed it'.[142] From a legal perspective, one should not be carried away by the phrase 'in their defence', since the positioning of the tank, or any other military equipment, in the vicinity of a hospital or another protected building constitutes a breach of the Geneva Conventions in itself. The description of this incident serves as rare evidence of alleged war crimes committed by each side. Moreover, the intentional positioning of the tank at that spot, if proven, would have given rise to suspicions of using the hospital and the protected persons within it, as a human shield, which is another act strongly prohibited under customary international humanitarian law.[143]

Examples usually used in the literature do not state clearly whether 'civil objects' or 'protected zones' can establish a 'human shield' to protect movable military targets, like a tank.[144] This however, appears to constitute State practice, according to the military manuals consulted in the

[139] D'Argent, "Non-Renunciation."

[140] Office of the Historian, *Vol. XVI*. Telephone Conversation Between President Johnson and the Under Secretary of State (Ball) (9 August 1964).

[141] ICRC, B AG 251 049-005.02, Consequences of the battles of 6,7,8,9, August 1964 (2 September 1964); PIO, Turkish Aircraft Raid Hospital Ambulances and Civilians at Pomos (9 August 1964).

[142] ICRC, B AG 251 049-005.02, Consequences of the battles of 6,7,8,9, August 1964 (2 September 1964).

[143] Henckaerts and Doswald-Beck, *Customary Study: Rules*, 337–338.

[144] Sivakumaran, *Law of Non-International Armed Conflict*, 421.

ICRC's customary international humanitarian law study,[145] and to have been also the view of the ICRC at the time, as inferred from the report. The ICRC's customary international humanitarian law study concludes that 'the use of human shields requires an intentional colocation of military objectives and civilians or persons *hors de combat* with the specific intent of trying to prevent the targeting of those military objectives'.[146] It is for this reason that in the ICRC's report the National Guard's affirmation that the tank was so well-camouflaged that the Turkish pilots could not have noticed, is highly problematic from a legal perspective. On the other hand, if the tank was indeed so well-camouflaged and could not have been seen from air, would suggest that what the Turkish pilots aimed at was the hospital. The ICRC concluded that it would have been impossible to establish the truth.[147]

The incident in Pomos points to a potential breach of the Geneva Conventions by both Turkey and Cyprus, giving rise to claims under international criminal law. Under the Geneva rules, one party's misconduct does not justify the misconduct of the other party. Today, it is a recognised rule under customary international humanitarian law that parties to both international armed conflicts and non-international armed conflicts must 'take all feasible precautions to protect the civilian population and civilian objects under their control against the effects of attacks'.[148] From the archives it is obvious that in the case of the Tylliria Raids the ICRC had paid close attention to such details, and the description of this incident in the archive constitutes a rare attempt by the ICRC to directly apply international humanitarian law in Cyprus.

Apart from the number of casualties reported by the Greek Cypriot side, the exact number of casualties during the Tylliria battles and air raids remains unknown. Indicative of the general lack of clarity is the fact that the grounds of the hospital in Pomos was one of the sites excavated as recently as 2019 in search of missing persons,[149] raising serious questions regarding the application of the international humanitarian rules concerning the treatment of the dead and the duty to account for missing persons.

[145] Henckaerts and Doswald-Beck, *Customary Study: Practice*, 2287.

[146] Henckaerts and Doswald-Beck, *Customary Study: Rules*, 340.

[147] ICRC, B AG 251 049-005.02, Consequences of the battles of 6,7,8,9, August 1964 (2 September 1964).

[148] Henckaerts and Doswald-Beck, *Customary Study: Rules*, 68.

[149] Christou, "Excavations in September."

A core humanitarian issue which in the following decades also became highly politicised on each side.[150]

On 9 August, Makarios gave an ultimatum that unless the air attacks stopped by 3:30 p.m., he would give an order for an attack against all Turkish Cypriot villages across the island. Meanwhile, the Greeks were considering the deployment of their heavily reinforced contingent, and the Cyprus Ministry of Foreign Affairs informed the USA that the Soviet Union was ready to intervene on the side of the RoC.[151] A major concern among US officials was the lack of willingness of States providing peacekeepers for UNFICYP to defend the island in case of a Turkish invasion, and President Johnson was considering all possible scenarios and outcomes, including 'to cordon off the island and let the thing settle down itself'.[152]

The armed violence in Tylliria inevitably triggered new deliberations at the UNSC, for a fifth time in eight months, since 26 December 1963. The legal arguments raised by Ambassador Rossides focused on the use of force by Turkey in breach of article 2(4) of the UN Charter, firmly distinguishing between the 'Turkish Cypriot community' and the 'Turkish rebels', affirming that it was the latter who were the target of the National Guard, in an effort to suppress 'the *rebellion*' taking place in Cyprus. A term he used repeatedly during this UNSC meeting.[153] The lengthy meeting at the UNSC concluded on 9 August 1964 with the passing of UNSC Resolution 193(1964), which expressed concern 'at the serious deterioration of the situation in Cyprus', and 'call[ed] for an immediate cease-fire by all concerned'.[154] Despite the ceasefire, 26 breaches were recorded from 15 August to 8 September. These included 11 cases of fire by Government forces, 14 cases of fire initiated by Turkish Cypriot fighters, 11 cases of fire of undetermined origin, as well as 23 cases of overflight, of which four were by Turkish aircraft, one by Greek aircraft, and 18 by aircraft of undetermined origin.[155] The most serious among the above

[150] Iakovou and Kornioti, "Missing Persons."

[151] Chrysostomou, "The Tylliria Battles."

[152] Office of the Historian, *Vol. XVI*. Telephone Conversation Between President Johnson and the Under Secretary of State (Ball) (9 August 1964).

[153] S/PV.1142, paras 90–112.

[154] UNSC Res 193(1964), Preambular paras 1 and 2.

[155] S/5950, para 92.

incidents was a machine-gun air attack by two Turkish airplanes on Polis wounding ten civilians on the morning of 10 August.[156]

In spite of the above breaches of the ceasefire, Resolution 193(1964) ended the most violent cycle of events pre-1974, which had commenced on 21 December 1963. The debate in New York, was one of the few instances where it can be deduced from the terminology used that in the eyes of the RoC government the island was going through a 'rebellion'; the first phase of a civil war under classical international law. Was this, however, 'just' a rebellion, or was it in fact an 'insurgency', as written years later by other officials?[157] Were legal considerations taken into account in the choice of specific terminology, at all? And did the Turkish Republic's direct engagement in hostilities in August 1964 change the status of the ongoing armed conflict from a non-international to an international one?

Legal Questions Deriving from Turkey's 1964 Intervention

The period from 21 December 1963 to 9 August 1964 can be roughly divided into three sub-periods; (1) the period of 'chaos' from 21 December 1963 to around 1 April 1964, when no formal State military force was active, (2) the period when the National Guard became operational, in its voluntary and conscription-based formations, roughly from 1 April 1964 up to 6 August 1964, and (3) the period of Turkish Air Force bombings in Tylliria, from 6 to 9 August 1964. Each of these periods give rise to intertwined legal questions on use of force, intervention, and conflict qualification. The Tylliria events particularly so, since they brought an 'international' element to the until then internal violence.

Existing literature often refers to a 'proxy war' throughout this period, emphasising Turkey's role in the establishment of TMT in 1958, and her constant material support to the Turkish Cypriot leadership.[158] On the other hand, one cannot disregard the fact that the other two Guarantor Powers, Greece and the UK, also played a role, albeit as seen their approach up to this point was considerably more subtle. Whereas the UK through its involvement in peacekeeping and in the offer of humanitarian assistance could easily retain an equal distance between the two communities on the

[156] S/5950, para 86.

[157] Tornaritis, *Constitutional and Legal Problems*, 20; Chrysostomides, *The Republic of Cyprus*, 92–93.

[158] Lovell, "Settling Protracted Social Conflicts," 19.

ground, Greece's obvious siding with the Greek Cypriot community was subjected to less legal limitations, since the Greek Cypriot community retained control of the formally recognised government of the Cypriot Republic, and with it the right to formally request assistance by other States. Terms such as 'proxy war', that have no legal weight yet have made it into the analytical vocabulary of the Cyprus conflict(s), while useful in describing a factual situation, do not serve a legal purpose. For decades Turkish and Greek interference in Cyprus have been at the epicentre of a mixture of political and legal arguments on each side, failing to provide a satisfactory legal analysis under the international/non-international armed conflict binary, or the distinction between *jus ad bellum* and *jus in bello;* use of force and conduct of hostilities, respectively.

As already explained, the prohibition of 'threat or use of force' under article 2(4) of the UN Charter, is intertwined with the customary principle of non-intervention under public international law. Though the only exceptions to the prohibition of the use of force may apply under articles 51 and 53 of the UN Charter, on the right to self-defence and on the regional enforcement measures respectively, the general rule remains that Turkey had no right to use force against the sovereign RoC. This is reinforced by the fact that the Turkish Cypriot community, as a non-state actor in the conflict, was not entitled to invite another State to intervene on their behalf.[159] Neither did Turkey have a right to intervene, despite the fact that Turkey constantly maintained during this period and thereafter, that she had a right to unilateral military intervention under article IV ToG, in spite of the plethora of voices to the contrary, from Hans Kelsen in 1959 onwards.

In his book, Necatigil expressed the view that justification under self-defence and article 51 of the UN Charter, would have been more suitable than an argument based on the ToG, in this instance, were it not for the 'conceptual hurdle' of the 'nexus of nationality'.[160] In other words, notwithstanding any feelings of proximity to Turkey by many Turkish Cypriots, Turkey could not intervene for their protection, since they were nationals (i.e. citizens) of another State. Moreover, in his analysis he refers to Turkey's use of force in August 1964 as a 'limited military action', but the word 'limited' is of no legal significance. Diplomatic language has

[159] Gray, *Use of Force*, 67–68, 105–107; Kritsiotis, "Theorizing International Law on Force."

[160] Necatigil, *The Cyprus Question*, 42–43.

developed a variety of terms to refer to an armed attack (intervention, invasion, or peace operation). As Klabbers observes, this is necessary to allow 'wiggle room' for political settlements, and it allows one to evade legal accountability it is hereby added, but judicial institutions focus on whether a specific behaviour is justifiable or not.[161] From that perspective, it still stands that the prohibition of the use of force is absolute, and not subject to different degrees.

Once an armed conflict is underway, no matter how short in duration and *regardless of who used force lawfully or unlawfully*, all parties involved are obliged to take all measures to protect those afforded protection under international humanitarian law. In that regard, in 1972, in a rare instance of invocation of international humanitarian law by the RoC pre-1974, Tornaritis claimed that during the Tylliria bombings Turkey had acted in breach of articles 16 (General protection of wounded and sick civilians), 18 (Protection of Hospitals), 20 (Protection of Hospital Staff), and 21 (Land and sea transport of wounded and sick) of Geneva Convention IV on the protection of civilians,[162] suggesting that the event constituted an international armed conflict. The statement, however, left outstanding the question of what the relationship of that international armed conflict was to the non-international armed conflict involving the RoC and the insurgent elements of the Turkish Cypriot community.

An 'internationalised armed conflict' refers to the process of transformation of an armed conflict from a non-international to an international one. The term is not to be understood as an intermediate third category of armed conflict.[163] Even though the notion of the transformation of a civil war into an inter-State war existed already in the eighteenth century, the earliest reference 'to internationalize a war' is traced to 1865 and Webster's American Dictionary of the English Language.[164] However, the first systematic study on conflict internationalisation was undertaken a century later by Law Professor, and as of 1980 ICRC member, Dietrich Schindler.[165] Schindler based his conclusions on observations drawn primarily from the Vietnam War, but in the 1970s he expanded his research to Bangladesh, Cyprus, and Lebanon, among others.

[161] Klabbers, "What's the Difference?" 505.
[162] Tornaritis, *Constitutional and Legal Problems*, 20.
[163] Harrison, "Internationalized Armed Conflicts," 1202.
[164] Mačák, *Internationalized Armed Conflicts*, 24.
[165] Schindler, "Internationalized Internal Armed Conflicts."

According to Schindler, there were two separate views on conflict internationalisation in the 1960s. The first stating that a civil war would become an international armed conflict once a foreign State intervenes militarily, and the second, holding that an internationalised civil war should be broken down into its international and non-international components.[166] When Schindler was writing in 1982 the dominant position was the latter, under which one had to maintain the international/non-international distinction, and examine an ongoing non-international armed conflict separately from the more recent international armed conflict, which started in parallel at some point in time. Like many current commentators, in his analysis Schindler would then demonstrate numerous alternative theoretical scenarios or combinations of alliances between the parties, to show how international humanitarian law should apply in each case.[167] Following a similar approach and the dominant logic of the 1960s, it can be concluded that Turkey's air attacks from 6 to 9 August 1964, would constitute a 'Four-Day War' between the RoC and Turkey, which was interconnected but *legally* distinguished, from the ongoing conflict between the RoC government and the Turkish Cypriot separatists.

Had the same facts taken place today however, the picture would be rather different. During the ICJ's *Nicaragua* judgment, and the 1990s cases before the International Criminal Tribunals for Rwanda and Yugoslavia, there were additional clarifications to Schindler's conclusions, especially on issues of State responsibility and individual criminal responsibility during such internationalised armed conflicts. The case of *Nicaragua* would have been of particular relevance to Cyprus had it come along about two decades earlier. In 1986 the ICJ stated that 'prohibited intervention' included *both* military action and 'indirect form of support for subversive or terrorist armed activities within another State'. This would include the type of support Turkey offered to the Turkish Cypriot community. Secondly, such 'forms of action' were 'wrongful in the light of both the principle of non-use of force, and that of non-intervention'.[168] Thus, had the *Nicaragua* judgement preceded Turkey's intervention both

[166] Schindler, "Internationalized Internal Armed Conflicts," 256.

[167] Schindler, "Internationalized Internal Armed Conflicts," 256–261; Mačák, *Internationalized Armed Conflicts*, 242–244.

[168] *Military and Paramilitary Activities in and against Nicaragua (Nicaragua v United States of America),* Judgement (Merits) [1986] ICJ Rep 14, para 205.

in the 1960s and the 1970s, the RoC would have additional legal arguments favouring its position.

Furthermore, according to Mačák's recent and detailed study on 'internationalised' armed conflicts, for an international armed conflict to 'absorb' an ongoing non-international armed conflict, there would be a need for the two 'allied conflict parties' to forego any autonomy they may have and act 'with a single use of force'.[169] Subject to additional research, it could be the case that this did happen in July and August 1974. In August 1964, however, Turkey only undertook a series of attacks from air, while the Turkish Cypriot fighters acted independently on land. Thus, whatever in kind support arrived from Turkey, there is little evidence of the Turkish Cypriot leadership and the Turkish Republic acting as a 'single force'. Admittedly, the constant active involvement of the Turkish Embassy in Nicosia, which is discussed in the following Chapter, prevents the drawing of any safe conclusions. Thus, it is the arrival of Turkish troops *on* the island and their mingling with local fighters on 20 July 1974 that could be seen more clearly as the moment of completion of an 'internationalisation' in the sense described by Mačák. This analysis is rather theoretical. Nonetheless, it helps illustrate the significance of drawing the missing factual and legal links between the events discussed in this book and the events of 1974.

Lastly, the events of August 1964 raised also important questions regarding the continuation of the validity of the 1960 treaties of Guarantee and Alliance. Even though the abrogation of these treaties was one of the political priorities of the Greek Cypriot leadership at the London Conference of February 1964,[170] Elihu Lauterpacht supported that both treaties remained in force.[171] This was despite the fact that the RoC had stated already in December 1963 that it considered the treaties void.[172] Another effort to denounce the same treaties followed in April 1964, in a letter from Makarios to Turkish Prime Minister Inonu. The declaration was accepted by Greece, but not by Turkey and the UK.[173] After the Tylliria events the issue resurfaced at the end of August, when the Greek and Turkish contingents were due to undertake a troop rotation and the

[169] Mačák, *Internationalized Armed Conflicts*, 87–104.

[170] Clerides, *My Deposition Vol. 1*, 203–209.

[171] Soulioti, *Fettered Independence: Documents*, 267.

[172] Clerides, *My Deposition Vol. 2*, 95–112.

[173] Nicolet, "Turkish Cypriot Failure in 1964," 65.

Cypriot government refused to allow the rotation of the Turkish troops, on the basis that following Turkey's attack the ToA was no longer in force.[174]

Under the customary law of treaties there is a general presumption against the unilateral termination of a treaty by one of the parties.[175] This customary rule was later inserted in article 54 of the 1969 Vienna Convention on the Law of Treaties, under which a treaty is only to be terminated either in conformity with the provisions of the treaty concerning its termination, or following a consensus to do so among *all* contracting States. According to article 56 of the same Convention, there are two exceptions to this general rule. Denunciation or withdrawal are allowed either (i) in cases where it can be established successfully that the parties implied the possibility of accepting denunciation or withdrawal, or (ii) when such possibility is implied by the nature of the treaty.

Neither the ToG nor the ToA contain provisions concerning their termination. The lack of termination clauses in treaties relating to the sovereignty of post-colonial States was normal practice, as their termination would have led to instability in the relations of European powers.[176] In Cyprus that would be the interests of the UK, Greece and Turkey, but also the broader power-dynamics in the context of the Cold War. Considering that both the ToG and the ToA are embedded in the constitutional architecture of the Republic, it is difficult to prove an implied acceptance of denunciation or withdrawal by all parties.

Since treaty law and customary international law are unable to resolve the issue, one then must turn to the 'general principles of law' in search of an answer. In this case, each community relied on two different, diametrically opposed principles. The Turkish Cypriots argued that under the *pacta sunt servanda* principle, the principle underlining contractual relations, the Greek Cypriots had already agreed to the London-Zurich Agreements and the three treaties and therefore, were bound by their obligations under the Agreements. The Greek Cypriots, on the other side, turned to the *rebus* sic *stantibus* principle, according to which a fundamental change in circumstances would repeal a previously made Agreement.[177] Paragraph 1 of article 62 of the Vienna Convention on the Law of Treaties

[174] S/5920, para 3.
[175] McNair, The Law of Treaties, 493–494.
[176] Chatterjee, "The Legacy of Bandung," 664.
[177] Adams and Cottrell, *Cyprus Between East and West*, 78–79.

generally restricts the application of the *rebus* principle, stating that 'A fundamental change of circumstances [...] may not be invoked as a ground for terminating or withdrawing the treaty', subject to minimal exceptions. As an alternative to denunciation, in cases of a 'fundamental change of circumstances' the Convention allows a treaty's suspension (article 62(3)), offering the parties time to work towards a resolution to the dispute, for an 'uncertain duration' that later may become of a permanent nature and eventually lead to termination.[178]

Whether Turkey's attack on Cyprus in August 1964, was a serious enough change of circumstances to justify the application of the *rebus* sic *stantibus* principle to the treaties of Guarantee and Alliance is a valid question. The further one looks back at the development of public international law, the broader is the view that treaties are abrogated with the outbreak of hostilities. By the first half of the twentieth century, however, McNair was of the view that 'war' does not end treaty obligations previously assumed by the parties to the conflict as such. He did add, however, that political treaties, including treaties of alliance, are generally considered abrogated with the outbreak of war.[179] Such was the case when the UK annexed Cyprus from the Ottoman Empire in 1914, since the secretly agreed-upon alliance of the 1878 Nicosia Treaty was abrogated once Britain and the Ottoman Empire joined WWI on opposing sides. With this example in mind, it could indeed be argued that there is enough reason to justify that the ToA between Cyprus and Turkey was abrogated in 1964, and if not in 1964, then certainly in 1974. Indeed, since 1974 the two States are formally in a frozen state of war, without any diplomatic relations, and with Turkey not recognising the RoC in most international fora. However, before giving a final answer, one would still need to consider the position and practice of Greece as the third party to the ToA.

The RoC did try to argue against the validity of the ToG and the ToA also outside the context of the military developments on the island. The year 1964 coincided with the drafting of the 1969 Vienna Convention on the Law of Treaties. There, the RoC raised the argument that according to the draft Vienna Convention the ToG was null and void, since it conflicted with *jus cogens* norms (i.e. absolute rules) of public international law. According to Ambassador Jacovides, who from 1982 to 1996 held a highly prestigious appointment as member of the International Law

[178] Giegerich, "Article 62," 1174.
[179] McNair, *The Law of Treaties*, 696–703.

Commission, the ToG conflicted with the principles of sovereignty, non-intervention, peaceful settlement of disputes and the prohibition of the use of force.[180] The merit of the legal argument was overall accepted by commentators then and later.[181] However, as seen from the above analysis, international law does not favour the termination of treaties already in existence, and the argument is of little factual importance. To date there has been no formal and binding pronouncement on the matter. Considering that elements of all three treaties are still being implemented today at least to a certain degree, it appears that the treaties are at the very least suspended. If that is the case, then whether they are to be terminated or revised will depend on a potential future resolution of the Cyprus Question. As McNair had written of such situations, it is 'a matter for politics and diplomacy',[182] not law.

In September 1964, U Thant stated that UNFICYP found itself 'in the midst of a bitter civil war'.[183] To what extent this was a political or legal statement, or both, is impossible to determine. It is worth noting here that in principle, the role of the UN Secretary-General involves carefully treading the path between law and diplomacy,[184] assuming that the two can be easily distinguished from one another. Nevertheless, the statements of UN Secretary-Generals have always carried varying degrees of persuasive authority, subject to the power balances within the Security Council and each Secretary-General's approach to the tasks at hand.[185] It appears that at the time, at least at a political level, there was a clear understanding that the severity of the situation had reached the legal threshold of 'civil war'.

Due to the continuous tension, the initial release from service for the voluntary members of the National Guard was postponed from early August to November 1964,[186] but even then, according to the UN, those men remained available as 'Home Guards', a rural militia active in their

[180] Jacovides, *International Law and Diplomacy*, 43–54; Zotiades, *Intervention by treaty right*, 25–35.

[181] Chrysostomides, *The Republic of Cyprus*, 72–73; Crawford, *The Creation of States*, 167–168.

[182] McNair, *The Law of Treaties*, 534–535.

[183] S/5950, para 221.

[184] Chesterman, *Secretary or General?*.

[185] Johnstone, "The Role of the UN Secretary-General," 447–451.

[186] Chrysostomou, *Establishment of the National Guard*, 305.

respective villages.[187] Thus, their formal release from duty in late 1964 could hardly be assessed as a positive step towards demilitarisation. In the meantime, the Republic had to deal also with internal issues of law and order. One last major development in the turbulent 1964 took place in November that year, with a fundamental impact on the constitutional functionality of the Republic.

Constitutional Survival Through Necessity

The lack of participation of the Turkish Cypriots in the State apparatus since late December 1963, either out of personal choice or due to the restrictions imposed to them by the Turkish Cypriot leadership, further deteriorated the performance of the already dysfunctional State mechanism, including the administration of justice. Thus, the legal principle *salus populi suprema lex*, the well-being of the people is the supreme law, was relied upon by the Legislature in July 1964, and the Judiciary five months later, to ensure the 'constitutional survival'[188] of the RoC.

According to the UN, initially both sides engaged in a practice of arbitrary arrests 'motivated by non-legal considerations'.[189] By the end of 1964, there was a reduction in such incidents, following instructions by the government to the police to stop arresting Turkish Cypriots upon the mere suspicion of their involvement in the ongoing violence. In some cases, it was the Courts that assumed a corrective role by discharging wrongfully arrested Turkish Cypriot citizens brought before them. Detainees accused of serious criminal acts and murders were either released due to 'lack of appropriate judges and courts' or subjected to indefinite detention.[190] This situation contradicts the need to preserve judicial guarantees in penal cases during non-international armed conflicts, which is one of the core minimum standards protected under common article 3 of the 1949 Geneva Conventions I-IV.

The administration of justice was affected due to a variety of factors, including the Turkish Cypriot judges' personal insecurity in the Greek Cypriot quarters of each town, general difficulties in travelling through checkpoints, or pressure from within the Turkish Cypriot community to

[187] S/6102, para 141.
[188] Polyviou, *Cyprus on the edge*.
[189] S/6102, para 106.
[190] HORM, Session 1963–1964, 9 July 1964.

not interact with the other community.[191] Case reports from that time confirm that 'with one or two exceptions, no Turkish or mixed cases were tried by the Turkish Judges' in any of the District Courts, from 21 December 1963 onwards. Exceptionally in Nicosia, where the Court was ordinarily located in the Turkish quarter, Turkish Cypriot judges were able to continue working on cases concerning their own community. At least some Turkish Cypriot judges were still attending court as usual, following efforts by Judge Wilson, the President of the High Court, to facilitate the maintenance of good working conditions until his departure from the island in May 1964.[192] Overall, the violence and the resulting physical segregation of the two communities made it difficult to follow through with most Constitutional provisions by the summer of 1964. In recognition of the above, in September 1964 UN Secretary-General Thant commended the Judiciary for their efforts to continue responding to their duties:

> It is gratifying to record that throughout the political crisis and inter-communal violence in the island the members of the country's judiciary, both Greek Cypriot and Turkish Cypriot, have to a large degree succeeded in maintaining, as far as is humanly possible, the objectivity and detachment that their high office demands.[193]

To resolve some of the difficulties posed, on 9 July 1964 the Administration of Justice (Miscellaneous Provisions) Law of 1964 (Law 33/1964) was published in the official gazette of the Republic, following its adoption by the House of Representatives. According to its long title, the purpose was to 'remove certain difficulties, arising out of recent events, impeding the administration of justice and to provide for other matters connected therewith' (English translation as provided in *Mustafa Ibrahim;* delivered entirely in English, as per normal practice at the time). The preamble focused on the impossibility of the functioning of the Supreme Constitutional Court and the High Court, adding that the legislative provisions enclosed in the new law were to remain in effect 'until such time as the people of Cyprus may determine such matters'. In essence, Law 33/1964 established a new Supreme Court, which merged the

[191] *Mustafa Ibrahim and others (1964)*, 250–252.
[192] Necatigil, *The Cyprus Question*, 62.
[193] S/5950, para 136.

jurisdiction of the constitutionally provided for Supreme Constitutional Court and High Court, under a reformed Supreme Court of a five to maximum seven-judge bench, without any reference to communal quotas. Law 33/1964, though now considerably amended, is still in force today.

The Judiciary's Position on Internal Violence

Like all laws passed after 21 December 1963, Law 33/1964 was passed in the absence of the Turkish Cypriot MPs, and its constitutionality was challenged before the reformed RoC Supreme Court in the landmark case of *The Attorney-General of the Republic v. Mustafa Ibrahim and others.*[194] If UNSC Resolution 186 ensured the international survival of the Republic, the *Ibrahim* case is the moment that safeguarded the survival of the domestic legal order. The case constitutes a turning point for the RoC, and indicates how international developments are in fact only a small fraction of the institutional and socio-political impact internal violence and armed conflict can have on a given society. An aspect often neglected by international legal scholarship in its analysis of armed conflict.

The case concerned five Turkish Cypriots arrested, charged, and prosecuted for the possession of arms and explosives with the intent of preparing war, and for using armed force against the authorities of the Republic, under the Explosive Substances Law (Capital 54), the Firearms Law (Capital 57; now repealed) and the Criminal Code (Capital 154). Each of the respondents was accused of committing the offences on 25 April 1964 in the Kyrenia, Limassol, and Paphos districts, carrying on 'a *war or warlike* undertaking against the Greek Community of Cyprus'.[195] When each of the District Assize Courts involved released the defendants on bail, the Attorney-General's Office submitted an appeal before the newly established Supreme Court of the Republic, to challenge these decisions.

Counsel for the Respondents, A. M. Berberoglu, raised three preliminary objections to the Appeal, which lie at the epicentre of this case's historical significance. The three Justices hearing the case, decided unanimously that Law 33/1964 was constitutional, on the basis of the DoN as applicable under Constitutional law. The judges gave concurrent judgments addressing the issues at hand from different perspectives, and the case remains a central point of reference in the Constitutional Law of

[194] *The Attorney-General of the Republic* v. *Mustafa Ibrahim and others* (1964) CLR 195.
[195] *Mustafa Ibrahim and others*, 243 (emphasis added).

the RoC ever since. Today the DoN is formally recognised as a direct source of Cypriot Constitutional Law, and *Ibrahim* is the leading case in the interpretation of Law 33/1964.

The purpose here is not to offer yet another account of the DoN in the Cypriot legal order. Instead, using the three preliminary objections as guidance, the objective is to offer clarifications on points of law, and also to draw additional factual information on this period, with a focus on the interplay between law and politics. As already mentioned, there were no major trials considering the vast majority of killings, abductions or enforced disappearances during this period. This reinforces *Ibrahim*'s uniqueness in portraying the judicial point of view regarding the situation on the island from December 1963 onwards.

The first preliminary objection raised by Berberoglu was that Law 33/1964 was unconstitutional, since its adoption did not follow the constitutionally prescribed procedure, in absence of the Turkish Cypriot MPs and a Turkish language publication of the text of the law in the Official Gazette of the Republic. Assessed as one of the weakest points of legal reasoning in the judgement as a whole,[196] the argument failed the legal test, since Law 33/1964 was an ordinary law that did not require separate majorities under the Constitution, and the quorum of the House could be satisfied with only 17 out of 35 Greek Cypriot MPs being present, as prescribed by articles 77 and 78 of the Constitution. Moreover, as per Judge Vassiliades, article 82 of the Constitution, which requires each law or decision of the House of Representatives to be published in the Official Gazette of the Republic, made no explicit reference to the language of publication, despite the fact that both Greek and Turkish are official languages of the Republic. Having said that, Judge Vassiliades did not omit to add that it was 'with greatest difficulty and the utmost strain', that he eventually accepted the Attorney-General's position that not publishing the law in Turkish was due to the lack of Turkish Cypriot officers in the civil service.[197]

The second preliminary objection was that the three-judge panel of the Supreme Court was in violation of the articles of the Constitution providing for the allocation of cases to judges belonging to the same community as the defendants. The UN Secretary-General reports confirm that UNFICYP had arranged for Turkish Cypriot judges, lawyers, Court staff,

[196] Kombos, *Doctrine of Necessity*, 171.

[197] *Mustafa Ibrahim and others*, 208–209, 215.

and witnesses to be escorted as long as such an arrangement would be necessary.[198] Hence, when *Ibrahim* was before the Supreme Court, there were two Turkish Cypriot Supreme Court judges,[199] who could have sat on the case, including the most senior among them and the Court's President, Judge Zekia. Judge Triantafyllides clarified in his judgement that 'the full bench was given an opportunity to consider, in camera, whether it should have sat for the hearing of these appeals',[200] eventually opting for the three-judge formation. As estimated by later commentators, this could have been a strategic choice to safeguard the application of the DoN, by avoiding the inevitability of two dissenting opinions.[201] An outcome which would have led to additional obscurity and ambiguity on an already highly controversial matter, as suggested by the earlier experience of the 1962 inquiries on the criminal provocations in Nicosia, during which officials were under immense pressure not to derogate from the political position of their respective community. It must be noted, that the offer of assistance to Turkish Cypriot judges to attend hearings lasted as late as 2 June 1966, when according to testimony by Turkish Cypriot judge Ulfet Emin, shared by Necatigil and confirmed through the UN archive, only one judge managed to pass through police control, eventually removed from his chambers at 'gun point'.[202] There is no available full description of the incident, and sources seem to disagree on whether pressure on the judges to leave their posts was exercised by Greek Cypriot or Turkish Cypriot officials. Either way, one cannot deny that these were probably the very last high-ranking Turkish Cypriot officials to abandon their posts.

The third and final preliminary objection raised by Berberoglu argued that 'necessity' was not justified under the circumstances, since the Council of Ministers had not issued a Proclamation of Emergency under article 183 of the Constitution. It is due to this last preliminary objection that the judges had the opportunity to elaborate in some detail on the ongoing situation. Article 183(1) provides that a Proclamation of Emergency may be declared in 'case of war or other public danger threatening the life of the Republic or any part thereof'. Judge Triantafyllides, stated that even

[198] S/5950, para 126.

[199] *Mustafa Ibrahim and others*, 244.

[200] *Mustafa Ibrahim and others*, 242.

[201] Kombos, *Doctrine of Necessity*, 168.

[202] Necatigil, *The Cyprus Question*, 63; S/7350, paras 154, 176; Doc S/7611, paras 169–174.

though the Council of Ministers had not declared a state of emergency, 'contrary to glaring fact, that no such emergency exists, strongly indicates that the present emergency is one which could not be met within the express provisions of the Constitution', adding that:

> At a time when by a resolution, dated 4th March, 1964, of the Security Council of the United Nations an International Force has been dispatched to Cyprus to assist in the return to normality and a U.N. Mediator has been assigned to try and work out a solution of the Cyprus Problem, it would be an abdication of responsibility on the part of this court to close its eyes to the realities of the situation, because, for any reason, no Proclamation of Emergency has been made under Article 183, and to hold that everything is normal in Cyprus. To pretend that the administration of justice could have functioned unhindered as envisaged under the Constitution, because a measure that could have been taken, under a provision of limited application, such as Article 183, has not in fact been taken, would be unreasonable.[203]

In the above extract, Judge Triantafyllides' reference to the fact that there was no emergency declaration 'for any reason' reminds us that 'the reason' in question may be external to the law. Triantafyllides hints that the reason is a political one, as indicated also by the fact that the actual power to declare an emergency lies with a political organ, the Council of Ministers. Whether the government at the time had considered the possibility of declaring an emergency under article 183 is unknown. There is no indication in *Ibrahim*, or in the Records of the Plenary Minutes of the House of Representatives, that they did. Since the records of the Council of Ministers have not been studied for the research which produced the present book, no conclusions can be drawn with certainty. Had it been considered, however, it is hereby estimated that this would have been mentioned at least by authors who held high-ranking official positions in the government, such as Stella Soulioti and Glafcos Clerides.

The DoN is distinguished from the declaration of a state of emergency, since the one is no substitute for the other.[204] Article 183 of the Constitution has never been used in the RoC, even though the circumstances could have justified it easily, as admitted by Attorney-General Tornaritis in 1980.[205] Turkish Cypriot academic and politician, Kudret Ozersay has also

[203] *Mustafa Ibrahim and others*, 225–226.
[204] Kombos, *Doctrine of Necessity*, 11.
[205] Tornaritis, *Constitutional and other Legal Problems*, 74–76.

argued that a declaration of emergency under article 183 of the Constitution could be an alternative remedy to the DoN, of which the Greek Cypriot officials made no use.[206]

Importantly, there is no universal obligation under international law to make such a declaration, even after the issue of Declarations of Emergency gained a more prominent role in public international law, once the International Covenant on Civil and Political Rights came in force in 1976.[207] Part of the problem lies with the overall legal culture of the 1960s, as already explained in the context of the study of the ILA in the previous chapter, as well as the problematic way in which governments usually handle so-called de facto emergencies; situations in which an emergency evidently exists based on the facts, but the responsible government does not proceed with issuing a formal legal declaration.[208]

The judgement of Judge Vassiliades took a realist approach throughout, with an overall emphasis on describing the situation on the ground:

> There is ample material on record, to show the conditions prevailing in the Republic at the material time and the circumstances under which the respondents were arrested. Indeed anybody living in the island since the 21st of December, 1963, must have had sufficient occasion, some way or another, to acquire knowledge of the warlike emergency, harassing the people of Cyprus, during the last, nearly, ten months now.[209]

Judge Vassiliades not only referred to a 'warlike emergency', but the information provided below further illustrates the relevance of the international legal framework of the laws of armed conflict. His judgement constitutes a unique authoritative account of what was happening in Cyprus in 1964, from a judicial perspective. The vocabulary he employed is telling in itself:

> There existed within the territory of the Republic of Cyprus, the following conditions:
>
> (a) a *state of revolt*; i.e. armed *rebellion* and *insurrection* against the established Government of the Republic;

[206] Özersay, "The Excuse of State Necessity," 54.
[207] McGoldrick, "Public Emergency Powers and International Law."
[208] ILA, "Second Interim Report (1988)," 148–149.
[209] *Mustafa Ibrahim and others*, 201.

(b) *armed clashes* between *organised groups* resisting the authority of the State, and the *forces authorised by the Government* to assert the authority of its organs;

(c) *loss of life*; damage to property interruption of communications; and upsetting of law and order in the affected areas, with all the consequent repercussions on life in general, within the territory of the State;

(d) *assertion of authority and actual physical control, over areas of State territory*, by the *insurgents* and their political leaders and commanders, to the exclusion of the authority of the established Government of the Republic;

(e) *presence, with the consent of the Government, of international troops within the State territory*, under a Commander acting for, and upon orders from an authority outside the State i.e. the Secretary-General of the United Nations and the Security Council thereof, for the declared purpose, inter alia, of preventing armed clashes between combatants, with a view to the maintenance of peace and the prevention of bloodshed; without, however, exercising government authority, or assuming in any way government responsibility;

(f) *inability of the State-Government*, pending a political settlement in international circles, *to combat the insurgents* in order to re-establish its authority and resume its responsibilities in the affected areas, owing to the presence and intervention of the said foreign troops; and corresponding uncertainty, as to when the one or the other of the combating forces may eventually prevail, so as to assume the responsibility of government in the maintenance of law and order in the territory of the Republic; and

(g) duration of such conditions over a *period of several months*.[210] (all emphasis added)

There are a number of conclusions one can draw from the above, even though the statement was only made in *obiter*, without any legally binding force. Firstly, the reference to 'existed' in the past tense, suggests that Judge Vassiliades, distinguished between the first half of 1964, when active fighting was almost continuous and the respondents were arrested, from the situation at the time he delivered his judgement on 10 November 1964. It had already been three months since a ceasefire was signed in the aftermath of the events in Tylliria.

Furthermore, the wording emphasised in the above passage, relates to the criteria used in the process of conflict qualification, as discussed previously. Most striking perhaps is Judge Vassiliades' unhindered recognition of the 'inability of the State-Government, pending a political settlement in

[210] *Mustafa Ibrahim and others*, 201–202.

international circles, to combat the insurgents'.[211] Considering the caution with which judges choose the wording of their decisions, the choice of words is not to be taken lightly. On the other hand, the interchangeable reference to 'revolt', 'insurrection' and 'rebellion',[212] suggests these terms were probably not used with due care for their exact legal meaning. This does not, however, diminish the fact that the judges were firmly aware of the potential legal implications of the seriousness of the situation before them. In the literature consulted for this research there is no reference to this specific point of the *Ibrahim* judgement. Only Chrysostomides has made an extremely brief, two-page-long comparison between 'insurgency' and 'belligerency', retaining a significant scope of ambiguity.[213]

As expected, opinions between Greek Cypriot and Turkish Cypriot commentators regarding *Ibrahim* differ. Turkish Cypriot commentators have been highly critical of the DoN and disagree with its application, since it offered a legal justification to the Greek Cypriot-controlled government of the RoC to proceed with a number of questionable legal reforms, analysed in the next chapter. Necatigil purported that the judges in *Ibrahim* were 'only tapping a slender stream of authority, particularly academic opinion, to develop an existing doctrine, or rather to create a new spurious doctrine'.[214] Kombos, on the other hand, is an example of a Greek Cypriot academic who has also been critical towards the DoN, primarily for its continuous predominance in Cypriot public law despite its supposed temporary nature. He has expressed the view that the judgement 'is an example of solid and thoughtful legal argumentation that can be regarded as the leading and most important contribution of the Cypriot legal system to legal science in general'.[215]

The 1949 Geneva Conventions During the Ibrahim *Case*

Despite the fact that the wording in *Ibrahim* reflected to a significant extent the law of armed conflicts, the 1949 Geneva Conventions are completely absent from the judgement. In November 1964, the RoC House of Representatives had not yet ratified the 1949 Geneva Conventions,

[211] *Mustafa Ibrahim and others*, 202.
[212] *Mustafa Ibrahim and others*, 201, 249.
[213] Chrysostomides, *The Republic of Cyprus*, 92–93.
[214] Necatigil, *The Cyprus Question*, 60.
[215] Kombos, *Doctrine of Necessity*, 6.

despite the ICRC's efforts to promote compliance with their provisions throughout 1964. In the detailed report accounting for the August 1964 battles and air raids in Tylliria, the ICRC delegate had mentioned that according to Minister of Justice Stella Soulioti, the government would adhere to the Geneva Conventions, while she had also proposed the establishment of a Cyprus Red Cross Society, to replace the Cypriot Branch of the British Red Cross.[216]

The bill on the ratification of the Conventions was for the first time on the agenda of the House of Representatives Plenary on 3 September 1964, roughly two weeks after the events in Tylliria. According to the minutes, however, the bill was not yet ready for debate and voting. Following another delay in October, an interim Report was eventually presented in a House plenary session on 7 January 1965, following meetings of the Parliamentary Committees on Foreign Affairs and on Legal Affairs, and it was agreed to further postpone the drafting of the final report, to allow the Attorney-General to offer clarifications on a number of unspecified points of law. The Law on the ratification of the Geneva Conventions (Law 40/1966) was eventually adopted 18 months later, on 7 July 1966, without any comments by MPs and any further information on the process made available through the minutes. Subsequently, the RoC submitted an Instrument of Ratification to the Federal Political Department of the Swiss Political Department on 18 July 1966.[217]

The reception of the Instrument of Ratification seven months after the ICRC delegation had already withdrawn from Cyprus puzzled its recipients since the RoC had already *acceded* to the Conventions, according to their records. As a result, the Swiss Political Department inquired with the ICRC whether in the latter's view the date of accession should be revised.[218] In turn, the ICRC stated that in order to avoid 'provocation of prejudicial interpretations regarding the application of the Conventions', they considered the RoC bound by the Conventions as of 23 May 1962.[219] Lack of clarity must have persisted, however, since Jean Pictet also addressed the

[216] ICRC, B AG 251 049-005.02, Consequences of the battles of 6, 7, 8, 9 August 1964 (2 September 1964); ICRC, B AG 251 049-005.02, Note 264 – Concerning the Cyprus Red Cross and the establishment of a national Red Cross (12 July 1965).

[217] ICRC, B AG 041-088, Copy of Instrument of Ratification by RoC MFA (18 July 1966).

[218] ICRC, B AG 041-088, Letter of Swiss Political Department to ICRC President, 1 September 1966).

[219] ICRC, B AG 041-088, Letter from ICRC to Swiss Political Department, Division of International Organisations (3 October 1966).

matter through a letter dated 15 November 1966 in his capacity as ICRC Director-General, reiterating the original position of the ICRC.[220] The letter to which Pictet was replying to was not available in the file consulted at the ICRC archive. It appears that after this exchange the issue was considered settled.

The position of the ICRC can be justified on the basis that under international law accession and ratification are two out of a number of different ways through which a State can express its consent to be bound by a treaty. States are under no legal obligation to ratify a treaty, unless this is demanded by the treaty itself. The 1949 Geneva Conventions I-IV (arts 61/60/140/156) provide that an accession takes effect six months after the date on which a notice of accession is received by the Swiss authorities. Thus, in practice, the lack of a ratification by the RoC simply prevented the applicability of the Conventions at the domestic legal level, but did not remove the State's international obligations.

Considering once again the facts of *Mustafa Ibrahim and others*, had the RoC ratified the 1949 Geneva Conventions shortly after it had acceded to them in 1962, Counsel for the Respondents, in addition to the three preliminary objections that had actually been raised, would have been able to also argue that: (1) the ongoing situation in Cyprus was a non-international armed conflict under common article 3, (2) his clients had to be afforded 'all the judicial guarantees which are recognized as indispensable by civilized peoples' in the wording of common article 3; and, (3) that Law 33/1964 failed to provide for those guarantees. It would then have been for the Prosecution to rebut that argument, potentially once again with recourse to the DoN. Arguments on the basis of common article 3 would require a more substantial engagement of the Court with armed violence. Had arguments on either side been raised on the basis of common article 3 *domestically* then, one can speculate that today we would be debating different legal issues in a potentially different factual context.

The Broader Significance of the Ibrahim Case

The value of *Ibrahim* does not lie solely in being the authority case on DoN in the RoC. The case also illustrates the difficulty of the Judiciary to effectively deal with the intensity of the internal violence of the kind

[220] ICRC, B AG 041-088, Letter from ICRC Director-General to Swiss Political Department (15 November 1966).

observed in Cyprus, and the level at which political arguments may be embedded or not in the use of legal language. Moreover, considering the criteria for the threshold of qualifying internal violence as a non-international armed conflict, the case is valuable in indicating that first, the Turkish Cypriot leadership did have control over a portion of the territory of the State, discussed in more depth in the next chapter, and second, that the criminal justice system and the State apparatus more broadly were unable to fully control the ongoing situation.

Reference to the DoN cannot be avoided in any discussion on Cypriot constitutional law, given its dual historical and legal significance. What is less known, however, is the doctrine's broader relevance and impact in cases of internal violence and internal armed conflict. By the mid-twentieth century the DoN was employed in a number of colonial and post-colonial contexts that follow the common law tradition. The earliest cases in fact derive from the US Civil War, and there has been a long list of cases across various other jurisdictions since; Pakistan, Uganda, Nigeria, the Seychelles, and more recently Fiji, and Canada.[221]

The best-known part of *Ibrahim*, which has attracted the broadest attention, is found in a list of criteria construed by Judge Josephides, illustrating when the DoN shall be invoked:

> I interpret our constitution to include the doctrine of necessity in exceptional circumstances, which is an implied exception to particular provisions of the constitution; and this in order to ensure the very existence of the State. The following prerequisites must be satisfied before this doctrine may become applicable:
>
> (a) an imperative and inevitable necessity or exceptional circumstances;
> (b) no other remedy to apply;
> (c) the measure taken must be proportionate to the necessity; and
> (d) it must be of a temporary character limited to the duration of the exceptional circumstances.
>
> A law thus enacted is subject to the control of this court to decide whether the aforesaid prerequisites are satisfied, i.e. whether there exists such a necessity and whether the measures taken were necessary to meet it.[222]

Central among the cases mentioned in the bibliography is the 1966 South Rhodesian case of *Stella Madzimbamuto v Lardner-Burke*.

[221] Kombos, *Doctrine of Necessity*, 45–134.
[222] *Mustafa Ibrahim and others*, 265.

Following the declaration of an emergency on 5 November 1965 by the Governor of the Crown colony of Southern Rhodesia, after the unlawful unilateral declaration of independence by the colony's all-white regime in 1965, the case was an application by a woman for the unlawful detention of her husband, who continued being detained even after the first state of emergency expired in February 1966. The case reached the Privy Council, the highest court of appeal within the British Empire, in 1968, and dealt with numerous issues, including the rules that govern illegal regimes, and the effects of war on State sovereignty under the DoN.[223] The comparative analysis undertaken by the judges is an impressive account of the various constitutional and other problems across the post-colonial world. Therein, *Ibrahim* was recognised as 'The high-water mark of the doctrine', but the Court distinguished the situation in Cyprus, recognising the validity of *Ibrahim*, but eventually concluding that Judge Josephides' criteria did not apply to the unlawful regime of Southern Rhodesia.[224]

The situation in Southern Rhodesia was also relied upon by the RoC at the time, who supported that like in Southern Rhodesia, in Cyprus too the 'minority' Turkish Cypriot community was trying to 'block the will of the majority of the country'[225] for *enosis*. From a historical perspective, this indicates once again the plethora of linkages and convergences between the unresolved disputes that have their route in the post-colonial world. As stated by Kombos, the law's 'polycentric and multidisciplinary character'[226] is a commonality between constitutional and public international law. Hence, more research is due combining comparative constitutional and international legal perspectives, to expanding our understanding of non-international armed conflicts and internal disturbances more broadly.

Conclusion

The improved organisation of the Greek Cypriot forces in the spring of 1964, combined with the self-organisation of the Turkish Cypriots within the areas under their control, suggest that the threshold for a

[223] Brookfield, "Courts, Kelsen, and the Rhodesian Revolution."

[224] *Madzimbamuto v Lardner-Burke* [1969] 1 AC 645; [1968] 3 ALL ER 561 (Privy Council), 681–682, 691; Wolf-Phillips, "Constitutional Legitimacy."

[225] A/PV.1344, para 161.

[226] Kombos, *Doctrine of Necessity*, 8.

non-international armed conflict was reached and that those who were not involved in the fighting should have been afforded the limited protections under common article 3 of the 1949 Geneva Conventions. The provisions of international humanitarian law however, only label a situation in a specific way; 'international armed conflict', 'non-international armed conflict' or 'internal disturbances below the threshold of a non-international armed conflict'. None of the three terms encompasses the level of the monumental changes that would take place domestically, as a result of the physical segregation between the two communities and the direct impact this had on the administration of the State.

In December 1964, few days short of the first anniversary of the 'Bloody Christmas', the UN Secretary-General assessed the situation as follows:

> Acute political conflict and distrust between the leaders of the two communities, and the passions stirred among the members of the two groups combine to create a state of *potential civil war*, despite the present suspension of active fighting. This situation adversely affects the entire economy of the island and causes some serious hardship for certain sections of the population, notably segments of the Turkish Cypriot community. The life and economy of the island remain disrupted and abnormal, and it would be unrealistic to expect any radical improvement until a basic political solution can be found. (emphasis added).[227]

From the certainty of the existence of a 'civil war' in September 1964, by the end of the year the UN Secretary-General changed his wording to a 'potential civil war'. In light of the relative quietness of the period that followed August 1964, perhaps diplomatic efforts would benefit more if the severity of the violence experienced in the previous months was toned down. There is limited doubt that the active involvement of the ICRC and UNFICYP contributed to a reduction in violence and the alleviation of the humanitarian situation. Nevertheless, the reduced intensity of the following years did not reverse the physical segregation, neither reduced the heightened levels of mistrust between the two communities, nor restored 'law and order' and led to a 'return to normal conditions'.[228]

[227] S/6102, para 237 (emphasis added).
[228] UNSC Resolution 186 (1964), para 5.

References

Books

Adams, Thomas W and Alvin J Cottrell. *Cyprus Between East and West.* John Hopkins Press, 1968.

Chesterman, Simon. *Secretary or General? The UN Secretary-General in World Politics.* Cambridge University Press. 2010.

Chrysostomides, Kypros. *The Republic of Cyprus: A study in International Law.* Martinus Nijhoff 2000.

Chrysostomou, Aggelos. *Από τον Κυπριακό Στρατό μέχρι και τη δημιουργία της Εθνικής Φρουράς* (1959–1964) (From the Cyprus Army until the establishment of the National Guard (1959–1964). 2015a.

Clerides, Glafcos, *Cyprus: My Deposition Vol 1.* Alithia Publishing, 1989.

Clerides, Glafcos, *Cyprus: My Deposition Vol 2.* Alithia Publishing, 1989.

Crawford, James, *The Creation of States in International Law.* 2nd edn, Oxford University Press, 2007.

Gibbons, Harry S. *The Genocide Files.* Charles Bravos Publishers, 1997.

Gray, Christine. *International Law and the Use of Force.* 3rd edn, Oxford University Press, 2008.

Hadjilyras, Alexander-Michael. *Η Κυπριακή Δημοκρατία και οι Θρησκευτικές Ομάδες* (The Republic of Cyprus and the Religious Groups). 2012.

ICRC. *Commentary on the First Geneva Convention for the Amelioration of the Condition of the Wounded and Sick in Armed Forces in the Field.* Cambridge University Press, 2016.

ICRC. *Commentary on the First Geneva Convention for the Amelioration of the Condition of the Wounded and Sick in Armed Forces in the Field.* Cambridge University Press, 2016.

Ierodiakonou, Pavlos. *Εθνική Φρουρά: Από τα Πέτρινα Χρόνια στο Σήμερα* (National Guard: From the stone years to today). Cultural Academy 'Kypropedia', 2016.

Jacovides, Andrew. *International Law and Diplomacy.* Martinus Nijhoff, 2011.

James, Alan. *Keeping the peace in the Cyprus Crisis of 1963–64.* Palgrave, 2002.

Kızılyürek, Niyazi. *Μια ιστορία βίας και μνησικακίας: Η γένεση και η εξέλιξη της εθνοτικής διένεξης στην Κύπρο Vol 2* (A story of violence and resentment: The genesis and evolution of the ethnic conflict in Cyprus), Translated by Michalis Theodorou. Heterotopia, 2019.

Kombos, Constantinos. *The Doctrine of Necessity in Constitutional Law.* Sakkoulas, 2015.

Kyriakides, Stanley. *Cyprus: Constitutionalism and Crisis Government.* University of Pennsylvania Press. 1968.

Mačák, Kubo. *Internationalized Armed Conflicts in International Law.* Oxford University Press, 2018.

McNair, Arnold D. *The Law of Treaties.* Reprinted 2003, Oxford University Press, 1961.

Miller, Linda. *Cyprus: The Law and Politics of Civil Strife*. Center for International Affairs, Harvard University, 1968.
Mirbagheri, Farid. *Cyprus and International Peacemaking*. Hurst & Co, 1998.
Necatigil, Zaim M. *The Cyprus Question and the Turkish position in International Law*. 2nd edn, Oxford University Press, 1993.
Oppenheim, Lassa. *International Law: A Treatise Vol II: Disputes, War and Neutrality*. Edited by Hersch Lauterpacht, 7th edn, Longmans, 1952.
Packard, Martin. *Getting it Wrong: Fragments from a Cyprus Diary 1964*. Author House, 2008.
Patrick, Richard. *Political Geography and the Cyprus Conflict, 1963–1971*. University of Waterloo, 1989.
Pictet, Jean. *Commentary on the First Geneva Convention for the Amelioration of the Condition of the Wounded and Sick in Armed Forces in the Field*. ICRC, 1952.
Pictet, Jean. *Commentary on the Fourth Geneva Convention relative to the Protection of Civil Persons in Time of War*. ICRC, 1958.
Polyviou, Polyvios G. *Cyprus on the Edge: A study in constitutional survival*. 2013.
Sivakumaran, Sandesh. *The Law of Non-International Armed Conflict*. Oxford University Press, 2012.
Sant Cassia, Paul. *Bodies of Evidence: Burial, Memory and the Recovery of Missing Persons in Cyprus*. Berghahn Books, 2007.
Soulioti, Stella. *Fettered Independence: Cyprus, 1878–1964 Vol 1 - The Narrative*. University of Minnesota Press, 2006.
Soulioti, Stella. *Fettered Independence: Cyprus, 1878–1964 Vol 1 - The Documents*. University of Minnesota Press, 2006.
Tornaritis, Criton G. *Constitutional and Legal Problems in the Republic of Cyprus*, Press and Information Office, 1972.
Tornaritis, Criton G. *Cyprus and its Constitutional and other Legal Problems*, 2nd edn, 1980.
Tudor, Margot. *Blue Helmets Bureaucrats: United Nations Peacekeeping and the Reinvention of Colonialism, 1945–1971*. Cambridge University Press, 2023.
Varnava, Marilena. *Cyprus Before 1974: The Prelude to Crisis*. I.B Tauris, 2019.
Zotiades, George B. *Intervention by treaty right: Its legality in present day international law*. Jus Gentium Series of Publications on International Law, 1965.

Chapter and Edited Volumes

Bothe, Michael. "Peacekeeping". In *The Oxford Commentary on the Charter of the United Nations Vol 1*, edited by Bruno Simma, Daniel-Erasmus Khan, Georg Nolte and Andreas Paulus. 3rd edn, Oxford University Press, 2012.
Chatterjee, Partha. "The Legacy of Bandung". In *Bandung, Global History, and International Law*, edited by Luis Eslava, Michael Fakhri, Vasuki Nesiah. Cambridge University Press, 2017.

D'Argent, Pierre. "Non-Renunciation of the Rights Provided by the Conventions." In *The 1949 Geneva Conventions: A Commentary*, edited by Andrew Clapham, Paola Gaeta, and Marco Sassòli. Oxford University Press, 2015.

Giegerich, Thomas. "Article 62. Fundamental change of circumstances." In *Vienna Convention on the Law of Treaties: A Commentary*, edited by Oliver Dörr and Kirsten Schmalenbach. 2nd edn, Springer, 2018.

Henckaerts, Jean-Marie and Louise Doswald-Beck. eds., *Customary International Humanitarian Law Vol I: Rules*. Cambridge University Press, 2005.

Henckaerts, Jean-Marie and Louise Doswald-Beck. eds., *Customary International Humanitarian Law Vol II: Practice*. Cambridge University Press, 2005.

Ipsen, Knut. "Combatants and Non-combatants." In *The Handbook of Humanitarian Law in Armed Conflicts*, edited by Dieter Fleck. 2nd edn, Oxford University Press, 2008.

Klabbers, Jan. "Intervention, Armed Intervention, Armed Attack, Threat to Peace, Act of Aggression, and Threat or Use of Force: What's the Difference?" In *The Oxford Handbook of the Use of Force in International Law*, edited by Marc Weiller. Oxford University Press, 2015.

Kritsiotis, Dino. "Theorizing International Law on Force and Intervention." In *Oxford Handbook on the Theory of International Law*, edited by Anne Orford and Florian Hoffmann. Oxford University Press, 2016.

Lattanzi, Flavia. "Humanitarian Assistance." In *The 1949* Geneva Conventions*: A Commentary*, edited by Andrew Clapham, Paola Gaeta, and Marco Sassòli. Oxford University Press, 2015.

Lovell, David W, "Settling Protracted Social Conflicts: Trust, Identity, and the Resolution of the 'Cyprus Issue'". In *Contemporary Social and Political Aspects of the Cyprus Problem*, edited by Jonathan Warner, David W Lovell and Michalis Kontos. Cambridge Scholar Publishing, 2016.

Moir, Lindsay. "The Concept of Non-International Armed Conflict." In *The 1949 Geneva Conventions: A Commentary*, edited by Andrew Clapham, Paola Gaeta, and Marco Sassòli. Oxford University Press, 2015.

Nicolet, Claude. "Turkish Cypriot Failure in 1964." In *Cyprus: 40 years on from Independence: Proceedings of a Conference in the University of North London on 16–17 November 2000*, edited by John Charalambous, Alicia Chrysostomou, Denis Judd and Heinz A. Richter. Bibliopolis, 2002.

Nishat, Nishat, "The Right of Initiative of the ICRC and Other Impartial Humanitarian Bodies." In *The 1949 Geneva Conventions: A Commentary*, edited by Andrew Clapham, Paola Gaeta, and Marco Sassòli. Oxford University Press, 2015.

Venturini, Gabriella. "The Temporal Scope of Application of the Conventions." In *The 1949 Geneva Conventions: A Commentary*, edited by Andrew Clapham, Paola Gaeta, and Marco Sassòli. Oxford University Press, 2015.

Watts, Sean. "Who is a Prisoner of War?" In *The 1949* Geneva Conventions*: A Commentary*, edited by Andrew Clapham, Paola Gaeta, and Marco Sassòli. Oxford University Press, 2015.

JOURNAL ARTICLES

Brookfield, F. M, "The Courts, Kelsen, and the Rhodesian Revolution." *The University of Toronto Law Journal* 19, No. 3 (1969): 326–352.

Chrysostomou, Aggelos, "Μάχες Τηλλυρίας (7–11 Αυγούστου 1964) Το Υπουργικό Συμβούλιο της Κυπριακής Δημοκρατίας συνεδριάζει" (The 'Tylliria Battles' (7–11 August 1964) The Council of Ministers in Session). *Εθνική Φρουρά & Ιστορία* 35 (2015): 49.

Dzehtsiarou, Kanstantsin "*Georgia* v *Russia (II)* (App No 38263/08) European Court of Human Rights (Grand Chamber) (Judgement, Merits, 21 January 2021) (note)" *American Journal of International Law* 115, No. 2 (2021) 288–294.

Harrison, Andrea. "Internationalized Armed Conflicts in International Law." Review of *Internationalized Armed Conflicts in International Law*, by Kubo Mačák. *International Review of the Red Cross* 101, No. 912 (2019): 1201–1205.

Harroff-Tavel, Marion, "Neutrality and Impartiality – The importance of these principles for the International Red Cross and Red Crescent Movement and the difficulties involved in applying them" *International Review of the Red Cross* 273 (1989): 536–552.

Harroff-Tavel, Marion, "Action taken by the International Committee of the Red Cross in situations of Internal Violence" *International Review of the Red Cross* 33, No. 294 (1993): 195–220.

ICRC, "Humanitarian Aid to the Victims of Internal Conflicts: Meeting of a Commission of Experts in Geneva" *International Review of the Red Cross* 3, No. 23 (1963): 79–91.

Johnstone, Ian, "The Role of the UN Secretary-General: The Power of Persuasion Based on Law" *Global Governance* 9, No. 4 (2003): 441–458.

McGoldrick, Dominic. "The Interface between Public Emergency Powers and International Law" *International Journal of Constitutional Law* 2, No. 2 (2004): 380–429.

Kalyvas, Stathis, "How Civil Wars Help Explain Organized Crime – and How They Do Not" 59(8) *The Journal of Conflict Resolution* 59, No. 8 (2015) 1517–1540.

Kaoullas, Lambros, "Το έλλειμμα ασφαλείας και η κοινωνικοποίηση του μονοπωλίου της βίας" (The security deficit and the communalization of the monopoly of violence). *Εθνική Φρουρά και Ιστορία* 35 (2015): 30–47.

Özersay, Kudret. "The Excuse of State Necessity and its implications on the Cyprus Conflict." *Perceptions* IX, No. 4 (2004–2005): 31.

Schindler, Dietrich, "International Humanitarian Law and Internationalized Internal Armed Conflicts" *International Review of the Red Cross* 230 (1982) 255–264.

Theodorides, John, "The United Nations Peace Keeping Force in Cyprus (UNFICYP)" *International and Comparative Law Quarterly* 31 (1982): 765–783.

Tsagourias, Nicholas, "Consent, Neutrality/Impartiality and the Use of Force in Peacekeeping: Their Constitutional Dimension" *Journal of Conflict and Security Law* 11, No. 3 (2006): 465–82.

Wolf-Phillips, Leslie, "Constitutional Legitimacy: A Study of the Doctrine of Necessity." *Third World Quarterly* 1, No. 4 (1979): 97–133.

Other

Bell, Christine "Ceasefire" (December 2009) *MPEPIL* (December 2009) https://opil.ouplaw.com/view/10.1093/law:epil/9780199231690/law-9780199231690-e263?prd=EPIL, accessed 15 December 2021.

Christou, Jean, "Excavations in September to locate remains of victims of 1964 battle of Tylliria" (*Cyprus Mail*, 30 July 2019). https://cyprus-mail.com/2019/07/30/excavations-in-september-to-locate-remains-of-victims-of-1964-battle-of-tylliria/, accessed 30 June 2021.

Iakovou, Natasa and Nadia Kornioti, "Missing Persons in Cyprus: Observations from the past and recommendations for the future." PRIO Cyprus Centre Report 7 (*PRIO Cyprus Centre*, 2019). https://cyprus.prio.org/Publications/Publication/?x=4294, accessed 10 January 2025

ILA, Committee on the Enforcement of Human Rights Law, 'Second Interim Report of the Committee' (1988) 63 *International Law Association Conference Report* 129.

Archival Material

CIA, Doc No CIA-RDP79T00429A001400020022-6, Memorandum: Cyprus, 26 December 1963 (Released 4 February 2004) < https://www.cia.gov/readingroom/document/cia-rdp79t00429a001400020022-6> 12 May 2021.

Hansard, HC Deb 14 January 1964 vol 687 col 35.

HORM, Session 1963–1964, 1 June 1964a.

HORM, Session 1963–1964, 15 June 1964b.

HORM, Session 1963–1964, 9 July 1964.

ICRC, B AG 041-088, *Adhésion aux Conventions de Genève de 1949 de la République de Chypre* (15/11/1962–15/11/1966).

ICRC, B AG 200 049-004, Troubles à Chypre, décembre 1963. Correspondance, rapports de délégation de Pierre Gaillard, premier partie (27/12/1963–17/01/1964a).

ICRC, B AG 200 049-005, Troubles à Chypre, décembre 1963. Correspondance, deuxième partie (18/01/1964–18/01/1964b).

ICRC, B AG 251 049-001, *Offre de services du CICR au gouvernement chypriote* (27/12/1963–28/12/1963b).

ICRC, B AG 251 049-004, *Mission d'une délégation du CICR à Chypre, du 31 décembre 1963 au 27 novembre 1965, activités diverses de la délégation en faveur des victimes des troubles entre chypriotes grecs et chypriotes turcs, première partie* (16/01/1964–02/12/1965a).

ICRC, B AG 251 049-005.02, Mission d'une délégation du CICR à Chypre, du 31 décembre 1963 au 27 novembre 1965, activités diverses de la délégation en faveur des victimes des troubles entre chypriotes grecs et chypriotes turcs, deuxième partie (15/06/1964–25/11/1965b).

ICRC, B AG 251 049-006, Mission d'une délégation du CICR à Chypre, du 31 décembre 1963 au 27 novembre 1965, activités diverses de la délégation en faveur des victimes des troubles entre chypriotes grecs et chypriotes turcs, troisième partie (15/06/1964–26/11/1965c).

ICRC, B AG 251 049-009, Mission d'une délégation du CICR à Chypre, du 31 décembre 1963 au 27 novembre 1965, activités diverses de la délégation en faveur des victimes des troubles entre chypriotes grecs et chypriotes turcs, sixième partie (13/01/1963–29/11/1965d).

Johnson, Lindon B and Ismet Inonu, "Document - Correspondence between President Johnson and Prime Minister Inonu, June 1964, as released by the White House, January 1, 1966." *Middle East Journal* 20, No. 3 (1966): 386.

LBJ Presidential Library, *Recordings and Transcripts of Telephone Conversations and Meetings,* Telephone conversation between President Johnson and Dean Rusk #3623 (4 June 1964) <https://www.discoverlbj.org/item/tel-03623> accessed 24 June 2021.

Office of the Historian, US State Department, *Foreign Relations of the United States, Vol XVI, Cyprus; Greece; Turkey (1964–1968)* https://history.state.gov/historicaldocuments/frus1964-68v16/d56, accessed 24 June 2021.

PIO, Αστυνομική Ανακοίνωσης (Police Announcement) (21 December 1963a).

PIO, Statement by Gendarmerie (21 December 1963b).

PIO, Statement by Gendarmerie (22 December 1963c).

PIO, Joint appeal by the President and the Vice-President of the Cypriot People (21 December 1963d).

PIO, Turkish Cypriots continue their unprovoked attacks (24 December 1963e).

PIO, Ο Αρχιεπίσκοπος συνόδευσε το Τουρκικόν Νοσοκομειακόν Προσωπικόν εις την Βρεττανικήν Αρμοστεία (The Archbishop has escorted the Turkish Hospital Staff to the British High Commission) (26 December 1963f).

PIO, Statement by the Minister of Interior Mr. Polykarpos Yorkatzis (27 December 1963g).
PIO, Turks kill Greek monks (1 January 1964a).
PIO, Turks raid Nicosia Armenian Church (29 January 1964b)
PIO, Maronite Detained by Turkish Terrorists (12 June 1964c).
PIO, Turkish Aircraft Raid Hospital Ambulances and Civilians at Pomos (9 August 1964d).
UNA, S-0869-0003-03-00001, *Items in Peace-keeping Operation – Cyprus – General Instructions for UNFICYP, 13 March 1964* (Released 6 June 2006a) https://search.archives.un.org/general-instructions-for-unficyp-2 accessed 28 September 2021.
UNA, S-0869-0003-08-00001, *Items in Peace-keeping operations, Cyprus - Background notes on reports of build-up of arms and troops in Cyprus, July 1964* (Released 6 June 2006b) https://search.archives.un.org/background-notes-on-reports-of-build-up-of-arms-and-troops-in-cyprus-july-1965 accessed 28 September 2021.
UNA, S-0869-0001-07-00001, *Items-in-Peace-keeping operations – Cyprus - United Nations Force Regulations, 07 April 1964*, UN Doc No. ST/SGB/UNFICYP/1, 25 April 1964 (Released 6 June 2006) https://search.archives.un.org/united-nations-force-regulations-2 accessed 28 September 2021.

UN Reports on Situation in Cyprus

S/5514 (13 January 1964).
S/5516 (17 January 1964).
S/5593 and Addenda 1- 3 (12, 17 and 26 March 1964).
S/5634 Report enclosing Exchange of Letters Constituting an Agreement between the UN and the Government of the RoC Concerning the Status of UNFICYP (31 March 1964).
S/5653 Note by Secretary-General and Aide-memoire concerning some questions relating to the function and operation of the United Nations Peace-Keeping Force in Cyprus (11 April 1964).
S/5671 (29 April 1964).
S/5679 (2 May 1964).
S/5764 (15 June 1964).
S/5920 Report by the Secretary-General to the Security Council on the Developing situation with Regard to the Projected Rotation of Turkish National Troops in Cyprus (29 August 1964).
S/5950 (10 September 1964).
S/5950/Add.2, Addendum covering developments from 10 to 15 September 1964 (15 September 1964).

UN Verbatim Records

UNSC S/PV.1095 (18 February 1964a).
UNSC S/PV.1098 (27 February 1964b).
UNSC S/PV.1099 (28 February 1964c).
UNSC S/PV.1102 (4 March 1964d).
UNSC S/PV.1142 (8 August 1964e).

Correspondence

UNSC S/5488 Letter from Cyprus Permanent Representative to UN to UNSC (26 December 1963a).
UNSC S/5491 Letter from Turkey Permanent Representative to UN Secretary-General (27 December 1963b)
UNSC S/5508, Letter by UK Permanent Representative to UNSC (9 January 1964f)
UNSC S/5514 Letter from UK Permanent Representative to UNSC (13 February 1964g).
UNSC S/5545 Letter from Cyprus Permanent Representative to UNSC (15 February 1964h).
UNSC S/5550 Letter from Cyprus Permanent Representative to UNSC (17 February 1964i).
UNSC S/5556 Letter from Turkey Permanent Representative to UNSC (19 February 1964j).
UNSC S/5859 Letter from Permanent Representative of Turkey (8 August 1964k).
UNSC S/5861 Letter from Cyprus Charge d'affaires (8 August 1964l).

Court Cases

The Attorney-General of the Republic v. Mustafa Ibrahim and others (1964) CLR 195.
Madzimbamuto v Lardner-Burke [1969] 1 AC 645; [1968] 3 ALL ER 561 (Privy Council).
Military and Paramilitary Activities in and against Nicaragua (Nicaragua v United States of America), Judgement (Merits) [1986] ICJ Rep 14.
Georgia v Russia (II) (Application No 38263/08) (Grand Chamber) Judgement (Merits), (ECtHR) 21 January 2021.

CHAPTER 5

Politics Before Everything, 1965–1968

The ceasefire of August 1964 and the invocation of the DoN in November that year led to a standstill in inter-communal relations. The ICRC and the UN kept monitoring the situation, with the ICRC delegates becoming increasingly frustrated in their middle-man role and the way humanitarian needs were exploited for political gain. The situation led ICRC delegate Jacques Ruff in March 1965 to exclaim in one of his reports: 'The situation here is extraordinary. Politics before everything.'[1] Around the same time, the UN Secretary-General, described the situation as a 'tense and fragile truce', which was likely to continue 'as long as there is a hostile confrontation within the Island and as long as the territory of the Republic is cut up by front lines and fortifications'.[2] The term 'truce', a temporary pause in fighting, is key in understanding the environment in Cyprus from 1965 to 1968. International humanitarian law provides no time limits concerning the beginning or the conclusion of a non-international armed conflict, and interruptions in fighting do not suspend or terminate the obligations of parties under common article 3 of the 1949 Conventions.

Many of the practices and the mechanisms employed in the first half of 1964 by early 1965 started obtaining a sense of *de facto* permanence. Primary among them, UNFICYP's presence, the evolution of the National

[1] ICRC B AG 251 049-005.02, Note 209 – General Considerations (18 March 1965).
[2] S/6228, para 67 (emphasis added).

N. Kornioti, *Law's Politics: The Cyprus Troubles, 1960–1968*, https://doi.org/10.1007/978-3-031-93369-1_5

Guard into the official armed forces of the State and the application of the DoN. Hence, the period from September 1964 to July 1974 has generally attracted less interest from researchers, notwithstanding limited research on the socio-economic dynamics formed after the violent months of 1964 and the initiation of inter-communal and multilateral negotiations. Most research on the military developments is constrained to the single most significant incident of violence during this period, which took place in the villages of Ayios Theodoros (Larnaca District) and Kophinou in November 1967. This in itself has led to deep chronological gaps, casting an even darker shadow over a complete decade of Cypriot history, which could have otherwise helped bridge the continuities observed from the early 1960s to the early 1970s. Therefore, the concluding chapter of the book seeks to shed light on the less clear aspects of the historical narrative, always in conjunction with relevant legal and diplomatic developments.

Cypriot Society After 1964

The first post-independence census of December 1960 is the sole authoritative source to this day providing an overview of the population of the RoC island-wide.[3] In 1960, the island had a total of 577,615 inhabitants (49.4% Male, 50.6% Female), of whom 3,602 resided in the SBAs, the areas 'retained' by the UK. The population was divided into seven 'races', the term used in the official documents, as follows (Table 5.1):

From the above one can see how reducing the population to two broad communities constitutionally, failed to reflect the cultural diversity among the Republic's population. Notably among them the 'Gypsies',[4] who with less than 1000 individuals did not reach the constitutional threshold to identify as a separate 'group', but also did not qualify as a separate 'religious group' in line with the wording of article 2(3) of the Constitution. This group were included in the Turkish Cypriot community, since the majority spoke Turkish and were of the Muslim faith, without any recognised minority protections regarding their distinctive culture and traditions. Even though their status as a separate minority group in the RoC is today recognised under European Union law, like with other small historical communities their experience is majorly absent from mainstream narratives of Cypriot history.

[3] RoC Statistical Service, *Census of Population and Agriculture 1960 Vol. I*, Table IV.

[4] Trimikliniotis and Demetriou, "The Cypriot Roma," 241.

Table 5.1 RoC Population per ethnic group (RoC Census December 1960)

Group	*Individuals*
Greeks	442,521
Turks	104,350
British	20,955
Armenians	3628
Maronites	2708
'Gypsies'[a]	502
Other[b]	2921
TOTAL	577,615[c]

[a]'Gypsies' is the term used in the document. According to one commentator, 'Cyprus Gypsies' have not adopted the ethnonym 'Roma'. See: Akçali, "The 'Other' Cypriots," 77

[b]The available documents do not define 'Others'. It is presumed to include Latins and non-British foreigners

[c]This is the total mentioned on the document, but there is a discrepancy of 30 persons between this number and the total deriving from the individual groups above (577,585). The last column on the document was not visible. Judging from other documents in the census, it is hereby assumed that the missing column refers to 'Unknown/ Not Stated'

The census of 1960 informs further that the vast majority of the population of Cyprus could read and write, with the highest illiteracy levels observed among women from both communities in rural areas. Most economically active individuals were working in the areas of agriculture, manufacturing, and construction, with 'other' overpassing construction by some 1500 individuals. These numbers however, do not correspond to the productivity levels in each industry. Even though in the early 1960s the island enjoyed the second highest income per capita in the Mediterranean region, failing to introduce modern technologies in areas like agriculture and farming led to a productivity of merely 16% of the Gross Domestic Product (GDP), despite the fact that these two industries employed roughly 44% of the population.[5]

The persisting uncertainty and lack of security after December 1963 had adverse consequences for the economy of the Republic. In 1964, import duties fell, violence paralysed economic activity in urban and rural centres adjacent to the Turkish Cypriot-controlled areas, unemployment increased sharply, and public revenue from taxes dropped.[6] The tourist

[5]Varnava, *Cyprus Before 1974*, 77–82.

[6]HORM, Session 1963–1964, 30 March 1964, Speech by Minister of Labour and Social Insurance, Tassos Papadopoulos; HORM, Session 1964–1965, 28 December 1964, Speech by Minister of Finance, Renos Solomides, 338.

industry was profoundly affected with only 7722 foreign visitors in the first half of 1964, compared to 49,585 arrivals 12 months earlier.[7] Foreign experts who provided technical assistance towards the implementation of development programmes withdrew their services, and economic recovery seemed unlikely. Nevertheless, once violence subsided, immediate steps were taken to reduce unemployment, promote industrial growth, and foster the promotion of private initiatives. The successful implementation of these policies led British High Commissioner Sir Norman Costar to remark in 1969:

> Cyprus is the only country I know which has flourished economically on a civil war [...]. One might almost say that Cyprus has put all of its nonsense into politics and kept it out of economics.[8]

Despite considerable increase in military expenditure, it took the RoC economy no more than two years to recover. Internally, temporary measures were taken to assist those using property in 'adversely affected areas'. At the international level, new trade agreements were signed with countries of the Soviet bloc, an oil refinery was built in Larnaca, and targeted initiatives supported the hospitality and tourism industry. By the end of 1965, the government's statistical data indicated the lowest unemployment rate since 1958, and steady growth in all sectors of industry.[9]

Nevertheless, neither the policies initiated, nor the data selected at the time took into account the isolated Turkish Cypriot community. According to Ozay Mehmet, Turkish Cypriot Canada-based Emeritus Professor in Development Economics, discussions on the Cyprus conflict(s) have been dominated by legal experts and political scientists, with the former searching for the 'magic wand in constitution making', and the latter 'dwell[ing] on the politics of identity and ethnicity', underestimating how the economic vulnerability of the Turkish Cypriot community contributed to their increasing separatist tendencies.[10] Similarly, in comparing the cases of Cyprus and Ireland, international law expert John Reynolds has argued that self-determination on both islands was 'implemented in the form of a narrow nationalist project without a clear redistributive socioeconomic

[7] Varnava, *Cyprus Before 1974*, 77–82.
[8] Varnava, *Cyprus Before 1974*, citing TNA, FCO 9/785, Costar to FCO, 26 March 1969.
[9] Varnava, *Cyprus Before 1974*, 84–85.
[10] Mehmet, *Sustainability of Microstates*, 22–23.

policy'.[11] The vast majority of displaced persons in the enclaves were unemployed and sustained through financial relief and assistance from Turkey, without any official statistical data for this specific group of persons having been identified to date. Indicatively, however, one author supported that by the end of 1964, the average income of a Turkish Cypriot living in an enclave equated a mere 24% of the average Greek Cypriot income, in direct contrast to 86% at the end of 1963.[12]

It must be noted that the UN Secretary-General's periodical reports from this period, engage consistently and in relative detail with economic developments at the time, across sectors and with reference to the parallel economy that was gradually evolving in the Turkish Cypriot enclaves. A limited number of initiatives and schemes involved both communities, developed with the assistance of UNFICYP as a means towards fostering collaboration with the ultimate objective being the return to 'normal conditions'.

Economic relations are more often than not a significant factor in obtaining a better understanding of the shifting social dynamics during a non-international armed conflict, or internal disturbances, as indicated in research from the 1990s wars in former Yugoslavia and Rwanda.[13] Hence, domestic socio-legal policies are of particular importance in internal conflicts, where all aspects of social relations among the local population can have a tremendous impact on worsening or ameliorating a violent situation.

The Effective End of Bi-communality

The formal records of the plenary minutes of the House of Representatives on 17 December 1963, contain a note informing that this was the last plenary session with the participation of both Greek Cypriot and Turkish Cypriot MPs, before the 'intercommunal disturbances of December 1963'.[14] Nothing else from the discussions recorded on that day or during the preceding period, suggests the eventual turn of events four days later. According to Emilianides, however, there was a general decline in Parliamentary meetings in 1963, compared to preceding years.[15]

[11] Reynolds, "Peripheral Parallels?" 255.
[12] Hoffmeister, *Legal Aspects*, 19.
[13] Anghie and Chimni, "Third World Approaches," 196–197.
[14] HORM, Session 1963–1964, 17 December 1963, p. 130.
[15] Emilianides, *Co-Existence*, 26–27.

As indicated in the minutes, parliamentary debates at the time took place in both formal languages of the RoC, each MP speaking in the language of their own community, with simultaneous interpretation in the other language, not unlike common practice in international intergovernmental fora. The last point on record from December 1963 is a request by Turkish Cypriot MP Halit Ali Riza to postpone the discussion on one of the topics on the agenda, to allow time for the translation of all relevant materials into the Turkish language. This pending matter was never again formally addressed. At least not in plenary.

Following the events of December 1963, the House of Representatives resumed work on 10 January 1964. The first point on the agenda was the approval of the annual budget. It was only when the President of the House, Glafcos Clerides, asked the Turkish Cypriot Secretary to read out the Report of the Budget Committee in Turkish, that the Greek Cypriot Secretary replied that the Turkish Cypriot Secretary and all other Turkish Cypriot MPs were absent, adding that there was no need to read out the Turkish text. The President of the House agreed, and the budget was approved without a plenary discussion on the substance. According to article 77 of the RoC Constitution, the quorum for the House of Representatives plenary sessions was a mere one third of all MPs without communal qualification, which could be satisfied with only 17 Greek Cypriot MPs in attendance. With only 15 Turkish Cypriot MPs in total, out of 50, the Turkish Cypriot MPs could not satisfy the required minimum on their own. Nonetheless, it took the House three whole years to put the issue of the quorum on the agenda and settle the matter formally during the 1966/1967 parliamentary session.

The ongoing violence dominated the work of the House of Representatives throughout 1964. With only two Greek Cypriot parties represented in the first ten-year-long Parliament of the RoC, an 'internal confusion' was observed among the MPs of the larger 'Patriotic Front' (*Πατριωτικό Μέτωπο*) party. Most of these MPs were united in support of Makarios' government, but represented a range of ideologies across the political spectrum, from the conservative right up to Social Democracy, while Communism remained the distinctive political line of the second party, AKEL.[16] The Turkish Cypriot MPs, all of whom came from the 'Turkish National Party' of Fazil Kutchuk, represented the third political

[16] Emilianides, *Towards Catastrophe*, 17–20.

party in Parliament until 17 December 1963. They never returned to their seats, notwithstanding one single attempt to do so in July 1965.

Throughout the 1960s the Legislature was generally marginalised, due to the instability that existed and by virtue of the Presidential system of governance assigned to the Republic through its Constitution. Public debates were usually brief, and agreement over new bills was often reached in advance of the formal voting in plenary.[17] Whereas the recorded minutes of the Plenary sessions are valuable in filling gaps in the historical record, the relative lack of scrutiny during plenary debates precludes an in-depth assessment of the legal reforms that took place during that time. This was crucial since the absence of the Turkish Cypriot MPs allowed the adoption of a series of legal reforms, which radically changed the bi-communal character of the Cypriot Republic. A process that some have termed the 'hellenisation' of the Republic,[18] or the establishment of a 'second *de facto* Greek state'.[19]

Within 20 days from the Supreme Court's *Ibrahim* judgement, discussed in the previous Chapter, the House of Representatives passed a new Municipal Corporations Law (Law 64/1964), to resolve the problem which had occurred following the expiration of the colonial Municipal Law on 31 December 1962. This new law completely disregarded article 173(1) of the Constitution, which provided for separate municipalities in the five biggest urban centres of the island, re-establishing instead the municipalities that were in existence on 1 January 1958, bypassing, therefore, the previously unchallenged unilateral declaration of Turkish Cypriot municipalities during the bi-communal violent upheaval of 1958.

The next major reform, perhaps the most radical among them, took place on 30 March 1965. It concerned the dissolution of the Greek Communal Chamber and the establishment of a Ministry of Education in its place, re-allocating the Greek Chamber's responsibilities primarily to the new Ministry (Law 12/1965). As already discussed, the two Communal Chambers were constitutional bodies, which according to article 87 of the Constitution, held the power to pass legislation on religious, educational and cultural matters of communal nature. The Preamble of Law 12/1965 justified this reform on the basis that the Greek Communal Chamber (i) could not exercise its responsibilities and functions 'as things stand', while

[17] Emilianides, *Towards Catastrophe*, 38–39.
[18] Hoffmeister, *Legal Aspects*, 17–19.
[19] Kızılyürek, *Resentment*, 590.

(ii) the exercise of its functions was vital for the functioning of the State. Moreover, (iii) the Greek Communal Chamber had invited the House of Representatives to transfer the responsibilities of the Chamber to the (direct) authority of the Republic 'as soon as possible', elevating its status, as this (iv) had 'become necessary' (hinting on the DoN) 'until the Cypriot people expresse[d] its opinion on these matters'.

Since not all responsibilities of the Communal Chambers under the Constitution related to education and the portfolio of the new Ministry, section 3 of Law 12/1965 allocated some responsibilities to other existing ministries. Notably, however, any task that was not allocated to another Ministry was transferred directly to the Council of Ministers, which was subsequently empowered to assign the task in question to any organ, authority or individual they decided to. Law 12/1965 does not list expressly the tasks delegated to the Council of Ministers, but one obvious example deriving from a comparison of the constitutional and the legislative texts, are the issues pertaining to charitable and sporting foundations, bodies and associations. This move raises questions concerning civic life within the Greek Cypriot community, since from the years of 'Palmerocracy' onwards, when most political activity was restricted, such organisations played a fundamental role in the island's political life. Furthermore, not only the law explicitly contradicted article 46 of the Constitution which states that the RoC is to have a total of ten Ministries, but it also appears to have seceded part of the legislative powers of the Greek Communal Chamber directly to the Executive, interfering with the doctrine of the separation of powers and reducing the checks and balances that a legislative body could potentially exercise upon the Executive. Lastly, Law 12/1965 deepened further the chasm the DoN had already created between the black letter of the Constitution and its practical application, in complete disregard for the principle of bi-communality.

By 1965 it was also time for the RoC to hold its second round of elections, following those held on 13 December 1959, when Cypriots were called to choose the State's leaders prior to independence. Amidst the ongoing situation and the absence of the Turkish Cypriot community from political life, abiding to the constitutionally assigned procedure was not possible. Thus, the House of Representatives passed a law which extended the presidential and the parliamentary terms of office for up to 12 months (Law 38/1965). A law which was renewed twice, in 1966 (Law 48/1966) and 1967 (Law 46/1967), with the first Presidential elections since the establishment of the Republic eventually held in 1968.

The first parliamentary elections after independence were held as late as 1970, with the first Parliament completing a full decade-long term.

These laws made no reference whatsoever to the office of the Vice-President or the term of the Turkish Cypriot MPs. Already in the previous year, on 27 June 1964, the ICRC delegate in Cyprus had informed his Headquarters that according to information received by the Director-General of the Ministry of Foreign Affairs, the RoC government no longer recognised Kutchuk as the Vice-President of the RoC and from then on, he was simply the head of a rebel formation *(le chef d'une fraction rebelle)*. With the separate electoral catalogues and the separate administration of elections also being abolished in 1965 (Law 39/1965), the 'communal distinction was written off'.[20]

These developments did not leave unconcerned anyone with a vested interest in developments in Cyprus. The UN Secretary-General issued *ad hoc* reports to inform the UNSC. Among the Guarantor Powers, the UK and Turkey protested the reforms, while there is no record of Greek efforts to defend them either. It is at this point that Turkish Cypriot MPs attempted to return to the House of Representatives, requesting the UN Secretary-General's good offices to enable their attendance to the Parliamentary plenary session that would discuss the bill extending the terms of office of the Greek Cypriot MPs and the RoC President. A meeting between a delegation of Turkish Cypriot MPs and the President of the House of Representatives was arranged in the afternoon of 22 July 1965, where Glafcos Clerides conveyed to the Turkish Cypriot delegation the conditions upon which the Turkish Cypriot MPs would be allowed to attend the plenary.

(a) The Turkish Cypriot members would resume their seats permanently rather than only for the purpose of the present debate;
(b) The Turkish Cypriot members would accept that the laws enacted by the House of Representatives would be applied to the whole of Cyprus, including the Turkish areas, by the Government using the normal authorized administrative organs;
(c) While the Greek Cypriot members would regard attendance at the House by the Turkish Cypriot members as implying recognition by them of the present Cyprus Government, the Turkish Cypriot members would not be called upon to make a statement to that

[20] S/6569, para 4.

effect, and the Greek Cypriots would likewise refrain from making any such statement on the record of the House;
(d) It must be understood that the provision in article 78 of the constitution concerning separate majorities had been abolished and every member of the House would have one vote for all decisions.[21]

Such conditions were unacceptable to the Turkish Cypriot MPs, who by accepting them would have put themselves in a direct confrontation with the leadership of their own community. The bill was eventually adopted the next day, after only one Greek Cypriot MP, a well-known lawyer and future long-term mayor of Nicosia Lellos Demetriades, challenged the gravity of such unilateral moves, by suggesting that the extension of the terms of office should be put before the electorate through a referendum, in place of the anticipated elections.

Within a fortnight, on 5 August 1965, the House of Representatives made legislative arrangements that would allow the election of one 'Religious Group Representative' for each of the Armenian, Maronite, and Latin religious groups with standing before the House and any other authority or organ of the Republic (Law 45/1965). These religious group representatives to this day are vested with the power to address issues relevant to each of their respective religious groups, filling in gaps created in their representation following the dissolution of the Greek Communal Chamber.[22] The last stroke in terms of the legal reforms undertaken by the RoC government during this period came in June 1967, when a new law on the functioning of the Public Service Commission—the body tasked with appointments of public servants—abolished the requirement for the appointment of both Greek and Turkish members, under the usual 70:30 ratio, as originally provided for by article 124 of the Constitution. A point which Makarios' had raised in his 13 points for constitutional amendment in 1963, and was therefore, at the core of inter-communal disagreement. Contrary to all other laws mentioned above, Law 33/1967 contains no preamble stating that its adoption had 'become necessary' under the DoN, potentially indicating an increase in confidence of Greek Cypriot MPs through the use of less cautionary wording.

In direct contrast to the Greek Cypriots, in the aftermath of 1963–1964 the Turkish Cypriots held a firm grasp on the 1960 constitutional order.

[21] S/6569, paras 7–16.

[22] Hadjilyras, *The Religious Groups*, 91–92.

A stance aiming to ensure that their community would not be reduced to minority status within the RoC. For this reason, despite their apparent isolation within the enclaves, the Turkish Cypriot leadership maintained by analogy the application of the provisions of the original 1960 Constitution, to the extent this was possible. Once the terms of office of the President and the Greek Cypriot MPs were extended, the Turkish Cypriot MPs passed two 'communal laws' of their own, extending the terms of office of the RoC Vice-President and the members of the House of Representatives, providing for interim provisions concerning the election of the members of the Turkish Communal Chamber. The intention was to facilitate the Chamber's constitutional functioning and to reiterate that the community's fundamental rights, as enshrined in the RoC Constitution, were still in force.[23] While these two legislative instruments have no legal standing under RoC law, they serve as evidence of the earliest efforts by the Turkish Cypriot community to self-organise and adapt to a new reality, which would soon become the 'new normal'. In the face of separatism, the fact that holding onto the RoC Constitution was the only means to maintain legitimacy is a paradox worthy of more detailed research, especially in view of public perceptions of the issue.

Commentators from both communities have observed and admitted that the legal reforms on the side of the Republic gradually aligned the constitutional legal order to the 13 constitutional amendments suggested by Makarios in November 1963 and had sparked the violence in the first place.[24] Necatigil identifies a total of seven laws purporting to the abolition of the 1960 Constitutional framework.[25] The laws mentioned here, plus the National Guard Law (Law 20/1964), the Police (Amendment) Law (Law 21/1964), and the Administration of Justice (Miscellaneous Provisions) Law (Law 33/1964), which were adopted before the Supreme Court's *Ibrahim* judgement. Whereas, admittedly, in spring 1964 the establishment of the National Guard, the merging of the Police and the Gendarmerie forces, and the Administration of Justice laws could be justified as emergency measures, from March 1965 onwards it is difficult to justify the radical legal reforms undertaken exclusively by reference to the conflict. Besides, the more changes to the constitutional order were made,

[23] Kyriakides, *Constitutionalism and Crisis*, 118–119.

[24] Necatigil, *The Cyprus Question*, 53–56; Emilianides, *Towards Catastrophe*, 73; Kızılyürek, *Resentment* (n 48) 590–591; Varnava (n 9) 44–50.

[25] Necatigil, *The Cyprus Question*, 56–60; Necatigil, *The Cyprus* Conflict, 31–34.

the harder it became to see such measures as 'temporary'. The gradual abolition of the bi-communal structures by the Greek Cypriot-led government on the one side, and the opportunity to establish self-governing territorial 'pockets' by the Turkish Cypriot leadership on the other, portrayed a rapid move towards a point of no return.

International lawyer Anthony Anghie has pointed out in his own research that regardless of the exact nature of a state of emergency, law plays an integral role in managing it.[26] In Cyprus this was no different. Legal literature has also established that de facto emergencies can either 'inflate' a normalcy onto an emergency, or 'deflate' an emergency into normalcy.[27] This 'deflation' characterises the RoC during this period and thereafter. It is in the very nature of emergencies to adversely impact democratic decision-making, human rights and the rule of law, creating tensions between the State's 'internal' and 'external' sovereignty,[28] while the sovereign decision-maker acts both within and outside the law. In other words, the law cannot fully explain or regulate emergencies, and legal issues serve as only one aspect of a far greater picture.

The Enclaves and the Turkish Cypriot Community

While the above legislative reforms were taking place, the Turkish Cypriot community continued living in isolation from the rest of the island's population, both in and outside the self-administered enclaves. It has already been illustrated how in the immediate aftermath of the violence of December 1963 bridges of communication were built between the two communities for humanitarian purposes, upon the initiative of the ICRC and the British-coordinated Joint Task Force, later replaced by UNFICYP. However, the ceasefire of 9 August 1964, while instrumental in bringing an end to the ever-increasing violence, did not bring a restoration of 'law and order' or 'normal conditions'. On the contrary, the continuous segregation of the Republic's population, combined with the legal reforms and the lack of political and diplomatic progress, led to routine division.

Territorial control is a fundamental aspect of general public international law and the law of armed conflict, including in situations of internal

[26] Anghie, "Rethinking Sovereignty" 306.
[27] Greene, *Permanent States of Emergency*, 52–62.
[28] von Laffert, *Zypern und Fragen*, 138–141.

violence. Daily life within the enclaves is perhaps the most neglected aspect from this period's historiography. Therefore, the limited scope of knowledge we have today on the formation of the enclaves, daily life therein and the impact their existence has had on the island as a whole is a major gap in comprehensively evaluating the social, the political and the diplomatic events of the 1960s. Moreover, *de facto* territorial control is of particular significance under the classical understanding of 'civil war' and under common article 3, since when exercised by non-state armed groups is one of the recognised indicators establishing whether a non-international armed conflict exists, under the criteria of both 'organisation' and 'intensity'. On the other side, whereas territorial control can strengthen the argument in favour of recognising that a conflict has crossed the threshold of applicability for common article 3, the absence of territorial control should not be interpreted automatically as non-application of common article 3.[29] The exact threshold of this requirement has always been unclear, even after Additional Protocol II to the 1949 Geneva Conventions was adopted in 1977.

Under public international law an 'enclave' is an isolated part of a State circumscribed by a single foreign State, the 'host State', which prevents a direct link with the territory of the State to which it belongs, the 'home State', unless through the territory of the host State. It is acknowledged, however, that historically enclaves have existed also as 'internal' or 'administrative enclaves', within historically set boundaries.[30] In that sense, 'enclaves' in Cyprus constitute the SBAs, where the UK is the 'home State' and the RoC the 'host State'.[31] The Turkish Cypriot enclaves during this period, on the other hand, were neither 'enclaves' in the legal sense of the term, nor 'historical administrative entities', despite the traditionally higher concentration of Turkish Cypriot citizens in many of these areas. In 1963–1964, the Turkish Cypriot enclaves became 'new *de facto* geopolitical fields'[32] through the use of force, and had no autonomous legal standing whatsoever, other than being territory over which the Republic's authorities had lost control at some point since December 1963.

Among the plethora of disciplines that have engaged with the Cyprus Question, it appears that only anthropological research has addressed

[29] Moir, "The Concept of Non-International Armed Conflict," 407.

[30] Irmscher, "Enclaves."

[31] Irmscher, "Enclaves," para 7.

[32] Patrick, *Political Geography and the Cyprus Conflict*, 99.

different aspects of the topic with some consistency.[33] This is in addition to the well-known study of Vamik Volkan in psychology, on the psychological effects of inter-communal conflict particularly in the Turkish Cypriot community, following a visit to his native Cyprus in the late 1960s.[34] The most detailed study on the enclaves to date, however, remains Richard Patrick's assessment of the conflict from the perspective of political geography. His research was the result of his doctoral research in the early 1970s, and contains information he obtained through fieldwork and a series of interviews with high-ranking political figures from the Turkish Cypriot community. These limited secondary sources, combined with archival material compiled from the field reports of the ICRC's Cyprus mission and the UN Secretary-General's reports to the UNSC, help to reconstruct significant aspects of life in the enclaves and the Turkish Cypriot community at large here.

Though ethnically defined regions pre-existed the establishment of the RoC to a certain extent a legacy of Ottoman societal structure, after 21 December 1963, the RoC security forces allowed entry and exit from the enclaves through designated checkpoints. Greek Cypriot government officials and private individuals were allowed entry by the Turkish Cypriot leadership only in 'rare and special cases [...] as a matter of political principle with little attempt at justification on practical grounds'.[35] Despite the checks, however, many locations were not accurately demarcated and changes could occur at short notice.

The perceived boundaries represented agreements achieved through 'local understandings' and 'compromises' among local officials from both communities, 'between instructions from distant superiors and a desire to live and let live'.[36] These were based on a number of practical considerations, including local patterns of ethnic settlement, land ownership, communication, transportation, and levels of inter-communal hostility. *Mukhtars* or military commanders could also negotiate such local arrangements, following UNFICYP facilitation. Some of these agreements could qualify as 'special agreements' under IHL, which broadly interpreted are

[33] Bryant and Hatay, "Guns and guitars"; Bryant and Papapdakis, *Politics of Memory.*; Loizos, *Unofficial Views.*

[34] Volkan, *A psychoanalytic history.*

[35] S/7611, para 109.

[36] Patrick, *Political Geography and the Cyprus Conflict*, 86–87.

understood to have imposed additional humanitarian rules on the parties to the conflict.

Communication between the territories under the control of the Republic and the enclaves had to be maintained as much as possible. For this reason, UNFICYP was driven to draw a list of politically and legally neutral terms when referring to Turkish Cypriot officials, in order to avoid formal recognition of their governance and compromise the rights of the Republic over those territories. Thus, on the one side there was the 'Cypriot Government' and on the other the 'Turkish Cypriot leadership', there were the RoC 'District Officers' and the 'Local Turkish Cypriot leadership', as well as the 'Cyprus Police' and the 'Turkish Cypriot police element'. This obsession with 'etiquette' has been a continuous obstacle towards challenging the usual terminology and critically assessing the situation as a whole, since deviating from the normally accepted terms is subject to constant and severe criticism from various sides. In a legal context this is especially harmful, since legal arguments are dependent on words which, as seen throughout this book, are rarely static in meaning. Over the decades this has led to a cacophony of politico-legal arguments of decreasing substantial value repeated in a loop. These terms survive, even dominate one could argue, inter-communal and diplomatic discussions to this day.

In the earliest period of the conflict, archival evidence mentions that individuals who strayed off the territory controlled by their own community would often go missing. Later, Greek Cypriots who entered the enclaves unintentionally would usually be detained, questioned and searched, to be eventually released following interventions by UNFICYP. Overall, Greek Cypriots avoided places largely inhabited by Turkish Cypriots, as reflected by the fact that Greek Cypriots would rarely visit relatives detained in the Turkish Cypriot sector of Nicosia, despite ICRC willingness to arrange such visits for people from both communities. Instead, the transit of Greek Cypriots through Turkish Cypriot-controlled territories would only take place under UNFICYP escort and supervision.

On the other hand, even though the Greek Cypriot position is that the Republic's authorities never precluded Turkish Cypriots from entering the areas under the control of the Republic, there is considerable evidence that Turkish Cypriot citizens were subjected to strict, occasionally humiliating, checks. According to UNFICYP, complaints by Turkish Cypriots would sometimes be unsubstantiated, but serious incidents have also been witnessed and reported by UNCIVPOL. One such example was the arrest of 20 Turkish Cypriot men by the Cyprus Police in Larnaca, for wearing clothing resembling military uniforms. Upon their release they were examined by an UNFICYP doctor, who confirmed that their wounds were consistent with complaints for ill-treatment and assault. However, as seen below, the movement of Turkish Cypriots was also strictly regulated by their own leadership on the basis that such control was allegedly necessary for security purposes.[37]

According to interviews by Patrick to Osman Orek, fist Minister of Defence of the RoC, and Rauf Denktash, initially President of the Turkish Communal Chamber and decades-long leader of the Turkish Cypriot community, the enclaves followed a five-level administrative structure under a 'civil-military synthesis'. The smallest units were the Turkish Cypriot villages—or Turkish Cypriot quarters within a mixed village or town—which grouped with other neighbouring villages or quarters composed larger clusters. Each cluster had its own 'headquarters' manned by a 'police sergeant' and a 'fighter officer', who led a battalion-like formation of fighters. Many clusters together formed 'sub-regions' with stationed full-time 'fighter units'. Two or more sub-regions, depending on geographical proximity, would form a single region. In practice, this led to seven *de facto* Turkish Cypriot district authorities, each with its own 'district officer' based in Nicosia, Chatos, Famagusta, Larnaca, Limassol, Paphos, and Lefka.[38] This territory covered about 54 square miles (140 sq km) in total; a mere 1.5–2% of RoC territory.[39] If a non-international armed conflict can exist without any territorial control,[40] then any arguments that the territory controlled by the Turkish Cypriot leadership is negligible and cannot substantiate the existence of a non-international armed conflict lose significance.

The fifth level of administration was the 'policy-making coalition' which directed the community island-wide, and was based at the headquarters of the Turkish Cypriot leadership in Nicosia. Regarding the community as a whole, civil affairs were directed by a General Committee of former Turkish Cypriot ministers and MPs. The Turkish Communal Chamber legislated according to the competences it already had under article 87 the

[37] S/7611; S/7350; S/7611; S/7969.
[38] Patrick, *Political Geography and the Cyprus Conflict*, 84–86.
[39] Necatigil, *The Cyprus Question*, 53–54; Chrysostomides, *The Republic of Cyprus*, 91.
[40] Moir, "The Concept of Non-International Armed Conflict," 407.

RoC Constitution, and RoC Turkish Cypriot public servants retained their positions and continued working for the Turkish Cypriot *de facto* administration, with a standard monthly salary subsidised by Turkey. In terms of military affairs, Supreme Command was exercised by a General of the Turkish army, who was attached to the Turkish Embassy, and carried the *nom de guerre* 'Bozkurt'. 'Bozkurt' was identified by the UN as member of staff at the Turkish Embassy, who had arrived to Cyprus prior to the 1963 events. According to the UN he left the Island on 24 February 1967.[41] His exact hierarchical relationship with the Turkish Ambassador was unclear, but Patrick purported that the General was in no way subordinate to the Ambassador. Below him, each enclave was governed by a *Bayraktar*, usually a Turkish Army officer, who according to some sources was appointed directly by the Turkish Republic's Special War Bureau.[42]

In February 1964, the ICRC delegate in Cyprus informed the ICRC Headquarters that it was TMT that gave the orders and determined the policy within the enclaves.[43] One of their aims was the promotion of 'Turkish consciousness', through the imposition of movement restrictions outside the enclaves, fines and other sanctions for those associating with Greek Cypriots.

Like Turkey's military intervention in August 1964, the type of direct involvement analysed here also constitutes unlawful intervention under international law. By the end of 1964 and until 1968, the total number of Turkish Cypriot 'armed elements' was estimated at about 12,000 men.[44] As mentioned previously, Turkish Cypriot fighters did not wear distinctive uniforms, in part due to the RoC's policy to prohibit the import of fabric and other materials that could be used for the sewing of uniforms. Nonetheless, new military clothing among the Turkish Cypriot fighters was observed by UNFICYP in the first half of 1965.[45] In June 1965 used military uniforms of US origin, some with ranking insignia, were found among the items delivered by one of the Turkish Red Crescent shipments to Cyprus. By the end of 1965, an 'increasingly professional' organisation of the Turkish Cypriot fighters was reported, potentially enhancing the level of 'organisation' observed among them.

[41] S/7969, para 33.

[42] Kızılyürek, *Resentment*, 600.

[43] ICRC, B AG 251 049-004, Report No 3 for the period 1–15 February 1964 (16 February 1964).

[44] S/6102, para 136; S/7191, paras 48–52; S/7969, paras 34, 116.

[45] S/6426, paras 33, 87.

Reliable statistical data on displacement from this period has not been found for either community, and the limited existing information varies across sources. Speaking of exact numbers becomes harder considering the mass emigration of Turkish Cypriots after 1963, that after 1960 there is no official RoC census on the Turkish Cypriot population, and that the very first census on the population in the occupied northern territory of the island was held as recently as 1996.[46] In December 1963, the total number of *displaced Turkish Cypriots inside and outside the enclaves* was estimated by UNFICYP at 25,000, of whom 21,000 were accommodated in larger Turkish Cypriot communities inside and outside the enclaves, and 4000 found shelter in camps for displaced persons within enclaved territories.[47] A year later, the UN Secretary-General reported that the population within the enclaves amounted to about 59,000 individuals, which is equivalent to 57% of the whole Turkish Cypriot population under the census of 1960. Among them, there were approximately 13,600 displaced.[48]

The above figures do not coincide with Chrysostomides, who agrees with UN figures on the number of persons within the enclaves, but has claimed that 79,000 Turkish Cypriots (65% of the community) resided outside the enclaves. If correct, this number would inflate the total of Turkish Cypriots beyond the official 1960 census figures. Based on the numbers provided by UNFICYP and the 1960 census, the remaining Turkish Cypriots outside the enclaves must have been approximately 45,350 individuals, concentrated in areas with an originally high Turkish Cypriot population. Though seemingly free, these individuals were also isolated and faced similar practical problems to those enclaved. This was facilitated by the bi-communal Constitution, since Turkish Cypriots were by default not integrated with the Greek Cypriot community within the State's administrative structure. Moreover, the Turkish Cypriot *mukhtars* refused to take an oath of allegiance to the Republic, and subsequently, the government refused to recognise their authority. This was further exacerbated by the new Municipal Corporations Law (Law 64/1964) passed in November 1964. Eventually, the government dissociated itself from any responsibility towards the welfare of those Turkish Cypriots continuing to reside under its control, holding the position that these Turkish

[46] Hatay, *Is the Turkish Cypriot Population Shrinking?* 23.

[47] S/6102, para 45.

[48] S/6102.

Cypriots could share strategic information with TMT and the Turkish Cypriot leadership. Overall, it appears that the number of displaced persons fluctuated over the years, depending on political and military developments. By the early 1970s the Turkish quarters in 72 mixed villages and 24 Turkish Cypriot villages were completely deserted. Only eight mixed villages remained mixed, albeit with a reduced number of Turkish Cypriot residents.[49]

Whatever the security concerns of the Republic vis-à-vis the Turkish Cypriot population remaining under its control, common article 3 of the 1949 Geneva Conventions states that within an internal armed conflict 'Persons taking no active part in the hostilities [...] shall in all circumstances be treated humanely, without any adverse distinction founded on race, colour, religion or faith, sex, birth or wealth, or any other similar criteria'. To that, one should not omit to add the extensive human rights provisions of the RoC Constitution, including non-discrimination on the basis of community under article 6, which binds all state organs in the process of exercising their duties. Hence, it appears that the Republic failed to apply any due process in view of the protection of the rights of its Turkish Cypriot citizens during this period. A silver-lining to the predicament of those who remained in their villages, in spite of the risks that choice involved, was that they retained relative freedom and access to their land and farms, and therefore, were self-sustained and able to participate in some limited commercial activities.

On the other hand, life within the enclaves has often been described as 'life under 'siege', in secondary sources,[50] but also in the ICRC archives. As soon as violence erupted in December 1963, the RoC government imposed a series of economic restrictions to the enclaves, primarily by prohibiting certain materials from entering the enclaves and confiscating any such materials found at the checkpoints. Moreover, all UN Secretary-General reports from 1964 to 1968 consistently refer to the lack of postal services in the enclaves, problems with regular access to public utilities like electricity and water, issues with public revenue, and the payment of social insurance benefits such as retirement pensions, to eligible Turkish Cypriots. Where solutions were available, politically motivated hurdles would usually arise. For instance, where governmental postal services were accessible to Turkish Cypriots, they would still be prevented from using them by

[49] Patrick, *Political Geography and the Cyprus Conflict*, 75.
[50] Bryant and Hatay, "Guns and guitars."

their own leadership, in order to not 'recognise' the authority of the government. A parallel non-governmental postal network was soon established, but in 1965 a Turkish Cypriot man was convicted for conveying 383 letters in contravention of the privilege of the Postmaster-General, under the Post Office Law (Capital 303). In their judgement, the Supreme Court evaded discussing the contextual background to the case, but reduced the disproportionately high fine imposed at first instance, in recognition of the humanitarian issues at stake.[51]

Living conditions differed from one enclave to another, depending on factors such as population density, soil morphology, freedom of movement, and each region's standard of living before December 1963. Between 20 and 30 July 1964, the ICRC mission organised an island-wide inquiry on the living conditions of the Turkish Cypriot community, assessing the needs of approximately three quarters (75%) of the total Turkish Cypriot population, in and outside the enclaves. People were distinguished in five categories: (i) the 'refugees', some of whom managed to move along with their cattle, (ii) the 'unemployed', including those whose profession could practically not be exercised, such as construction and factory workers, dockers, and track drivers, (iii) dependents of dead or missing persons, (iv) the 'middle class', small in number and the only ones who could still make some purchases to cover their needs, and (v) the 'combatants', who included more or less all able men residing within the enclaves aged 17 to approximately 40 years old.

Lack of housing, inadequate infrastructure, nutrition, and access to medical services were problems that arose across regions immediately. In one of his reports the ICRC delegate in Cyprus expressed surprise to the fact that in the months between December 1963 and September 1964, there were no epidemics, serious diseases or nutritional deficiencies developed among the population. Moreover, the lack of employment within the enclaves led most able-bodied men to enlist as fighters, before conscription became compulsory for all male secondary school students (predominantly minors) and graduates. This meant that it was especially difficult for the ICRC to distinguish between civilians and combatants, and therefore, to prevent any relief items reaching the combatants, who were not meant to enjoy the protections and humanitarian assistance afforded under international humanitarian law to women, children, and elderly civilians. These Turkish Cypriot fighters, who were tasked primarily

[51] *Mehmet Halil Hamouza* (1965).

with guarding the boundaries of the enclaves, continued residing with their families and 'naturally' sharing meals with them.[52]

By late 1965, there were increased incidents of Turkish Cypriots displaced persons occupying Greek Cypriot-owned houses and government buildings in the Turkish Cypriot-controlled neighbourhoods in Nicosia, as well as in disputed areas along the Green Line.[53] In 1966, the government started repairing or building houses, in an effort to start encouraging those displaced to return to their villages. The scheme, however, failed to attract interest due to security concerns, but also because the Turkish Cypriot leadership actively deterred members of their community from returning, and sanctioned those who attempted to do so.[54]

The most densely populated areas were the displaced persons camp in Mandres (Hamitkoy) within the broader northern Nicosia enclave, and the Kokkina (Erenkoy) enclave on the north-west coast. In Mandres, housing was the most significant issue. With the government refusing to facilitate the building of permanent structures and with the transfer of building materials being restricted, the ICRC suggested the building of traditional mad-brick houses, which offered good isolation from heat and cold. Efforts to that effect were initiated in 1965, but it was not before June 1966 that tents were no longer in use.

In Kokkina the unhospitable, rocky, sea-side landscape made living conditions particularly difficult. With an original population of only 300 inhabitants, after the fighting in August 1964 the population almost doubled from 850 persons to 1400. This had an extreme impact on the living conditions of those stranded there, with daily calorie-intake reduced by half for all, while some families found shelter in caves 'under sub-normal conditions'.[55] In the first half of 1967, as many as 1200 individuals in Kokkina still lived in tents, with the addition of wooden floors for the winter months being the sole improvement managed. Owing to its strategic position as a bridgehead to Turkey, this was one of the last areas to benefit from the government's relaxation measures in the second half of the 1960s. People there were exempt from any initiatives encouraging the

[52] ICRC, B AG 251 049-005.02, Note 111 (2 August 1964).

[53] S/7001paras 69–73; ICRC, B AG 251 049-005.02, No 237 – Blockade of the Turkish quarter of Nicosia (4 May 1965).

[54] S/7350 para 123; ICRC, B AG 251 049-005.02, Note 274 – Activity Report (27 September 1965).

[55] S/5950.Add. 2, para 4; ICRC, B AG 251 049-005.02, Note 125 – Activities of the Delegation (15 September 1964).

return to 'normal conditions'. Until January 1968, entry and exit from the enclave was completely restricted and people were sustained exclusively on humanitarian relief delivered fortnightly, subject to the restrictions imposed by the RoC authorities.

Access to healthcare was another widespread problem. ICRC medical experts arrived to Cyprus to conduct a medical needs assessment and make recommendations from late August to early September 1964. Difficulties arose from the beginning, when the exact number of Turkish Cypriot medical practitioners could not be determined. According to government figures there were 119 registered Turkish Cypriot doctors, while the figures provided by the Turkish Cypriot representatives contained only 40. This could be explained at least in part by the mass emigration of Turkish Cypriots upon the eruption of violence. Medical conditions were assessed as 'unfavourable' overall, but quality of services ranged from 'primitive' (in the eyes of a Swiss expert) to 'excellent', depending on the region. In urban settings there were usually hospitals accessible at various degrees. In isolated areas, the situation was particularly challenging. In the Louroudjina enclave and the nearby villages of Kochatis and Marki for instance, no medic or nurse was identified among some 3000 individuals, while in Lefka there were only three doctors—a General Practitioner, a Paediatrician, and a Gynaecologist—attending to a population of 6000 persons, without access to laboratories and other basic equipment.

In Polis, the Greek Cypriot doctor continued executing his duties 'as the case was before the start of the troubles'.[56] Despite the freedom of movement in that area, Turkish Cypriots would visit him only if escorted by the UN out of fear for disappearances. On his part, the doctor could not visit the villages despite his good intentions, ever since he was 'welcomed' with gunfire on one such occasion. As an intermediate solution, it was agreed that the doctor would provide his services once a week at the town's Turkish school. Seriously ill persons from isolated areas like this one would be transported by UNFICYP to the nearest hospital, and in some individual cases, the government allowed exceptions to movement restrictions.

In parallel, UNFICYP had developed a process of routine meetings between local leaders from both communities to alleviate tensions and find commonly agreed solutions to daily problems, in Larnaca, Limassol, Paphos, and some rural areas. The initiative was quite successful. Especially

[56] ICRC, B AG 251 049-005.02, Note 128 (18 September 1964).

in Limassol, there was no serious incident of violence for a whole year from May 1964 to May 1965. This trend was interrupted when the National Guard took action against fortified Turkish Cypriot houses in the city, and two days later a Turkish Cypriot parade took place with participants dressed in military uniforms.[57]

The territorial pocket-structure of the enclaves made extremely difficult the continuous supervision of regional developments by the military and the civil Turkish Cypriot leadership, based in Nicosia. This is evident by the diverse living conditions and policies followed locally, and the enhanced role and relevant level of discretion enjoyed by the village *mukhtars* of each community in their local agreements with UNFICYP. In terms of fighting too, according to a testimony recorded by Kizilyurek, the Turkish Cypriots fought organised in local groups, and only in Tylliria in August 1964 fought in unity.[58]

By mid-1966 the CIA reported that while 'miserable' in some areas, the overall situation in the enclaves had to a certain extent improved for the majority of their inhabitants, despite efforts by Turkey to exaggerate the Turkish Cypriot 'plight' in diplomatic forums.[59] It is estimated here that this diversity of experience from one region to another is one of the factors that allowed the decades-long vagueness about this period, leading to the urban myths and anecdotal stories still dominating public discourse. The Turkish Cypriot leadership presented the undeniably extreme suffering experienced in some regions like Kokkina, as representative of the experience of the whole of the community. Conversely, the Greek Cypriots have consistently played down the severity of the events preceding the 1974 Turkish invasion, even though members of their own community, albeit less in number, were also displaced and exposed to adversity. This diversified state of affairs is not immune from an examination through a legal lens.

Legal Issues Relevant to Communal Segregation

One of the main controversies in the respective narratives from this period is the Greek Cypriot view that the Turkish Cypriots withdrew and

[57] S/6426 paras 86–88.

[58] Kızılyürek, *Resentment*, 544.

[59] CIA, Doc No CIA-RDP79-00927A005300040003-9, Current Intelligence Weekly Special Report Cyprus: A Status Report, 27 May 1966 (Released 8 February 2008).

abandoned their official positions and villages in pursuit of *taksim*.[60] The Turkish Cypriots on the other hand, maintain that the Greek Cypriot community pursued a 'campaign of extermination against the Turkish Cypriots'[61] (since 1998 a codified crime against humanity) so as to declare *enosis* with Greece. Each side has built its respective narrative based on political arguments, often disguised under a legal form. For six decades these legal claims have rarely been substantially scrutinised, and each side accepts its set of legal arguments as absolute, undeniable truths. A closer look at the facts shows a rather nuanced reality, which blurs the perceived parameters of the legal arguments made.

Legal argumentation, as traditionally understood, aims to determine one 'winning' and one 'losing' party. In criminal trials, circumstances that may improve or worsen the position of the accused are taken into account as mitigating or aggravating circumstances. On the geopolitical field, such mechanisms to weight and balance the legal arguments are missing. Thus, over the years, the respective community leaderships in Cyprus have taken full advantage of the inherent shortcomings of international mechanisms for legal enforcement and accountability, and the lack of an appropriate formal forum that could potentially examine their claims. Decades-long diplomatic negotiations have proved a poor substitute to address the insecurity, mistrust, and sense of injustice deepening the chasm between the two communities. Given the different international standing of each community, the governing Greek Cypriot community on the one side and the insurgent Turkish Cypriots on the other, the legal analysis calls for a separate assessment of each group's positions and actions.

The hardship faced by the Turkish Cypriot civilians was not unknown, as shown in the archives. The topic of 'The coercion of citizens of the Republic by Turkish terrorists to abandon their houses and their property and to be held without their consent away from them', was discussed for the first time at the House of Representatives on 30 March 1964. Only three MPs took the floor, most prominently Titos Fanos and Georgios Santis, who raised concerns about the 'peaceful and law-abiding Turkish citizens',[62] recognising the violation of their human rights, as well as the

[60] PIO, *Toward a Unified Cyprus: The myth of Turkish Cypriot "Isolation"* (4th edn, PIO 2010); The publication makes no reference to the period before 1974.

[61] ICRC, B AG 200 049-005, Collection of press clippings and information bulletins, Special News Bulletin No. 9 'Kuchuk Cables UN' (22 January 1964).

[62] HORM, Session 1963–1964, 30 March 1964, 47.

duty of the RoC to protect them and offer assistance for their safe return to their homes. As commented by Kizilyurek, the Greek Cypriot MPs on the one side tried to show empathy, but on the other they were too concerned with allocating responsibility solely to the Turkish Cypriot 'rebels' or 'insurgents', failing to engage more critically with the situation as a whole.[63] Indeed, Turkish Cypriots would usually leave their homes only after members of their community were killed, abducted, or harassed, expecting to return within months.[64] This not only indicates a failure on behalf of the State to provide for the adequate protection of its citizens, but it also contradicts one of the loudest mainstream Greek Cypriot narratives that survives today. Namely, that the members of the Turkish Cypriot community 'just left', or that all Turkish Cypriots had conspired against the dissolution of the RoC.

It has to be acknowledged that an overview of plenary debates shows that space for scrutiny of the Executive in the two-party House of Representatives during this time was exceptionally narrow. Similarly, ICRC reports state explicitly that moderate voices in both communities were unable to declare their views in public.[65] Varnava has also pointed out how Makarios shifted continuously between exercising pressure and moderation towards the Turkish Cypriot community,[66] echoing others who have written how 'charismatic nationalist statesmen' in the 1960s, would also be responsible for the level of inequality and violence that followed in many post-colonial States.[67]

To speak of human rights violations requires a strong human rights infrastructure in the society in question and in the corresponding legal culture. It is a fact that human rights in the 1960s did not aspire to the same level of relevance they do today. Despite the adoption of the Universal Declaration of Human Rights by the UNGA in 1948, it would take almost three decades for international lawyers to endorse human rights as an inalienable part of international law.[68] Despite the strong liberal character of the RoC Constitution, with its extensive list of fundamental rights, this culture of a lack of interest in human rights became inherent to the

[63] Kızılyürek, *Resentment*, 577.

[64] Patrick, *Political Geography and the Cyprus Conflict*, 76–78.

[65] ICRC, B AG 251 049-004, Note 113 - Weekly report (10 August 1964); ICRC Archive, B AG 251 049-005.02, Note 274 – Activity Report (27 September 1965).

[66] Varnava, *Cyprus Before 1974,* 109.

[67] Gassama, "The Deceit and the Conceit," 127.

[68] Moyn, *The Last Utopia*, 178–179.

approach taken vis-à-vis the Turkish Cypriot community and eventually penetrated the long-term policy of the RoC in terms of inter-communal relations. The establishment of a Ministry of Education that replaced the Greek Communal Chamber *only*, left exposed those Turkish Cypriots who resisted the separatist policies of their own leadership. Even after 1974, Turkish Cypriots who refused to relocate to the Turkish-occupied north of the island continued to be marginalised, becoming virtually invisible to the mainstream society, and deprived of basic civil rights such as the right to vote for decades thereafter.[69]

As indicated through the archives, it seems that the RoC government relied on one other major factor in justifying its overall disposition towards the Turkish Cypriot community. This was no other than the oppression of the members of that community by their own leadership, as shown in a letter from Makarios to the UN Secretary-General's Special Representative in November 1964. Therein Makarios included a list of sanctions imposed by the Turkish Cypriot leadership on those residing in the enclaves if, for example, they were seen conversing or entering into negotiations with Greek Cypriots, appeared before 'Greek Cypriot Courts', bought goods from Greek Cypriots, or entered the 'Greek Cypriot sector', for reason other than 'passing through', including 'for promenade', 'amusement' or 'friendly association with Greek Cypriots'.[70]

Admittedly, such detailed list has not been found elsewhere in the material consulted. However, ICRC reports from June 1965 did state that the Turkish Cypriots were subjected to 'menaces of all kinds' from within their own community, including fines and deprivation of assistance, expressing the conviction that the situation would have been very different had the Turkish Cypriot politicians allowed people to return to their ordinary work. ICRC delegate Max Stalder expressed the view that had Makarios managed to exercise control over the Greek Cypriot irregulars who, in his words, were equally feared by Greek Cypriot civilians, members of both communities would have been encouraged to restart working together.[71] Similar claims were made in the same month by the UN Secretary-General, with reference to a 'deliberate policy of

[69] *Aziz v Cyprus*, ECtHR, 2004.

[70] S/6102, Annex III – Letter dated 12 November 1964 from President Makarios to the Special Representative.

[71] ICRC, B AG 251 049-004, Final report by Max Stalder (6 June 1965) p. 5.

self-segregation'.[72] Evidently, therefore, in 1965 the conditions for peaceful coexistence were there, but the political will was clearly lacking.

The position of the Turkish Cypriot community is that life in the enclaves was life under 'siege'. 'Siege' is not an exclusively legal term. It does however carry, like 'enclaves' and many others, legal relevance that in a legal context ought to be examined. A siege is an ancient method of warfare, an 'operational strategy', which while lawful *per se*, attaches to rules of conduct which aim at protecting the civilian population within a besieged area, from either 'bombardment' or 'starvation'.[73] It is evident from the above that the RoC government had, by virtue of its sovereign rights over its own territory, extensive control over various elements which directly impacted daily life within the enclaves.

The living conditions of the Turkish Cypriot community were especially difficult in summer 1964. On 5 August 1964 for instance, the water supply was cut off for days in the Turkish Cypriot quarter of Paphos, during the days of the Tylliria Air Raids.[74] This is an act of great severity, especially considering the level of heat in the Mediterranean during the summer months, but also because it can easily be interpreted as a 'reprisal' against the civilian population, which is an unlawful act in itself. Days later Makarios explained that this was due to piling unpaid utility bills by the Turkish Cypriot community, which the UN eventually settled.[75]

According to the literature, irregulars on both sides would sometimes deliberately damage equipment across the water network, even though neither electricity nor water could be completely cut off by the government, as that would have also disturbed the network for Greek Cypriot quarters and villages. On at least one occasion the government had refused to repair Turkish Cypriot telephones, and on another, the RoC Ministry of Foreign Affairs rejected the delivery of 400 tons of flour as humanitarian relief, because the harvest season was about to finish and 'the Turks [were] not missing corn'.[76] Nevertheless, the ICRC was careful to point out the absurdity of the situation on both sides, reporting in the same document that the Turkish Cypriot leadership had asked for a delivery of

[72] S/6426, para 106.

[73] Kraska, 'Siege' *MPEPIL* (December 2009), paras 1, 4–8.

[74] UNA, S-0869-0003-08-00001, Summary of Military Action in Cyprus, 5–8 August 1964, 14 July 1964 (Released 6 June 2006), para 7.

[75] ICRC, B AG 251 049-005.02, UN Press Release (Unofficial record, 18 August 1964).

[76] ICRC, B AG 251 049-004, Note 103 – Activities of the delegation (6 July 1964).

40 Kg of typhoid vaccines, when the half of that amount would have sufficed to vaccinate the entire island population.

The very term 'besieged' was used by the ICRC with reference to the '"besieged" Turkish quarters' in August 1964,[77] and the UN Secretary-General with reference to the temporary 'siege of the Turkish School in Polis' (without quotation marks), earlier that year.[78] In the aftermath of the Tylliria battles, in September 1964, the Secretary-General stated that the '*economic blockade*' had led to 'serious shortages of many essential products in the Turkish Cypriot sector', concluding:

> [It] seems warranted that the economic restrictions being imposed against the Turkish communit[y] in Cyprus, which in some instances have been so severe as to amount to veritable siege, indicate that the Government of Cyprus seeks to force a potential solution by economic pressure as a substitute for military action.[79]

Some relaxation of the strict economic restrictions observed in the summer of 1964 took effect shortly before the above report was published. Whether this was the result of diplomatic pressure, internal scrutiny or due to Turkey's brutal show of power is unknown.

It appears that a policy of 'blockade' was occasionally employed on an ad hoc basis, as indicated through an ICRC report of 1965, which states that a 'blockade' of the Turkish Cypriot sector in Nicosia, was used as 'collective punishment', an act prohibited under international humanitarian law, and it was of an 'essentially political' (i.e. not military) character.[80] Legally, a siege is distinguished from a blockade. The latter constitutes a separate method of warfare, where the objective is to prevent enemy or neutral vessels and/or aircraft from entering or exiting areas under the control of an enemy State. Thus, the legal framework does not fit the Cypriot context, and the various reports do not employ the terms of 'siege' and 'blockade' in the narrow legal sense of the terms. Nevertheless, the examples mentioned above offer clarity on some of the oppressive practices employed.

[77] ICRC, B AG 251 049-005.02 (n 152) (quotations in the original).

[78] S/5764, para 35.

[79] S/5950, para 99 (emphasis added).

[80] ICRC, B AG 251 049-005.02, No 237 – Blockade of the Turkish quarter of Nicosia (4 May 1965).

If agreed that the violence in Cyprus after 1963 amounted to a non-international armed conflict, both the RoC and the Turkish Cypriot leadership were bound internationally to treat everyone under their respective control 'humanely, without any adverse distinction', according to common article 3 of the 1949 Geneva Conventions. The only remaining caveat not directly addressed so far is that for common article 3 to apply to the Turkish Cypriot leadership and fighters they had to be identified as 'combatants'. Admittedly, the meaning of the term 'combatants' is clearer and has originally been reserved, for international armed conflicts.[81] However, after common article 3 was adopted in 1949, Jean Pictet did mention that the term was used also with reference to members of irregular armed forces, without prejudice to their non-official status under public international law.[82]

Traditionally, corresponding to the three levels of 'civil war', the members of irregular armed forces would be termed 'rebels', 'insurgents' or 'belligerents', and as already seen, if the irregular forces were recognised as 'belligerents', then that would give another State the right to intervene on their side in the 'civil war'. Thus, when Chrysostomides and Emilianides held the view that the Turkish Cypriot fighters were not 'belligerents',[83] they had in mind that the Turkish Cypriot fighters had no recognised international status under public international law, and therefore, Turkey (or any other State) had no right to intervene on their behalf. However, under the 1949 Geneva rules the distinction between the three is redundant and the 'label' attached to irregular forces fighting a State's recognised government is of minimal importance among the other indicators that fall under the criteria of 'organisation' and 'intensity'. It is known that States are generally reluctant to recognise belligerent status to irregular forces, exactly with the purpose to discourage external intervention. Therefore, by foregoing the distinction after 1949, anyone fighting in a non-international armed conflict would be held accountable in accordance with common article 3 and the 'minimum standards of humanity', without allowing recourse to the formalities enclosed in controversial and dubious technical terminology.

[81] Ipsen, "Combatants and Non-combatants."

[82] Pictet, *Commentary GCIII 1960*, 44.

[83] Chrysostomides, *The Republic of Cyprus*, 92–93; Emilianides, *Towards Catastrophe*, 63 fn 100.

Having established that there was a non-international armed conflict and that Turkish Cypriot fighters can be seen as combatants under international humanitarian law, the question of the RoC's legal responsibility under international humanitarian law, in general, and common article 3, in particular, remains. Overall, the RoC government was bound to protect anyone on its territory under human rights law, according to its Constitution and the ECHR, at the very least. This responsibility as not shared with the Turkish Cypriot leadership. However, both the RoC and the Turkish Cypriot leadership had a responsibility not to act in a way which contravened the minimum protections provided for by common article 3, and individuals on both sides who committed unlawful killings, rapes or other crimes should have been subjected to the domestic criminal justice system of the RoC. There is evidence in the literature that the RoC government was aware of the asymmetry in the legal responsibility carried by each community. The Greek Cypriot community through their control over the internationally recognised State of the RoC, and the Turkish Cypriot leadership, as a separatist group. This knowledge had delayed the Republic's ratification of a number of international human rights instruments which would allow individual petitions for human rights violations before the mechanisms available under the ECHR and the International Covenant on Civil and Political Rights.[84]

Shifting Diplomatic and Military Balances

In parallel to the new social, political, and legal realities that took shape on Cyprus from December 1963 onwards, the diplomatic process barely progressed in the last quarter of 1964. It was not until March 1965 when the publication of a report by the first UN Mediator for Cyprus, Dr Galo Plaza, stirred the waters leading to a new diplomatic rift and a negotiating stalemate among all parties involved. In the period that followed, the RoC increased its military expenditure and faced internal problems within the High Command of the National Guard. In terms of the enclaves, the situation remained stable, but always volatile.

Shortly after the publication of the Galo Plaza report, the ICRC delegation decided that its presence was no longer needed. The ICRC was satisfied that UNFICYP was capable of handling the humanitarian needs on the ground, despite the fact that UNFICYP's humanitarian efforts

[84] Hargrove, Jacovides, Tamkoç and others, "Cyprus: Prospects for Settlement," 113, 128.

were not always effective, given the peacekeepers' lack of resources and training on such matters.[85] Tension had not completely dissolved and shooting incidents still occurred, yet at this juncture, diplomacy came to dominate any discourse, leaving aside any other questions of legality and accountability.

Diplomacy over Law

Dr Galo Plaza Lasso, was appointed Mediator for Cyprus by UN Secretary-General U Thant on 16 September 1964, in accordance with paragraph 7 of UNSC Resolution 186. A former President of Ecuador (1948–1952), Plaza was already familiar with the realities in Cyprus since at the time of his appointment he had already been holding the position of UN Secretary-General Special Representative in Cyprus for the preceding four months. During the first six months of his mission as Mediator, he completed three rounds of consultations among Nicosia, Ankara, Athens, and London, and on 26 March 1965 he submitted an extensive report (S/6253) to U Thant and the UNSC. The report, which determined the diplomatic atmosphere for the following months, was ill-received by multiple key actors and has been preoccupying analysts ever since.

The report is a valuable historical document due to its lengthy and comprehensive description of the situation on the island. Starting with an extensive description of the background information to the violence, from the London-Zurich Agreements up to 1965, it then describes the general atmosphere, making an accurate and insightful reference to a 'physical' and a 'psychological' Green Line, which held people divided. In addition, the report offers a detailed overview of the respective positions held by each community and the Guarantor Powers, and addresses the issue of self-determination with reference to the unsatisfactory arrangements under the 1960 treaties, and the controversy over the future constitutional architecture of the State. A unitary structure supported by the Greek Cypriots, against a federal structure supported by the Turkish Cypriot community. The report also elaborates on the importance of offering adequate protection to individual and minority rights, and the 'inevitably' relevant question of guarantees for any potential settlement agreed upon.

At no point does the report undertake a robust legal analysis or refers to law other than in respect of the contested legal points between the two

[85] Tudor, *Blue Helmets Bureaucrats*, 229–234.

communities. It offers no qualification of the level of violence as an 'international' or 'non-international' armed conflict, or 'internal disturbances' and it provides no relevant legal framework applicable to the ongoing situation. One minor exception here is Plaza's identification of the protection of human rights and fundamental freedoms, 'as having the highest relevance to any settlement of the Cyprus problem',[86] with a minimal general reference to the UN Charter and the 1948 Universal Declaration of Human Rights.

This gives us the opportunity to reflect more extensively on the role of diplomacy in cases of long-term armed violence and frozen conflicts. The term 'diplomacy' is traced back to 1796 and British parliamentarian Edmund Burke, and it encloses the methods of communication between State officials, designed for the promotion of foreign policy objectives, by direct or tacit adjustment. Its objective is to enable States to pursue their interests 'without resort to *force, propaganda, or law*',[87] and its *raison d'être* derives from issues relevant to hostility, security, and the maintenance of relations with a 'potential adversary'.[88] This is not to say that the law has absolutely no role to play. As evidenced through references to U Thant's reports on Cyprus to the UNSC, the law has a rather subtle role to play in diplomatic practice.[89] In the 1960s, the interplay between law and diplomacy was the result of a 'dual track' approach inherited by U Thant from his predecessor Dag Hammarskjöld, which was both 'legalistic' and 'political', and consequently tolerated extensive flexibility in diplomatic negotiations and policy implementation, as shown in studies on the 1960s crisis in the Congo.[90]

Mediation and the use of the UN Secretary-General's good offices is an integral part of UN diplomacy and the negotiations on the Cyprus Question. Mediation is a traditional pacific dispute settlement mechanism, mentioned in the UN Charter, and whose significance in war had already been recognised long before the establishment of the UN, under the 1899 and 1907 Hague Conventions.[91] 'Good offices' has been described us an 'attenuated form of mediation', not listed under the Charter, where the

[86] S/6253 - Galo Plaza Report, para 158.

[87] Berridge, *Diplomacy: Theory and Practice*, 1.

[88] Tom Farer, "Diplomacy and International Law," 493.

[89] Koskenniemi, 'The Place of Law in Collective Security' (1996) 17(2) *Michigan Journal of International Law* 455.

[90] Özsu, "Georges Abi-Saab and the Congo Crisis." 603.

[91] Oppenheim, *International Law*, 8–11.

party mandated to offer its 'good offices' is tasked with encouraging the parties to the dispute to initiate or resume negotiations.[92] In Cyprus, over the years, this role has been assumed by a long list of UN Secretary-General representatives.

From an international relations perspective, the law comes *at the end of a negotiatory process* to 'seal the deal', through the drafting of a legally binding agreement setting out the agreed-upon settlement between the parties to the conflict. Law does not play a determining role during the negotiations. At the same time, both lawyers and international relations experts have long-accepted that they may employ different terminology to describe similar events and phenomena, but in a way that better reflects the objectives and the priorities of each discipline. Terminology therefore, can be 'confusing, often inconsistent, unscientific, and in a perpetual state of flux', contradicting any law-oriented notions of certainty.[93] According to the literature, the appropriate label or level of formality depends on the objectives of the negotiating parties. For example, in some instances an informal agreement between the parties may be preferred by representatives of the Executive power, in order to avoid the need for ratification of an international agreement, and subsequently, to also avoid domestic scrutiny by the Legislature and the undesirable public debate which usually follows.[94] Hence, what for lawyers constitutes the core of the legal profession, meaning the detailed study, scrutiny and cross-referencing of legal texts, for international relations experts and diplomats is a factor that can be emphasised or played down depending on the circumstances surrounding a negotiation process and the objectives at hand.

This brief parenthesis on the disposition of lawyers, international relations experts and diplomats towards language and legally charged terminology is more than just a matter of semantics. The aim is to show how the different priorities between diplomacy and law has contributed to our piecemeal, almost abstract, understanding of this period of Cypriot history.[95] Every round of negotiation since the 1960s has been more abstract and detached from the events in question than the previous, adding layers of fog over the details that make all the difference when a legal assessment is underway. The present book has sought to offer

[92] Tomuchat, "Article 33."

[93] McNair, The Law of Treaties, 22.

[94] Berridge, *Diplomacy: Theory and Practice*, 72–76.

[95] Dobell, "Policy or Law for Cyprus?."

clarifications on various instances, dominant among them being the juxtaposition of the legally defined international/ non-international armed conflict dichotomy, and that of the daily usage of terms like war/civil war, and civil war's sub-classifications.

Closing the parenthesis, despite its carefully construed language and comprehensive analysis of all events, parties on both sides of the conflict found grounds for dissatisfaction with Plaza's Report. Initially, the RoC government was positive, since the report embraced the sovereignty and independence of the RoC, by referring to a 'majority' and a 'minority' with an emphasis on the protection of 'minority rights', and suggesting changes to the form of guarantees provided under the ToG. On 12 April 1965, however, the RoC government notified the UN that they could not support the Mediator's view on self-determination,[96] since it effectively suggested the abandonment of any aspirations for *enosis*. The Greek government was not so explicit, and though cautiously positive towards the report, Greece stressed that they would 'respect the right of the people of Cyprus to decide freely about their own future'.[97] The report received a negative reaction from Turkey, who complained that the Mediator had overstepped his mandate by expressing views and making suggestions concerning the substance of the problem.[98]

The controversy has been analysed extensively across the literature, and is considered a key moment of the 1960s. According to Varnava's study, one of Turkey's core disagreements was the suggestion on prioritising inter-communal negotiations, since they held the view that the Cyprus issue should remain a primarily Greco-Turkish affair.[99] According to Necatigil, the proposal of guaranteeing the minority rights of the Turkish Cypriots through an appointed UN Commissioner was also not acceptable, obviously conflicting with the long-term position of the Turkish Cypriot leadership that they would not accept their community's status to be reduced to that of a 'minority group'.[100] Contrary to the highly legalistic diplomatic debates in London and New York in early 1964, it would appear that the 'uneasy truce' observed as of September 1964 made strong legal expertise hardly relevant or in fact desirable, six months later.

[96] S/6275/Add.1.

[97] S/6280, para 6.

[98] S/6267; S/6267/Add.1.

[99] For a historical analysis see: Varnava, *Cyprus Before 1974*, 23–42.

[100] S/6279.

Nevertheless, despite its misgivings, the Galo Plaza report gave renewed confidence to the RoC government which, according to ICRC delegate Ruff, was no longer motivated to 'come across as conciliatory', was 'as armed as ever', and was convinced that time worked in their favour.[101]

By October 1965, Makarios submitted to the UN Secretary-General a Declaration, stating the Cypriot government's intention to adopt a Code of Fundamental Rights and Freedoms in accordance with the Universal Declaration of Human Rights, to ensure the autonomy of all 'minority communities'. To let them participate in Parliament 'in accordance with the recommendation of the United Nations Mediator', and to accept 'for a reasonably transitional period', 'the presence in Cyprus of a United Nations Commissioner', to observe and advise on Human Rights.[102] The Declaration was accompanied by a Memorandum, containing a chart of Fundamental Rights and Freedoms, with additional protection for 'groups of individuals who possess characteristics differentiating them from the main body of the people of Cyprus – whether they be termed minorities, ethnic groups or communities'.[103]

Not everyone was convinced of the good intentions behind the above proposal, some arguing that it was a strategic move to attract UNGA support during the Assembly's forthcoming annual session.[104] Makarios 'Charter of Minority Rights' was circulated to the UNGA on 11 October 1965. The document was not well-received by the Turkish Cypriot leadership or Turkey.[105] The UNGA's 20th Session was once again a major test for the international integrity of the RoC government, despite the fact that UNSC Resolution 186 had secured the legitimacy of the Greek Cypriot-controlled government, more than a year and a half earlier.

At the 20th Session of the UNGA (July to December 1965), the 'Cyprus Situation' was commented upon in 20 Plenary meetings, by predominantly African and Asian member States. Cyprus was also on the agenda of the UNGA's First Committee on Disarmament and International Security from 11 to 17 December 1965, where member States had the

[101] ICRC, B AG 251 049-005.02, Note 232 – Assistance by the Turkish Red Crescent (21 April 1965).

[102] A/6039, 3–5.

[103] A/6039, 3–5.

[104] Miller, *Cyprus: Law and Politics*, 91–92.

[105] A/6052, 6–10.

opportunity to discuss the matter in more depth, and prepare a draft Resolution presented and voted for in Plenary on 18 December 1965.[106]

UNGA Resolution 2077(XX) took '*cognizance* of the fact that the Republic of Cyprus [remained] an equal Member of the United Nations' and 'should enjoy, full sovereignty and complete independence, without any foreign intervention or interference' (para 1). The Plenary Records indicate, however, an overall reserved position among UN members. From those who took the floor, most restated their regret for the lack of a solution and their relief for the end of violence, as well as their willingness to support a resolution which would guarantee the rights of both communities, recognising the Republic's territorial` integrity and sovereign equality. The topic of Cyprus, would often be referred in conjunction with other long-term unresolved conflicts of 'exceptional gravity', such as Korea, Vietnam, Palestine, the division of Germany, and Kashmir.[107] The resolution passed with 47 votes in favour, predominantly from former colonies and Non-Aligned Movement members, with Greece and Yugoslavia being the only European States to vote in favour. A clear manifestation of Makarios' long-term successful relations with the leaders of other former colonies. Only five states voted against (Turkey, USA, Albania, Iran and Pakistan), while 54 States abstained. Among them the remaining four permanent members of the UNSC; China, France, the Soviet Union and the UK.

Many states made use of their right to elaborate on their vote. Among them, Malaysia, who had abstained, stated that sovereignty was not a matter of degree, and that all States have their sovereignty constrained to a certain degree through international legal obligations. An obvious rejection of the RoC's argument that its three constituting treaties were a major obstacle to being an 'equal' to other States. On the other hand, even though Lebanon had voted and spoken in favour of the resolution, its UN delegation felt compelled to submit an explanatory letter to the body, clarifying that its vote should be interpreted 'towards the preservation of the State of Cyprus as an independent Republic and not as a step towards its union with any other State'. The clearest indication of the overall atmosphere came from Spain who had also abstained and commented that 'a draft resolution with such a large number of abstentions, representing a mass manifestation of non-adherence, cannot produce very

[106] Cyprus Question, UNGA Res 2077(XX) (18 December 1965).
[107] A/PV.1350 (6 October 1965); A/PV.1355 (11 October 1965).

important results'.[108] The abstention of four out of five permanent UNSC members alludes to the same conclusion. As correctly observed in 1968, in the broader scope of things, the fact that it was the UNSC and not the UNGA that maintained primacy over the Cyprus Question, and that none of its permanent members supported UNGA Resolution 2077(XX), indicated the resolution's limited significance. With the exception of Turkey's military intervention in 1964, Miller estimated, UN members were generally reluctant to authorise major shifts in the *status quo*, while at the same time the UN was reluctant to 'adjudicate' the legal claims of the parties to the conflict.[109]

This cautionary approach by other states and experts did not preclude the Greek Cypriot politicians from presenting UNGA Resolution 2007(XX) to the public back in Cyprus as a major diplomatic victory. In a speech to the House of Representatives on 7 January 1966, Spyros Kyprianou, the Republic's Minister of Foreign Affairs, acknowledged and refuted all major points of concern raised at the UNGA. He emphasised that the abstaining States proceeded in this way knowing that with their stance they indirectly facilitated the approval of the Resolution.[110] The approach taken by the Minister failed to consider that the States which supported the RoC had their own vested interests in avoiding precedents that could be detrimental to their own national interests, such as India's clear opposition to partition, in light of the unfolding situation in Kashmir.[111]

Supporting the RoC was likely to set a precedent that newly established States would be able to unilaterally decide when the framework of their independence would no longer suit them. Challenging the sovereignty of the RoC, would open the doors to challenging the sovereignty of other new States facing internal disturbances or armed conflict. Supporting Turkey's position, could dangerously narrow the scope of the principle of non-intervention in the affairs of another State. To become too vocal against Turkey, would give rise to accusations of undermining the human rights of the marginalised Turkish Cypriot community, at a time when States, in the context of the civil rights movement and the apartheid regime in South Africa, were heavily scrutinised on the positions they held

[108] A/PV.1402 (18 December 1965).
[109] Miller, *Cyprus: Law and Politics*, 20–21.
[110] HORM, (1965–1966) 7 January 1966.
[111] A/PV.1358 (12 October 1965) para 47.

on such matters. Abstention was indeed, the least detrimental option, if no other vested interests dictated otherwise. The survival of the RoC was therefore, not based on the undisputable rightness (or righteousness) of the Greek Cypriot politicians, but rather it was contingent to the predominant international political climate of the 1960s.

The marginalisation of international law and the turn to international relations and policy in the Cold War, was driven by a preference for flexible principles and case-by-case negotiated settlements, which allowed for the use of language as a means to justify political acts, as opposed to adjudicating disputes.[112] In addition to side-stepping many relevant elements of international law, the case-by-case approach led to an isolation between similar cases, which precluded a broader understanding of overarching trends and issues of common concern.

Military Controversies and Further Interventions

Improving the defensive capacity of the National Guard became a priority in the last quarter of 1964. Efforts to secure equipment for 'Akritas', had already been underway as early as 2 January 1964, under precautionary measures in order not to attract the attention of the British forces. Secret shipments from Greece followed in February 1964, including heavy equipment like second-hand armoured vehicles used by the Greek Army from 1945 to 1960. Bilateral meetings between Greek and Greek Cypriot officials on the matter continued up to the events in Tylliria in August 1964. In addition to formal governmental agreements, there were also private arms import initiatives, as well as the setting up of amateur mechanical workshops.[113]

The structure of the Turkish Cypriot military elements did not change radically during this period. The number of fighters was estimated at a constant 12,000 men, despite changes in recruitment policies. An improved 'combat effectiveness' was reported, due to continuous training and instruction, including courses on combat leadership, which appeared to produce a 'command structure', especially in Nicosia and the enclave

[112] Koskenniemi, *Gentle Civilizer*, 413–509; Chatterjee, "The Legacy of Bandung," 657, 665.

[113] Chrysostomou, *Establishment of the National Guard*, 273 -278; Ierodiakonou, *Stone years*, 98.

expanding in its northern suburbs.[114] It was later reported that such training appeared to be guided by professional military personnel from Turkey, other than the officers and soldiers present on the island as members of the Turkish national contingent.[115]

The renewed confidence after Plaza's report was evident at all levels of government, as indicated by MP Georgios Tzirkotis' triumphant statement of 3 June 1965, that 'There is no internal danger for us anymore',[116] referring to the Turkish Cypriot community. During that time the military situation on the island was described as 'generally calm', and the ceasefire was 'largely maintained', even though 'war-like' activities and living conditions in some regions persevered.[117] Considerable changes in the capacity of the National Guard were also reported in mid-1965:

> It is felt that with the acquisition of certain modern weapons, including armour, and with the training of personnel in their use, the National Guard has acquired a substantial striking-power, which is continuously growing in effectiveness. Moreover, the large- scale acquisition of military transport has given the National Guard the ability quickly to reinforce any area of the island, and has improved its operational mobility in general.[118]

In the first half of 1966, there was a notable increase in shooting incidents, often initiated by 'trigger happy' individuals on both sides.[119] From only 17 shooting incidents reported in March 1966, an overwhelming 289 incidents were reported in December.[120] The UN also noted Turkish Cypriot psychological provocations in the form of 'battle noises' and military exercises near the Nicosia-Kyrenia road, while the UN convoy was passing through. As stated by U Thant:

> [A]rms have not been laid down; the map of the Island is still dotted with military posts and police checkpoints; the military confrontation persists; only a tenuous quiet prevails.[121]

[114] S/6426, para 31; S/7001, paras 26–29.
[115] S/7969, paras 30–31.
[116] HORM, (1964–1965) 3 June 1965.
[117] S/7001, para 2.
[118] S/6426, para 25.
[119] S/7350, paras 68–70.
[120] S/7611, para 81.
[121] S/7001, para 100.

Special reference is due to an incident in the villages of Mora and Melousha, east of Nicosia, where on 23 and 24 July 1966 UNFICYP observed preparations for a joint operation by the National Guard and the Cyprus Police, aiming to prevent Turkish Cypriot fighters from expanding their positions in the region.[122] UNFICYP initiated negotiations both locally and with the National Guard Headquarters in Nicosia in an effort to prevent an escalation, when an allegedly irregular police patrol drove through the streets of a Turkish Cypriot village while the National Guard stood nearby, with UNFICYP noting that the National Guard had taken initiative without giving the UN an opportunity to find a peaceful solution to the disagreement between the parties. The incident carried tactical similarities to the infamous Kophinou operation of 1967, though contrary to that incident, this time escalation was prevented successfully.

Changes in the pattern of violence were also observed, with a rapid increase in other types of criminal activity. Cases involving both Greek Cypriots and Turkish Cypriots fell under the responsibility of UNCIVPOL, which acted in liaison with the Cyprus Police. Only in the second half of 1966, UNCIVPOL investigated more than 200 cases, of which 19 involved homicide offences, 55 shootings at persons working in the fields, an unknown number of cases concerning alleged defectors from both communities, including Greek Cypriots who had crossed into the Turkish Cypriot sector of Nicosia, 24 bomb explosions, 5 booby-trap explosions, and a number of forest fires amounting to alleged arson.[123] In these cases, UNCIVPOL acted as liaison between the Cyprus Police and the Turkish Cypriot 'police elements', but prosecutions in many cases were impossible, due to obstacles in conducting criminal investigations within the enclaves. These observations are in line with general observations during armed conflict, that the committing of war crimes, crimes against humanity and genocide are often underpinned by ordinary crimes,[124] emphasising again the significant role of public order and the domestic criminal justice system at times of extended armed violence.

One other type of ordinary criminal activity observed was the engagement of peacekeepers and other foreign nationals with the illicit smuggling of humans, arms and relevant materials, usually in exchange of a

[122] S/7611, paras 49–61.
[123] S/7611, paras 85–104.
[124] Schabas, *Unimaginable Atrocities*, 43–44.

fee.[125] Peacekeepers caught in such activities were under the exclusive criminal jurisdiction of their respective national States, and those found guilty were dismissed from service.[126] Foreign nationals who were not peacekeepers on the other hand, fell under the jurisdiction of the Cypriot courts.[127] The effectiveness of the criminal justice system was doubted however, when in one such case a French national, convicted with a 12-year prison sentence for sabotage, was released after serving just one year of his sentence.[128] Such cases would often be the source of irritability at the highest political and diplomatic levels.[129]

Following the Turkish air raids of August 1964, the Soviet Union accepted to provide additional equipment, strictly under a commercial agreement to avoid any political undertones, which would give rise to arguments that the Soviet Union was taking a clear position in support of the RoC. Under the agreement, there were three shipments of military rockets destined for Cyprus, to be delivered via Alexandria with the consent of Egyptian President Gamal Abdel Nasser. In Alexandria, National Guard officers would receive training in deploying the system. In the meantime, Greece offered to the RoC training-aircraft that could be adjusted to serve as combat planes. Cyprus had asked Syria to host the aircraft given its geographical proximity, but the request was rejected.[130]

UNFICYP had made an agreement with the RoC on 10 September 1964 to be informed of arms' shipments arriving at Limassol port.[131] However, given its limited mandate, UNFICYP was not authorised to inspect arms shipments to the island, and even though they were aware that Limassol was not the only port through which arms were imported, it was not until December 1966 that the RoC confirmed the import of arms from Czechoslovakia, intended for use by the Cyprus Police.[132] This could not be avoided since during unloading the cargo at the Limassol

[125] S/7611, paras 13–14; Tudor, *Blue Helmets Bureaucrats*, 247–253.

[126] S/5634, Annex I, para 11; S/7969, para 12.

[127] *Keith Marley* v *the Republic* (1964) CLR 143.

[128] UNSC Letter from Permanent Representative of Cyprus to the Secretary General (7 March 1966) UN Doc S/7182; S/7350, para 83; S/7969, para 88.

[129] HORM, (1963–1964) 1 June 1964, 79; See also: S/7182 (n 352).

[130] Ierodiakonou, *Stone years*, 98–101.

[131] S/6102, para 129.

[132] UNSC Report by the Secretary-General (Addendum) (13 December 1966) UN Doc S/7611/Add.1.

port on 2 December 1966, one of the containers broke down and accidentally uncovered its contents.[133]

On 15 December 1966 there was a parliamentary question addressed to the Minister of Interior Yiorkadjis, now also Minister of Defence, on whether the National Guard was tasked with surveilling the arms' storage of the Cyprus Police.[134] In reply, the minister confirmed that the police faced extensive shortages in equipment, since it was known to the higher Command of the National Guard that the police force were burdened with tasks 'heavier than the ordinary'.[135] Part of this targeted effort to strengthen the Cyprus Police included the establishment of a 'para-military tactical reserve' of 500 men, a 'Cypriot Army Unit' *(Σώμα Κυπριακού Στρατού)*, which would be positioned within the ranks and under the control of the police. Given the controversy, the equipment delivered from Czechoslovakia was eventually stored by the Cyprus Police, and was handed over to UNFICYP almost five decades later, in 2014.[136]

The admitted engagement of the Cyprus Police in activities beyond its ordinary mandate is of particular significance in determining the intensity of violence in late 1966. As mentioned in the Mora/Melousha incident above, the police were increasingly participating in joint operations with the National Guard. Ierodiakonou has claimed that in at least some of the police operations during this period, it was the National Guard that should have been deployed, yet this was avoided so as not to provoke an intervention by Turkey. The fact that many incidents were handled by the police, in spite of views that their intensity was 'heavier than the ordinary', distorts our present-day understanding on how severe those incidents really were. Had the National Guard intervened more often, in retrospect, we would have been prone to assume that the level of intensity was higher. Subsequently, the historical narrative of the period expanding from 1964 to 1967 would have been more coherent.

As seen, the presence of the Greek and Turkish contingents was integral to the very existence of the RoC, as stipulated by the ToA. However, the presence of foreign forces along with the growing political instability in Greece, where the Colonels' Regime had taken power in April 1967,

[133] UNSC Report by the Secretary-General (Addendum) (13 December 1966) UN Doc S/7611/Add.1; Ierodiakonou, *Stone years*, 112–113.

[134] HORM, (1966–1967) 15 December 1966, p. 319.

[135] HORM, (1966–1967) 20 January 1967.

[136] Ierodiakonou, *Stone years*, 112–113.

had direct impact on military and political developments on Cyprus. The controversy with the Czechoslovakian arms, as well as the changing type of violence observed, derived from increasing political disputes within the Greek Cypriot community, and the so-called 'military issue' *(στρατιωτικό ζήτημα)*. This concerned the command of the National Guard. By April 1967, the CIA estimated that there was a total of 31,000 'Greek Cypriot forces' counting both military and paramilitary units and including 'reserves'. Compared to the Turkish Cypriots, the Greek Cypriots appeared to have 'tactical superiority' and better equipment. They were also weakened, however, by a 'dichotomy of objectives and underlying mistrust between [Greek] Cypriot officials', which prevented Makarios and his government from taking decisions freely. The government's decision-making freedom, in the view of the CIA, was further restrained by the presence of British and peacekeeping forces on the island.

The Turkish Cypriots on the other side, despite the improvements in organisation noted by the UN, were estimated at 10,000 irregular fighters 'badly armed, poorly trained, and with declining morale'.[137] Most of them were concentrated in isolated villages, which precluded their effective resistance in case of attack. According to the CIA, the Turkish Cypriots were only supported by the 650 men of the Turkish national contingent, contradicting earlier reports stating that approximately 1000 regular Turkish army personnel were on the island, in addition to the Turkish national contingent.[138] This was still disproportionately less than the estimated number of 5750 Greek soldiers (8500 in 1966)[139] who had infiltrated Greek/Greek Cypriot positions on the island in 1967.[140] Contrary to Turkey, however, at a first glance, Greece—as well as Egypt and potentially Syria, as seen above—did have the right to offer support upon the request of the internationally recognised Cyprus government, The asymmetry between the rights of Turkey and Greece to intervene, derived once again directly from the different status of the Greek Cypriot and the Turkish Cypriot leadership under international law.

[137] CIA, Doc No CIA-RDP79T00826A001800010020-4, Greek and Turkish Military Capabilities, 3 April 1967 (Released 19 January 2006).

[138] CIA, Doc No CIA-RDP79-00927A005300040003-9, Current Intelligence Weekly Special Report Cyprus: A Status Report, 27 May 1966 (Released 8 February 2008).

[139] CIA, Doc No CIA-RDP79-00927A005300040003-9, Current Intelligence Weekly Special Report Cyprus: A Status Report, 27 May 1966 (Released 8 February 2008).

[140] CIA, Doc No CIA-RDP79T00826A001800010020-4, Greek and Turkish Military Capabilities, 3 April 1967 (Released 19 January 2006).

The Kophinou Operation

The second half of 1967 was turbulent. Frequent shooting incidents reoccurred from July to October 1967, following a prior 'spell of calm and reduced tension', which even allowed the resumption of direct air and sea travel between Cyprus and Turkey in May 1967, after a two-year pause.[141] The catalyst event that drew a line to the rising tensions this time was the so-called 'Kophinou Operation'.

Reporting on the first half of 1967, the UN Secretary-General stated that despite the numerical increase in shooting incidents during those months, there were less deliberate breaches of ceasefire. On the other hand, there was an increase of incidents that required the direct involvement of UNFICYP, while its relationship with both the National Guard and the Turkish Cypriot armed groups generally deteriorated. In spring 1967, UNFICYP was involved in minor incidents with Turkish Cypriot 'police elements' and with the National Guard.[142] On 16 April 1967, the National Guard fired against an UNFICYP helicopter after the latter had just taken off from Kokkina/Erenkoy, to transfer a seriously ill person on humanitarian grounds, following instructions to fire at any unidentified aircraft.[143] By the second half of 1967, there was a 25% increase in incidents that denied UNFICYP freedom of movement, in a way which prevented it from complying with its mandate.[144]

Larnaca district, where Kophinou and the surrounding villages are located, was a hotspot for military action in the first half of 1967. Violent incidents were recorded in the village of Mari, 16 kilometres east of Kophinou, and along Artemis Avenue in Larnaca, which by-passes one of two Turkish Cypriot quarters in that town. Violence along Artemis Avenue continued in the second half of 1967, while there was also a sharp return of violence in the towns of Limassol and Paphos, which had been largely calm in the previous year. New levels of politically motivated criminal activity was reached on 12 October 1967, when a civil aviation aircraft of Cyprus Airways crashed near the island of Kastellorizo, during an ordinary London-Athens-Nicosia flight, killing all 66 passengers on board.[145] Rumour had it that the attack targeted Georgios Grivas, but the

[141] S/8286.
[142] S/7969.
[143] S/7969.
[144] S/8286, para 21.
[145] HORM, (1967–1968) 12 October 1967; HORM, (1967–1968) 8 February 1968.

investigations undertaken with the involvement of the London Metropolitan Police were inconclusive. Despite the many casualties, today the incident is largely forgotten.

Kophinou has been historically an almost exclusively Turkish Cypriot village. According to the 1960 census had only 18 Greek Cypriot residents, out of a total of 728. Geographically, it is located a few kilometres inward of the south-east coast of the island, at a central junction intersecting the Nicosia-Limassol and Larnaca-Limassol roads. From the earliest days of the conflict, a considerable number of Turkish Cypriots had found refuge there, in search of safety from potential reprisals in the mixed villages of the surrounding region. This constituted Kophinou a Turkish Cypriot enclave of strategic importance. A short 4 kilometres south of Kophinou stands the adjacent village of Ayios Theodoros, which in 1960 had a population of 685 Turkish Cypriots and 525 Greek Cypriots. Within a range of 15 kilometres, there were a number of other mixed villages, which suggests that had the Turkish Cypriots obtained prime control in that region, then they would have been able to establish an even larger enclave preventing direct access between the capital Nicosia and the second largest city of Limassol.[146] Something that had already been the case between Nicosia and the considerably smaller town of Kyrenia, since December 1963.

The first shooting incident in Kophinou was recorded in May 1964, without casualties. The next incidents on record took place more than two years later, between December 1966 and July 1967.[147] During this time, to avoid further tension, the Cyprus Police decided to divert the route of its periodic patrols in the region, by avoiding the use of the main road passing through the Turkish quarter and into the village. The decision for the change had been taken on the Police Force's own initiative, keeping UNFICYP informed of patrols in advance, in order to ensure that the latter would observe the process. As of September 1967, there were various efforts to restore the free movement of the Cyprus Police in the region, with UNFICYP proposing a timetable to progressively achieve this by 2 November. Despite a personal intervention by U Thant, the Turkish government informed that a timetable would only be accepted on the condition that the National Guard withdrew from the positions it had been holding on Artemis Avenue in Larnaca, since May 1967.

[146] Ierodiakonou, *Stone years*, 119.

[147] Hart, *Two NATO allies at the threshold of war*, 39.

High-level meetings on the above issue were held in the presence of Makarios, Yiorkadjis, Grivas, and the UN Secretary-General's Special Representative and the UNFICYP Commander, on 13 and 14 November 1967. There, UNFICYP informed of their readiness to resume escorted patrols with the Cyprus Police, but a formal request by the RoC authorities was never submitted. Hence, UNFICYP's Commander in Kophinou was taken by surprise when on 14 November he was informed that the National Guard would resume patrols with the Cyprus Police towards Ayios Theodoros, a short 25 minutes in advance of the operation. The short notice from the National Guard was in the form of an ultimatum, that unless UNFICYP provided protection at the scheduled time of 13:15, then protection would be provided by the National Guard, instead. By that time, UNFICYP had already observed 'large-scale military movements' in the area, and had ruled out the possibility to join the National Guard in any action against the Turkish Cypriots, as that would constitute a clear breach of the peacekeeping principles of neutrality and impartiality.[148]

The patrol eventually took place jointly by the police and the National Guard as planned without any problems, and a second one followed on the morning of 15 November, again without incident. When a second patrol was initiated that day at 14:00, the entrance into Kophinou from the main road was barricaded by a tractor installed there by Turkish Cypriot fighters guarding the village. The patrol was also stronger, including a group of the National Guard's infantry. At the sight of the tractor the soldiers removed the road block and deployed in the vicinity, at which point three shots and automatic fire came, according to the UN report, from the side of the Turkish Cypriots. The exchange of fire in Kophinou, triggered parallel shooting in the neighbouring village of Ayios Theodoros, over which the National Guard established full control by early evening.

In Kophinou the fighting continued until 20:30, and although the National Guard had cleared most Turkish Cypriot positions, they were yet to obtain full control. UNFICYP was informed at 21:45 by the Ministry of Foreign Affairs of the Republic that a ceasefire had been ordered, yet sporadic shooting continued until the early hours of 16 November. According to the UN, civilians who had been captured and removed from the village by the National Guard, were eventually released and handed over to UNFICYP at 5:00 a.m 16 November. Later accounts of the events

[148] S/8248.

in Kophinou refer to brutal and extensive use of force by the National Guard, and numerous civilian casualties. The UN Secretary-General's report, however, makes no extensive reference to the damages and the casualties from the Kophinou operation, other than 'seventeen unidentified dead and seven wounded'.[149]

According to UN estimations, the 'magnitude' of the operation suggested that the operation was planned in advance. This is now confirmed through secondary literature, explaining that a military plan had been discussed by the RoC Defence Council as early as 31 October 1967. According to Ierodiakonou, the generalisation of the fighting was part of the plan, in order to allow the deployment of heavier equipment by the National Guard. The overall aim was an operation of a limited duration, to restore movement between Kophinou and Ayios Theodoros, without provoking a Turkish intervention.[150]

The National Guard protested against UNFICYP for its failure to prevent the violence, while UNFICYP counter-protested against 'the forcible and deliberate' disarming of UNFICYP soldiers, the use of UNFICYP positions by the National Guard, and the disabling of UNFICYP's radio equipment. One week later, the National Guard apologised for its interference with UNFICYP, expressing its readiness to compensate any damages caused.[151] It is important to clarify that any exchange of fire between State or non-State forces with peacekeeping forces does not take place outside the law. The prevailing view today is that when a peacekeeping force is fighting against State forces, the troops' conduct is governed by the laws of armed conflict applicable in an international armed conflict, but the law remains unclear regarding fighting between peacekeepers and non-State irregular forces.[152]

The Kophinou operation, while not long in duration, was a catalyst in terms of the diplomatic and political balances on the island. Between 17 and 19 November, UNFICYP and CIA reported a series of incidents in different areas. These included, exchange of fire between National Guard and Turkish Cypriots around the Kokkina and Limnitis enclaves, and overflights of unidentified and Turkish aircraft over the Karpas Peninsula and Nicosia. More incidents took place along the Green Line in Nicosia,

[149] S/8248, para 18.
[150] Clerides, *My Deposition Vol 2*, 205–207; Ierodiakonou, *Stone years*, 124.
[151] S/8248.
[152] Clapham, "The Concept of International Armed Conflict," 8–10.

with civilians sustaining injuries, and an attack against UNFICYP peacekeepers by Turkish Cypriot fighters was also recorded.[153]

On 22 and 24 November, the UN Secretary-General appealed to the governments of Cyprus, Greece and Turkey to seize any military preparations and resort to peaceful means of dispute resolution, in line with the UN Charter.[154] Before the end of the month restoration work had already started in Kophinou and the surrounding villages and to the surprise of the UN, the relationship between the Greek Cypriot and the Turkish Cypriot villagers in Ayios Theodoros had 'rapidly returned to normal' for the first time since July 1967.[155]

At the diplomatic level, the fighting immediately sparked a series of communications in Nicosia and New York. The situation gave Turkey the opportunity to put on the table a number of demands, including the removal of all Greek soldiers in excess of the 950 allowed under the ToA, and the disbandment of the National Guard, among others. The excessive number of Greek soldiers on the island gave Turkey a unique opportunity to focus on reaffirming the terms of the 1960 London-Zurich Agreements. A point for which Greece could expect the least support internationally.[156] Thus, Greece had no choice but to agree to this term. The first group of Greek soldiers left the island on 8 December 1967, and the withdrawal of the rest of the troops was concluded in the first quarter of 1968.[157]

New Parameters

The events of November 1967 led to a series of rapid developments that set the scene for the following years. Among them, the establishment of the 'Provisional Cyprus Turkish Administration' (PCTA), while intra-communal relations within the Greek Cypriot community deteriorated further. In the last quarter of 1967, there were a number of changes in the general approach of the Turkish Cypriot leadership, not with regard to their legal claims and positions, but in view of internal governance of the

[153] S/8248/Add.1, S/8248/Add.2; S/8260; CIA, Doc No CIA-RDP79T00826 A002900250001-7, The Cyprus Situation, 18 November 1967 (Released 9 July 2002).

[154] S/8248/Add.3; S/8248/Add.4.

[155] S/8446, paras 40–51.

[156] Ehrlich, *Cyprus 1958–1967*, 103–105.

[157] S/8446, paras 25–27.

Turkish Cypriot community. In 1968 the Cyprus Question entered a distinct new phase, which would last until the summer of 1974.

As stated previously, following his address before the UNSC in New York on 28 February 1964, Rauf Denktash did not return to Cyprus. He did, however, return secretly on 31 October 1967.[158] Even though he was caught and arrested upon arrival, the Republic's authorities agreed that he could not be prosecuted due to lack of sufficient *admissible* evidence that could prove Denkatsh's role against the legal government of the State beyond reasonable doubt. Glafcos Clerides, who had been tasked by Makarios to interrogate Denktash, admitted that the decision also had a political element, since in case of conviction Denktash would become a 'political prisoner', a 'hero to the Turkish Cypriot community', and 'a hot potato to hold'.[159] Hence, Denktash accepted a new offer to return to Ankara. Following this brief incident, the events in Kophinou and the removal of the surplus of Greek troops from the island, the next major development was the announcement of the establishment of a de facto Turkish Cypriot administration, the PCTA, in the evening of 28 December 1967. Four years and a week since 'the troubles' had started.

The alleged objective of the PCTA, as inferred by section 1 of its constitutive document, the 'Basic Law',[160] was to handle the affairs of 'all Turks living in Turkish areas' (the enclaves) 'until all provisions of the 16 August 1960 Constitution of the Republic of Cyprus are applied'.[161] The Basic Law consisted of 19 short provisions, covering Legislative, Executive and Judicial matters, all of which were aligned, as much as possible, to the provisions of the RoC Constitution. Sections 2 to 6 provided for a 'House of the Provisional Turkish Administration', in which the formerly elected Vice-President of the RoC House of Representatives would preside, and the Turkish Cypriot MPs and members of the Turkish Communal Chamber would sit. They would have all the corresponding legislative powers under the RoC Constitution, while all laws passed by the RoC House of Representatives before 21 December 1963 would remain in force. Executive power was to be exercised by an 'Executive Council', presided by the RoC Vice-President, closely resembling the RoC Council

[158] S/8286, paras 87–89.

[159] Clerides, *My Deposition Vol 2*, 202–204.

[160] Necatigil, *The Cyprus Question*, 65–68.

[161] For the full original text: S/8323 - Annex I, Press Release by the Cyprus Turkish Information Centre (29 December 1967).

of Ministers. However, section 13 of the Basic Law provided for the establishment of a separate 'Organization' by the Executive Council, that would be in charge of 'Defence and Security Services'. It is hereby estimated that such 'outsourcing' of executive power aimed at formalising the role of TMT or other links with Turkey, but no further information on this particular provision has been found in any primary or secondary sources consulted. The last sections provided for matters relevant to the Judiciary.

Upon this development in Cyprus, the UN Secretary-General submitted an emergency report to the UNSC, noting that he was given no advance notice on the establishment of the PCTA. The Turkish Cypriot leadership made no formal public statement on the exact purpose of the PCTA. It was the Secretary-General of the Turkish Ministry of Foreign Affairs who stated that the establishment of the PCTA was not to be construed as 'an attempt to foster the partition of Cyprus or to create a separate Turkish state in the island'.[162] On the same day, Makarios communicated a brief statement to the UN Secretary-General, according to which the RoC government was 'facing the situation calmly'. The view of the government was that the PCTA was unlawful, 'flagrantly unlawful', that any act deriving from it was 'entirely null and void' and 'devoid of any legal effect'.[163] The Republic saw it as contrary to the resolutions of the UNSC, undermining the UN good offices, and constituting an intervention in the internal affairs of the Republic by Turkey. In an effort to minimise the impact of this development, the RoC government asked all diplomatic missions in Cyprus to refrain from any visits or contacts with members of the PCTA, warning them that doing so would have been contrary to their accreditation.[164] Greece also followed up with a letter to the UN Secretary-General, concerned that the move undermined agreements made in the aftermath of the Kophinou operation and the ongoing process of disarmament.[165]

For the Turkish Cypriots, the establishment of the PCTA was an 'evolutionary organic development' and a 'constitutional arrangement' within the area of RoC constitutional law.[166] Even though this makes for an interesting legal argument in view of the extent to which the 1960 Constitution

[162] S/8323, para 3.
[163] S/8318.
[164] Varnava, *Cyprus Before 1974*, 136–137.
[165] S/8320.
[166] Necatigil, *The Cyprus Question*, 68.

had already been altered at that point, one cannot overlook the fact that the decision neither involved the recognised government of the RoC, which throughout this period was the strongest card played by the Greek Cypriot leadership, nor was the PCTA established through the proper legislative procedure. Of course, the same could be said for the series of laws the House of Representatives had passed from 1964 onwards, but the Greek Cypriot-led government had a legal advantage due to the invocation of the DoN domestically, and the international recognition it enjoyed. The British agreed that the establishment of the PCTA was indeed contrary to the provisions of the Constitution, despite its close alignment to its original text.

Challenging any issues of legality would potentially lead to counter-challenges regarding the legality of the RoC government's actions from 1964 onwards, and in particular all reforms based on the DoN.[167] The British, too, therefore, maintained an approach where the law would be invoked only when deemed appropriate in the pursuit of specific interests, provided it would not lead to further complications. Despite a legal exchange between the RoC Attorney-General and an unnamed 'Turkish legal expert',[168] the eventual choice not to engage in an in-depth legal analysis set a precedent for decades to come.

Humanitarian issues were also put aside. The suffering of individuals was only an insignificant fragment of the overwhelming number of legal and political concerns and interests involved. Therefore, the only legal arguments that 'survived' over the decades were largely abstract issues, highly contested by their very nature; sovereignty, state equality, self-determination, peace and security. Internationally, such issues are the 'bread and butter' of diplomatic circles and experts in international relations and law. Internally however, *domestic* politics exploit the abstractness to capitalise on the uncertainty, the fear, the mistrust, and the suffering experienced by the electorate.

UNSC Resolution 244 of 22 December 1967, apart from renewing UNFICYP's mandate, enabled UN Secretary-General U Thant to initiate new efforts towards a resolution. These efforts defined the course of action in the first half of 1968, during which all parties involved embarked on

[167] Varnava, *Cyprus Before 1974*, 137.

[168] S/8446, paras 76–84.

pre-negotiatory exchanges, aiming towards the first round of inter-communal negotiations in search of a constitutional solution.[169]

The first quarter of 1968 was reportedly one of the quietest periods since December 1963, leading to cautious optimism on the side of the UN Secretary-General:

> The three-month period covered by this report has been one of the quietest since the disturbances that broke out in December 1963 and, as described in the preceding chapters, inter-communal, incidents have diminished considerably. It is to be hoped that the crisis of last November, which could easily have transformed Cyprus and a broader area in the Eastern Mediterranean into a theatre of war accompanied by widespread loss of life and great destruction may have brought about a realisation to both Greek and Turkish Cypriots of the urgent need to compose their differences.[170]

On 12 January 1968, Makarios announced the lifting of restrictions on the movement of all Turkish Cypriots residing in all enclaves, apart from Nicosia and Kokkina. This was contrary to initial plans to restore freedom of movement across all regions, and was the result of the announcement on the establishment of the PCTA. Simultaneously, Makarios announced the organisation of the second ever presidential elections in the RoC. The announcement of presidential elections was accompanied by a declaration by Makarios, that the government would no longer pursue a policy towards 'what is desirable', meaning *enosis*, but rather it would turn its efforts towards 'what is feasible', meaning a solution along the framework of an independent Cypriot Republic.[171]

Despite the change in policy, Makarios was re-elected President on 25 February 1968 under the original 1959 electoral law, since Attorney-General Tornaritis had advised against the application of Law 39/1965 on the unified electoral roll. On the same day, the Turkish Cypriot leadership decided to organise separate vice-presidential elections since, in the view of Kutchuk, holding presidential elections only would be in violation of the Constitution.[172] He was reappointed 'Vice-President' without opposition, when his contender, Judge Mehmet Zekia, the former President of the Supreme Court, had to withdraw his nomination, despite the support

[169] Polyviou, *Conflict and Negotiation*, 62–101; Varnava, *Cyprus Before 1974*, 142–154.
[170] S/8446, para 148.
[171] S/8446, para 85; Clerides, *My Deposition Vol 2*, 213–215.
[172] S/8446, paras 94–98.

he enjoyed among the Turkish Cypriot electorate and the enthusiasm his potential nomination led to among the Greek Cypriots.[173] In total, there were three 'parallel elections' up to 1974, the other two being the parliamentary elections of 1970, and the next presidential elections of 1973.

Even before 12 January 1968, signs of progress were noticeable, such as the entry of a team of 19 technicians and seven vehicles of the Cyprus Electricity Authority in the Turkish Cypriot quarter of Nicosia, to make repairs on the electrical grid. This was in spite of the continuous lack of support by the Turkish Cypriot leadership towards initiatives that would seem to encourage governmental administration in the enclaves. At the same time, the government rejected schemes that would appear to give authority to a 'separate' Turkish Cypriot 'administration', or would need to channel government services through the Turkish Cypriot leadership.[174]

Despite acknowledgement that the government would have to assist the Turkish Cypriots residing out of the enclaves, there is no evidence of action in that direction.[175] On the contrary, two laws passed in early 1968 aiming to financially support those adversely affected by the events from 21 December 1963 onwards, explicitly provided that such schemes would apply to Greeks, Armenians, Latins, and Maronites only, excluding all Turkish Cypriots, including those who resided in the areas under the control of the Republic. Law 34/1968 on the Exemption from Immovable Property Tax in particular, abolished an earlier law of 1967 which made no explicit discrimination on communal grounds.

Already in December 1966, the government had established a Pancyprian Committee of Citizens Affected by the Turks (Παγκύπρια Επιτροπή Τουρκοπλήκτων), tasked with investigating the financial impact of the conflict on ordinary citizens, through questionnaires disseminated in each district. The results were presented in Parliament on 13 April 1967. Estimated monetary and actual damages were calculated at over 1 million Cyprus Pounds, and outstanding mortgage payments to and from Turkish Cypriots at nearly 1 million Cyprus Pounds.[176] The discussion continued on 4 May 1967, when MP Andreas Ziartides asked whether the name of the Committee should be reconsidered and changed to 'persons suffering from the rebellion', since:

[173] Varnava, *Cyprus Before 1974,* 142; Kızılyürek, *Resentment*, 679–680.
[174] S/8446.
[175] PIO, Highlights of the Speech Made by Minister of Labour (16 April 1967).
[176] HORM, (1966–1967) 13 April 1967.

> once the rebellion is over and once normality resumes then it will become obvious that the problem extends to the other community to a significant degree, and that the State, as a State of all Cypriots, will have to concern itself with dealing with the problem holistically.[177]

Ziartides' comment was dismissed, but the long-term adverse impact these discriminatory policies had on the Cypriot conflict-related narratives is undeniable.[178] Such an approach was short-sighted, both internally and internationally. Even if policies engaging with the Turkish Cypriot community had been met with resistance or mistrust, the effort would have increased trust among the Republic's citizens and reinforce a positive international image of the Republic in the longer-term.

The remaining restrictions on movement in Kokkina and Nicosia, and a travel ban imposed on male Turkish Cypriot students studying in Turkey in 1966, were lifted on 8 March 1968. Small-scale building activity on maintenance and repairs started without implementing any long-term solutions for the displaced and those living in overcrowded enclaves like Kokkina, where people continued to depend on humanitarian assistance under similar conditions as before.[179] Kizilyurek describes how Makarios' change of policy 'slightly opened the gates of the ghetto', and some Turkish Cypriots started working for Greek Cyprio employers, while some others left the enclaves and returned to their villages. However, not everyone felt safe to return under RoC control, and according to some sources, police officers prevented known TMT members from resettling back to their villages.[180]

In June 1968, in his thirteenth periodical UNFICYP report to the UNSC, U Thant referred five times to the 'emergency' that had started in December 1963.[181] A 'plot-twist', considering that less than four years earlier it was again U Thant who had referred to a 'bitter civil war'.[182] Considering that in June 1968 the two communities would enter the first round of formal negotiations the choice of the word 'emergency' suggests that all parties involved were once again prioritising diplomacy over law.

[177] HORM, (1966–1967) 4 May 1967.
[178] Demetriou, "Struck by the Turks."'
[179] S/8446, paras 119–123.
[180] Kızılyürek, "Stone years of the Turkish Cypriots," 17.
[181] eg S/8622.
[182] S/5950, para 221.

Conclusion

The complete restoration of freedom of movement in March 1968 and the commencement of inter-communal negotiations a few months later, indicated that during this period the material conditions existed to potentially put a final end to the cycle of violence that had started in December 1963. On the other hand, the continued segregation of the island's population, the continuous presence of UNFICYP, the non-restoration of the constitutional legal order and the establishment of the PCTA, as well as the lack of complete control by the RoC over the whole of its territory, suggest that at this point a return to violence was equally possible. The irreparable damage done to inter-communal relations was evident in the difficulties that existed in restoring a sense of normalcy.

In the period following 1968, the Greek Cypriots sunk deeper into intra-communal violence. The absolute leadership of Makarios was at stake, with some circles turning decisively against him after his shift towards the 'feasible' and his abandonment of *enosis*. According to Emilianides, by 1970 and just around the second ever parliamentary elections held in the RoC, 'It was obvious that the Republic of Cyprus was facing an internal crisis that reached the *threshold of a civil war* among the Greek Cypriots'.[183] A similar observation on a looming 'civil war among the Greek Cypriots' had already been made by the ICRC delegate on 27 September 1965.[184] Eventually, the events caught up with the state of uncertainty that persisted, and the normalised abnormality in the relations between the two communities was disrupted anew in summer 1974.

References

Books

Berridge, Geoff R. *Diplomacy: Theory and Practice*. 4th edn, Palgrave, 2010.

Chrysostomides, Kypros. *The Republic of Cyprus: A study in International Law*. Martinus Nijhoff 2000.

Chrysostomou, Aggelos. *Από τον Κυπριακό Στρατό μέχρι και τη δημιουργία της Εθνικής Φρουράς (1959–1964)* (From the Cyprus Army until the establishment of the National Guard (1959–1964). 2015.

[183] Emilianides, *Towards Catastrophe*, 104–108.

[184] ICRC B AG 251 049-005.02, Note 274 – Activity Report (27 September 1965).

Clerides, Glafcos, *Cyprus: My Deposition Vol 2*. Alithia Publishing, 1989.

Ehrlich, Thomas. *Cyprus 1958–1967*. Oxford University Press. 1974.

Emilianides, Achilles C. *Κοινοβουλευτική Συνύπαρξη Ελληνοκυπρίων και Τουρκοκυπρίων (1960–1963)* (Parliamentary Co-Existence of Greek Cypriots and Turkish Cypriots (1960–1963). Epiphaniou, 2003.

Emilianides, Achilles C. *Πορεία προς την καταστροφή: Κοινοβουλευτική Ιστορία 1964–1976* (Towards Catastrophe: Parliamentary History 1964–1976). Aegaeon, 2007.

Greene, Alan, *Permanent States of Emergency and the Rule of Law: Constitutions in an Age of Crisis*. Hart, 2018.

Hadjilyras, Alexander-Michael. *Η Κυπριακή Δημοκρατία και οι Θρησκευτικές Ομάδες* (The Republic of Cyprus and the Religious Groups). 2012.

Hoffmeister, Frank. *Legal Aspects of the Cyprus Problem: Annan Plan and EU Accession*. Martinus Nijhoff, 2006.

Ierodiakonou, Pavlos. *Εθνική Φρουρά: Από τα Πέτρινα Χρόνια στο Σήμερα* (National Guard: From the stone years to today). Cultural Academy 'Kypropedia', 2016.

Kızılyürek, Niyazi. *Μια ιστορία βίας και μνησικακίας: Η γένεση και η εξέλιξη της εθνοτικής διένεξης στην Κύπρο Vol 2* (A story of violence and resentment: The genesis and evolution of the ethnic conflict in Cyprus), Translated by Michalis Theodorou. Heterotopia, 2019.

Koskenniemi, Martti. *The Gentle Civilizer of Nations: The Rise and Fall of International Law 1870–1960*. Cambridge University Press 2001.

Kyriakides, Stanley. *Cyprus: Constitutionalism and Crisis Government*. University of Pennsylvania Press. 1968.

Loizos, Peter. *Unofficial Views: Cyprus: Society and Politics*. Intercollege Press, 2001.

McNair, Arnold D. *The Law of Treaties*. Reprinted 2003, Oxford University Press, 1961.

Mehmet, Ozay. *Sustainability of Microstates: The Case of North Cyprus*. University of Utah Press, 2010.

Miller, Linda. *Cyprus: The Law and Politics of Civil Strife*. Center for International Affairs, Harvard University, 1968.

Moyn, Samuel. *The Last Utopia: Human Rights in History*. Harvard University Press. 2012.

Necatigil (Nedjatigil), Zaim M. *The Cyprus Conflict: A lawyer's view*. 2nd edn, K Rustem and Brother. 1982.

Necatigil, Zaim M. *The Cyprus Question and the Turkish position in International Law*. 2nd edn, Oxford University Press, 1993.

Oppenheim, Lassa. *International Law: A Treatise Vol II: Disputes, War and Neutrality*. Edited by Hersch Lauterpacht, 7th edn, Longmans, 1952.

Patrick, Richard. *Political Geography and the Cyprus Conflict, 1963–1971*. University of Waterloo, 1989.
T. Hart, Parker. *Two NATO allies at the threshold of war. Cyprus: A Firsthand Account of Crisis Management, 1965–1968*. Duke University Press, 1990.
Pictet, Jean. *Commentary on the Third Geneva Convention relative to the Treatment of Prisoners of War*. ICRC, 1960.
PIO, *Toward a Unified Cyprus: The myth of Turkish Cypriot "Isolation"*. 4th edn, Press and Information Office, 2010.
Polyviou, Polyvios G. *Cyprus, Conflict and Negotiation, 1960–1980*. Duckworth. 1980.
Schabas, William A. *Unimaginable Atrocities: Justice, Politics, and Rights at the War Crimes Tribunals*. Oxford University Press, 2012.
Tudor, Margot. *Blue Helmets Bureaucrats: United Nations Peacekeeping and the Reinvention of Colonialism, 1945–1971*. Cambridge University Press, 2023.
Varnava, Marilena. *Cyprus Before 1974: The Prelude to Crisis*. I.B Tauris, 2019.
Volkan, Vamik. *Cyprus – War and Adaptation: A psychoanalytic history of two ethnic groups in conflict*. University Press of Virginia, 1979.
von Laffert, Gerd. *Die völkerrechtliche Lage des geteilten Zypern und Fragen seiner staatlichen Reorganisation*. Peter Lang. 1995.

Chapters and Edited Volumes

Bryant, Rebecca and Yiannis Papadakis, eds., *Cyprus and the Politics of Memory*. (I.B Tauris, 2012).
Chatterjee, Partha. "The Legacy of Bandung". In *Bandung, Global History, and International Law*, edited by Luis Eslava, Michael Fakhri, Vasuki Nesiah. Cambridge University Press, 2017.
Clapham, Andrew. "The Concept of International Armed Conflict." In *The 1949 Geneva Conventions: A Commentary*, edited by Andrew Clapham, Paola Gaeta, and Marco Sassòli. Oxford University Press, 2015.
Farer, Tom. "Diplomacy and International Law." In *The Oxford Handbook of Modern Diplomacy*, edited by Andrew F Cooper, Jorge Heine and Ramesh Thakur. Oxford University Press. 2013.
Gassama, Ibrahim J. "Bandung 1955: The Deceit and the Conceit." In *Bandung, Global History, and International Law*, edited by Luis Eslava, Michael Fakhri, Vasuki Nesiah. Cambridge University Press, 2017.
Ipsen, Knut. "Combatants and Non-combatants." In *The Handbook of Humanitarian Law in Armed Conflicts*, edited by Dieter Fleck. 2nd edn, Oxford University Press, 2008.
Moir, Lindsay. "The Concept of Non-International Armed Conflict." In *The 1949 Geneva Conventions: A Commentary*, edited by Andrew Clapham, Paola Gaeta, and Marco Sassòli. Oxford University Press, 2015.

Reynolds, John. "Peripheral Parallels? Europe's Edges and the World of Bandung." In *Bandung, Global History, and International Law*, edited by Luis Eslava, Michael Fakhri, Vasuki Nesiah. Cambridge University Press, 2017.

Tomuchat, Christian. "Article 33." In *The Oxford Commentary on the Charter of the United Nations Vol 1*, edited by Bruno Simma, Daniel-Erasmus Khan, Georg Nolte and Andreas Paulus. 3rd edn, Oxford University Press.

Trimikliniotis, Nicos and Corina Demetriou, "The Cypriot Roma and the Failure of Education: Anti-discrimination and Multiculturalism as a post-accession challenge." In *The Minorities of Cyprus: Development patterns and the identity of the internal-exclusion*, edited by Andrekos Varnava, Nicholas Coureas and Marina Elia. Cambridge Scholars Publishing, 2009.

Journal Articles

Anghie, Antony, "Rethinking Sovereignty in International Law" *Annual Review of Law and Social Science* 5 (2009): 291–310.

Anghie, Antony and BS Chimni, "Third World Approaches to International Law and Individual Responsibility in Internal Conflict" *Studies in Transnational Legal Policy* 36 (2004): 185–210.

Akçali, Emel, "The 'Other' Cypriots and their Cyprus Questions" *The Cyprus Review* 19, No. 2 (2007): 57–82.

Bryant, Rebecca and Mete Hatay, "Guns and guitars: Simulating sovereignty in a state of siege," *American Ethnologist* 38, No. 4 (2011): 631–649.

Demetriou, Olga, "'Struck by the Turks': reflections on Armenian refugeehood in Cyprus." *Patterns of Prejudice* 48, No. 2 (2014) 167–181.

Dobell, William M, "Policy or Law for Cyprus?" *International Journal: Canada's Journal of Global Policy Analysis* 31 (1976): 146–158.

Hargrove, Lawrence, James H. Wolfe, Andrew Jacovides, Metin Tamkoç and Matthew Nimetz, "Cyprus: International Law and the Prospects for Settlement" *Proceedings of the Annual Meeting American Society of International Law* 78 (1984): 107–132.

Koskenniemi, Martti, "The Place of Law in Collective Security." *Michigan Journal of International Law* 17, No. 2 (1996): 455–490.

Özsu, Umut, "Organizing Internationally: Georges Abi-Saab, the Congo Crisis and the Decolonization of the United Nations," *European Journal of International Law* 31, No. 2 (2020): 601–619.

Other

Hatay, Mete. Is the Turkish Cypriot Population Shrinking? An overview of the ethno-demography of Cyprus in the light of the preliminary results of the 2006 Turkish Cypriot Census – *PRIO Report 2/2007*. PRIO Cyprus. 2007.

Irmscher, Tobias, "Enclaves" *MPEPIL* (September 2007) https://opil.ouplaw.com/view/10.1093/law:epil/9780199231690/law-9780199231690-e1037 accessed 3 August 2021

Kızılyürek, Niyazi, *"Τα πέτρινα χρόνια των Τουρκοκυπρίων, 1964–1974: Μια προσωπική μαρτυρία"* (The stone years of the Turkish Cypriots). 61 Χρονικό, 26 April 2009.

Kraska, James. "Siege" *MPEPIL* (December 2009) https://opil.ouplaw.com/view/10.1093/law:epil/9780199231690/law-9780199231690-e407, accessed 19 August 2021

Archival Material

CIA, Doc No CIA-RDP79-00927A005300040003 9, Current Intelligence Weekly Special Report Cyprus: A Status Report, 27 May 1966 (Released 8 February 2008) https://www.cia.gov/readingroom/document/cia-rdp79-00927a005300040003-9, accessed 12 May 2021

CIA, Doc No CIA-RDP79-00927A005300040003-9, Current Intelligence Weekly Special Report Cyprus: A Status Report, 27 May 1966 (Released 8 February 2008) https://www.cia.gov/readingroom/document/cia-rdp79-00927a005300040003-9, accessed 12 May 2021

CIA, Doc No CIA-RDP79T00826A001800010020-4, Greek and Turkish Military Capabilities, 3 April 1967 (Released 19 January 2006) https://www.cia.gov/readingroom/document/cia-rdp79t00826a001800010020-4, accessed 12 May 2021

CIA, Doc No CIA-RDP79T00826A002900250001-7, The Cyprus Situation, 18 November 1967 (Released 9 July 2002) https://www.cia.gov/readingroom/document/cia-rdp79t00826a002900250001-7, accessed 12 May 2021

HORM, Session 1963–1964, 17 December 1963.

HORM, Session 1963–1964, 30 March 1964.

HORM, (1964–1965) 3 June 1965.

HORM, Session 1964–1965, 28 December 1964.

HORM, (1965–1966) 7 January 1966.

HORM, (1966–1967) 20 January 1967.

HORM, (1966–1967) 13 April 1967.

HORM, (1966–1967) 4 May 1967.

HORM, (1967–1968) 12 October 1967.

HORM, (1967–1968) 8 February 1968.

ICRC, B AG 200 049-005, Troubles à Chypre, décembre 1963. Correspondance, deuxième partie (18/01/1964–18/01/1964).

ICRC, B AG 251 049-004, Mission d'une délégation du CICR à Chypre, du 31 décembre 1963 au 27 novembre 1965, activités diverses de la délégation en faveur des victimes des troubles entre chypriotes grecs et chypriotes turcs, première partie (16/01/1964–02/12/1965).

ICRC, B AG 251 049-005.02, Mission d'une délégation du CICR à Chypre, du 31 décembre 1963 au 27 novembre 1965, activités diverses de la délégation en faveur des victimes des troubles entre chypriotes grecs et chypriotes turcs, deuxième partie (15/06/1964–25/11/1965).

PIO, Highlights of the Speech Made by Minister of Labour (16 April 1967).

RoC Statistical Service, Census of Population and Agriculture 1960 Vol. I: Population by Location, Race and Sex (RoC Printing Office, 1960) Table IV https://library.cystat.gov.cy/Documents/KeyFigure/POP_CEN_1960-POP(RELIG_GROUP)_DIS_MUN_COM-EN-250216.pdf, accessed 20 December 2021.

UNA, S-0869-0003-08-00001, Items in Peace-keeping operations, Cyprus - Background notes on reports of build-up of arms and troops in Cyprus, July 1964, Summary of Military Action in Cyprus, 5–8 August 1964, 14 July 1964 (Released 6 June 2006) https://search.archives.un.org/background-notes-on-reports-of-build-up-of-arms-and-troops-in-cyprus-july-1965, accessed 28 September 2021

UN Reports on Situation in Cyprus

S/6102 (12 December 1964)

S/6228 (11 March 1965)

S/6253 Report of the United Nations Mediator on Cyprus to the Secretary-General (Galo Plaza Report) (26 March 1965)

UNSC S/6279 Note by the Secretary-General (9 April 1965a)

S/6426 (10 June 1965)

S/6569 Report by the Secretary General on Recent Developments in Cyprus (29 July 1965a)

S/6586 (2 August 1965)

S/6569.Add.1 (5 August 1965b)

S/6569.Add.2 (10 August 1965c)

S/7001 (10 December 1965)

S/7350 (10 June 1966)

S/7611 (8 December 1966)

S/7611/Add.1 (13 December 1966)

S/7191 (10 March 1966)

S/7969 (13 June 1967)

S/8248 Special Report (16 November 1967)

S/8248/Add.1 (18 November 1967a)
S/8248/Add.2 (20 November 1967b)
S/8248/Add.3 (22 November 1967)
S/8248/Add.4 (23 November 1967)
S/8286 (8 December 1967)
S/8323 Special Report (3 January 1968)
S/8446 (9 March 1968)
S/8622 (11 June 1968)

UN Verbatim Records

UNGA A/PV.1344 (30 September 1965)
UNGA A/PV.1350 (6 October 1965)
UNGA A/PV.1355 (11 October 1965)
UNGA A/PV.1358 (12 October 1965)
UNGA A/PV.1402 (18 December 1965)

Correspondence

UNSC S/6275/Add.1 Note Verbale from Permanent Representative of Cyprus to Secretary-General (12 April 1965b)
UNSC S/6267 Exchange of Letters between the Permanent Representative of Turkey and the Secretary-General regarding the Report of the United Nations Mediator on Cyprus (2 April 1965c)
UNSC S/6267/Add.1 Exchange of Letters between the Permanent Representative of Turkey and the Secretary-General regarding the Report of the United Nations Mediator on Cyprus (7 April 1965d)
UNSC S/6280 Letter from MFA of Greece to Secretary General UN Doc (8 April 1965e)
UNGA A/6039 Letter from Permanent Representative of Cyprus to Secretary-General, enclosing Declaration on Minority Rights by Makarios (11 October 1965a)
UNGA A/6052 Letter by Permanent Representative of Turkey (15 October 1965b)
UNGA A/6224 Letter from the Charge d'affaires of Lebanon to the UN Secretary-General (28 December 1965c)
UNSC S/7182 Letter from Permanent Representative of Cyprus to the Secretary General (7 March 1966)
UNSC S/8260 Letter from the Permanent Representative of Cyprus addressed to the President of the Security Council (23 November 1967a)

UNSC S/8318 Letter by Cyprus Permanent Representative enclosing Statement by Makarios (29 December 1967b)
UNSC S/8320 Letter from the Permanent Representative of Greece to Secretary-General (2 January 1968)

Court Cases

Keith Marley v *the Republic* (1964) CLR 143.

CHAPTER 6

Epilogue

By early 1968, a complete decade after the earliest inter-communal violence of 1958, the two communities found themselves at an impasse. While politicians started negotiating a potential solution, analysts and experts shared their own views on what the future held for the eastern Mediterranean island. Linda Miller concluded her study uncertain of the form a settlement on Cyprus would have, but rather optimistic that the legal norms encompassing it would 'promote orderly self-rule', in the same way the law succeeded in limiting the violence and the impact of the conflict.[1] Adams and Cottrell doubted that a peaceful resolution between the two communities would be possible, if the two were 'left to their own devices'.[2] Stanley Kyriakides, on the other hand, advised that any settlement should be devised in such a manner that the majority would understand they had no 'absolute moral right to rule', and the minority would stop believing they had 'a right to perpetual veto'.[3]

The fundamental reforms to the constitutional order, the four years of Turkish Cypriot isolation and the exponential growth of militarism, put

[1] Linda Miller, *Cyprus: The Law and Politics of Civil Strife* (Center for International Affairs, Harvard University 1968) 65.

[2] Thomas W Adams, Alvin J Cottrell, *Cyprus Between East and West* (The Johns Hopkins Press 1968) 78.

[3] Stanley Kyriakides, *Cyprus: Constitutionalism and Crisis Government* (University of Pennsylvania Press 1968) 170.

N. Kornioti, *Law's Politics: The Cyprus Troubles, 1960–1968*,
https://doi.org/10.1007/978-3-031-93369-1_6

the two communities before a series of *faits accomplis*. Despite the first formal inter-communal round of negotiations in 1968, the deadlock continued into the 1970s and the darkest moments of Cypriot history were yet to unfold. The 1968 negotiations were led by Glafcos Clerides on the Greek Cypriot side, and by Rauf Denktash on the Turkish Cypriot side. The two leaders would sit across from each other at many rounds of negotiations over the following decades, until the ill-fated referendum for the plan agreed upon with the support of UN Secretary General Kofi Annan in 2004.[4]

The aim in 1968 was to re-negotiate the least functional aspects of the Constitution, and to address in particular the challenges arising on the question of local administration and self-governance. Ironically, on the eve of the coup d'état and the following Turkish invasion in July 1974, Constitutional Law experts Professors Orhan Aldikachti and Michael Dekleris from Turkey and Greece, respectively, had found a formula for a workable Constitution which was eventually never politically endorsed and implemented.[5]

Very little is known about day-to-day life in the RoC from the restoration of freedom of movement for the Turkish Cypriots in 1968, up to July 1974. There is no known complete body of work describing how the Turkish Cypriot enclaves co-existed with the Republic's authorities. Historians, political analysts and lawyers have shown little interest in this intermediary period, except for the events surrounding the wave of terror which spread within the Greek Cypriot community.[6]

The late 1960s saw the revival of EOKA's most extremist pro-*enosis* wing in the form of 'EOKA-B', led by EOKA's 1955 leader and Cyprus National Guard Commander Georgios Grivas. Their activities, closely linked with the military dictatorship in Greece, led to the bombing of governmental buildings, kidnappings and assassinations, including the persecution of left-wing political figures. Yet, the most high-profile assassination was that of Polykarpos Yorkadjis in 1970. The Republic's first Minister of Interior, who assumed also the role of Minister of Defence in 1964, and one of the leading figures behind the 'Akritas Plan'. About a

[4] Pericleous, *The Cyprus Referendum*.
[5] Polyviou, *Conflict and Negotiation*.
[6] Brendan and Craig, *The Cyprus Conspiracy*.

week ahead of his assassination there was the first assassination attempt against Makarios, allegedly organised with the involvement of the former. Two more failed attempts against Makarios took place before the coup of 15 July 1974. Within this environment, the Turkish invasion of 20 July 1974 and the de facto partition of the island came to epitomise the fear, suffering, and uncertainty of the preceding decade.

Between 1964 and 1974, the RoC never gained back control over the territory of the enclaves. Only after 1974, all enclaves in the southern half of the island—apart from Kokkina—fall within the territories controlled by the Republic. The Green Line, which divides Nicosia's core in half still stands, despite the establishment of checkpoints as of April 2003. It was after 1974 and the transfer of populations that ensued that we are left with the image of Cyprus we have today—that of a 'Greek south' and a 'Turkish north'. The division gave the opportunity to the Turkish Cypriot leadership to re-group and, following a number of amendments within their internal administration and governance, to eventually unilaterally declare the establishment of the at present still internationally unrecognised Turkish Republic of Northern Cyprus on 15 November 1983.[7]

References

Books

Adams, Thomas W and Alvin J Cottrell. *Cyprus Between East and West.* The Johns Hopkins Press, 1968.

Bryant, Rebecca and Mete Hatay, *Sovereignty Suspended: Building the so-called state.* University of Pennsylvania Press, 2020.

Kyriakides, Stanley. *Cyprus: Constitutionalism and Crisis Government.* University of Pennsylvania Press, 1968.

Miller, Linda. *Cyprus: The Law and Politics of Civil Strife.* Center for International Affairs, Harvard University, 1968.

O'Malley, Brendan and Ian Craig, *The Cyprus Conspiracy: America, Espionage and the Turkish Invasion* (I.B Tauris 1999).

Pericleous, Chrysostomos. *The Cyprus Referendum: A Divided Island and the Challenge of the Annan Plan.* I.B Tauris, 2019.

Polyviou, Polys. *Cyprus. Conflict and Negotiation, 1960–1980.* Duckworth, 1980.

[7] Bryant and Hatay, *Sovereignty Suspended.*

CHAPTER 7

Conclusion

In the 1960s, the experience of the Algerian War of Independence and the unhindered continuation of the Vietnam War, demonstrated the need to reassess and improve the humanitarian-oriented legal instruments adopted in the aftermath of WWII. Already in 1965, the Twentieth International Conference of the Red Cross in Vienna passed a resolution urging the ICRC to enhance its assistance to victims of non-international armed conflicts.[1] It would take almost a decade until negotiations for the 1977 Additional Protocols were initiated, upon the recommendation of the ICRC. In 1966, Jean Pictet published a short study entitled 'Principles of International Humanitarian Law', where he distinguished more clearly between the 'Hague law' branch of international humanitarian law as 'the law of war properly so-called', and the 'Geneva law' as 'humanitarian law properly so-called'.[2] This was one of the earliest references to a branch of public international law recognised as 'international humanitarian law'. In parallel, over the next years the UN would encourage the application of international human rights law in armed conflict. The year 1968 was designated as the Year of Human Rights, during which the UNGA proceeded with passing a Resolution on the Respect for Human Rights in Armed Conflicts (Resolution 2444 (XXIII), 19 December 1968). Thus, many of

[1] Sivakumaran, *The Law of Non-International Armed Conflict*, 43.

[2] Pictet, Jean "Principles of International Humanitarian Law." Alexander, "A Short History," 118.

N. Kornioti, *Law's Politics: The Cyprus Troubles, 1960–1968*,
https://doi.org/10.1007/978-3-031-93369-1_7

the legal rules we take for granted today did not exist or were still in their infancy in the 1960s, and it is in that perspective that the Cyprus Question, to a significant extent, remains a problem of its time.

In revisiting this period from a new prism, the book sought to present the Cyprus Question beyond the minutiae of high-level diplomacy. No doubt, the complete division of the island since 1974 has contributed to the Greek Cypriot and the international community's amnesia regarding the 1960s. As seen here, however, it can hardly be argued that the violent and uncertain 1960s have no impact on the present. A parallel aspiration of the book was to link the insular experience of Cyprus more directly with other developments from around the world during the same period. As a result, the book oscillates between the domestic and the international legal and historical realm. The benefit of this approach was to highlight how our present discourse and perspective are the result of the multidimensional interplay of both local and global factors, among which the law is one out of many elements.

The main question that guided the research behind this book was straight forward. Whether internal violence in Cyprus in the 1960s was of such severity that it could amount to a 'non-international armed conflict' under common article 3 of the 1949 Geneva Conventions. The answer is hardly a simple yes or no. In the last report falling within the chronology of this book, UN Secretary-General U Thant informed the UNSC that exchanges of fire were 'almost a daily occurrence over the past four years'.[3] However, armed violence in itself does not constitute 'non-international armed conflict'. To determine the answer *legally*, legal doctrine requires a rigorous assessment of the dual criteria of 'intensity of violence' and 'level of organisation' for *all* parties involved. Archival material has shed light on the sub-criteria constructing both intensity and organisation. Moreover, the archives revealed that the term 'civil war' had been used to describe the situation in Cyprus on multiple occasions. The fact that the Greek Cypriot leadership employed the term 'rebellion' and 'insurgency', is indicative of an awareness of the legal framework, as also proven by the separate judgements of the *Ibrahim* case. Therefore, it was only with the passing of time, and with the new *status quo* following the events of 1974, that the interrelation between the above terms was eventually left to lapse. However, a dry factual analysis is hardly satisfactory.

[3] S/8446, para 62.

By enriching the book with additional information on the general disposition towards the Geneva Conventions during decolonisation, by expanding the usual vocabulary and by knitting the history of Cyprus into the history of other regions of the world, the present book attempted to illustrate how and why the vocabularies and the narratives relating to armed violence in Cyprus evolved. The complete marginalisation of humanitarian law and humanitarianism broadly speaking was potentially a political choice, but also a symptom of the broader disposition of public international law's characteristic State-centeredness. Moreover, international law and global humanitarianism entail inherent biases, which cut directly through the cultures of all Cypriot ethno-religious groups.

Perhaps the biggest ambiguity in concluding lies in the follow up question. If there was a civil law in Cyprus in the 1960s, has it ended? International humanitarian law offers no guidance on when a non-international armed conflict ceases to exist. The ICRC's 1962 Expert Commission on Common Article 3 concluded that the provision was to remain applicable to 'situations arising from the conflict and to the participants in that conflict' even after the internal armed conflict may have ended, 'whatever the form or the conditions of the settlement may be'.[4] A non-international armed conflict may end only if one of the parties is defeated and ceases to exist, or a lasting cessation of armed confrontations suggests that a factual 'peaceful settlement' assessed on the ground, and not a formal legally binding 'peace agreement', exists.[5] Thus, if neither of the two parties is subjected to defeat, the question of whether a non-international armed conflict has ended, in absence of a legally binding peace agreement, is a matter of politics and diplomacy, not law.

Fluctuations in intensity, such as the ones witnessed in Cyprus from 1963 to 1968, are normal during an internal armed conflict. Even if intensity falls below the threshold of classification of a non-international armed conflict, this does not automatically end it.[6] The lack of shooting incidents in Limassol from spring 1964 to spring 1965, for instance, would not suffice to declare the end of the conflict. Moreover, along the axis of intensity, the experience of the enclaved Turkish Cypriots in Kokkina, who lived on a narrow strip of rocky coastland under substandard conditions without the right to exit the enclave for almost five years, stands directly across the

[4] ICRC, "Victims of Internal Conflicts." 83.
[5] ICRC, "Armed Conflict defined."
[6] ICRC, "Armed Conflict defined."

intensity experienced by those living in regions where no severe incidents of violence took place. Such extreme contradictions not only blur the time of assessing an end to an internal armed conflict, but also contribute to a vagueness in memory. The space in between the two extremes allows ample room for political and diplomatic manoeuvring and manipulation.

The Turkish invasion of 1974 complicates the status of violence experienced in the 1960s, since the invasion did lead to an international armed conflict between the RoC and Turkey. An ongoing status with implications for the whole island to this day. The two theoretical positions when a non-international and an international armed conflict overlap have already been elaborated. Either the non-international armed conflict is submerged in the international one, or the two armed conflicts co-exist in parallel. Such 'internationalised' armed conflicts are a clear challenge to the binary nature of armed conflict under international law, as the majority of conflicts around the world at the moment are estimated to fall in the void between the two available classifications.

The 'historical turn' in public international law has been instrumental to this research, in understanding the peculiar Cypriot sovereignty as part of a global system which continued sustaining its oppressive 'civilisational' prejudices, even after the majority of the former 'non-self-governing territories' became UN members. Legal history and TWAIL have served firstly, as a linkage bringing together the common aspects of the post-colonial experience, and secondly, as an informative source on the imperial and colonial mechanisms that impacted Cypriot law, politics and history. Among them, the concepts of 'guarantees and 'community', first introduced for the protection of the interests of European powers in the late Ottoman and early post-Ottoman period, stand out in their implementation during Cyprus' independence. It was within the context given to the architecture of Cypriot independence by TWAIL that the meaning and significance of the Republic's 'fettered independence' can be fully appreciated.

Along with a distinct historical narrative, each community has also built a respective set of legal arguments, which are often symmetrically antithetical and mutually exclusive. In a courtroom such hard cases are resolved on the basis of public policy or legal principles. However, the inter-communal aspect of the Cyprus Question has never been addressed by an international court or another extra-judicial mechanism, in great contrast to the multitude of intra-state cases and individual petitions concerning Cyprus and Turkey before the ECtHR after 1974. Apart from the obvious fact that many judicial mechanisms that exist today were not available then, this is also the direct result of three additional issues. Firstly, the consistent asymmetry of the two communities under international law, where only the Greek Cypriot community has international standing because of the continuous recognition of the RoC. Secondly, the prioritisation of diplomacy over law, where the law only plays a secondary role in dispute resolution. And thirdly and inevitably, the additional complexity of the Cyprus Question, which after 1974 entails the adverse consequences of an unresolved international armed conflict.

Almost five decades after the events in this book, Kizilyurek concluded that the two communities, had 'neutralised' each other.[7] Indeed, the more one obtains a deeper understanding of the island's history, the more they can see how each community's plans and actions in the pursuit of opposing political objectives had driven them together to a standstill and then division. Neither *enosis* nor *taksim* have been achieved, and neither community has exclusivity over victimhood. It is in this context that Koskenniemi's reflections on the politics of international law and its argumentative practice,[8] offered a perspective, a vocabulary and a legal framework, through which the recurring loops of violence in Cyprus could be studied anew. This time through a legal lens where traditional legal claims to an objective truth are left aside, offering a distancing from the common legal urge to identify a guilty party.

Cyprus is no longer an appealing case study for international lawyers. The 'discipline of crisis' as it has been aptly described by ICJ judge, Prof. Hilary Charlesworth,[9] seems unable to make itself relevant to a decades-long 'comfortable conflict'.[10] The constraining parameters that guide legal scholarship and practice, including traditional legal notions of neutrality and objectivity, and the inflexibility of legally defined terminology, confines international law to the margins. As a result, international law is yet to evolve into something beyond being 'employed as a *post hoc* explanation of behaviour that is not intended to be convincing and is not taken very seriously by either advocates or critics', as stated in Richard Falk's powerful critique in 1971.[11]

[7] Kızılyürek, *Resentment*, 580.
[8] Koskenniemi, *From Apology to Utopia*.
[9] Charlesworth, "A Discipline of Crisis."
[10] Adamides and Constantinou, "Comfortable Conflict."
[11] Falk "Introduction," 16.

In the 1960s Richard Falk was leading the Civil War Studies Project of the American Society of International Law (ASIL), and like other international law scholars of his generation observed developments in Cyprus and elsewhere as they happened. The ASIL project is the same project which gave us Linda Miller's informative 1968 study on Cyprus.[12] In her acknowledgements she thanks, among others, Thomas Ehrlich, whose detailed book covering Cyprus from 1958 to 1967,[13] became one of the foundational books of Harvard's International Legal Process school of thought. A movement which was particularly interested in the way decision-makers would use international law during crisis situations.[14] This association between Cyprus and legal scholarship in the late 1960s was one of the unexpected and almost accidental discoveries of the research. It makes one wonder whether the vibrant interest in non-international armed conflicts was eventually lost due to political or intellectual reasons, or because as the years passed by international scholars had to move on, standing true to their obsession with crisis.

There is a slight paradox between Charlesworth's and Falk's views. The first is firmly set in the present, and the second is oriented towards the past. A closer reading of Charlesworth position, however, reveals that she does not speak of law itself. Rather she focuses on how international lawyers speak of and engage with the law. She argues that the usual approach to law narrows considerably the fundamental questions and enquiries made.[15] Falk on the other side, critiques law's inability as a discipline to have a substantial impact on current events. International lawyers' obsession with crises comes to fill in the void created by their discipline's inability to deliver its promise of a more just world as a crisis unfolds. This could also explain why politics and diplomacy, and not law, determine the final outcome. To truly overcome the constraining crisis-centred outlook of international law Charlesworth proposes the creation of 'an international law of everyday life' that would take into account the experience and the perspectives of ordinary non-elite people. It is this ordinary experience that the present book sought to untangle from underneath multiple layers of law, politics and historical narratives.

[12] Miller, *The Law and Politics of Civil Strife.*

[13] Ehrlich, *Cyprus 1958–1967*, 120.

[14] Bianchi, *International Law Theories*, 101–102.

[15] Charlesworth, "A Discipline of Crisis," 377.

References

Books

Bianchi, Andrea. *International Law Theories: An inquiry into different ways of thinking*. Oxford University Press, OUP 2016.

Ehrlich, Thomas. *Cyprus 1958–1967*. Oxford University Press, 1974.

Kızılyürek, Niyazi. *Μια ιστορία βίας και μνησικακίας: Η γένεση και η εξέλιξη της εθνοτικής διένεξης στην Κύπρο Vol 2* (A story of violence and resentment: The genesis and evolution of the ethnic conflict in Cyprus). Translated by Michalis Theodorou. Heterotopia, 2019.

Koskenniemi, Martti. *From Apology to Utopia: The Structure of International Legal Argument*. Reissue with New Epilogue. Cambridge University Press, 2005.

Miller, Linda. *The Law and Politics of Civil Strife*. Center for International Affairs, Harvard University 1968.

Sivakumaran, Sandesh, *The Law of Non-International Armed Conflict*. Oxford University Press. 2012.

Chapters and Edited Volumes

Adamides, Constantinos and Costas M. Constantinou. "Comfortable Conflict and (Il)liberal Peace in Cyprus." In *Hybrid Forms of Peace: From Everyday Agency to Post-Liberalism*, edited by Oliver P Richmond and Audra Mitchell. Palgrave, 2012.

Richard A. Falk. "Introduction." In *The International Law of Civil War*, edited by Richard A. Falk. John Hopkins Press, 1971.

Journal Articles

Alexander, Amanda, "A Short History of International Humanitarian Law," *European Journal of International Law* 26 (2015): 109–138.

Charlesworth, Hilary, "International Law: A Discipline of Crisis" *The Modern Law Review* 65, No. 3 (2002): 377–392

ICRC, 'Humanitarian Aid to the Victims of Internal Conflicts: Meeting of a Commission of Experts in Geneva' *International Review of the Red Cross* 3, No. 23(1963): 79–91.

Pictet, Jean, "The Principles of International Humanitarian Law" *International Review of the Red Cross 66* (1966): 455

Other

ICRC, *How is the Term "Armed Conflict" defined in International Humanitarian Law? International Committee of the Red Cross Opinion Paper 2024* (16 April 2024) https://www.icrc.org/en/document/icrc-opinion-paper-how-term-armed-conflict-defined-international-humanitarian-law, accessed 10 January 2025.

UN Documents

S/8446, Report on the United Nations Operation in Cyprus (9 March 1968).

Appendix I: Article 3 Common to Geneva Conventions I–IV 1949

In the case of armed conflict not of an international character occurring in the territory of one of the High Contracting Parties, each Party to the conflict shall be bound to apply, as a minimum, the following provisions:

(1) Persons taking no active part in the hostilities, including members of armed forces who have laid down their arms and those placed 'hors de combat' by sickness, wounds, detention, or any other cause, shall in all circumstances be treated humanely, without any adverse distinction founded on race, colour, religion or faith, sex, birth or wealth, or any other similar criteria.

To this end, the following acts are and shall remain prohibited at any time and in any place whatsoever with respect to the above-mentioned persons:

(a) violence to life and person, in particular murder of all kinds, mutilation, cruel treatment and torture;
(b) taking of hostages;
(c) outrages upon personal dignity, in particular humiliating and degrading treatment;
(d) the passing of sentences and the carrying out of executions without previous judgement pronounced by a regularly constituted court, affording all the judicial guarantees which are recognised as indispensable by civilised peoples.

N. Kornioti, *Law's Politics: The Cyprus Troubles, 1960–1968*,
https://doi.org/10.1007/978-3-031-93369-1

(2) The wounded and sick shall be collected and cared for.

An impartial humanitarian body, such as the International Committee of the Red Cross, may offer its services to the Parties to the conflict.

The Parties to the conflict should further endeavour to bring into force, by means of special agreements, all or part of the other provisions of the present Convention.

The application of the preceding provisions shall not affect the legal status of the Parties to the conflict

Appendix II: Security Council Resolution 186 (4 March 1964)

The Security Council,

Noting that the present situation with regard to Cyprus is likely to threaten international peace and security and may further deteriorate unless additional measures are promptly taken to maintain peace and to seek out a durable solution,

Considering the positions taken by the parties in relation to the Treaties signed at Nicosia on 16 August 1960, 4.

Having in mind the relevant provisions of the Charter of the United Nations and its Article 2, paragraph 4, which reads: "All Members shall refrain in their international relations from the threat or use of force against the territorial integrity or political independence of any State, or in any other manner inconsistent with the purposes of the United Nations",

1. *Calls upon* all Member States, in conformity with their obligations under the Charter of the United Nations, to refrain from any action or threat of action to worsen the situation in the sovereign Republic of Cyprus, or to endanger international peace;
2. *Asks* the Government of Cyprus, which has the responsibility for the maintenance and restoration of law and order, to take all additional measures necessary to stop violence and bloodshed in Cyprus;
3. *Calls upon* the communities in Cyprus and their leaders to act with the utmost restraint;

N. Kornioti, *Law's Politics: The Cyprus Troubles, 1960–1968*,
https://doi.org/10.1007/978-3-031-93369-1

4. *Recommends* the creation, with the consent of the Government of Cyprus, of a United Nations Peace-keeping Force in Cyprus. The composition and size of the Force shall be established by the Secretary-General, in consultation with the Governments of Cyprus, Greece, Turkey, and the United Kingdom of Great Britain and Northern Ireland. The Commander of the Force shall be appointed by the Secretary-General and report to him. The Secretary-General, who shall keep the Governments providing the Force fully informed, shall report periodically to the Security Council on its operation;
5. *Recommends* that the function of the Force should be in the interest of preserving international peace and security, to use its best efforts to prevent a recurrence of fighting and, as necessary, to contribute to the maintenance and restoration of law and order and a return to normal conditions;
6. *Recommends* that the stationing of the Force shall be for a period of three months, all costs pertaining to it being met, in a manner to be agreed upon by them, by the Governments providing the contingents and by the Government of Cyprus. The Secretary-General may also accept voluntary contributions for the purpose;
7. *Recommends further* that the Secretary-General designate, in agreement with the Government of Cyprus and the Governments of Greece, Turkey and United Kingdom, a mediator, who shall use his best endeavours with the representatives of the communities and also with the aforesaid four Governments, for the purpose of promoting a peaceful solution and an agreed settlement of the problem confronting Cyprus, in accordance with the Charter of the United Nations, having in mind the well-being of the people as a whole and the preservation of international peace and security. The mediator shall report periodically to the Secretary-General on his efforts;
8. *Requests* the Secretary-General to provide, from funds of the United Nations, as appropriate, for the remuneration and expenses of the mediator and his staff.

Index[1]

A
Alliance, Treaty of (ToA), 31, 100–102, 116, 117, 121, 175, 176, 242, 248
Army, 69, 77, 100, 101, 116–118, 133, 135, 142n44, 151, 153, 155, 160, 161, 165, 167, 217, 238, 243
Attorney-General, 101, 108, 122, 123, 136, 180, 181, 183, 187, 251, 252

B
Bandung, 63–65, 64n143, 68
Bi-communal/Bi-communality, 109–111, 125, 205–212

C
Civil war, 3, 5, 51–62, 79, 108, 121, 125, 132, 141, 152, 170, 172, 173, 177, 191, 204, 213, 229, 234, 254, 255, 268
  See also Non-international armed conflict/Internal armed conflict
Clerides, Glafcos, 38, 73, 120, 183, 206, 209, 249
Colonialism
  decolonisation, 3, 4, 6, 43, 61, 62, 64, 67, 72, 75, 99, 269
  post-colonial, 14, 19, 44, 59, 64, 65, 80, 96, 100, 175, 189, 190, 225, 270
Colony/ies, 10, 31, 33–36, 39, 57–59, 61–81, 95, 98, 99, 104, 190, 236
  Crown colony, 31, 33, 61–79, 94, 98, 99, 104, 190
Commander, 69, 101, 116, 149, 185, 214, 246, 278

D
Denktash, Rauf, 37, 73, 145, 146, 216, 249

[1] Note: Page numbers followed by 'n' refer to notes.

N. Kornioti, *Law's Politics: The Cyprus Troubles, 1960-1968*,
https://doi.org/10.1007/978-3-031-93369-1

E
Egypt, 36, 61, 70, 243
Emergency, 15, 49, 57, 68–80, 101, 105–108, 113, 116, 136, 138, 144, 151, 161, 183, 184, 190, 211, 212, 250, 254
Enclaves, vii, 141, 150, 154, 156, 162–166, 205, 211–223, 226, 227, 230, 238, 240, 245, 247, 249, 252–254, 269
Enosis, 32, 33, 36, 37, 62, 68, 69, 78, 95, 125, 131, 190, 224, 234, 252, 255, 271
EOKA, 15, 35, 49, 58, 64, 68–81, 105–106, 116, 123, 131, 135, 151, 161, 264
Establishment, Treaty of (ToE), vii, 98, 99, 101, 105, 140, 143
European Convention on Human Rights (ECHR), 47, 49, 71–76, 80, 105, 106, 108, 141, 151, 230

F
Famagusta, 118, 155, 216
Fighters, 57, 73, 131, 134, 135, 144, 151, 152, 156, 164–166, 169, 174, 216, 217, 220, 229, 230, 238, 240, 243, 246, 248
First World War (WWI), 26, 29, 31, 36, 45, 66, 80, 176

G
Galo Plaza, 230, 235
Geneva Conventions 1949 I-IV, 2, 7, 48, 53, 103–105, 121, 137, 141, 151, 155, 161, 164, 165, 167, 168, 178, 186–188, 191, 213, 219, 229, 268, 269
  Geneva Convention I, 56, 158
  Geneva Convention II, 53
  Geneva Convention III, 54, 74, 162, 166
  Geneva Convention IV, 74, 166, 172
Greece, viii, 2, 32, 36, 59, 62, 63, 69, 70, 72, 73, 75–77, 80, 93, 96, 97, 100, 105, 112, 117, 121, 123, 136, 143, 144, 151, 161, 170, 171, 174–176, 224, 234, 236, 238, 241–243, 248, 250, 278
Green Line, 137, 152, 221, 231, 247
Grivas, Georgios, 69, 70, 161, 244, 246
Guarantee, Treaty of (ToG), 96–98, 101, 102, 143, 164, 171, 175–177, 234

H
House of Representatives, 58, 103, 104, 107, 112, 113, 119, 120, 147, 148, 159, 160, 179, 181, 183, 186, 187, 205–211, 224, 225, 237, 249, 251

I
Imperialism, 6, 25
Independence, 2, 10, 36, 38, 40, 59, 61, 63, 67, 69, 93–125, 131, 136, 140, 149, 151, 190, 208, 209, 234, 236, 237, 270, 277
Internal disturbances/internal violence, 13, 15, 46, 55, 60, 105, 107, 111, 121, 135, 138, 158, 170, 180–186, 188–191, 205, 213, 237, 268
International armed conflict, 46, 56, 59, 110, 121, 138, 168, 171–174, 191, 229, 234, 247, 270, 271

International Committee of the Red Cross (ICRC), 18, 19, 28–30, 30n26, 48, 52, 53, 55–57, 60, 61, 74, 104, 104n40, 121, 122, 131, 134, 138–143, 149, 150, 155, 157, 158, 163–165, 167, 168, 172, 187, 188, 191, 201, 209, 212, 214, 215, 217, 219–222, 225–228, 230, 235, 255, 267, 269, 276
International Court of Justice (ICJ), 41, 60, 99, 107
International Criminal Court, 8, 45, 122
International criminal law, 8, 43–45, 50, 58, 168
International humanitarian law, 5, 7, 12, 43–45, 48–53, 55, 57, 58, 72, 74, 75, 80, 102–109, 137, 139, 152, 155–157, 162, 166–168, 172, 173, 191, 220, 228, 230, 267, 269
International human rights law, 43, 44, 46–49, 75, 105, 108, 267
Internationalised armed conflict, 172–174, 270
Intervention, Third party, 40, 41, 57, 60, 64, 96, 97, 136, 164, 170–173, 176, 177, 185, 217, 229, 236, 237, 242, 247, 250
Invasion, 3, 4, 30, 139, 147, 160, 169, 172, 223, 270

J
Judiciary, 17, 113, 114, 178–186, 188

K
Kutchuk, Fazil/Vice-President, 37, 94, 100, 101, 107, 111–113, 117, 118, 120, 122, 132, 136, 145, 160, 163, 206, 209, 211, 249, 252
Kyrenia, 19, 136, 152, 153, 180, 245

L
Larnaca, 118, 152, 202, 204, 216, 222, 244, 245
Lausanne, Treaty of, 32, 63
Legislature, 9, 17, 113, 118, 178, 207, 233
Limassol, 222
London, 16, 17, 38, 69, 71, 93, 94, 133, 139, 140, 143, 144, 150, 231, 234
London-Zurich Agreements, 75, 115, 175, 231

M
Makarios III, Archbishop/President, 3, 17, 62, 64, 68, 73, 77, 80, 93, 94, 100, 101, 107, 111–113, 117, 120, 122, 124, 132, 134, 138, 144, 156, 160, 161, 169, 174, 206, 210, 211, 225–227, 235, 236, 243, 246, 249, 250, 252–255, 265
Mukhtars/community leaders, 32, 214, 218, 223
Municipalities, 78, 115, 116, 118–120, 207

N
National Guard, 153, 156, 157, 159–165, 168–170, 177, 201, 211, 223, 230, 238–248
New York, 18, 76, 94, 136, 144, 145, 150, 170, 234, 248, 249

Nicosia, 33, 76, 78, 79, 94, 118, 121, 123, 131–137, 139, 140, 144, 150, 153, 156, 159, 162, 164, 165, 174, 176, 179, 182, 215, 216, 221, 223, 228, 231, 238, 240, 245, 247, 248, 252–254, 277
Non-international armed conflict/ Internal armed conflict, 2, 5, 7, 46, 51–61, 105, 110, 121, 137, 150, 158, 161, 163, 168, 171, 172, 174, 178, 188–191, 201, 205, 213, 216, 219, 229, 230, 234, 267–270, 272
See also Civil War

O
Ottoman Empire, 25, 27, 29, 31, 176

P
Paphos, 118, 151, 152, 180, 216, 222, 227, 244
Partition, 32, 77, 98, 237, 250
Police Force/Cyprus Police, 71, 116, 132, 160, 215, 216, 240–242, 245, 246

R
Religious groups, viii, 30, 32, 36, 66, 111, 114, 152, 160, 202, 210

S
Second World War (WWII), 2, 10, 26, 27, 35, 36, 38, 39, 43, 45, 47, 48, 52, 57, 61, 67, 68, 80, 97, 267
Secretary-General, 18, 42, 71, 94, 145, 148, 149, 152, 153, 155–157, 177, 179, 181, 185, 191, 201, 205, 209, 214, 218, 219, 226, 228, 231–233, 235, 244, 246–248, 250–252, 268, 278
Security, 39, 41, 50, 71, 73, 75–79, 96, 100, 107, 113, 135, 147–149, 151, 161, 177, 203, 214, 216, 219, 221, 232, 251, 277, 278
Self-determination, 11, 58, 62–68, 70, 77, 95, 99, 118, 204, 231, 234, 251
Soulioti, Stella, 16, 17, 97, 120, 140, 183, 187
Sovereignty, 7, 27, 31, 32, 41, 42, 44, 59, 64, 65, 67, 73, 94–96, 98, 102, 109, 110, 146, 175, 177, 190, 234, 236, 237, 251, 270
Soviet Union, 144, 145, 169, 236, 241
Supreme Constitutional Court (SCC), 113, 117–119, 123, 179, 180
Supreme Court, 99, 103, 107, 179–182, 207, 211, 220, 252
Syria, 241, 243

T
Taksim, 32, 68, 78, 95, 125, 131, 224, 271
Territorial integrity, 11, 40, 65, 96, 99, 100, 102, 136, 149, 236, 277
Third World Approaches to International Law (TWAIL), 11–13, 62, 270
TMT, 76, 77, 79, 151, 152, 156, 164, 170, 217, 219, 250, 254
Tornaritis, Criton, 101, 104, 106, 108, 172, 183, 252
Turkey, viii, 2, 31, 45, 55, 59, 63, 64, 72, 76, 77, 93, 94, 96, 97, 99,

100, 105, 112, 117, 121, 136, 143–146, 163, 164, 166, 168–178, 205, 209, 217, 221, 223, 228, 229, 234–237, 239, 242–244, 248, 250, 254, 270, 278
Turkish Red Crescent, 141, 142, 165
Turkish Republic of Northern Cyprus (TRNC), vii, 136, 265
Tylliria, 152, 163–170, 172, 174, 185, 187, 223, 227, 228, 238

U

United Kingdom (UK), 2, 17, 18, 31, 36, 39, 51, 57, 59, 63, 71–75, 77, 79, 80, 93, 94, 96–99, 104, 143, 145, 149, 170, 174–176, 209, 213, 236, 278
United Nations Force in Cyprus (UNFICYP), 18, 19, 40, 42, 43, 136, 143, 146–149, 152–154, 154n94, 159, 163–166, 169, 177, 181, 191, 201, 205, 212, 214–218, 222, 223, 230, 240–242, 244–248, 251, 254, 255
United States of America (USA), 10, 18, 94, 144, 145, 163, 169, 217, 236

V

Villages, viii, 32, 78, 79, 118, 132, 134, 150–152, 156, 164–167, 169, 178, 202, 216, 219, 221–224, 240, 243–246, 248, 254

The manufacturer's authorised representative in the EU is Springer Nature Customer Service Centre GmbH, Europaplatz 3, 69115 Heidelberg, Germany. If you have any concerns regarding our products, please contact ProductSafety@springernature.com

Printed and bound by CPI Group (UK) Ltd, Croydon, CR0 4YY
30/09/2026
02225583-0010